Glory Was Not
Their Companion

Glory Was Not Their Companion

The Twenty-Sixth New York Volunteer Infantry in the Civil War

Paul Taylor

McFarland & Company, Inc., Publishers
Jefferson, North Carolina, and London

The present work is a reprint of the illustrated case bound edition of Glory Was Not Their Companion: The Twenty-Sixth New York Volunteer Infantry in the Civil War, *first published in 2005 by McFarland.*

"...the noble Twenty-sixth, which amid many discouragements and under some adverse circumstances, has seen as much hard service, endured as many privations uncomplainingly, stood as bravely and lost perhaps as heavily in battle as any regiment this state has sent into the field. It has rarely, if ever, been mentioned in official dispatches and received but a scant measure of commendation from any other quarter; but when its thinned and more than decimated ranks shall come back to their homes, (alas! that so many homes shall welcome no more the loved ones they sent forth,) their true merit will be appreciated, and the hard-earned laurels they have won shall not be denied them."
—William Johnson Bacon, prominent citizen and judge of Utica, New York, writing in the spring of 1863

LIBRARY OF CONGRESS CATALOGUING-IN-PUBLICATION DATA

Taylor, Paul, 1959–
Glory was not their companion : the Twenty-Sixth New York Volunteer Infantry in the Civil War / Paul Taylor.
p.   cm.
Includes bibliographical references and index.

ISBN 978-0-7864-4924-8

1. United States. Army. New York Infantry Regiment, 26th (1861–1863). 2. New York (State)—History—Civil War, 1861–1865—Regimental histories. 3. United States—History—Civil War, 1861–1865—Regimental histories. 4. New York (State)—History—Civil War, 1861–1865—Registers. 5. United States—History—Civil War, 1861–1865—Registers. I. Title.
E523.526th.T395   2010   973.7'447—dc22   2004030137

British Library cataloguing data are available

©2005 Paul Taylor. All rights reserved

No part of this book may be reproduced or transmitted in any form or by any means, electronic or mechanical, including photocopying or recording, or by any information storage and retrieval system, without permission in writing from the publisher.

Front cover: "The Mud March" by Giovanni Ponticelli, circa 1863 *(detail),* courtesy of West Point Museum Art Collection, United States Military Academy

Manufactured in the United States of America

McFarland & Company, Inc., Publishers
Box 611, Jefferson, North Carolina 28640
www.mcfarlandpub.com

Contents

Acknowledgments vii
Preface 1

1. From the Pastoral Fields of Oneida County 3
2. A Long, Hot Washington Summer 14
3. On to Fort Lyon 33
4. Marching Orders! 43
5. A First Taste of Death 58
6. *Maryland, My Maryland* 73
7. The Fredericksburg Campaign 90
8. Into the Mud: January 1863 104
9. A Less-Than-Glorious Finale: Chancellorsville and Home 112
10. 1863–1865 and the Postwar Years 125
11. Author's Afterword 130

Appendix A: Command Within Campaigns and Post Assignments 133
Appendix B: Regimental Roster 135
Chapter Notes 207
Bibliography 215
Index 221

Acknowledgments

I've had the distinct pleasure of realizing time and again just how kind Civil War enthusiasts can be. Given the relative obscurity of the Twenty-sixth New York, it's clear to me that this work may not have been as thorough had so many individuals not stepped forward to share their knowledge and personal collections. With so little primary source material pertaining to the Twenty-sixth existing in the public realm, this generosity was most gratifying. In particular, I'd like to thank Mr. Don Wisnoski of Chadwicks, New York, and Mr. Charles Rogers of Northridge, California, for their contributions of the various letters and diaries from their personal collections. A kind thank you is also given to Leah Kemp and Anne Schaetzke of the Rochester, New York, Museum and Library for fastidiously transcribing the fragile Warren Firman diary for me, as well as to Ms. Sue Greenhagen at SUNY Morrisville for alerting me to numerous clippings from the *Utica Saturday Globe*. Jim Gandy of the New York Military Museum in Saratoga Springs was equally supportive by providing numerous portraits and sharing the museum's Twenty-Sixth NYSV newspaper clippings collection. I'd also like to thank Steve Zerbe of Cherry Hill, New Jersey, for his superb assistance in obtaining hard copy of source material that time and distance precluded me from getting. Near the end of this journey, a number of people graciously gave of their time and expertise to critique portions of the manuscript. To wit, I'd like to acknowledge Mr. Ted Alexander, staff historian at the Antietam National Battlefield Park; Mr. Ed Raus, staff historian at the Manassas National Battlefield Park; Mr. Donald Pfanz, staff historian at the Fredericksburg and Spotsylvania National Battlefield Park; as well as to C. P. Weaver, editor of *Thank God My Regiment an African One: The Civil War Diary of Nathan W. Daniels*. Their insights and comments all helped to shape the final product. I certainly cannot forget to mention Kim Shearer and the reference staff at the Macomb County, Michigan, Public Library. They must have processed dozens of interlibrary loan requests for me over a 12-month period. Their speed and efficiency is cheerily noted and, believe me, went a long way toward making this work possible! Last, but certainly not least, special thanks goes to my wife, Miriam, and my three children, Kimberly, Christopher, and Sofia. Their love, support, and neverending patience is the glue that holds it all together.

Preface

I never had the opportunity to learn of and then research a bloodline ancestor who wore the blue or gray. To the best of my knowledge, there simply weren't any. The closest my family had to a bona-fide Civil War veteran was a paternal great-great-grandfather who signed up for the emergency Pennsylvania militia during Lee's invasions of the North, but nothing beyond that. My wife, on the other hand, had at least two ancestors who served in the Union army.

A short time after discussing the war with my wife's uncle, who is the family genealogist, I received in the mail from him several pages of notes on a man named Francis Crigier. The papers mentioned that he had enlisted late in 1861, was captured at Second Bull Run, paroled, and then reenlisted in 1864 with the Third New York Light Artillery. No mention was made anywhere as to what regiment he was in during the Second Bull Run engagement. Some initial research revealed that state records had initially misspelled his name, but seeing what they had led me to surmise that his unit was the Twenty-sixth New York Volunteer Infantry. A visit a few years later to the National Archives' Civil War Pension Records department confirmed his service.

Wanting to learn more about this man, I began to do some cursory research into the history of the Twenty-sixth New York. It didn't take long to realize that the written record for this regiment was minimal, at best. No formal regimental history had ever been penned by a veteran of the unit, nor had there ever been a detailed, modern telling of his service. The few published books that were relevant to the Twenty-sixth's story were long out-of-print and exceptionally rare. Unpublished primary source material at institutions was also scarce. Numerous repositories across New York and elsewhere simply had very little, if anything, in their collections pertaining to this regiment. A research trip to central New York revealed 21 historical repositories in Oneida County that owned Civil War manuscript material. Though primary sources were found there regarding any of the other Oneida regiments, not one file was to be had relating to the Twenty-sixth.[1] I thought I might have uncovered a small cache when I learned of the New York regimental files within the Grand Army of the Republic papers now housed at the New York State Archives. Those regimental files were described as containing personal reminiscences from the veterans of their respective units, but alas, the Twenty-sixth's file contained but seven pieces of paper listing little more than the names of its officers and battles. This was the typical situation at most institutions I contacted. It seemed that the history and travails of this New York regiment had been relegated to the dustbin of history.

The foray into the history of this regiment became one of twists and turns, especially when it came to learning of those events that Civil War veterans themselves often glossed over, or neglected to write about in the years after the war. I discovered that it was not all gallantry and glory, but that like all soldiers in all wars, there were ample amounts of drunkenness, cowardice, and other behavior that the nineteenth-century regimental historians usually overlooked.

I knew nothing of the Twenty-sixth New York Volunteer Infantry prior to beginning this journey. There was no personal or professional agenda to promote, and despite the marriage connection to Francis Crigier, no long-dead ancestor to memorialize. As such, I have been able to research and write their history from the objective viewpoint of an impartial observer. Yet, by the time this work was completed, I felt I was intimately acquainted with many of the regiment's veterans. On more than one late-night session at the keyboard, I imagined the ghost of one or more of these men attempting to reach out to me, requesting that I augment or possibly correct something. Theirs is a story of men young and middle-aged, American and European, farmer and tradesman, poor and well-off, all of whom were among the first to step forward and answer their fledgling nation's call. They did their best and played their small role in a much bigger production whose results helped to shape and mold America into the shining beacon of today. For that we should all be grateful.

1

From the Pastoral Fields of Oneida County

The cry of "war!" spread throughout the land in the late winter and early spring of 1861. Young men North and South braced for a cultural and military explosion that some feared would ruin the youthful United States of America, while others relished just such a dramatic possibility. Many southerners felt that secession from the Union was their last option, not necessarily liked but certainly needed, as they believed that decades of unfair tariff laws and industrial modernization had firmly and unfairly tilted political clout to the northern states. Forgotten by these citizens was any consideration of eliminating their agrarian society that was born on the backs of tens of thousand human slaves. Radical abolitionists in the north were more than ready to pick up the musket if it meant the end of slavery in all parts of the United States, though the majority of northern citizens cared most about the preservation of the country. While many disapproved of slavery in a philosophical sense, most northerners seemed to care for the rights of the African as little as their southern countrymen.

In the gentle farmlands of central New York State, the populace of Oneida County peaceably went about their daily lives as farmers and merchants. Named after the Oneida Indian tribe, Oneida County lies in the very center of New York State. Formed in 1798, it contains approximately 1,200 square miles and lies about 100 miles from Albany, the state's capital. Over 106,000 people called the county home in the days before the Civil War. Possessing one of the finest agricultural areas in the state, Civil War-era Oneida offered numerous opportunities to farmers, with the primary crops being wheat in the county's valleys with dairy and cattle raising up in its hills. The town of Utica and villages along the Oriskany and Sauqoit creeks were home to most of Oneida County's manufacturing.[1]

The preservation of the Union, at the price of leaving the slaves in bondage where they stood, was a proposition that seemed to be as fervent in central New York state as anywhere else in the north. Typical of that sentiment was a member of Oneida County's Millard family, writing in 1860 that, "The Union will not be dissolved. Slavery will be allowed to remain unmolested where it now is. The Federal Compact requires it and the people have no idea of disturbing that compact for their honor is bound with it and it seems tribe for the best good of all it is not practicable to do otherwise but the bounds are fixed. "Thus Far And No Farther" is now the Motto. Slavery must stand where it is Extension is out of the question." By early 1861, compromise from all parties was rapidly fading and war seemed inescapable.

The citizens of Oneida County met the inevitable coming of war with ample amounts of patriotic fervor, money, and men ready to enlist. As early as February 1, 1861, 500 citizens attended a rally in Utica, consisting of "all who believe a real and substantial difficulty exists in the administration of the Federal government." Such gatherings were held elsewhere throughout the county and were filled with speeches peppered with pro–Union remarks.[2]

With diplomacy having failed, Confederate forces at Charleston, South Carolina, opened fire on Union-held Fort Sumter on April 14, 1861, igniting a war that would claim hundreds of thousands of lives before its closure four years later. The next day, President Abraham Lincoln called for 75,000 volunteers to suppress the rebellion, with an enlistment period of only three months. Most men adamantly believed that the war would be well over by that time, what with one great battle somewhere providing the ample margin of victory. Lincoln had the foresight to know that the huge volunteer service was necessary, for at the beginning of the conflict the nation's regular army stood at little more than 16,000 men, most of whom were scattered throughout the far West. To further complicate matters, over 25 percent of the regular army's officers had resigned their positions in order to offer their swords to the fledgling Confederacy.[3]

After hearing Lincoln's first plea for volunteers in mid–April, men from each and every northern state answered the call to duty. The Empire State was no different as Gov. Edwin D. Morgan placed the call for 17 regiments consisting of 780 men each to serve the state for a period of three months. Since New York was the largest state in the Union, its quota of men was also numerically the greatest, with a total of 649 officers and 12,631 enlisted men as its share of the aggregate. Morgan, acting on his own, quickly followed up on the initial request by calling for 21 more regiments of 780 men each on April 25, giving the Empire State a total of 38 regiments to be formed.

Nationalistic zeal was high with most young men believing the war would be short-lived. Preservation of Union and flag were the paramount reasons for enlisting, for at this stage of the conflict, slavery had yet to be considered by most in the North as a primary reason to fight. William Holstead of North Bay, New York, soon to become part of the Twenty-Sixth New York Volunteer Infantry, summed up the fighting sentiment of many in a letter left for his parents: "Mother, I leave this to let you know that I have gone to help defend the American flag." Though patriotism seemed to be the common thread for most, such was not the case for all. Practical reasons for enlisting were as diverse as the young men's backgrounds. "My sympathy for the south is as strong as ever," wrote 34-year-old recruit Charles McClenthen of Rochester, New York, "but I believe the more men the north can bring into the field at once, the shorter will be the duration of the war; and I also believe all the troops raised in the north will be necessary for defensive operations." Though McClenthen's predictions would be somewhat off the mark, he would end his term of service honorably and as his regiment's unofficial chronicler.[4]

Mustering In

Sensing that the scope of the conflict would be larger than initially anticipated, Lincoln issued a call for another 60,000 volunteers on May 3. Men from all over central New York State had been hastening to the president's appeal. In Hamilton, the Union Guards formed and elected 22-year-old George Arrowsmith as their captain. Capt. Anton Brindle recruited the Utica Grenadiers. At Oriskany Falls, John Palmer recruited what the local paper termed "the best young men that part of the country affords." The women of Oneida County did their part as well, forming in May a Utica chapter of what would soon be nationally known as the Ladies' Soldiers Relief Association, whose mission would be to ensure that adequate supplies of food and clothing were getting to the local troops.[5]

The methods of enlistment then in place were rushed and often lacked any sense of order. Few men were rejected due to physical frailties and doctors and enlistment officers often took the recruit's word regarding his age. Recruiting of companies commenced immediately and what became known locally as the First Oneida infantry regiment was mustered into federal service on May 17, 1861. This regiment would soon be christened the Fourteenth New York Volunteers.[6]

Colonel William H. Christian (USAMHI).

On the same day as the Fourteenth, New York accepted the Twenty-Sixth New York Volunteers for service of 90 days. Like the Fourteenth, they were also being formed primarily in Oneida County, with the local moniker of the Second Oneida Regiment. As with most regiments, the Twenty-Sixth consisted of 10 companies, which were designated by the letters A through I, and K. The nickname Second Oneida was a bit of misnomer though, since four of those 10 companies were recruited from outside of Oneida County. Nearby Madison and Tioga counties each contributed a company, and due to a bookkeeping error, two companies from Rochester (Monroe County) that had been initially recruited for the Thirteenth Infantry were ultimately sent to the Twenty-Sixth to round out the regiment. By virtue of state Special Order 196, William H. Christian was confirmed as the regiment's colonel. Richard H. Richardson, who had helped to raise a company known as the Washington Continentals, was mustered in as the lieutenant colonel. Gilbert S. Jennings of Rochester, was accepted as the regiment's major. For ministering to the ailments of the flesh, 28-year-old Dr. Walter B. Coventry filled the regimental surgeon's position, and for the spiritual needs of the soul, Ira P. Smith became the regiment's first chaplain.

Unfortunately for the fledgling regiment, the new reverend brought some unneeded controversy to camp in addition to the Word. A central New York newspaper was surprised at his appointment when they learned of it, remarking in a column, "If this be the 'Rev.' Ira Smith we have in our mind, he is not fit to associate with respectable soldiers." Apparently, the good reverend's calling had traversed the spiritual spectrum, first as a Methodist minister, then a Universalist, and lastly as a Baptist preacher. Each time, Smith was forced to leave his flock due to his alleged "degraded passions." The paper concluded, "If Col. Christian knew the character of the man he was appointing, he belies his own name." Smith resigned his position two months later.[7]

William Henry Christian had been a regular army veteran of Colonel Jonathan Stevenson's California campaign during the Mexican war, enlisting as a private in Company K of Stevenson's First New York Volunteers, and then rising to the rank of sergeant from 1846 to 1848. During those days, Christian earned a highly respected military reputation despite the fact that he had never actually been in combat. Christian stayed in California after the war ended hoping to cash in on the "gold fever" that was then raging throughout that land. He stayed in California for seven years and taught in the first English school on the Pacific Coast. While in California, Christian learned the science of engineering and upon his return to Utica in 1854 was made city surveyor. When Lincoln's call went out for volunteers, the then 36-year-old Christian traveled to Albany to petition Governor Morgan for permission to raise a regiment of volunteers. Due in large measure to Christian's military background, permission was promptly granted and Christian set up a recruiting office in Utica to begin the process.[8]

Corporal Orlando B. Preston, whose Company K hailed from Camden, New York (New York State Military Museum).

Once a company was formed, the young and not-so-young men headed off to training camp. In the case of the Second Oneida, the new privates ranged in age all the way from 18 to the early 40s, with most being in their early 20s. Ethnicity was as diverse as the young men's ages. In addition to native-born Americans, men who immigrated to New York from all over Europe joined the ranks. Utica's Company C was typical. Its 107 enlistees boasted 82 native-born Americans but also had recruits from Ireland, Canada, England, Wales, Scotland, Italy, Baden, and Switzerland. The regiment's new recruits also included a significant number from Utica's *Deutschtum*, or German ethnic community. As with other nationalities, German immigrants had come to this land seeking to maintain their cultural roots while realizing the debt they owed to their new homeland. That debt would soon show itself in the many German-Americans who would enlist in the Twenty-Sixth New York. That was especially true in Captain Brindle's Company E. Brindle held the distinction of being the regiment's eldest volunteer at 50 years of age and his muster rolls showed that fully one-half of the 106 men who served in this Utica company were German-born. Ceremony and brass bands accompanied the men as they left town, regardless of their nationality. Utica's Company B headed off to training camp to the sounds of the local band playing *The Girl I Left Behind Me*.[9]

Captain John Kingsbury initially enlisted as First Sergeant of Company B. (Kathleen Dietrich Collection—USAMHI).

Once the various companies were organized, they quickly set out for the military barracks at Elmira, where their initial drilling and training would occur. Located just six miles north of the Pennsylvania border on rolling farmland in the southwest part of the state, the camp was initially set up as a rendezvous and training point for all new recruits mustered from western New York State. Three years later in 1864, the Elmira barracks would be converted into a prisoner-of-war camp for captured Confederates. In short order, rebel prisoners would nickname the place "Hellmira," and it would become the North's most infamous prison camp for southern prisoners of war.

Patience was not a virtue nor a commodity in ample supply during those April and May days of enlistment and training. The U.S. government wanted the green recruits mustered and ready for action as quickly as the state did. Capt. Washington Eliot of the regular army sent a note to the already Elmira-based William Christian on May 20 asserting that, "If your Regt. is organized complete & all present, I will ready to muster it into the service of the U.S. tomorrow at 9 A.M. I would like to confer with you as to the necessary arrangements." With everything in order, the ceremony occurred the next morning as scheduled. The proceedings for the Twenty-Sixth New York and the other new regiments were later recalled by U.S. 2nd Lt. William Averell, who was one the army's mustering officers present during those early days at Elmira: "The regiment was in line and as the roll of each company was called the men answered to their names and stepped to the front and then altogether with uncovered heads and uplifted right hands, repeated the words of the oath of allegiance and obedience, sentence by sentence, after the mustering officer." Once the enlisted men were completed, then the officers stepped forward and repeated the ceremony. Cheers abounded upon the completion of each regiment. Despite the pageantry, the mustering ceremony included

1st Lieutenant Martin Dunham mustered in as a sergeant, Company B, on May 21, 1861 (Christopher H. Jordan Collection—USAMHI).

a soon-to-be-discovered major error, only four days after their Oneida County comrades from the Fourteenth New York Infantry.[10]

By the time of the Twenty-Sixth's arrival at Elmira in late May, the peaceful village was in the process of being turned into an armed camp, with as many soldiers as civilian residents. The logistics of providing shelter and food were enormous. Barrel factories were converted into sleeping quarters and hospitals. Any manner of public building, as well as a good number of private residences, were transformed into temporary quarters for the endless parade of new recruits. Several of the recruits even found themselves private lodging, courtesy of the federal government, at the local Revere hotel.[11]

The first half of June 1861 was spent learning the basics of military drill and parade at the Elmira military post. Carpenters and laborers gathered from the town had constructed additional barracks so that a total of six now rimmed the village. Journalists from around the state who observed the handiwork reported that the facility was the finest in all New York. Zeal and enthusiasm were everywhere and rarely was a negative comment muttered about the incessant repetition of martial exercises that would hopefully turn the Oneida boys into a well-oiled fighting unit. The local public seemed equally intent in watching the battalion drills as hundreds of them turned out on a daily basis to watch. Seemingly fascinated by the martial exercises, Elmira had taken on a carnival atmosphere as patriotic music filled the air throughout the day and well into the night. It was in these early, heady days of the war that the regiment suffered its first casualty. That distinction belonged to Private Charles Darla, who, while being far away from Confederate bullets, drowned on June 9 while bathing in a nearby stream.[12]

News from camp was eagerly anticipated by family and friends back home. George Arrowsmith, who had now become captain of the Twenty-Sixth's Company D, began what would turn into a lengthy correspondence to the *Utica Morning Herald and Daily Gazette* under the pseudonym of "Aliquis."

Highlighting the stay was the formal presentation to the Twenty-Sixth of its regimental colors, which was undertaken with much pageantry by the local citizenry. The flag was described as measuring almost 10 feet by six feet. Made of the finest silk, it contained 34 silver stars set against a dark blue background, and was heavily fringed with twisted gold silk. The pole was made of highly polished rosewood, with a glittering brass eagle perched at the head of the staff. Since the banner had

A volunteer regiment on parade at the camp at Elmira, New York (*Harper's Weekly*).

been started and finished prior to the regiment receiving its official designation, the inscription was to the "Central New York Battalion," which is how the then-forming unit was known prior to its formal mustering. Colonel Christian replied to the gathered throng that the flag would not soon be forgotten by his men, and thanked the townspeople for their kindness. An added measure of pride was given to the new recruits when they all noticed that the student body of the local women's college had also ventured out to witness the ceremonies.[13]

The local civilians were not the only bystanders who were impressed with the martial performance of the Twenty-Sixth. Watchful eyes from the army's adjutant generals office were also present and reporting the shape of the new regiments. The Second Oneida received solid marks from 2nd Lt. William Averell, who had been sent to report on the progress at Elmira. "The Twenty-Sixth are supplied with arms, accouterments, uniform clothing, and camp and garrison equipage; are in good order and under fine discipline, considering the short time they have been in service," reported Averell. "They could take the field at short notice." And so it would be. A few days later, when Colonel Christian announced to the assembled companies that the regiment was instructed to ship out to Washington, a long cheer erupted from the ranks. Action at last! Caps were hung from the tips of bayonets amidst the clapping and huzzahs. This announcement also served to separate the truly anxious from those of weaker mettle. Though desertions at Elmira had been minimal to this point, 14 men ran through the picket guards on June 16, with sidearms at the ready if they needed to be used. Christian dispatched 20 men and a captain to round them up, but as darkness had set in, the hunt failed. Nevertheless, most of the men ultimately returned back to camp by the 19th. With a full regiment at the ready, the Oneida boys were deemed fit for active duty, and prepared to march.[14]

Despite the praise of others, "fit for duty" was considered by some soldiers as a highly subjective assertion. The quality of army food was hotly debated amongst many recruits from central and western New York, but it appears to not have been an issue with the Second Oneida. Their cooks and commissary quickly garnered a reputation for serving up some of the finest food in Elmira, with Maj. Gilbert Jennings remarking that their commissary was "the right man in the right place!"[15]

But on two other critical matters, all were in unison agreement about the despicable quality. At this nascent stage of the war, the Oneida boys were yet to be clothed in the standard Union uniform of dark blue field jacket and light blue trousers. The federal army was procuring standard uniforms as quickly as possible but quartermasters quickly found themselves behind the curve as men poured into the recruiting stations. Instead, they marched off to glory wearing the shoddy, dark gray jackets and trousers of the New York state militia, which were trimmed with black braid. Their overcoats were of marginal, but still serviceable quality, and like their uniforms, were not known for their long-term durability. Apparently hastily ordered, poorly made, and ill-fitting, the uniforms were derisively known by the New Yorkers as the "penitentiary uniform." Decades later, two grizzled, old veterans of the Twenty-Sixth New York Infantry still remembered them with disdain: "I am satisfied that the men who furnished the uniform to the first regiments organized in the state of New York have gone to a place where clothes are not needed," wrote Capt. Edmund Shurley. Anson Cleveland, a musician with the regiment, concurred with Shurley: "[We were] clad in suits that even Governor Morgan and Senator Conkling were ashamed of."

Weapons quality was also called into question. June 4 saw the issuing of muskets in which new Enfield rifles were expected. To everyone's dismay, .69 caliber, 1840-era percussion muskets were handed out, which caused more than one eyebrow to be raised in suspicion.[16]

Friday, June 21, 1861, dawned overcast and rainy as the New Yorkers boarded a 20-car, two-locomotive train amidst a cheering crowd. Many a tear was shed on the train station platform as wives, mothers, and sisters bid their men goodbye. With the previous attempts at desertions fresh in the officers' minds, lookouts were stationed everywhere in order to make sure that all boarded who were supposed to board. They were fully packed with three days' provisions and 15,000 rounds of ammunition for their southeasterly journey. The train left the station at 9:00 am, beginning a journey that was slow and monotonous. It took a full 20 hours to reach the village of Williamsport, Pennsylvania, where the men at last exited the cramped cars. A tremendous ovation and sumptuous meal prepared by the ladies of the town awaited the New Yorkers, who were delighted to stretch their weary bodies in the Pennsylvania sun. Headed by their brass band, the Twenty-Sixth proudly marched through the town streets. Soon the order was given to load their rifles and to prepare to march to Baltimore where southern sympathies remained strong. All thoughts were on the Sixth Massachusetts militia, which had been attacked by hostile, pro–Confederate demonstrators only two months prior.[17]

★ ★ ★

Prior to reaching Baltimore on April 19 en route to Washington, Col. Edward F. Jones of the Sixth Massachusetts had received word that his Bay Staters were in for a rude welcome at Baltimore. Orders were given for a hasty march through the town, but upon beginning their trek, they were showered with numerous rocks and bottles from the angry mob. The Bay Staters increased their steps to the double-quick, which seemed to enrage the crowd even further, who now believed that the

Off to war (*Century Magazine*).

soldiers would not fire or had no ammunition. Pistol shots were numerously fired into the uniformed ranks, and one soldier fell dead. The order "Fire" was given, and it was executed. Several of the civilians fell, and the Sixth Massachusetts again advanced at the double-quick. The mayor of Baltimore, George William Brown, arrived and placed himself at the head of the column beside Captain Follansbee. The mayor pleaded with the soldiers not to again open while also assuring them they would be protected. How he expected to accomplish this in the middle of the riot was not made clear, but soon his patience was exhausted. Jones alleged that the mayor then seized a musket from the hands of one of the soldiers, fired and dropped one of the throng, while a policeman who was in advance of the column also shot a man with his pistol. Brown later denied both of those assertions but did remark that he had "learned by experience that the safest and most humane manner of quelling a mob is to meet it at the beginning with armed resistance." The Massachusetts men finally reached the safety of their train, which was now parked at the other end of town. After getting under way, Colonel Jones conducted a head count and realized that 130 of his men were missing, including the entire regimental band. To add further insult, all the units' baggage had been stolen.[18]

★ ★ ★

With bayonets gleaming in the sun, the grim-faced Twenty-Sixth arrived at Baltimore around 2:00 P.M. Their brief stay in the Old Line State found them winding their way through Entaw and the intermediate streets before reaching Camden Station. Ultimately, they passed through physically unmolested, but like the Sixth Massachusetts before them, were on the receiving end of dubious remarks and hisses. Strict orders were given to ignore any verbal insults from the mob, and with further instructions not to accept any offerings of refreshments or water. As might be expected, several new recruits failed to heed the command and ended up viciously ill from tainted water.

Late in the afternoon of the 22nd, another train was boarded and the New Yorkers began the final leg of their journey to Washington, D.C. Arriving late in the afternoon, the men quickly realized the errors of packing so many personal articles in their knapsacks. The heat was oppressive at the young nation's capitol and every pound strained the back as the regiment unloaded from the train. Despite thermometer readings of 102 degrees in the shade, the New Yorkers were exuberant to be at the end of their monotonous trip. In celebration, a number of them foolishly discharged their muskets out the windows of their train as it pulled into the station, nearly hitting some of the watchful Eighth Massachusetts in the process. As the men unloaded from the cars, a correspondent from the *Washington Evening Star* observed that the regiment seemed to be entirely composed of "well developed, sinewy men." What was also obvious was that the weight of their backpacks was straining every grain of those well-developed muscles. To make matters worse, it was learned upon disembarking that an unwelcome three-mile march to their designated campground was forthcoming. With the heat so intense, many of the raw soldiers soon fell out of the marching column while others simply passed out, but fellow soldiers from other regiments pitched in and soon the regiment bivouacked for the night north of the capital building at Meridian Heights. Their camp was called "Camp Van Valkenburgh" in honor of Gen. Robert Van Valkenburgh, who befriended the unit back in Elmira. Many of the exhausted New Yorkers didn't even bother to erect their tents, opting to sleep where they fell in the open air of Washington. The next morning, Colonel Christian reported their arrival to Col. John K. Mansfield, inspector general of the army, who was also in charge of the district's defenses.[19]

Within days, the young soldiers were playing tourist in order to see the town's grand buildings. Twenty-two-year-old Pvt. DeWitt Staring of Company A was one of many who visited the capitol building, which was still under construction. He described the senate chamber as "the best sight I ever witnessed." Duty and its attendant rigors was never far away, though. "We have got to sleep with our guns loaded and by our side in case of any alarm," continued Staring, bemoaning the fitful rest that such alarms caused. Such an warning occurred almost immediately, during the Twenty-Sixth's second night in the capital. Though it ultimately proved to be false. Staring wrote how "we were in line of battle in 5 minutes after the Col. called us out, so you can see how we rest." Such were a young New Yorker's challenges in defending Washington.[20]

Washington, D.C.

The fledgling nation's capital in 1861 was a far cry from the major metropolitan center it would become within several decades. Fetid smells, intolerable dust in the summer, and mud everywhere in the winter were the physical characteristics that most visitors remembered. Cattle, pigs, and sheep seemed to have the run of the town, grazing wherever they pleased. It seemed that the various regiments also camped where they pleased, with little rhyme or reason to the layout. Oliver O. Howard, future Union general, but at that time the colonel of the Third Maine, recalled the Washington scene in that first summer of the great conflict: "Regiments crowned every height; officers in uniform thronged the streets and crowded the hotels. There appeared to the looker-on great confusion; not yet any regular, well-appointed force. Everybody talked; newspapers published and sometimes magnified idle rumors; they made and unmade reputations in a day. No one seemed to know what was to be done or what could be done."[21]

Culturally, the Union capitol was much more southern in its habits and customs than that of a major northern town, due in large measure to its geographic location. Confederate Virginia lay just over the Potomac River and while neighboring Maryland was technically a neutral border state, Lincoln was well aware of its significant secessionist sympathies, as evidenced by the bloody skirmishing in Baltimore of the previous months. Little wonder that the president viewed the safety of Washington as a preeminent concern. By early June, the oath of allegiance had been given to all employees within the capitol and its adjoining navy yard. Capt. James Dahlgren had administered the pledge to the various mechanics and laborers at the yard, without any type of distinction to the men's skin color. With a new army slowly being raised to protect Washington, attention could now turn toward the capital's physical defenses.[22]

2

A Long, Hot Washington Summer

The Twenty-Sixth settled into their positions on Meridian Heights with little difficulty. The initial euphoria, however, quickly turned into boredom with seemingly nothing to do in the way of confronting the enemy. The young men who so eagerly marched off to war with visions of gallantry and quick battlefield victory soon learned the daily lessons of a monotonous camp life. After only several weeks in Washington, the day after day routine of drill and parade exercises soon caused the average soldier, wrote Pvt. William Bacon, to become "lazy and shiftless in the extreme, and its effects demoralizing to the last degree, unless one's principles are firmly grounded and adhered to." Bacon then made his real point: "The idea I had was that we should march right on to bear the brunt of battle, and at the expiration of about a year return home covered with glory and honor, or die a patriot's death. The probability however is that little fighting will be done, and we shall lie around this city to protect it." The tedium often showed its effects in drunkenness and numerous late-night brawls with either civilians or soldiers from other regiments. These altercations were becoming so habitual that the local Washington newspaper was able to devote almost a column per day decrying the rowdy exploits of its volunteer defenders. Unfortunately for Colonel Christian, his New Yorkers were not immune from the less-than-favorable press. In one account, it was reported that an unidentified assailant belonging to the Twenty-Sixth attempted to stab a Massachusetts corporal with a bayonet near the corner of Ohio Avenue and Thirteenth Street. Though no reason for the fight was given, the article observed that several nearby soldiers pounced on the New Yorker and gave him a thorough thrashing, much to the delight of the civilian onlookers. Pvt. Timothy Gaffney, though, found it easy enough to explain his regiment's brawling in a letter home:. "[T]hey are a Blood Thirsty set of men and becaus [sic] they cannot get at the enemy they are fighting among themselves."[1]

The fact that the regiment had yet to be paid did not help attitudes, either. Plus, there was a growing rumor circulating among some men that what they viewed as a 90-day federal enlistment was evolving into two years without their just consent. This issue would come to head a month later. In late June, Pvt. Albert Collier wrote home bemoaning the life of the new recruits: "[T]ell Johnny that i think a soldiers life a hard one and that i think he is the best off to be at home ... they was a going to pay us as soon as we got to Elmirey [sic] and have not got it yet and i think it a shame ... they say now that they will not pay any thing unless we stay in for too [sic] years...."[2]

Just because the Twenty-Sixth left New York with a full compliment of men did not mean that recruiting had stopped. The army knew that more men would soon be needed so the recruiting office in Utica was still open for business. Getting those still-eager recruits to Washington was becoming a trickier matter, however. M. M. Jones, a civilian recruiter stationed in Utica, wrote to Colonel Christian on June 25 bemoaning the lack of transportation. "What shall I do?" lamented Jones. "I am beset to send on recruits for your Regt. to Washington, but know of no way of doing it without paying fare." With no means to carry out his authority, Jones concluded his missive: "As I am sort of godfather to your Regt. *here* hope you will send no more recruiting officers here without clay, or straw, or tolls, or something."[3]

Even with more men on the way, the Union Quartermasters Department had been completely unprepared for the massive pouring of men into Washington. The small, professional staff within that department consisted of only 37 officers when the war broke out. Unfortunately, close to one-fourth of those resigned their posts to join the Confederacy while most of the others had been stationed out West. Months were to pass before they were brought East and reassigned. Other valuable officers were lost when those men accepted combat command. With the quartermaster's department totally overwhelmed and embarrassed, many recruits still wandered around without guns, proper uniforms, and questionable food.[4]

Several soldiers of the Twenty-Sixth who were tired of waiting for proper clothes went into Washington and purchased their own uniforms, choosing those that suited their own taste and convenience. Those tastes were as varied as the states and towns that the men had come from. Still others were forced to don trousers or shirts that were in a very ragged and torn condition. This individual solution to the uniform dilemma of purchasing any reasonable uniform from any practical source even became temporary government policy. By early summer, Quartermaster Gen. Montgomery Meigs had ordered the purchase of ready-made clothing rather than force improperly clothed regiments to remain in camp. Meigs acknowledged the "slop shop clothing that I did not wish to buy," but the situation was so dire that he ordered his subordinates to purchase any durable cloth of a modest color and to have it quickly turned into uniforms. The general

Capt. George Arrowsmith (Applegate— "Reminiscences and Letters of George Arrowsmith").

received some political heat from his decision but later defended it by remarking that anyone "who saw sentinels walking post about the capital of the United States in freezing weather in their drawers, without trousers or overcoats" would not blame the quartermasters department for attempting to clothe them.[5]

The rations issue was not as severe as the uniform one; nevertheless the consistency was sometimes questionable. Captain Arrowsmith explained, "[W]e frequently take some long fasts, just long enough to make us relish the pork, bread, and coffee when we get it." A want of basic supplies was also present. The men slept on the ground, utilizing knapsacks and stumps for pillows. Waterproof blankets were an especially popular commodity in short supply. Tents were often so short that the sight of legs and feet protruding from the opening was routine. "Bayonets serve for forks and candlesticks, brush houses for kitchens, ammunition boxes for seats and tables," continued Arrowsmith, "while at times there are vague rumors that shoes and boots will have to be used to make soup and jerked beef."[6]

It wasn't entirely a case of drill and lying about camp. There was apparently ample time for the as-yet-untrained army to react to intentionally set false alarms. One balmy June evening showcased how almost the entire army could be awoken and in battle line due solely to the long roll of an unwitting 18-year-old drummer boy. William Harrar, the drummer boy for Oneida County's Fourteenth New York Infantry, was instructed to sound the call to arms after he was ordered to accompany a superior officer to the parade ground around midnight. Half-asleep soldiers fell out of their tents, grabbing their rifles along the way, while officers sounded the call to fall in. The Twenty-Sixth, which was camped next to the Fourteenth, was ordered deployed for skirmish duty. A battery was also moved near a shallow crossing on the Potomac, lest the Confederates try a crossing there. The rebel drums soon joined in and for a few moments, heartbeats quickened in the chests of the New Yorkers. The nervous soldiers maintained their positions throughout the night, though it was apparent by dawn that the whole charade was a false alarm. Word of the event soon reached the president. Lincoln sensed that a stunt had been pulled and quickly summoned all of his colonels and field officers to the White House at 10:00 A.M. to find out who was the culprit. Colonel Christian was questioned very closely by the president but was fortunately able to prove that the call came from a camp to the left of the Twenty-Sixth. Ultimately, everyone returned to their camps still unclear as to who the prankster was. Not until 25 years later, while together and smoking their pipes and reminiscing, did Harrar reveal his account to William Christian.[7]

The deed was well-forgotten by the time the nation's birthday rolled around. July 4, 1861, was a day of dress parade for the Twenty-Sixth New York. A show of the grand army in the making had been organized by Maj. Gen. Charles Sandford to celebrate the nation's birthday. The martial highlight would be an energetic parade along Pennsylvania Avenue which would consist of all the New York regiments who were still encamped on the Washington side of the Potomac. Lincoln stood along with General-in-Chief Winfield Scott on a canopied platform in front of the White House as they watched 21,000 New Yorkers in full uniform parade down the avenue. The day was extremely hot and humid, but according to one civilian, "[T]he men appeared strong, active, and vigorous and in the very best of spirit." Colonel Christian, astride his black charger, marched his men in the second

2. A Long, Hot Washington Summer   17

Washington, D.C., parade, July 4, 1861 (A. Waud sketch—Library of Congress).

brigade past the reviewing stand. Smart, sharp salutes were delivered by the still gray-clad regiment as they marched by. Even Lincoln noticed their out-of-place uniforms, as he purportedly asked an assistant "what rag-mill that body of men represented" when the New Yorkers marched by. Despite their seedy attire, the Twenty-Sixth was gaining a reputation as a well-oiled unit on the drill field and it showed on this day. Brass bands, broiling sun and picnics all around added to the Independence Day morning celebrations. To the average onlooker, it was army of massive proportions, embodying the American spirit that must march on Richmond immediately to stamp out treason.[8]

July 10 brought about a crucial and long-awaited piece in the well-armed, well-dressed soldier puzzle. Newer muskets were finally available to the New Yorkers! A morning march to the city arsenal was at hand, where the men exchanged their antiquated smoothbores for a more modern pattern. Despite the fact they did not receive the modern Enfield or Springfield rifles many had been expecting, all agreed the 1852 smoothbores were a vast improvement over what they had been issued.[9]

The next day, July 11, brought even more merriment to the New Yorkers. Payday! Having not received one cent since their arrival in Washington, the arrival of the U.S. paymaster was a blessed sight, indeed. Some had feared that they were never to be paid at all. The regiment's correspondent to the hometown and Democratic *Utica Daily Observer* wrote, "Soldiering one or two months without a cent of money—reduced to the utmost poverty—without a farthing to buy anything, not even to buy tobacco or pay postage on our letters to our friends,—made many of us think that the war had some other sufferings besides those of common every day life."[10]

Washington politics and the subsequent demand for military action had been brought fully to bear on General-in-Chief Henry Halleck and commanding Union Gen. Irvin McDowell. Though McDowell rightfully argued that his green army was still unprepared for battle, political realities prompted him to cross the Potomac River and bring his 35,000 men into the Virginia fields on July 16. Their goal was to engage the Confederate army under the command of Gen. Pierre Gustav Toutant Beauregard. Beauregard had his troops positioned near the railroad depot of Manassas Junction, some 25 miles to the west of Washington. The first major clash between the two fledgling armies was drawing near. The Twenty-Sixth New York was not assigned a place in McDowell's column; instead they were to be held back as part of the reserve. It was a role which they would become well acquainted with by the time they mustered out two years later.

By the morning of Sunday, July 21, the first major battle of the war was underway near a northern Virginia stream known as Bull Run. The Twenty-Sixth, which was still in Washington, was quickly reassigned to Col. John McCunn's recently organized four-regiment brigade, which was part of Irvin McDowell's Army of Northeast Virginia. After receiving orders from Gen. Winfield Scott, McCunn quickly marched his men along with three days' rations in their haversacks from their Washington camp. McCunn knew that their mission was one of support for

The slave pen, Alexandria, Virginia (*Gardner's Photographic Sketchbook*).

the army at Bull Run, but as was usually the case, the average private did not know their destination. Leaving around noon, they boarded a steamer to cross the Potomac. Unfortunately, their number was too great, forcing about one-fourth of the regiment to wait for the steamer to make a return trip. Once at Alexandria, Virginia, they were to take a train to the Manassas battlefield where the war's first great battle was underway. Upon arrival, they met their new comrades in McCunn's advance brigade, which consisted of the Twenty-Sixth, as well as the Fifteenth, Twenty-Fifth, and Thirty-Seventh New York. The dreary day provided an opportunity to witness firsthand the slavery horrors that most of the northern men had only read about. While marching through Alexandria, the regiment passed by the notorious human stockade with the words "slave pen" emblazoned at the top. Private Rightmire described it as a blood-chilling sight. "My ire was raised to highest pitch. I told my comrades if I ever got the chance, I would shoot to kill at so diabolical [an] institution."[11]

Alexandria, Virginia

Alexandria, which is located due south of Washington just across the Potomac River, had been seized by Union soldiers on May 24, 1861. That day marked the first bloodshed of the war in Virginia when an irascible pro–Confederate hotelier named James W. Jackson shot and killed Lt. Col. Elmer Ellsworth of the Eleventh New York Fire Zouaves. Ellsworth was attempting to remove the town's Confederate flag, which flew above Jackson's inn. Jackson had previously issued the public challenge regarding the flag "that whoever should attempt to remove it, would have to pass over his dead body." Upon killing Ellsworth, Jackson was immediately gunned down inside the hotel by a fellow soldier of Ellsworth's. News of the shootings spread like wildfire across the telegraphs throughout the land, with each man quickly becoming both hero and martyr to their respective sides.[12]

Prior to the war, Alexandria had been a thriving port town of almost 13,000 residents. Its existence went back to colonial times and the prosperity and prominence of the town was well-known to all. By late spring of 1861, the town had been reduced to a shell of its former glory, with a *New York World* columnist reporting that he had never seen a more forsaken people or desolate city. Pavements, once smooth, were now rough and dilapidated; cobblestones in piles alternated with mudholes and pitfalls. The greenery of the city, from trees and manicured lawns to colorful flower beds, all vanished under the footfalls of the advancing Union army. Businesses were closed as their owners had fled from the growing fear of war, while gray-clad soldiers, instead of civilians, had roamed the streets prior to the Union occupation.[13]

The few Confederates garrisoned at the town had vanished with the Yankee arrival, so now Alexandria bustled as both a federal supply depot and camp for the newly arriving Union soldiers. Those citizens with southern sympathies who still remained kept huddled to themselves inside their homes as they witnessed the telegraph office and railroad yards quickly fall under Union control. Alexandria soon became an armed camp for an ever-growing army. The need for the protection of Washington quickly began to reshape the topography of the land as massive construction of earthworks and forts soon began, with virtually every eminence crowned with some type of fort. A town of one-time sumptuous bounty and beauty became one of depravity and desolation.

★ ★ ★

Still waiting at Alexandria for the word to advance, many of the newly minted bluecoats were exhilarated that the perceived glory of battle was about to be experienced. Better to be on the battlefield to watch the rebels run and leave the dreary boredom of camp life well behind. Colonel Christian could hear the cannonading from the front and twice received orders to proceed, but both times the orders were countermanded as there was no train to take his force to the front. It was not until early evening that their west-bound train was found, so some soldiers of the Twenty-Sixth amused themselves throughout the afternoon of July 21 by trying to pry away pieces of the inn for souvenirs where Colonel Ellsworth had been killed almost a month prior. While waiting, the sounds of cannon could be clearly heard from the distant field, not only in Alexandria but back near their Washington camp as well. Excitement and anxiety was running high as the train set out but then the cars stopped unexpectedly at nearby Springfield Station. Sensing that battle might be at hand, Christian cautiously threw out a picket line. Exhilaration turned to groans as the regiment received a dispatch with the disturbing news that Union forces had been signally routed from the field and were now in full retreat back to Washington. The Twenty-Sixth was immediately ordered back to Alexandria where they took up a position in a grove about 40 rods west of Fort Ellsworth, (named after the late Union martyr, Colonel Ellsworth) atop Shuter's Hill so that they could help cover the retreat of McDowell's army. Abandoned homes and barns in the vicinity became the new barracks. Colonel Christian showed proper military discretion by not commenting directly to the press on the battle itself, but in a letter home opined that he felt the army had moved 10 days too early. In covering and observing the Union army's retreat, Christian wrote that, "every road leading from the action is crowded with returning troops. They came by squads, by companies and by regiments. Blackened faces and tattered uniforms designate those who suffered most severely." George Arrowsmith concurred with his colonel's assessment. "All parts of the North were represented in the rout—Zouaves with their gay uniforms torn, dirty and blood-soiled, soldiers without shoes, some without guns or knapsacks; others, more determined, carrying away three or four of each; some without eyes, some without ears, and others with various flesh wounds, riding limping, or running—such was the picturesque procession which went along the road all yesterday forenoon." They didn't realize it at the time, but the Alexandria hills around Fort Ellsworth would be their home for the next nine months.[14]

The days following the Bull Run disaster were filled with anticipation of a rebel attack on the capital. Pickets were thrown out virtually around the clock, but by the 26th it was apparent that no strike was forthcoming.

With the debacle at Manassas fresh in his mind, Lincoln felt a change in command was needed. On July 27, 1861, Irvin McDowell was dismissed and George McClellan was brought in as the new commanding general of the Division of the Potomac.

The 35-year-old McClellan had graduated second in his 1846 class at West Point and had developed an impressive military record since then. Due in part to

Alexandria and its environs (*Official Military Atlas of the Civil War*).

a small but significant victory in the western Rich Mountain campaign out in western Virginia, Lincoln decided to place "Little Mac" in command. Numerous treatises have been written over the decades debating the strategic brilliance or lack thereof of George McClellan. One aspect of his leadership, though, has been universally agreed upon, and that was his penchant for military training, administration, and organization. The Union's Army of the Potomac would end the war four years later as the greatest and most powerful army on the face of the earth. The seeds of that legacy began with General McClellan's initial training of that force.[15]

The reorganization and continuous developing of the capital's defenses prompted a change of camp for the Twenty-Sixth on July 27. Leaving Fort Ellsworth in able hands, the New York boys marched out to Camp Maxwell, about three miles farther west from the Episcopal seminary. More reinforcements were also on the way, as well. Word reached the camp that an additional 150 men had been recruited in Utica, and were expected to arrive in camp the following Sunday. The Second Oneida was again closing in on 1,000 men under arms.[16]

In addition to the new recruits, proper federal uniforms were finally available. Excitement was rampant in the camp on July 29 as the rumor spread that each man was to draw new clothes and that the paymaster was once again present. Gone were the dingy gray uniforms that had caused so much confusion for so many at Bull Run. Replacing them were the brand new dark blue jackets and light blue trousers of the burgeoning federal army. Pvt. Cornelius Rightmire of Company K merrily recalled, "We privates each drew eight dollars in silver. Now we did strut in our new suits with that silver in our pockets!" Getting paid was apparently still a bit more problematic for other soldiers, such as Pvt. Charles A. Smith, who had just enlisted in the Twenty-Sixth following a brief stint with the Eighth Ohio Infantry. Honorably discharged for ill health, Smith never received a dime's worth of pay for his time of service, prompting letters to the Ohio Adjutant General's office seeking redress. For those privates who did get paid, the new euphoria proved too exhilarating. The money prompted many to continue refining their taste for alcohol-induced trouble, as evidenced by George Childs of Company H, whose right hand was shattered when a drunken comrade discharged a loaded musket into it. Both men were reported to be on "benders," and ended up being among the 40 men held in Alexandria "slave-pens" for drunk and disorderly conduct.[17]

The feeling of martial pride and joy in the new clothes was short-lived, however. Some New Yorkers felt that new uniforms were a moot point since the regiment would be going home in a few days, or so they thought. The federal government clearly had other ideas. August brought the new army's first contentious confrontation regarding the actual term of enlistment, with some regiments, most notably the Seventy-Ninth New York and Second Maine Infantry regiments, forcefully asserting that 90 days was duty in full. After all, this was what they believed they had signed up for during those April days of enlistment. In the case of the Twenty-Sixth New York, the argument had some merit, for a review of the original muster documents, published in 1864, clearly revealed the term of service as 90 days. In a strange twist of fate, the Twenty-Sixth was one of a handful of New York regiments listed at 90 days with the exceptions of the militia. Apparently, the mustering officer, Capt. Washington L. Eliot, had mistakenly mustered in the Twelfth, Thirteenth, Twenty-First and Twenty-Sixth for only 90 days, though the term of enlistment was supposed to be two years. The mistake was not caught by the adjutant general's office, either. An army inspector to the Elmira recruitment camp back in early June wrote in his report that, "Two of these regiments (the Twenty-First and *Twenty-Sixth*) have been mustered into the service of the United States for three months. The remaining five are volunteers in the service of the State for two years." By August 2, their oversight

1st Lt. William E. Mercer resigned August 1861 during the Twenty-Sixth's first term-of-enlistment controversy (Dan Wisnoski Collection—USAMHI).

was rectified. On that day, the New York Adjutant General's office sent Special Order No. 325 to Colonel Christian ordering him on August 21 "to report with his command to the Adjutant General of the United States Army, for the remainder of the two-year term of enlistment."[18]

The camps were rampant with allegations regarding who was to blame and there were even some token threats of violence. "If they hold the 26th regiment we will have war in the camp; there will be blood and murder..." wrote Private Gaffney. In the end, most of the enlisted men dutifully accepted the longer term, though numerous officers refused to back down and threatened resignation. Colonel Christian took the men at their word, called his officers around, and stated that none were to remain except those who were prepared to serve the entire two years. The acrimony was rife, with the acting adjutant, David Smith Jr. somehow placing blame for the whole affair on Christian himself. Maj. Gilbert S. Jennings quickly came to his colonel's defense, accused Smith of being drunk on numerous occasions, once in uniform, and that only Christian's benevolence prevented Smith from being court-martialed. In all, a total of 14 officers from the Twenty-Sixth tendered their resignations, having concluded that the military life they had anticipated was not meeting up with the day-to-day reality. Their resignations were promptly accepted. Replacement officers were selected from those who were committed to the full service and their names sent to the governor of New York for approval. Among those chosen and accepted by the governor was 19-year-old William Bacon, who would soon serve as adjutant for the regiment. The Twenty-Sixth New York was far from being the only regiment to question their time of duty and though the matter had been peaceably settled within the regiment, the whole affair was a small stain on their service record.[19]

The time-of-enlistment issue was likewise of great concern with the Fourteenth New York Infantry. Also known as the First Oneida, it was a brother-in-arms regiment of the Twenty-Sixth, having been recruited primarily from Oneida County simultaneously with Christian's command. The discord within that regiment was similar to the Twenty-Sixth's, with Sgt. David Ritchie of the Fourteenth concluding that the turmoil had been brought about primarily "by *outside* mischief makers," in particular reporter(s) from *both* regiments' hometown newspapers. "Instead of endeavoring to inspire loyal soldiers with still greater zeal," wrote Ritchie, "they endeavor to cool their ardor in every possible way, however dishonorable." One correspondent had already been placed under arrest by saying that the war had gone far enough and that he would do everything in his power to see that the regiments came home quickly. The Fourteenth had been partially recruited in the town of Rome, a Democratic stronghold which lay about 17 miles northwest of Utica. That regiment was viewed by some Romans as their "hometown" unit, and therefore, they displayed only passing sentiment at best toward the Twenty-Sixth. A few days after the early August term-of-enlistment episode, a lieutenant from the Twenty-Sixth showed up in Rome trying to enlist more recruits into the Second Oneida. After a hard week, the officer had secured only one man. The Democratic *Rome Weekly Sentinel,* no friend of the Lincoln administration's position on the 90-day matter, gleefully editorialized on the recruiter's lack of success: "Disgusted by the disrelish of Romans for military glory, he departed with his solitary captive." The whole term-of-enlistment affair could have been far worse, however.

The federal government quickly announced that two years was the enlistment period and that any man who refused would be sent to hard labor.[20]

William Tecumseh Sherman, an army regular who was currently stationed in Washington and who was three and a half years away from his famous "March to the Sea," made clear his distaste for the entire class of volunteer soldier: "They may eat their rations and go on Parade," wrote Sherman, "but when danger comes they will be sure to show the white feather." Sherman had been promoted from colonel to brigadier general only days earlier and wasted no time in showing his disdain for those questioning the term of enlistment. When over 100 mutineers in his brigade reacted as had those in the Twenty-Sixth, he sent them off in leg irons to help build Fort Jefferson in the Gulf of Mexico. A local civilian wrote how he had "witnessed this evening the quelling of a mutiny among the 79th [NY] Regt. A strong force of Infantry and Cavalry and four pieces of Artillery were brought to bear upon them when they 'fell in' and were paraded on 14th St, the ring leaders picked out, 36 in number who will be punished, some of them probably shot." George McClellan was prepared to carry out the civilian's prediction. "I have the ringleaders in irons" wrote the stern general. "They will be tried and probably shot tomorrow; an example is necessary to bring these people up to the mark."

The show of force and governmental willpower had apparently gotten through to most of the men from Oneida County. Capt. John Babcock of the First Oneida summarized the realities to his sister by declaring that if the New York regiments did not accept the two-year service, "the Sec'y of War will either disband and send us home at the expiration of the three months or send us someplace where we won't care about going—They want no growling regiments near where others are for disaffection among troops will spread and a dissatisfied *volunteer* is a poor *soldier*—They have a way of sending fault finding troops to some point where fortifications & c. are being thrown up & instead of a musket give them a pick and a shovel to handle." On the other hand and despite the threats, George Arrowsmith's pen disagreed with Sherman and McClellan's caustic opinions. "The volunteers are now the only force the country can rely upon," wrote the captain in August 1861. Arrowsmith continued, "The regular army is now only a fossil relic of something that *once* was of some importance. Now, it is only of use as a police force, for which it is usually employed." Colonel Christian likewise agreed with his junior officer, wryly remarking that he "owned the corn" in expressing his preference for his volunteers.[21]

★ ★ ★

McClellan's first major reorganization of the army occurred in early August. The divisions and brigades were reformed, with experienced military men, chiefly West Pointers, at the head of most of them. As of August 4, 1861, the Second Oneida was made part of Brig. Gen. Samuel Heintzelman's brigade, which was now one of the 12 brigades that made up the Union army's Division of the Potomac. Their comrades in the brigade included the Sixteenth and Twenty-Seventh New York volunteers, the Fifth Maine, and Tibaldi's Battery A of the 2nd U.S. Artillery. Home was now Camp Vernon in Alexandria, near the old Episcopal seminary *(modern address of 3737 Seminary Road, Alexandria)*.

One of the first direct contacts with rebel cavalry for the Oneida men occurred on August 14. Capt. Thomas Davis of Company H and 50 men set out from camp on a routine picket and patrol mission. Near the small hamlet of Annandale, located about three miles south of Bailey's Crossroads, they encountered a small squadron of Confederate cavalry. Having not yet been detected, the boys in blue quietly rode around the edge of a wood where they expected to surprise the gray riders. At the last moment, the federal patrol was detected and the rebels quickly managed to get off two volleys, with no impact on the Oneida men. The Twenty-Sixth returned their fire, emptying several rebel saddles. The fire of the musketry alerted the nearby Confederate camp, which quickly sounded the long drum roll of alarm. Plainly hearing such a call told the New Yorkers that the enemy was in force and quite nearby, prompting Captain Davis to withdraw his unit back to camp and report their findings.[22]

Yet another camp move was forthcoming on the 15th when the Twenty-Sixth moved into the rear of Fort Ellsworth, about three-quarters of a mile from Alexandria along the Little River Turnpike. The new camp was christened "Camp Mary," and the purpose of the switch was to consolidate their position with that of their fellow regiments in Heintzelman's brigade. Though the new locale lacked the physical beauty of their prior countryside position at Camp Maxwell, the move was viewed by Captain Arrowsmith as being for the best, since he felt the affairs of their new brigade would be carried out with more responsibility and order. Despite Arrowsmith's approval of the move as being for the best, it was also viewed by most as a nuisance in the short run. Camp articles were merely tossed into large wagons, creating total confusion as to who owned what. Inevitably, it always seemed to rain, adding a layer of mud to everything. The solution, according to Arrowsmith, was to have "some women to scold the teamsters, it would be as good as an ordinary May Day."[23]

Mid-August brought about more blows delivered against the enemy by the Twenty-Sixth. Sunday, August 11, found the companies of Capts. Charles Jennings, William West, and George Blackwell on picket duty on the south side of Hunting Run, which runs in a southeasterly direction on the southern extreme of Alexandria. Starting from their camp on the northern edge of Hunting Run, the companies set out on the Mount Vernon Road, crossed a lengthy bridge over the run, and then took separate roads once on the other side. Orders were to throw out their pickets four to six miles south of the stream toward the enemy, and to simply wait and watch. Such was the dull drama of picket duty. The tired and bored guardsmen remained at their lonely posts until the following morning, at which time they were startled to hear the unmistakable sound of a large body of Confederate infantry approaching. The companies hurriedly returned to camp later on Monday at which time a now much-concerned Colonel Christian anxiously listened to their report. Who was guarding that important bridge? It lay only about one mile in from the Potomac, so if a large body of rebel infantry traversed that bridge with no warning, they could strike into the heart of the Union base at Alexandria and wreak considerable havoc. Highly alarmed, Christian immediately mounted his horse and charged off with Lieutenant Colonel Richardson and Major Jennings to investigate. Their fears were confirmed upon arrival. Only nine men of the Twenty-Seventh New York, who would be brushed aside by an enemy force of any size, guarded the huge wooden structure. Christian pounded his way to General Franklin's headquarters to alert his divisional commander of the potential danger. In explaining the scenario, Christian volunteered the Twenty-Sixth to assume responsibility for the road's security. Franklin agreed, and it was determined that one company could probably handle the matter.

That evening, Captain Arrowsmith and his Company C spent a most miserable night. Rain fell in torrents, and the poor New Yorkers were obliged to stand along the bridge as sentries, thereby garnering the full force of the storm in their faces. Captain Arrowsmith and Adjutant Bacon were on horseback and periodically rode out amongst the hills to sense if any rebel force was approaching. Red and yellow rockets shot off by the Confederates convinced the young officers that there were plenty of rebels out there, it was only a question of which direction were they heading.

The following morning, Arrowsmith returned his company to camp to resume their normal duties. Throughout the day, Colonel Christian pondered the bridge's security and slowly seemed to develop a different attitude. Rather than protecting it, Christian now felt that the bridge had to be destroyed. It occurred to him that the army's entire attitude up to that point had been one of not inconveniencing the enemy, and of attempting to avoid any type of property destruction. Christian rode to the tent of Col. Thomas Davies, who was in command of the brigade in place of the ailing Samuel Heintzelman, who had been seriously wounded at Bull Run and was still recuperating. Christian pointed out to Davies how one well-placed rebel cannon could sweep his entire force from the bridge and into the river. That being completed, the rebel force could march unimpeded into Alexandria and possibly precipitate another rout of the bluecoats as had happened only a month prior. Davies agreed, and dispatched two companies, one from the Twenty-Sixth and one from the Twenty-Seventh New York to complete the task. The torch was soon put to the oaken structure, and in short order, months of manual labor was reduced to ashes.[24]

Four days after their successful destruction of the Hunting Run bridge, the Twenty-Sixth was again detached for all-day picket and patrol duty. Three companies of the regiment were sent forward on the 21st to relieve those men from the Sixteenth New York, who were currently patrolling the designated area. One company was to patrol the Mount Vernon Road *(modern Old Mount Vernon Road)* a second was to man the barricade at the intersection of the Richmond Road and the old Fairfax Road, while the third company was to be broken down into platoons and sections. The platoon would command the intersection at the junction of the Richmond and Mount Vernon Roads, with various squads being thrown out on the same roads.[25]

The seemingly constant state of watchfulness and alarm knew no boundary with regard to time of day or day of the week. Sunday evening church services were rudely interrupted the night of August 25 when it was reported that a large body of Confederates was advancing on Alexandria via the Mount Vernon Road. The services were quickly dispensed with, and instead of leading their companies in the singing of Psalms, orders were issued to all captains to distribute ammunition. The Twenty-Sixth and their brigade comrades were ordered to be ready to march within five minutes. Troops ran helter-skelter to grab their muskets and cartridge belts as the drum roll sounded. But on this night, as with so many others, the alarm turned out to be a false one, allowing the young New Yorkers the opportunity to return to their Bibles.

Having reorganized the army to his current satisfaction, McClellan now realized that a stronger degree of order and martial discipline was needed. No longer would the drunken rowdiness that had been so prevalent on the streets of the capital be earlier that summer be tolerated. Passes would be required to leave camps, whether on furlough or to the hospital, and their issuance was rare. A provost marshal's department was created to sweep the streets of all the loitering soldiers who had no business in the town. Those without proper passes were arrested.[26]

Around this time the United States Sanitary Commission also began its mission, which in the Washington area was a far more benevolent one than that assigned to McClellan's provost department. Initially, the commission's task was to inspect the various regimental camps with the hope of instilling a sense of hygiene and sanitation to the sites. Despite the presence of the government's official Medical Bureau, the all-volunteer Sanitary Commission was officially endorsed by the federal government in June 1861. Though Lincoln sanctioned its creation, he often referred to the commission as his "fifth wheel on the coach," mistakenly believing that the commission's mission of mercy was being duplicated elsewhere. Its task was daunting, for sanitation within the volunteer camps turned out to be exactly what its inspectors had feared. Camp inspector Robert Tomes made his way to the Twenty-Sixth's camp in late August for what would be the first of three inspections for the Oneidans over the next eight months. The New Yorkers initially fared neither worse nor better than most of their new comrades. Though the camp's site was deemed appropriate, being elevated on a hillside for proper drainage, little else in the way of camp cleanliness passed muster. Drains were considered foul, camp streets were labeled as dirty or neglected, and the area between the tents was described as littered. The men's personal hygiene fared better, with the inspector noting that the men bathed frequently (twice a week) and under the proper, watchful eye of an officer, though their heads, neck and feet were washed daily. As this inspection was coming hot on the heels of early August's near-mutiny, the inspector dutifully noted that the spirits of the men were only "so-so." That was also the inspector's approach toward the overall health of the regiment, as he commented that the general health of the unit was "deteriorating slightly."[27]

With the health and sanitary matters of the camps now purportedly under control, McClellan then instituted boards of examination which were to determine the fitness for command of the various volunteer officers. His expectations were clearly laid out to these officers, creating much consternation among some of the ineffectual ones who had received their commands via political appointment. Colonel Christian had no concerns, due in large measure to his prior duty with the army in Mexico. The colonel responded to McClellan's directives on September 2 by clearly stating how the Twenty-Sixth New York would be handled on a daily basis. His written orders were as follows: "Reveille at sunrise, Squad drill from 5:30 to 6:30 A.M.—Surgeons call at 6:30 A.M.-Breakfast at 7 A.M.—Guard mounting at 8 A.M.—Police call at 8:30 A.M. at which time every company will clean its grounds about and opposite the tents.—Adjutants call at 9 A.M.—Company and skirmish drill at 9:30 A.M. until 11 A.M.—Dinner at 12 M.—Battalion drill at 3:30 P.M.—Dress parade (call-retreat) at sunset—Supper at 7 or 7:30 P.M.—Tattoo at 9 and taps at 9:30 P.M. when all noises in camp will cease and all lights be extinguished. The officer of the day will be responsible for the execution of these last orders. Guards are directed to adhere to the regulation for their government as published with army regulations, and officers of the guard are responsible for the proper observance of the rules, and will, until further orders read them to their guards. Captains of companies will read the articles of war to their respective commands every Sabbath, on which day their will be no squad or company drills." Observing the Sabbath was to become official Army of the Potomac policy. Four days later on September 6, McClellan announced to the army through General Order No. 7 that the army should display a more proper respect for the Sabbath. All work was to be suspended and no military movements undertaken on that day of the week.[28]

To help facilitate McClellan's new directives regarding regimental discipline, Colonel Christian, a pious man, held a meeting in his tent with all of the regiment's commissioned officers. Christian was also known as a teetotaler and was gaining a smart reputation within the ranks as a spit-and-polish disciplinarian. He asked his officers that they all sign a pledge of temperance, as an example to the rest of the troops. Christian offered to head the list. To his delight, all his officers readily agreed, and soon the same message was being circulated to the privates. More help of a higher order was also on the way.[29]

In order to facilitate proper spiritual observances for the multitude of young men in the army, it was common practice for each regiment to have its own regimental chaplain. It was this man's role to counsel his soldiers against the sins of drink and of the flesh that many found tempting being so far from home. Of course, during battle, the chaplain ministered to the wounded and dying as well. Since Ira Smith had resigned, the Reverend Dr. Daniel W. Bristol, a 48-year-old Methodist minister, arrived at the camp in October to serve as the new chaplain to the Twenty-Sixth.[30] Since the regiment's young men had gone through the spring and summer with minimal religious instruction, many of those soldiers found his presence most gratifying. In short order he was able to start up a regimental congregation of some 15 members and a temperance society of which he boasted at least 80 participants. The chaplain struck up a good friendship with deeply spiritual Adjutant William Bacon, who found in the chaplain a confidant and advisor. Bacon felt his situation was noticeably different from the prior summer when he wrote to his parents, "I have hardly been alone enough to read my Bible, and when I do read, it seems as if every body swore and cursed more than ever, and took peculiar pains to disturb me. Nevertheless I manage to read as often as possible, and find great relief in its sacred pages." Before long, Dr. Bristol was conducting evening services and afternoon temperance meetings for the Oneida boys, in addition to the regular morning services. Proper services meant the need for a chapel tent, especially during the coming winter. In addition, the much-desired tent would serve as an off-duty social gathering point for the young, single men. Judge William Bacon, father of the regiment's adjutant, set up a foundation back home to solicit the necessary donations. If the tent was procured, the War Department agreed to pay for the expense of transporting it to the regiment's camp.[31]

Picket duty, forage duty, and the occasional potshot at enemy horsemen had been the extent of the Twenty-Sixth's engagements through the long, hot Washington summer. Usually these types of daily events provided little in the way of battle, but offered plenty of good fodder for evening campfire discussions. In addition to rehashing the facts of the day, the rumor mills were also in full swing as to

Skirmishing between the pickets of the two armies in Virginia (*The Soldier in Our Civil War*).

what, when, and how the regiment's next action would transpire. According to Private Gaffney, one such rumor had the Twenty-Sixth being sent to Kentucky or Missouri since that was where the majority of the actual fighting was then occurring. The young private had no doubt what was in store for the gray-clad enemy should he and his fellow New Yorkers be sent west: "There will be some bloody battles there when we reach that place unless the rebels surrender for this is the crack regiment in Washington and Alexandria and all about this place."[32]

Despite the apparent routine in daily life, a Yankee lad could quickly find himself being led off to a rebel prison camp if he dropped his guard or did not pay constant attention to what was going on around him. Three young men of the Twenty-Sixth learned that lesson the hard way on September 5 while out on a foraging expedition near Mount Vernon. While out gathering corn for their evening meals, Sgt. John Norton and Pvts. David Jones and Hiram Richmond were suddenly surprised and captured by a Confederate cavalry patrol. Private Richmond wrote to his family from a Confederate prison a few months later and described his capture. "I was the only one at the Post at the corners, and had hardly time to fire the signal gun and retire some distance, when a troop of cavalry rode down and took what there was at the Corners. I kept secreted some distance from them, but was soon taken in charge; resistance would have been death, and not wishing to throw my life away at so cheap a bid, had but to give up my faithful musket." The rebels had fine mounts but a number of the horsemen lacked shoes and good clothes even at this early stage in the war. They quickly concluded that Yankee clothes would do and ordered the now highly embarrassed New Yorkers to strip.

The bluecoats' Union comrades came running to help, but only saw the rebel horsemen riding away with three near-naked figures in the rear.[33]

These brief contacts between the opposing enemies had been commonplace since Bull Run, and by September were an almost daily occurrence. Any kind of larger-scale advance, however, seemed to be nowhere on the horizon for either side, though camp rumor was usually rife with such pending announcements. Nevertheless, Union commanders viewed the Confederate cavalry patrols as annoying and meddlesome, so small infantry excursions into the field were becoming daily events. New Brig. Gen. Henry W. Slocum brought Colonel Christian into his headquarters on October 3 and outlined to him what the next advance would entail. Christian, for the first time in the war, would personally lead a detachment of companies from not only the Twenty-Sixth New York, but men of the Fifth Maine and the Sixteenth New York, along with Company F of the Twenty-Seventh New York. Slocum wanted a wide variety of men from his brigade in this expedition to test the mettle and discipline of all involved. A total of 300 men, as well as a company of cavalry, were to head south along the Mount Vernon Road to the vicinity of eighteenth-century Pohick Church, where rebel cavalry were reported to be in camp. That house of worship was well known to all men both blue and gray as a spiritual home of George Washington, who had served as a vestryman there prior to the Revolutionary War. The church was located only 10 miles south of Washington, so the entire expedition was treated as merely a one-day affair. Slocum viewed his orders as crystal clear. Not only did he relay his expectations and instructions to Christian verbally, but then in writing as well. Two hundred twenty-five of the men were to circle to the rear of the enemy's camp with orders to attack at 6:00 the following morning. The remaining 75 infantrymen, along with the cavalry, were to advance south along the Richmond Road, starting

Union soldiers at Mount Vernon (*New York Illustrated News*).

their advance four miles north of the church. They would then slowly drive in the Confederate pickets beginning at 5:45 a.m., thereby capturing the main body in between.

The final advance in the pitch-black night started off properly, with the main body of bluecoats passing through the tiny village of Occoquan. They emerged from the woods just at daybreak, near their destination of Pohick Church. With rebel pickets clearly visible, the men expected orders to charge, but at the last moment Christian called off his men, opting instead to send them off in another direction. To one New Yorker of the Twenty-Seventh Infantry, it appeared as if the intent was to let the enemy get away before they hurt someone. Watching the affair unfurl, Captain Arrowsmith was dismayed to realize that the large body of cavalry they were anticipating was merely an outpost of 15 to 20 riders, probably belonging to the Hampton Legion. Sensing the danger, the gray horsemen bolted away, leaving behind their commissary stores and a half-cooked breakfast, which the hungry federals quickly disposed of. After sacking the officers' quarters and taking what supplies they could use, the Union men began their march back to camp, having completed what one participant called, "as useless an errand as a body of tired men were ever sent upon."

General Slocum, a by-the-book disciplinarian, was not pleased in the least when he was given the results of the expedition. According to his report, Slocum felt that Christian let matters get out of his control from the outset. The march was disjointed; orders were not followed, resulting in no significant quantity of rebel cavalry being taken upon the bluecoats' arrival near the church. Worse yet, on the return march, Christian's efforts at discipline and order were sadly lacking. Men from each company wandered off everywhere, looting and robbing not only secessionist civilians but pro–Union homes as well. To top it all off, one of their own men was accidentally shot and killed by a comrade. Slocum was outraged at his subordinate officer for not controlling such behavior and issued a general order condemning all officers who allowed or participated in such depredations on private property. Eighteen officers of the Sixteenth New York felt that it was a slap of their face to be lumped in with the looters and coolly demanded a retraction from Slocum. The general was not fazed. Instead of retracting his denunciation, he placed every one of the junior officers under arrest and confined them to their tents. According to Slocum, "Within a day or two, the most humble apologies commenced pouring in, and finally every one was released. But it had a wonderful effect."[34]

In his final report to division commander Gen. William Franklin, Slocum urged a court of inquiry be convened to look into the matter. The matter finally ended up on McClellan's desk, who agreed with his subordinate. Charges were to be preferred against Christian, but apparently the whole matter fell through the cracks. Ultimately, the entire mess blew over with no formal proceedings forthcoming.[35]

Though Colonel Christian entered into federal service with a positive reputation from his younger Mexican War days, his Civil War career was off to an inauspicious start. Regardless of Christian's earlier reputation, Slocum had apparently seen enough. In November 1861, Christian and the Twenty-Sixth were transferred essentially only on paper from his brigade to Gen. James Wadsworth's Washington command, with the still-under-construction Fort Lyon as their primary base.

The disappointing expedition to Pohick Church notwithstanding, life in the regiment's camp was not entirely without some upside. The quantity and quality of food was about as good as it was ever going to get for the boys in blue. "We have plenty of fresh beef twice a week, and good pork, corned beef and bacon, with coffee, tea, sugar, rice, hominy, beans, molasses, and bread," wrote one Oneidan. "Our rations are more than most of us can stow away.... Take it all in all, we are having a grand time down in Dixie, and all we want is a chance to get a sight at Beauregard, or some of his representatives."[36]

The pleasant fall days were starting to give way to much cooler weather, signaling that the Twenty-Sixth was soon to enter their winter quarters. Before continuing regimental command responsibilities, the colonel had some other business to attend to. On November 5, Christian requested a two-day pass to return home so he could attend to "important private business." His camp was rife with rumor that the regiment's bachelor colonel was to be married, however, according to Captain Arrowsmith, who wrote home with tongue firmly planted in cheek, "no court-martial has yet been convened on the subject." The rumors soon proved to be true. On the 6th, he married Mary H. Timmerman back in New York City. Unfortunately for the newlyweds, no honeymoon could be forthcoming, for Christian was still on active duty, and those responsibilities included a new command. Despite the Pohick Church fiasco, Christian was detached as commander of the massive Fort Lyon on November 6, per Special Order No. 154. With the same order, the Twenty-Sixth's lieutenant colonel, Richard H. Richardson, was detailed as commander of nearby Fort Ellsworth for the period of November and December 1861. Richardson would also be taking two companies of the Twenty-Sixth with him. A new stage of the regiment's enlistment was underway.[37]

3

On to Fort Lyon

Fort Lyon was named after Union Brig. Gen. Nathaniel Lyon, who had been killed at the August 10, 1861, battle of Wilson's Creek, near Springfield, Missouri. The new garrison was intended to be the preeminent work guarding the southern flank of the capitol and would ultimately prove to be the second-largest fortress in Washington's entire network of defense. Situated on the high ground overlooking Hunting Creek, just south of Union-controlled Alexandria, the fort's primary role was to hold that ground as Confederate batteries could easily shell Alexandria and other smaller forts if they took it. In fact, such a scenario had long been a subject of great anxiety to federal authorities. Once the bluecoats had been able to secure their possession of the heights, construction of the works began immediately, beginning with infantry trenches to provide cover for the fort's carpenters and engineers. Maj. John Newton of the army's engineer corps initially laid out its trace during the summer of 1861. Construction began in early September with the Twenty-Seventh New York Infantry initially breaking ground, but soon the majority of the garrison's development fell on the backs and shoulders of the Twenty-Sixth. It was hard manual labor, what with the constant swinging of axes and hammers. The daily, exhausting "fatigue duty" warranted a special reward for the thirsty New York boys. "We get 25 cents per day for working and two gills of whiskey," wrote 20-year-old Pvt. Timothy Gaffney in October. Unfortunately for young Gaffney, his satisfaction was short-lived, as he would die in early January of injuries suffered while working on the huge bastion.[1]

It was quickly realized that vast tracts of forest would have to come down in order to provide an adequate field of fire for the fort's guns, much to the consternation of the local pro–Southern citizenry who owned the land. In no time, the entire field of vision became a vast wasteland. The *Alexandria Local News* observed in October that, "The once wooded heights all around, are now destitute of trees, and the landscape, dotted with frowning fortifications, earthworks, and entrenchments, has that hard, cold, stern look which is anything but pleasant either in nature or design."[2] This was the land that the Twenty-Sixth New York now called home.

Once completed, the fort's rolling grounds covered a full nine acres with a perimeter of 937 yards. Most of the fort conformed to the topography of the ground, which mostly consisted of a high plateau where the main parts of the works were situated. The fort's 40 guns, primarily consisting of 32 mounted pieces and six mortars, had a full, sweeping field of fire that overlooked Alexandria's railroad depot, Telegraph Road and the Little River Turnpike.[3]

★ ★ ★

Unfortunately, none of Fort Lyon is still in existence. Only the slightest ghostly outline of Fort Lyon's northeast trace can still be detected. High-rise apartment buildings and the Huntington Station of the Washington, D.C., metro and subway sit on the plateau where this mighty bastion stood. Nevertheless, one can visit this location, and with a panoramic view of Alexandria and Washington in the background, still appreciate the strategic position that this garrison once held.

Other than the daily picket duty, no military action of consequence was forthcoming through the winter of 1861-62. Fort Lyon still was not entirely finished, so that task, along with the monotonous picket duty, provided plenty of daily work for the Twenty-Sixth. According to Captain Arrowsmith, camp life was "excruciatingly dull," and in a letter back home wrote that, "[we] have almost forgotten what we came here for—the chief object of the campaign being, in appearance, to keep warm. All who have any good pretext are endeavoring to get leaves of absence...."[4]

Though relatively little action had occurred with the enemy, the regiment's ranks were being slowly thinned by desertion, disability and illnesses. Many of the young men, some who had never left their hometowns, were starting to realize the hard realities of military life. Disease was quickly becoming a bigger enemy for the young men now living together than the Confederates were. The rebels were often not to be found, but disease seemed everywhere. Such was the case for young Pvt. Charles Mason of Company I. The 21-year-old had been sick throughout the summer and according to his hometown newspaper correspondent was "dying by the inches" and should be sent home. When Mason finally succumbed in early September, his body was sent home where it was buried with full military honors. Sickness also knew no bounds with regards to rank or position. Even General McClellan was stricken, contracting typhoid fever during December and January, which kept the general bedridden for weeks.[5]

New recruits were soon needed to replace those discharged for illness and disability, as well as the near-mutiny in August. The enticement to young men between the ages of 18 and 45 was a $100 bounty, a handsome sum in those days. One thousand men under arms was the goal for the typical Union regiment at the outset of the war. Typical of those arriving was Pvt. Francis Crigier, a 21-year-old blacksmith from Sequoit, New York. In addition to the bounty, the new soldier would earn a rate of pay of $13 per month. Getting that pay in a timely fashion was apparently no longer as problematic as it had been back in the dog days of summer when the war first started. With new systems in place, the Twenty-Sixth's soldiers were now receiving their wages on a regular basis. The long line of sutlers' wagons passing by the camps and hawking their various wares inevitably followed the welcome arrival in camp of the paymaster. Arrowsmith viewed these peddlers with a stern eye, for to him they "appeared like a Hebrew funeral, old women with baskets and boys with pails, all sorts of sharks selling to the soldiers very poor specimens of everything at very high prices." Most men ignored the sutlers, however, and dutifully sent their earnings home to their families.[6]

New faces were now routinely appearing in camp; however the quantity of new recruits coming into the regiment was still not to General Slocum's liking. Maj. Gilbert S. Jennings had been dispatched to Rochester, New York, for some two months and his lack of recruiting results had caught the general's demanding eye.

Plus, with Christian at Fort Lyon and Lieutenant Colonel Richardson in command at Fort Ellsworth, every senior officer of the regiment was needed in camp. On November 12, Slocum wrote to Gen. Seth Williams requesting that Jennings be brought back.[7]

Despite the fact that the two senior officers of the Twenty-Sixth New York were in charge of the two most important forts guarding Washington's southern flank, Slocum's trust in Christian, and by extension, Richardson, was lacking. By the middle of November, he was visiting the forts daily, and sometimes brought McClellan along as well. Everything was inspected, from the soldiers' personal grooming to the brigade hospitals. In spite of the fiercely cold weather, the New Yorkers routinely turned out to cheer their commanding general.[8]

$100 Bounty.

AND PROBABLY A LAND WARRANT. Volunteers wanted for the 26th Regiment—a number of able-bodied men between the age of 18 and 45.
Pay per month, $13. Mileage to Washington—making the first month's income $20.
This Regiment is commanded by Col. Wm. H. Christian who served with credit in the Mexican War.
In addition to pay, each recruit will receive uniform, clothing and good board and lodging as soon enlisted.
☞ Pay will commence from the time of enlistment.
Apply at the Recruiting Office, Exchange Buildings.
E. R. P. SHURLY
Captain 26th Regiment N. Y. Vols.
Utica, Sept. 5, 1861.   [dtf]   Recruiting Officer.

Newspaper classified ad offering a bounty to recruits for the Twenty-Sixth New York (*Utica Morning Herald and Daily Gazette*).

George McClellan was slowly succeeding in restoring morale and confidence to the Army of the Potomac. Drill parades were a source of pride to his men, especially when conducted in front of the various Washington dignitaries and senators and congressmen from back home. They had been held frequently ever since Bull Run, but the grand review slated for November 20 would be the largest yet. Over 60,000 soldiers decked out in Union blue paraded out past the Potomac River to the tiny Virginia village of Bailey's Crossroads. Lincoln, McClellan and most of the cabinet watched as the federal troops proudly marched past. This first "grand review" was an all-day affair as the line of men snaked backed to the capital. Cannonading and brass bands were in action from dawn to dusk. Unfortunately for the Twenty-Sixth, they were not invited to participate, instead being relegated to picket duty for the day. As a unit that had gained a positive reputation for parade and drill sharpness, this slight was duly noted. Captain Arrowsmith was convinced he knew the real reason for the oversight: "We had no new clothes to go to the show in," meaning their existing uniforms were starting to get a bit ragged for the spit and polish required by the generals of the day. They would be ready for the next one, though, for in a matter of days, new dark blue overcoats and forage caps would be forthcoming, in preparation for the coming winter.[9]

Picket duty was fast becoming the main activity of the regiment, outside of the laborious construction at Forts Lyon and Ellsworth. Though little contact with the enemy had occurred, the Twenty-Sixth proudly viewed themselves as a hardworking regiment and with ample justification. One anonymous writer defended the regiment's perceived inaction in a letter written to the hometown *Utica Daily Observer* in late November 1861. "In addition to their usual military services, such as drill and picket duty, they have labored extensively in constructing a line of beautiful forts which overlook and command the Potomac.... Their stalwart arms have swung the axe to the laying low hundreds of acres of forest, which obstructed the range of our protecting cannon, or afforded cover to a threatening enemy.... Only think of twenty or thirty acres going down before the warrior's axe in a single night, which was done in one night by this regiment."[10]

Daily visits to the outer works around Washington convinced McClellan and his staff more than ever of their strategic importance and of the rapid need to complete them. Fort Lyon was especially high on both lists. By late November, Col. Orlando M. Poe's Second Michigan Infantry had been added to the 600 men under Colonel Christian at Fort Lyon, giving Christian the equivalent of a small brigade to command at his garrison. His responsibilities and instructions were straightforward. He was being given an adequate and efficient garrison at Fort Lyon so that Christian would have fatigue parties large enough to finish construction of the huge complex before any winter storms might halt the work. Warm weather aided the soldiers' efforts and before long, 30 guns were mounted and ready for action. By the end of the year, artillery practice with the heavy 32- and 100-pound guns was a daily occurrence. The distinct whistle of the balls and their heavy thud against the ground could be heard as far as two miles away.[11]

The U.S. Sanitary Commission paid another visit to the Twenty-Sixth on December 14, no doubt with the hope that camp cleanliness had improved since the initial visit in August. Inspector George Blake placed the current regimental

Edwin Forbes' sketch of an eastward view looking toward Alexandria, Va., which is in the far background. Fort Lyon can be seen on the far right perched atop the heights of Hunting Creek, with Fort Ellsworth atop Shooter's Hill on the far left. This was home for the Twenty-Sixth's men from November 1861 through May 1862 (*Century Magazine*).

strength at 854 men, noting that two companies were now camped at Fort Ellsworth with the remaining eight at Fort Lyon. Blake had to have been pleased if he had seen the regiment's prior report, for on almost all counts, the Twenty-Sixth showed progress. From cleanliness of the camp streets to sanitary conditions near the privy, health matters were improving. In fact, Blake wrote the overall general health of the regiment was noticeably improving. The soldiers' diet was also considered satisfactory, which consisted of fresh meat two times a week, desiccated vegetables were served three times a week, while fresh bread was a happy constant due to the nearby army bakery in Alexandria. Fresh fruits and vegetables, however, were never to be had which was duly noted in Inspector Blake's report.[12]

Life for the regiment was not all mud, inspections, and manual labor. Free time allowed the men ample opportunity to visit the capital for an evening of revelry, though a soldier had to make sure that his pass was in proper order lest he wind up in the local stockade.

The new year of 1862 was ushered in on the morning of January 1 with a full cannonade that seemed to many a mere continuance of the previous night's celebrations. To those who had experienced an excess of celebration, the morning explosions no doubt added an additional headache to the one already brewing within their skulls. A morning of light snow added a softer touch to the aural and visual landscape. Several formal ceremonies of the day were highlighted by the first raising of the United States flag over Fort Lyon. Chaplain Daniel Bristol offered a few brief remarks to his assembled flock and then at precisely 2:00 P.M., Mary Christian, the colonel's new wife, pulled on the flagpole ropes. All cheered enthusiastically as "Old Glory" lifted into the clear, blue sky. As the New Yorkers let loose with three hearty cheers for the new ensign, the fort's guns joined in with another roaring echo. When Fort Lyon's guns had finished, Lieutenant Colonel Richardson's guns across the valley at Fort Ellsworth continued the salute.[13]

January's winter quarters gave the regiment an opportunity to deal with wayward soldiers and their accumulating disciplinary issues. The prescribed method of meting out justice was that of the military court-martial. These courts quickly showed that not all enlistees were of the solid martial stock that local recruiters had hoped for. The Twenty-Sixth was not spared with three privates facing the docket in January 1862. Pvt. Stephen Richards led the way by facing charges of being absent without leave from November 13 though December 6, 1861. The 40-year-old also faced charges of forgery and habitual drunkenness. Though he pleaded not guilty, he was found guilty on all charges and sentenced to forfeiture of all pay, a dishonorable discharge, and one year at hard labor in the local penitentiary. Thirty-two-year-old George Childs was likewise charged with desertion. It seems the private had been present when the regiment had gone from Washington to Alexandria in preparation for a possible advance during the Bull Run battle of July 21, 1861. At Alexandria, however, Childs was nowhere to be found and was never seen again until being arrested as a deserter in Rochester, New York, some months later. Like Richards, Childs was found guilty and sentenced to forfeit all pay. The third and final case in the January 1862 triumvirate was that of Pvt. Eli Westfall , who, like the others, was accused of desertion. The 20-year-old had deserted from Elmira in May 1861 shortly after being mustered in and was not seen until he was arrested in the camp of a Pennsylvania regiment in December of that year. As was the case with his predecessors, Westfall was found guilty and sentenced to hard labor for the rest of his term and the forfeiture of all pay.[14]

Once the day's military drill and administrative duties were concluded, nighttime entertainment could be contemplated. Evening relaxation consisted of some song and dance, and on this end the regiment's brass band was acquiring quite a reputation as a well-rehearsed and cohesive unit. Their evening serenades at Fort Lyon were a calming antidote to the thunderous roar of the fort's 100-pound Parrot guns which were now being discharged daily during artillery practice. Every now and then, though, the cannon of friend and foe would also join in on the nightly festivities. One soldier stationed near Fort Lyon wrote in his journal, "On a fine moonlight night, the scene is charming. Now and then the sullen boom of artillery is heard down the river for an hour at a time, showing that the enemy are alive.... We sit on the piazza smoking our pipes on fine nights and listen to this music for hours." With apparently little in the way of military action to occupy their thoughts, Colonel Christian and his officers gathered up the regimental band and played hosts to a number of Washington dignitaries and other regimental officers at a grand ball held the night of January 7 at Alexandria's Liberty Hall. One of the guests referred to the event as "a gathering of the selectest character." After welcoming the guests, Christian and his new bride left for camp early on in the evening.[15]

In addition to having learned musicians, the New Yorkers were also hospitable hosts to the ever-increasing numbers arriving in and around Fort Lyon. A long, cold tempest in midwinter prompted the New Yorkers to open up their shelters to

The Twenty-Sixth's officers at Fort Lyon. This grainy but rare 1862 image is the only known photograph of specific members of the regiment taken in the field. From left to right: Col. William Christian, Lt. Col. Richard Richardson, Richardson's daughter and wife, Maj. Gilbert Jennings, and an unidentified "camp carer" (*Utica Saturday Globe*).

their fellow and tentless Second Michigan comrades, lest they be forced to freeze in the cold and rain. "Their kindness knew no bounds & will be long remembered," wrote one of the grateful Michiganders.[16]

On January 29, Lieutenant Colonel Richardson and the two companies of the Twenty-Sixth stationed across the valley at Fort Ellsworth were ordered to rejoin the regiment at Fort Lyon. Though rumors of movement for the Twenty-Sixth were a constant companion in their camp, the end of each wintry, February night still found the regiment camped inside Fort Lyon. "We are rolling on in the usual monotonous round of camp life,—roll call, guard mounting, drill, dress parades, tattoo and taps," wrote a soldier to the hometown *Utica Daily Observer*. They were more than ready to strike their blow for the Union, but Uncle Sam and Mother Nature kept the New Yorkers fort-bound.[17]

Springtime brought rumors as fresh as the new flowers; the regiment was going to be discharged soon or that battle and campaign were imminent. The truth of the matter was that the winter and early spring of 1862 saw the Twenty-Sixth continuing its dreary fatigue and picket duties at Fort Lyon. Among the dull responsibilities was escort duty, or the return of "property" unlawfully taken from the local citizenry. In the spring of 1862, Capt. Edmund Shurly of Company C received orders from Colonel Christian that he and his company were to return property to an Alexandria local named Mason, who was related to the Charles Mason of "Mason and Dixon" fame. Mason was a nearby resident, reasonably wealthy, and a well-known Confederate sympathizer. When Shurly arrived at the quartermaster's office, he learned much to his dismay that the goods being returned included a family of five slaves. When the captain protested such a reprehensible chore, he was advised that many such tasks were to be performed in Uncle Sam's service. Ultimately acquiescing, Shurly and Company C started out with their human cargo. No rush was needed and during the long march, many breaks and stops were taken. Captain Shurly, as well as most of the soldiers in his company, felt morally aghast at what they were doing. Was becoming an agent in the enforcement of the Fugitive Slave Act why they had volunteered? With about four miles remaining, Captain Shurly devised a scheme by which his human cargo could "escape." He told the negro father that his men would stop at the next creek and rest for about 10 minutes in the woods to the left of the wagons, and that he would pull the guard away from the wagon as well. That would give the family ample time to flee into the woods off to the right of the wagons. When Captain Shurly asked the slave if he thought his family could get away, the answer was unhesitating: "Just give me the chance, Captain. I know every part in these woods. If it were not for my wife and children, I would kill myself before being sent back to Massa Mason."

The plan worked as expected. When Shurly and his squad returned from their "rest," the slave family was gone. The New Yorkers went through the obligatory motions to find their fugitives, but clearly with half-hearted effort.

Mason was outraged when Shurly told him the news. The old man swore with one breath that he would have Shurly cashiered from the service. With the next, he told the captain that his son commanded a company of Confederate cavalry, and would give the New Yorkers a rough go of it on their march back to Fort Lyon. To Shurly's surprise, the old man apparently followed through on his threat to have him dismissed. Two days after the company's return, orders were handed down to place Shurly under arrest and for him to report straight to McClellan. Fortunately for the captain, McClellan was out, so Shurly made an impromptu decision to visit William H. Seward, Lincoln's secretary of state, whom the captain had met several times before the war. After hearing the young man plead his case, Seward promised to bring the matter immediately to President Lincoln's attention. One-half hour later, Seward returned, with orders from Lincoln to have Captain Shurley released. Seward explained to the young officer that, according to the president, "a U.S. officer was not worth his salt to return negroes to their owners." It was an experience that no officer in the Twenty-Sixth, or any other regiment for that matter, would ever have to repeat. Perhaps due to Shurly's incident, on March 3, 1862, Lincoln signed an act forbidding the return of slaves who had escaped from their rebel owners and made it to Union lines.[18]

Spring also brought forth the news, factual this time, of an impending campaign. The cries of "on to Richmond" filled the air in and around Washington's camps! Certainly the New Yorkers hoped to be part of the advance, but still no word came as to when, or even if, they would leave Fort Lyon. The anticipation began to wear on some men. Pvt. Thomas Huntly wrote home on April 7 declaring, "I think before mcclelan made a move there was three hundred thousand men around washington—it is still about our going away from here—now I think that that is played out now." Huntly then further greased the rumor mill. "There is a report that this regt. is to be discharged in a few days but we cannot tell anything about the truth of the report—but of course we all hope it is so."[19]

The inaction meant more of the same daily drudgery for the New Yorkers, for whom the boredom and cold wintry days was now reflected in the physical condition of their camp. April 22nd brought the third and final camp inspection report administered by the U.S. Sanitary Commission and its results could not have been a source of pride for Colonel Christian. Adequate drainage was still a problem at Fort Lyon, with the inspector noting that the "Camp and its suburbs

Surgeon Walter B. Coventry (Don Wisnoski Collection—USAMHI).

3. On to Fort Lyon

The Twenty-Sixth New York Volunteer Infantry on drill parade at Fort Lyon. Probably taken in late winter or early spring 1862 as the remnants of snow can be seen on the ground. (Brady—National Archives).

[are] very foul, especially in the ravines adjacent. Will be risky if occupied in the summer." The inspector further recorded that regimental surgeon Walter Coventry had urged Christian to change camps, "but to no effect." All other areas of camp cleanliness also received poor marks.

The discipline of the regiment's soldiers was still generally viewed as a positive. Battalion drills were conducted regularly and the men were observed as routinely being soldier-like in appearance. Unapproved absences from camp were another matter, however. The report recorded that guards were stationed only at the various bridges and that the men therefore wandered in and out of camp "at will." The report concluded with the belief that the general health of the regiment was deteriorating.[20]

The preparation of the army to advance down the Virginia peninsula brought about more reorganization. In May, the regiment was officially assigned to Gen. James Ricketts' newly formed brigade. The 44-year-old Ricketts had been a captain of artillery in the regular army and had been shot four times the previous summer at Bull Run. Captured on that field by the Confederates, Ricketts had not been exchanged until January 1862. In April, he was promoted to brigadier general of volunteers for his gallant conduct during the Bull Run battle. His first command would be the First Brigade of the Second Division in the newly created Department of the Rappahannock. Those units had been constituted April 4, 1862, from original First Army Corps, Army of the Potomac. The new department was to cover the area that entailed the geographic portion of Virginia east of the Blue Ridge and west of the Potomac River, the Fredericksburg and Richmond Railroad, which also included the District of Columbia, and the country between the Potomac and Patuxent Rivers. The Second Oneida, excited with the prospects of their new assignment, were restless as they anticipated their future. DeWitt Staring, recently promoted from private to quartermaster sergeant, had spoken for most when he wrote in late winter, "this Regt. is not satisfied by staying here in this mud hole and long for the day to come for us to march which I think is not far off." His prediction of impending action was not far off the mark. The winds of change were blowing strongly toward the Twenty-Sixth, and for many, the opportunity for battle was long overdue.[21]

4

Marching Orders!

Spring brought talk of new campaigns with it, but for the Second Oneida there were still administrative details at Fort Lyon to finish with. These duties included a few court-martials, one of which included Pvt. Frank Pierce of Company D. He had been absent without leave off and on since his Buffalo enlistment back in September. By the time he was located, the charges had been upgraded to desertion, theft of a horse, and three other charges. The speedy one-day trial resulted in guilty verdicts across the board for the 19-year-old. Hoping to send a message to other would-be deserters, Pierce was given a dishonorable discharge and a sentence of five years in the Washington, D.C., penitentiary.[1]

With such mundane matters behind them, it was time for the regiment's first campaign. May 2 finally brought the news that the Twenty-Sixth had been anxiously awaiting for months. Move out! George McClellan's "Peninsula Campaign" had gotten underway and it was rumored that the New Yorkers, as part of Irvin McDowell's corps d' armee, were finally heading south to reinforce "Little Mac." Knapsacks and personal belongings were hastily but happily packed at the news that so-called "real" action was in the offing! Before departing, however, there was the formal ceremony of being relieved at Fort Lyon by the Ninety-Fourth New York Volunteers. Immediately following the ritual of turning over the garrison, the unit marched straightaway to Alexandria's wharfs. The sleepy troops slowly moved out at 1:00 A.M. on the 3rd. At the Alexandria dock, the regiment boarded the steamers *South America* and *North America*, and then headed south to the Aquia Creek landings near Fredericksburg. The daylong 42-mile cruise down the Potomac River was uneventful, with most of the regiment opting to lounge or sleep on the decks of the boats.[2]

Landing that evening, they made their camp about three miles inland, and then proceeded further on to Brook's (Aquia) Station, located on the railroad just north of Fredericksburg. The forlorn area consisted of three dilapidated buildings; a dwelling, one station house and a grist mill. Here they found plain evidence of prior rebel encampments and batteries which to the New Yorkers' astonishment seemed to have been far more formidable in the newspapers than in person. Clearly, the rebels were now long gone from this place, leaving behind only a few graves of their comrades in gray.[3]

Having been camped near the Aquia Creek landings for five days, with nary a rebel in sight, new orders came from McDowell on the morning of May 9. The Twenty-Sixth was to immediately report to McDowell's Fredericksburg headquarters, a distance of some 15 miles. They arrived in Fredericksburg that afternoon

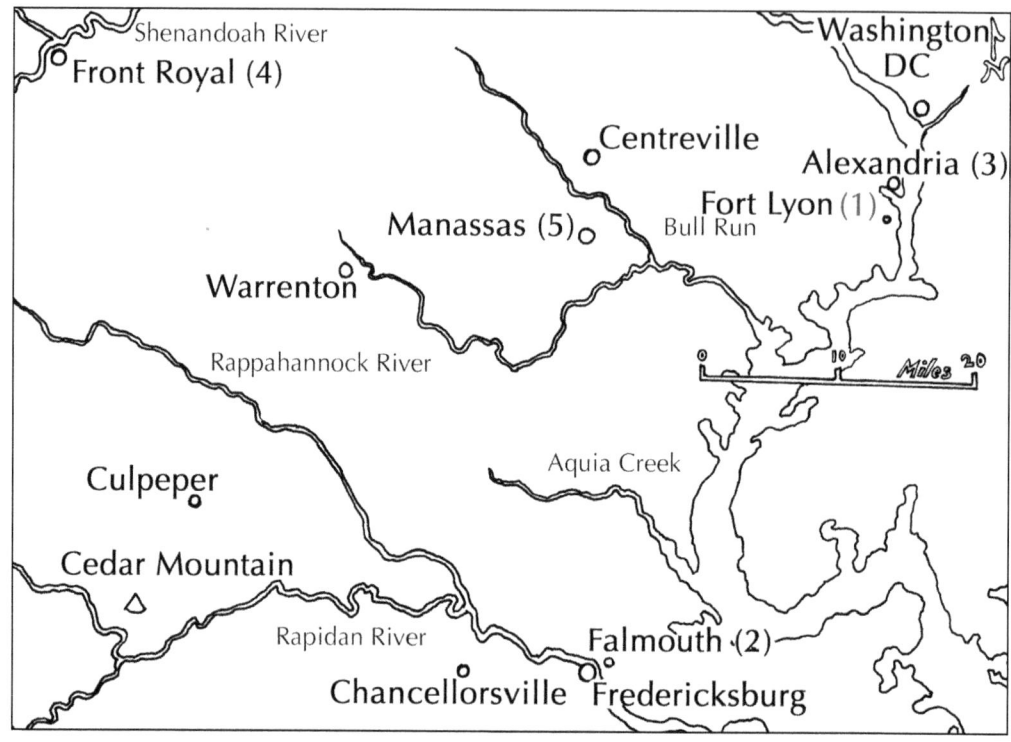

The 26th leave Ft. Lyon (1) on May 3, 1862 with orders to assist Gen. Irvin McDowell near Falmouth (2). There they sit until May 24, when they are ordered to return to Alexandria (3) and then make a forced march toward Front Royal (4) to assist Union armies battling Stonewall Jackson. The army returns to Manassas (5) on June 18 with little result.

after a long, hot, and dusty march and set up at Camp Mary Washington, situated on a wide plain about a mile from the Rappahannock. McDowell's corps had originally been sent south to protect the Orange and Alexandria Railroad and to guard the approaches to Washington. Later, McDowell was given permission to advance as far as the Rappahannock River. Ultimately, McDowell was to join up with McClellan, but his army had been parked at Fredericksburg for several weeks to still serve essentially as a buffer between Washington and the Confederate forces. Once McDowell could move, his men would assist McClellan and his beleaguered troops down on the peninsula, through a planned strike from the north on Richmond. For the time being, however, his corps' primary use had been to rebuild the rail and bridge network running from Aquia Creek over the Rappahannock River and into Fredericksburg, which the rebels had done their best to burn and destroy when they pulled back from the town.[4]

Mid-May found the regiment bivouacked at Camp James Ricketts opposite Fredericksburg; the camp was named in honor of their new brigade commander. Joining the Twenty-Sixth in Ricketts' new brigade were the Eighty-Eighth and Ninetieth Pennsylvania Infantry, and the Ninety-Fourth New York Infantry, which had just arrived from Fort Lyon. Ricketts' battery of six rifled cannons rounded out the fighting force. The camp was on the 1,300-acre plantation grounds of a Mr. Wallace, who was known to all as a rabid secessionist with two sons serving in the Confederate army. The New Yorkers were delighted to finally be in the field, and the fact that they were camped on private "secesh" property made for even-broader smiles on their faces. The new brigade commander had heard favorable comments regarding the Twenty-Sixth, but had never actually seen them in the field. To get better acquainted, he asked for a battalion drill. The months of hard drill work at Fort Lyon now paid off, for Ricketts later commented that it was one of the better-drilled units he had witnessed.[5]

Fredericksburg offered to the regiment the visage of an ancient town, dating its existence to colonial times. Businesses were mostly closed, presenting a somber scene to those Yankees who went into the town on a pass. Few local citizens seemed to appear in public, and those few that did tended to mull about on street corners. The lone eatery that still existed offered meager fare, which Captain Arrowsmith described as "some bacon, bread, butter, and tea; facetiously called a dinner for fifty cents." Whiskey was not to be had, except in sad recollections. Bacon and corn bread were the standard fare, perhaps a little tobacco, and as Arrowsmith summed up, "a little abuse of the Northerners by way of dessert."[6]

The New Yorkers quickly adapted to their daily march and bivouac routine. The marches were still new to the young soldiers, so the grumbling and grousing that would inject many marches in the months to come had yet to reveal itself. The soldiers knew not where they were going when the marching orders came, nor why. It was all still a grand adventure.

Upon stopping to set up camp, the bivouac spot took on the appearance of a bee colony, with each worker doing his preordained task. Every man was setting up the small shelter tents, which came in two parts and were designed to accommodate three or four. Packing and unpacking, every man carried all his worldly possessions on his back. Cooks began the task of setting up the open-air kitchens. Feeding upward of 750 men on the move was a sizeable task, and a joy, for it meant that fresh food was at hand.

As the senior regiment, the Twenty-Sixth was the lead regiment on the march and placed at the far right of any battle line.

An entirely new, and unexpected, set of marching orders were handed to the Twenty-Sixth on May 24. Stonewall Jackson's Valley Army had been wreaking havoc in the Shenandoah Valley and both Lincoln and Halleck now feared for Washington's safety. McDowell was ordered to suspend the planned reinforcement of McClellan and instead was instructed to send two of his four divisions to the Shenandoah to reinforce the federal forces there. One of the two divisions sent was under the command of Gen. Edward O. Ord, under whom was Ricketts' new four-regiment brigade. Believing that the march on Richmond was still forthcoming, McDowell reviewed Ord's division on May 20. Gen. James Shields' division, the other of two to be sent to stop Jackson, had arrived on the 22nd. Prior to leaving, Lincoln personally reviewed the division on May 24, having traveled to the Union camps with Secretary of War Edwin Stanton in order to personally discuss the situation with McDowell. After the appropriate pomp and circumstance, the Twenty-Sixth retired to pack up their camp. Marching back to Aquia Creek in the evening of the 24th, the brigade boarded transports at the landing and steamed the 40 miles back to

Alexandria on the 25th. Without pausing, the New Yorkers boarded trains at 11:00 P.M., which took them to Manassas Junction. Though not known to the Twenty-Sixth at the time, the hardest marches of their lives were just in front of them.[7]

Their orders called for a forced march from Manassas toward Front Royal and Strasburg, with the stated hope of ultimately bagging Stonewall Jackson and his ragged legions somewhere in the Shenandoah Valley. After concentrating all day at Manassas Junction, Ord's two divisions began to move out on May 28. The blue column continued all night through a terrific downpour, staying close to the Manassas Gap railroad. Upon arriving at Delaplane (Piedmont Station), the brigade was ordered to leave knapsacks and all excess baggage in order to further lighten the load. With three days' rations in hand, which consisted of only hardtack and a little ground coffee, they were to march rapidly toward Front Royal. On the following morning, cannon could be heard in the distance, arising from the skirmishing with Jackson's rear guard. Ricketts' brigade was immediately put in motion and crossed the Shenandoah River; but it was soon realized that Jackson's Confederates were at least a good 10 miles away at Strasburg. With Jackson having made his escape up the valley, the command went into camp on the Winchester Road. Arriving too late for any action, the regiment did appear in time to bear the brunt of another ferocious storm, without the benefit of tents or overcoats.

So severe was the deluge that two bridges across the Shenandoah River were washed away, which stranded the Twenty-Sixth New York, as well as the Second Maine Battery, from the remainder of their division. Further complicating matters was that McDowell's entire corps was now isolated from other commands that they were to hook up with.[8]

This was not a situation that many had envisioned. Captain Shurly of Company G had been on a pass into the village of Front Royal to procure tobacco when he saw the bridge fall, just as he was just about to recross. Shurly raced back to General Ricketts' tent to alert him of the collapse. "This is bad," remarked the general. "If the Confederates ascertain that the bridge is destroyed, your regiment and the battery will be captured." For close to three days the rains continued, causing continued isolation. Fortunately for the Twenty-Sixth, ample livestock was to be had from neighboring farms, despite unpopular orders from Irvin McDowell that farmers' animals were not to be touched. Starvation was not an issue, but illness soon became one, for the New Yorkers ate too hardily on the various farm animals they came across. Shurly ultimately came up with an idea. Having built rope ferries as a boy, he explained to Ricketts that if a long-enough rope could be found, as well as a boat, he could design a rope ferry to rescue the Twenty-Sixth. Ricketts readily agreed, believing that just about any plan was better than no plan. After a few days the rain ceased, allowing the captain to put his plan into action. Finding the rope was simple enough, but an adequate flat boat proved a greater challenge. None of the local residents proved helpful, all stating that Stonewall had burned every boat lest they fall into Yankee hands. Shurly found a local Negro who strongly suspected that the local miller might know of a boat. He was right. With ample threats from Shurly and his crew, the miller finally acquiesced and showed the New Yorkers a proper vessel for their task. A few hours later, the Twenty-Sixth New York was safely rejoining their comrades. Several days of rest allowed the sick men to regain their usual state of good health and buoyancy.[9]

On May 31, General Ord was relieved of his command due to an undisclosed illness. General Ricketts was given divisional command with Colonel Christian assuming temporary command of Ricketts' old brigade.[10] The long, hard marches and miserable weather were starting to affect others as well, both physically and mentally. Among them, Lt. Col. Richard Richardson fell ill near Front Royal with severe bouts of diarrhea. He was granted a furlough of one week on June 10 to recuperate his health back in Alexandria. It would be the first of Richardson's several absences from the field at crucial times due to various ailments.[11] Others decided that actual combat and forced marches were not to their liking and decided to simply desert the army. With the fighting apparently over, the Union army went into a wait-and-see posture. Of course, picket duty did not cease, and on this end, numerous rebel stragglers were rounded up by Union patrols. Many were sent from Strasburg to be guarded by the Twenty-Sixth at its current camp, since it was realized that getting food to those prisoners could become problematic with the bridges being out and the water level at the fords near record height. To effect the movement, Colonel Christian was ordered to send two companies of his regiment to Strasburg for the purpose of escorting the prisoners to his headquarters, on being notified in advance of the time when the prisoners could be sent.[12]

Realizing that Jackson was long gone, orders finally came on June 18 to begin the trek back to Manassas Junction. The New Yorkers solemnly struck their tents and boarded the freight cars headed east, knowing that their army's quest to defeat the elusive Stonewall had proven a dismal failure. The next several weeks were spent in camp on the plains of Manassas and from the commentary of the soldiers, a more dreary and tedious bivouac was not to be had.

Disappointment in the results of the march to Front Royal was apparent throughout the brigade's camps. The New Yorkers were at one point within hearing distance of Jackson's guns and were convinced that had they been permitted to march, they could have taken Stonewall's rear guard and destroyed his baggage trains. Such was the 20-20 hindsight that permeated those days. Of course, the daily routines of camp life, such as inspection and drill, continued to occur, but everyone knew that the next action seemed to be much farther to the south, near Richmond. "Manassas may now be regarded as a place well suited for being held for a great while by an army on either side," observed one of the regiment's officers, "for when a general gets once comfortably fixed in the big brick house, he is not much disposed to leave." The weather was stifling hot, with only the occasional shower and the men's thirst was rarely slaked due to little or bad water. Tedium was the rule, with some men relegating themselves to providing guided tours for the civilians from Washington who might still wish to visit the Bull Run battlefield of the previous summer.[13]

Inevitably, some men began to conclude that army life was not the gallant adventure they had originally envisioned. Desertion was a fact of life in all regiments, and the Twenty-Sixth was no exception. In fact, June 1862 would prove itself to be the regiment's single worst month for desertions as 25 men would permanently abandon their comrades during the month.

Nineteen-year-old Thomas Baker of Company F was one such young man who arbitrarily decided to forego the remainder of his enlistment. Unfortunately for the youthful private, Union authorities near New Berne, North Carolina, later apprehended him. Punishment for desertion technically included execution by firing squad, but actual punishments, if any, varied widely throughout the war. In spite of the wide range of punishments, Baker became one of the relatively few men actually condemned and shot during the war. Cpl. Nelson Wandell of the Ninth Vermont Infantry described Baker's execution on August 13, 1862: "A little after five [A.M.] we fell into line and marched out a little over a quarter of a mile south of here near an old scrubby tree. We formed three sides of a square. Our regt. on the right, a Co. of heavy Artillery next. Then a Co. of Rhode Island light artillery. Then Capt. Horns, Co. of the 12th N.Y. Cavalry. At half past six A.M.., the escort with the prisoner came and filed in the square and around it. First came the Provost Marshal Major Lawson, then the band of music, then the Coffin born by four men, then the prisoner with the Chaplain, then a Sergt with a file of ten men with loaded guns and bayonets fixed, then a Co. of the Provost Guard of the 15th Conn. The prisoner looked very pale but walked with a firm step, his hands tied in front, he did not appear to realize his awful situation. They filed around the inside of the square and up to the grave. The coffin was placed on the ground, the head towards and about ten feet from the grave, the prisoner stood beside it while the Chaplain read a portion of scripture and said a prayer. He then shook hands with Baker and bid him good by. Major Lawson shook hands with him and bid him good by. Then the sargent of the guard bandaged his eyes and seated him on the foot of his Coffin facing the guards. They were posted in front of and about twenty feet distance, at the order from the Provost Marshal, Ready. They all cocked their pieces at the command, aim and fire. The eight men on the left fired their pieces in the prisoner's breast and he fell back dead on his Coffin. After Dr. Carpenter pronounced him dead. We marched around the grave in review and then to camp and broke ranks."[14]

Despite such incidents, the Twenty-Sixth's overall health was in good shape, with the regiment's surgeon remarking that they had no more than a half dozen men who could not take up the march at once. Though the regiment as a whole was still in fine shape, its colonel suffered the first of several peculiar injuries in the line of duty. Christian had been in the field delivering or fulfilling orders near Warrenton when the strange accident occurred. The colonel alleged that he rode into a fenced area when all of a sudden the gate along the road abruptly closed, harshly trapping rider and horse in between the gate and its post. The heavy gate had apparently swung hard enough to give the luckless Christian a nasty bruise in his lower back and right groin area. Though it seemed an innocuous wound at the time, Christian would use this incident years later as the first basis for a post-war pension, which was ultimately rejected.[15]

The regiment's formal assignment with the Department of the Rappahannock came to an end in late June. The most recent failures in the Shenandoah Valley prompted Lincoln to consolidate the Mountain Department, the Department of the Shenandoah, and the Department of the Rappahannock into one new army. It would be known as the Army of Virginia, with its formal mission being the protection of Washington, D.C. In addition, the army was to demonstrate in the Culpeper and Charlottesville area northwest of Richmond in order to relieve the pressure then being exerted upon George McClellan's Army of the Potomac on the Peninsula. Forty-year-old John Pope would be its new commanding general.

4. Marching Orders!

Pope arrived at his new command with a rising military reputation acquired in the western theater's battles of Madrid and Island No. 10, both of which were small but important Union victories. His open flaunting of his successes, coupled with pointing out his new army's lack of it against the wily Robert E. Lee, did not sit well with the eastern men. Once Pope arrived in Washington, it is said that he promptly declared that his headquarters would be in the saddle, thereafter causing many of his soldiers to derisively proclaim that his hindquarters should have been where his headquarters were.

The war's slow progression also brought about realization in Washington that more men would be needed to suppress the rebellion. Another call for 300,000 volunteers went out to the various northern states. Recruiting had been fairly quiet back home in Oneida County but now picked up again. The county newspapers all trumpeted the news and urged their young men to step forth. Many central New York counties offered bounties for new volunteers and even wealthy citizens came forward, offering to privately match the public offerings. For the soldiers already in the trenches, these offerings from citizens of financial means urging *others* to join the fray were met with ambivalence, and often, disdain. "They are willing to do all they can toward getting others to enlist, and actually offer some boy two dollars per month if he will enlist; tell him that it is a glorious thing 'to die for one's country,' and that he will gain everlasting honor for himself if he will enlist," wrote H. C. Myers from the Twenty-Sixth's Virginia camp. "They seem to forget that the poor boy has not the interests at stake that they have. They enjoy the benefit of peace, and is it any more than right that they bear some of the losses of war?" This anger toward that segment of the citizenry would continue through the end of their service.[16]

Pope's new reorganization brought changes in corps, division, and brigade commands. Irvin McDowell still had the Third Corps. James Ricketts was formally promoted to command of McDowell's Second Division since Gen. E. C. Ord was now transferred to another department. Gen. Zealous B. Tower, a new face to most of the men, was given command of the Second Brigade, and it was into this brigade that the Second Oneida was placed. The 43-year-old Tower, an engineer officer by training, graduated first in his West Point class of 1841, and had recently been promoted to the rank of brigadier. The Ninety-Fourth New York and the Eighty-Eighth and Ninetieth Pennsylvania volunteers continued alongside the Twenty-Sixth in Tower's brigade. This was the order of battle under which the Twenty-Sixth New York Volunteers would fight the summer campaign.

Pope wasted no time putting his new force into motion. The New Yorkers spent the 4th of July preparing for the new campaign still encamped at Gainesville and Manassas Junction. Once they moved out, it quickly became apparent that Mother Nature was not in their corner. An exceedingly dry Virginia summer quickly created miserably filthy bodies and parched throats due to the scorching sun and choking dust. On the following day the bluecoats arrived in Warrenton where the Twenty-Sixth and the rest of the division would remain for over a week, awaiting orders for the next movement of the army. Warrenton was a small village that saw its Warrenton Branch Railroad serve as an important connector into the much-larger Orange and Alexandria rail line The village was described by George Arrowsmith as "one of the finest towns I ever saw, with fine mansions, flanked by lovely gardens, and streets well shaded." Arrowsmith was in a particular buoyant frame of mind, for just weeks earlier he had been promoted to assistant adjutant general, serving on General Tower's staff. The entire Twenty-Sixth enjoyed the rest as well, with the regiment as a whole still being in relatively good health, though Arrowsmith did remark that Maj. Gilbert S. Jennings was now recovering from a recent illness. A change of location and its attendant water supply often brought intestinal distress for the ranks. Scouring the nearby fields for blackberries seemed a popular method of relaxation for the troops, with Pvt. Warren Firman recording in his diary on July 12 that he had obtained 10 quarts in several hours. Other brigade comrades echoed similar sentiments. A Pennsylvanian from that state's Ninetieth Infantry, camped alongside the Twenty-Sixth New York, readily agreed with Arrowsmith's assessment on the beauty of the place. He went on to note, however, that the area's entire populace was "wool dyed sesech" and that the army would have to stay put a bit longer "to keep the rebels from destroying the crops or appropriating them for their own use." By the 12th, however, sickness was again becoming an issue in the brigade. It seemed that Tower's men were camped in a low-lying, swampy area a mile outside of town. According to Col. Adrian Root of the Ninety-Fourth New York, the "night vapors and miasma" were rapidly sickening his men and that "the other three regiments of the brigade were just as badly off." After much protestations from his officers, Tower granted all regiments permission to relocate to a higher, more open area.[17]

The prolonged bivouac at Warrenton finally ended on July 22, when orders came to move out. The regiment packed their tents and ended up camping at Waterloo Bridge on the Rappahannock River, about eight miles west of Warrenton. Here, General Pope finally assumed personal command of the army. Pope personally reviewed Ricketts' division, including the Twenty-Sixth, on August 1 and in spite of some regiment's impecunious state, complimented the division commander on the discipline and excellent bearing of his soldiers. He promised all that they would soon have "an early interview with the Sesesh [sic]." On the 5th of August, Ricketts' division broke camp and proceeded to march through Jeffersonville and finally halted outside of Culpeper on the afternoon of the 6th. The march had been over relatively flat ground, however the sun was brutally hot which resulted in noticeable straggling. The Twenty-Sixth was last in the marching column; therefore they were again forced to choke on the dust left by their brigade comrades. Water was becoming somewhat scarce, which made for an exhausting day. Still, the overall attitude in line was upbeat. Men speculated on the likelihood of action and debated back and forth about the extent of it. The New Yorkers remained outside of Culpeper on August 7.[18]

The Battle of Cedar Mountain

Real action finally appeared imminent for the New Yorkers. On the 8th of August, the regiment and the rest of their divisional companions received word they were to leave their Culpeper camp. Cavalry reports had indicated that that Jackson and his rebels had left their camps at Gordonsville and now crossed the Rapidan River, some 15 miles away. Pope had been anxiously trying to consolidate

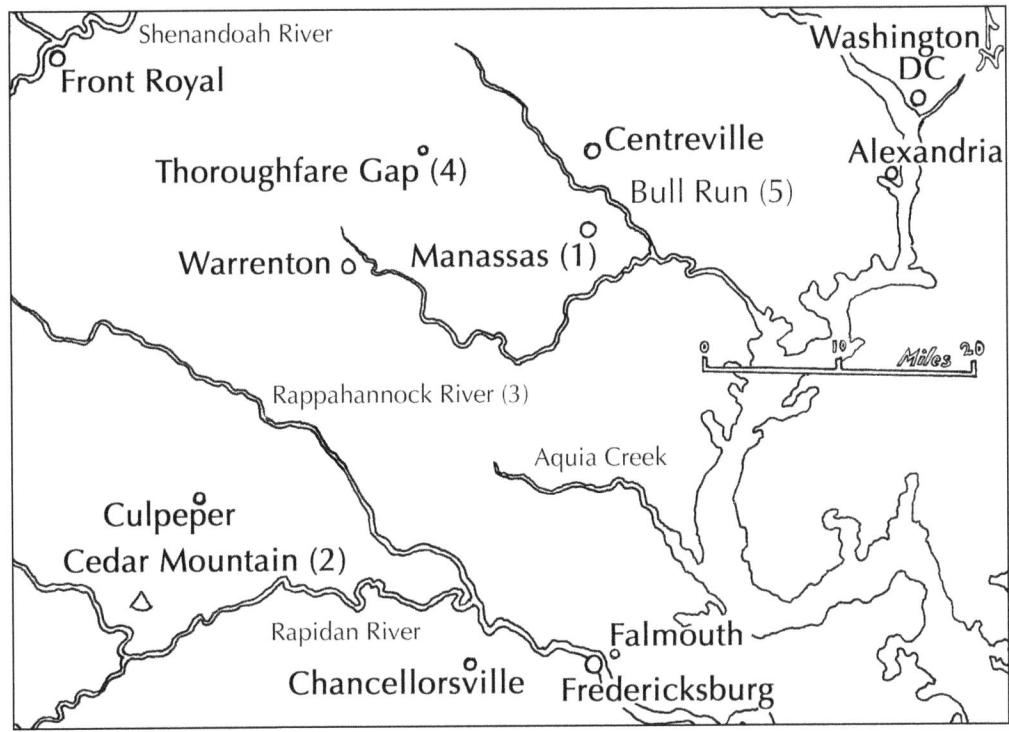

(1) The Twenty-Sixth moves out toward Richmond from Manassas on July 4, 1862. (2) They collide with Jackson's rebel on August 9 at the battle of Cedar Mountain. (3) Constant skirmishing with the rebels ensues along the Rappahannock in mid- to late August. (4) They are part of Ricketts' rear guard during the August 28 fight at Thouroughfare Gap. (5) A forced march follows. They arrive in time for the August 30th battle of Second Bull Run. Their brigade makes a gallant stand but is ultimately routed off the field.

his three corps near Culpeper, but so far, only Gen. Nathan Banks' corps was in the vicinity. The bulk of McDowell's Third Corps was still back at Warrenton and Franz Sigel's First Corps was also on the way. Leaving their camps at around 2:00 P.M., Ricketts' division marched through Culpeper, with its first stop along the Orange Road, in order to hold the junction of that thoroughfare and the Stevensburg Road. It would be almost a day later before the word came that many were anticipating.[19]

With Jackson advancing and battle expected, Banks' corps was ordered forward on the morning of August 9 to confront the enemy near an eminence just south of Culpeper called Cedar Mountain. Banks' object was to place his left flank on the mountain slope with his center and right in open ground northwest of the hill. The engagement began as an artillery battle with Pope ordering Banks to hold his advance position. Banks, believing he was going against inferior numbers, soon launched an infantry attack on his own accord with his corps. The Yankee surge initially caught the rebels off guard and drove them back through the woods almost to the breaking point. Jackson urgently ordered A. P. Hill's division to be brought up and then valiantly rallied his men, even drawing his sword for the only recorded time in the war. Hill's fresh troops arrived in the nick of time, launching a counterattack that crashed into Banks' now heavily outnumbered and exhausted bluecoats. The Union advance stalled and began to recede.

It was never Pope's intention to send Ricketts' division into the fight, opting instead to hold them as a reserve just south of the Orange and Stevensburg roads until it was known with certainty by which road Jackson's columns might advance. Now, matters had changed. With a heated battle well underway, Gen. John Pope spoke to the men of Ricketts' division at Culpeper, informing all of the great things he expected of them.[20] At 5:00 P.M. on August 9, Ricketts' division was ordered forward at the double-quick as a precautionary measure, with the lead elements finally reaching the front around 7:00 P.M. Ricketts and his men were unaware that Banks had launched his attack, but when they arrived two to three miles from Cedar Mountain, they passed by scores of exhausted men with blackened faces and sweat-stained uniforms headed in the other direction. The musket firing was plainly audible in the distance and according to one of Ricketts' men, "it sounded like corn popping." After gallantly pushing back Jackson's host earlier in the day, they were now slowly heading to the rear after giving way against overwhelming numbers. After conversing with Banks, McDowell had Ricketts form his battle line that ultimately placed Tower's brigade on the extreme right. Gen. George Hartsuff's Third Brigade followed close behind Tower as reserve. One of Hartsuff's men later recalled that Tower's brigade marched proudly into place in a giant cornfield with their fifes and drums playing a spirited rendition of *Dixie*. After arriving on the field near dusk, Tower immediately brought up Leppien's Maine battery and Matthew's Pennsylvania battery onto the hill, and placed the Twenty-Sixth New York and the Eighty-Eighth Pennsylvania to the right of these guns. This meant that the New Yorkers now held the far right of the Union line. Both sides were precariously positioned within musket range of the other side, so close that Tower's officers could hear the rebel officers shouting their orders. Yet no skirmishing was forthcoming during the black night as the New Yorkers lay on the damp ground. It was later alleged that since the Twenty-Sixth lay so close to the enemy gunners, a number of the New Yorkers were eager to make a dash for the enemy's cannon, but General McDowell, who was now on a different section of the field, vetoed the purported request. General Tower would have concurred, observing that, "No orders were given me to commence an attack, and this was probably prudent, as the position of the enemy, his strength, and the nature of the ground he occupied were unknown, and could not be ascertained in the night."[21]

Such a rash request displayed just how green a number of the New Yorkers were. Though they had been in the army for over a year, for most this was their first real combat. Now, with darkness at hand and even though rebel cannons were posted nearby, a number of the inexperienced soldiers made the costly mistake of lighting fires in order to make coffee or to read letters from home. Unbeknownst to the raw troops, the illumination from those campfires provided excellent targets for rebel artillery only 400 yards away. The result was predictable and disastrous. Confederate shells plowed into Tower's line, causing some casualties. Union batteries soon responded, and before long, a vigorous, artillery exchange was brought into play. By midnight, the infantry regiments of both blue and gray were lying on their arms and were forced to stay that way into the early morning hours of April 10.

The Union artillery was particularly effective, silencing the rebel guns within a matter of hours. Pvt. Charles McClenthen of the Twenty-Sixth's Company G described the barrage as "a perfect shower of shot and shell, that an ordinary sized thunder storm would be but 'a tempest in a teapot' compared to it," while Colonel Root of the nearby Ninety-Fourth New York described the scene as "indescribably beautiful, the shells could be seen shooting like meteors through the sky." Near 3:00 A.M. on the 10th, Tower's men were given orders to reform in the woods to the right of their initial position since McDowell's entire Third Corps was now in the process of reforming its lines. By 7:00 A.M. it was believed a new rebel movement was underway. The brigade promptly moved out under orders from McDowell to cover the Madison Road, with the Twenty-Sixth in the lead. Cavalry reconnaissance

Fife Maj. Samuel Benedick, one of the Twenty-Sixth's principal musicians (New York State Military Museum).

had already determined upon the brigade's arrival on the road that the Confederate threat was overestimated. Still playing it safe, Christian and his men were sent forward with two companies deployed as a skirmish line to investigate what was in their front. After pressing forward a full three miles, it was determined to Tower's satisfaction that the enemy was nowhere around. Under new orders from McDowell, the entire brigade was countermarched to their initial position in the reformed line. If any of the Twenty-Sixth were looking forward to the prospects of combat, they were to be disappointed. The Battle of Cedar Mountain was essentially over. The regiment had been fortunate, for their first serious battle had ended with no casualties. In fact, good fortune extended throughout Tower's brigade, as it finished the fight with the fewest casualties in all of Ricketts' division. Such luck, however, would not last forever.[22]

Dawn on the 11th brought about an opportunity for a much-needed breakfast. The men of Company C killed and dressed two hogs and one cow for their meal. A nearby farmhouse that had been deserted by its owners in the middle of the night provided ample quantities of flour, sugar, salt, and kettles to round out the hearty meal. The home's split-rail fence, as usual, provided the cooking fuel.[23]

Around 11:00 A.M. on the blistering hot morning of August 11, a truce was agreed to so that the dead and injured could be carried off the field. Jackson granted permission till 2:00 P.M., and later extended it to 5:00 P.M. at Pope's request. McClenthen surveyed the ground and saw for the first time the harvest field of death. Blue- and butternut-clad bodies lay everywhere, as well as numerous fresh mounds of earth marking the spot where some of the fallen had already been laid to rest. For close to a week, the Virginia temperatures had been brutally hot and now the stench of the dead filled the nostrils of burial parties. The position where the rebel batteries had been placed was soon discovered, the guns destroyed and the ground strewn with men and horses. Seeing scores of mangled and decaying bodies for the first time had varying effects on the Twenty-Sixth's soldiers. Twenty-one-year-old Pvt. William E. Bowen was aghast at what he witnessed: "I saw nine dead rebels; it was a sickening sight—worms were eating their ghastly remains." On the other hand, the older Charles McClenthen felt that, "This was a splendid sight, and as we seemed to be perfectly safe we enjoyed it hugely." To the private's consternation, he saw numerous rebel soldiers carting off guns and ammunition, while the bluecoats were under strict orders to touch nothing except for their dead and wounded. Regarding this bitter development, the private added, "of one thing I am certain, the battle field was inside the enemy's pickets. Our men were obliged to take off their belts and leave their arms before going on to it and were not suffered to take any of our arms, ammunition or equipment with which the field was strewn of it." Despite the hot and foul work of burying the dead, men from both sides exchanged courteous conversation when the opportunity arose and shared drinks from each others canteens. The civility extended to the generals as well. One private in Ricketts' division noticed that General Hartsuff and Confederate Gen. J.E.B. Stuart, who graduated together from the same West Point class, had spent two hours together under a shady tree talking of old times.[24]

Stonewall Jackson, however, would not spend his time looking up old acquaintances. He took full advantage of the truce, using it as a timeout from which he could easily remove his exhausted army from the field. Realizing through cavalry reconnaissance that Pope's entire Army of Virginia was now rapidly concentrating, Stonewall had no intention of forcing another engagement and chose to withdraw, hoping that the Union army might pursue him. The use of a cease-fire as an effective means for the enemy to withdraw was not lost on the ordinary Union soldier. "When will our generals stop this game?" asked McClenthen, as Jackson's Confederates slipped back across the Rapidan the night of the 11th. From Jackson's perspective, with the Rapidan between himself and Pope, the withdrawal would allow ample time to obtain reinforcements from Lee in Richmond, at which time another attack on Pope could be played out.[25]

With Jackson gone, Pope directed his army to advance toward the retreating foe, marching in fits and stops until they paused at the banks of the Rapidan River on August 15, well within cannon shot of Confederate batteries. Pope held the Rapidan line with Sigel's corps on the right, McDowell's corps in the center, and Gen. Jesse L. Reno's newly arrived division on the left. Banks' battered corps was still licking its wounds back at Culpeper. All told, about 40,000 men in blue pressed down on the rebel army. Tower's brigade marched to Mitchell's Station, where they made their camp. By this time, Lee was concentrating his forces along with Jackson's as rapidly as possible. The railroad bridge on the Rappahannock behind the Union army was the key choke point. Lee believed that Stuart's cavalry might actually destroy that bridge before Union forces could reach it. He planned to cross the Rapidan on the 18th and swing in behind Pope, so that their numerically superior forces might deliver a crushing blow to Pope's left flank before any sizable federal reinforcements arrived. Fortunately for Pope, he saw his danger and ordered parts of his army to fall back behind the Rappahannock via the railroad crossing on August 18. During the day, the Twenty-Sixth received orders to be ready to move at a moment's notice, but not to strike their tents until after dark. That evening, the usual fires were lit and roll calls taken. At around 11:00 P.M., the New Yorkers fell in line and quietly began the march back toward Culpeper.

The final act was the destruction of the railroad bridge over Cedar Run, a task that fell to Tower's rear-guard brigade. A contingent of pioneers was ordered to fire the bridge, to ensure that any rebel pursuit would be slow in coming. Unfortunately, the crossing fell before anticipated, killing a lieutenant from the Eighty-Eighth Pennsylvania who was supervising the detail.

Deception during a withdrawal was to be a constant Union trait during the coming campaign. Celerity, however, was not forthcoming. Tower's brigade was bringing up the rear of the entire army, so they had to deal with an interminable slow-paced march. Teamsters and wagons from Ricketts division, as well as those from other corps, clogged the route of retreat. Soldiers could barely begin their march before they were forced to stop again due to the bottlenecks. The unit ended up marching around the other side of Cedar Mountain from which they had originally advanced in order to free itself from the logjam. The morning of August 19 found Tower's rear guard forming a line of battle near the old Cedar Mountain battlefield, as they fully expected their adversary to cross the Rapidan once the Union pullback was detected. After waiting for several hours, it was decided that no action was forthcoming, so the Twenty-Sixth and their comrades moved out and continued the march to the next river. The bottlenecks of the previous day continued due to orders that the wagon trains were to precede the troops. Start and stop, start and stop throughout the hot summer hours. It was not until sundown of the 19th before Tower's brigade reached the Rappahannock. Hungry and worn out, Tower's brigade pushed on across the river, each man almost collapsing where he stood when the fall-out notice came. Private Firman, exhausted from the trek, scribbled in his diary that his company finally stopped around 11:00 P.M., having marched about 25 miles without rations, since they had run out the previous night. Relief would not be forthcoming, for due to a logistical blunder, the wagon trains had started out the previous day in *advance* of the troops. By midday on August 20, the Twenty-Sixth and their comrades in Tower's brigade were entrenched on the river along the right of Ricketts' division. McDowell's entire corps, with the exception of the Eleventh Pennsylvania who were thrown in advance on the south side of the river, now occupied the north bank of the Rappahannock at the railroad crossing. Sigel's corps occupied the right, General Banks' corps partly in reserve and partly on the left, and Reno's corps below, at Kelly's Ford. John Reynolds' division, formerly under McDowell's command, and which it was soon to rejoin, was coming up the river from Fredericksburg. The night of the 20th also brought the return of the much-awaited wagon trains. Private Firman, having been

Retreat of the Army of Virginia across the Rappahannock (*Century Magazine*).

able to wash his hands and face for the first time in days, recorded, "About 8 o'clock in the P.M. our rations came back to us which we hailed with few regrets."[26]

For the next three days each force remained on its respective side of the Rappahannock, with the Twenty-Sixth supporting the federal batteries. Pope knew that the Rappahannock was easily traversable at numerous points along the Union line, so he ensured that ample artillery was posted at key crossings to deter any threatened rebel attack. Sure enough, Lee's army attempted to cross the river at both the bridge and the numerous fords below, but without success. Each time, Union artillery succeeded in driving back the butternuts.

The Twenty-Sixth was involved in one such skirmish on the 21st when Confederate forces attempted to cross the Rappahannock at Clouce's Ford by erecting a pontoon bridge across the ford. The regiment lay on their northern bank along with the Eighty-Eighth and Ninetieth Pennsylvania, as well as the Twelfth and Thirteenth Massachusetts. When the rebel forces were halfway across, the unseen Union line rose and sent forth a ferocious volley, causing numerous pontoons and boats to drift downstream. Rebel gunners immediately responded with shell and canister, but were quickly silenced by Armstrong's Maine battery. In this engagement, as with most others during the three-day affair along the Rappahannock, the bluecoats suffered almost no loss, due in large measure to Union batteries and sharpshooters denying the rebels any type of advantageous ground from which to place their batteries. Despite the overall lack of involvement, every New Yorker was constantly forced to keep his head down, lest a screaming rebel missile remove it. During these cannonades, General Ricketts seemed to be everywhere, much to the approval of his men. From supervising the posting of infantry to the placement of batteries, James Ricketts was quickly earning the respect and admiration of his division. Unfortunately, the same could not be said of the Twenty-Sixth's colonel. How exactly William Christian conducted himself during those days remains cloudy. However, doubts about his fitness for command appeared shortly thereafter. Though Christian received nominal praise for his performance on the 21st, according to Private McClenthen, "Christian's conduct first gave cause for that suspicion of unfitness for command of which subsequent battles have afforded 'proof as strong as holy writ.'" Apparently, the strain of warfare was starting to take its toll on the colonel.[27]

★ ★ ★

The three-day engagement between blue and gray along the Rappahannock was primarily fought with artillery. Though under a consistent shelling, the lack of infantry skirmishing afforded the New Yorkers an opportunity for rest and to continue the never-ending quest for desirable food. Capt. Edmund Shurly wrote of a time in which a number of the foot soldiers made sure their stomachs were filled to the profound dismay of several officers. It seemed that the sutler assigned to the Twenty-Sixth had set up his tent near the banks of the Rappahannock, but the repeated marches had seriously depleted his stocks. After getting clearance from General Ricketts to return to Washington, a number of the regiment's officers approached the peddler about the prospects of obtaining some apples from their home state's Genesco Valley. The sutler did not disappoint the New Yorkers, for upon his return he proudly showed off several barrels of the prized fruit to a small group of officers. At that moment, an alarm sounded along the picket line, causing the officers to hurry away to their respective posts. The alarm proved to be a false one, and within the hour, the officers were leisurely returning to their prize. The various captains and staff, with Colonel Christian now among them, merrily eyed the barrels as the sutler proceeded to open them. To everyone's astonishment, the barrels proved to be empty! It was quickly ascertained that a few of the privates had spotted the booty, strategically cut holes in the bottom of the barrels when the officers had gone so that the apples would roll out, down the steep bank and into the river, where the fast-moving current brought them around the bend to the hungry, laughing bluecoats. Christian was incensed. "Captain," said the colonel, "you will arrest the men who committed this theft. By the gods, I will make these sour apples to them!" But no thief was ever apprehended. Only decades later, at a regimental reunion would Captain Shurly's tormentor reveal himself![28]

6

A First Taste of Death

Each day also brought new reports and observations of Confederate wagons and infantry marching further to the north. It was apparent that Lee was attempting to turn Pope's right flank, having previously failed in the Union's front and left.

August 23 brought about a fierce rainstorm that added to the growing misery felt by the New Yorkers. Rations were short, feet were sore, and the realization that one was about to be soaked to the skin only added to the somber moods. In fact, so severe was that day's deluge that the trestle bridge across the Rappahannock had been swept away and had then lodged against the railroad bridge. The pressure on that surviving bridge was such that it was now yielding to the pressure of the flood, and it too was in imminent danger of being carried off. Reports stated that the river had risen some six feet and all the crossing fords were gone. The rapidly rising river told Pope that it would be best to withdraw his army further and cease any plan of attack along the Rappahannock. The weather and river conditions would also prevent Lee's army from mounting any imminent strikes in his new rear. Therefore, Pope felt that he could concentrate his forces near Sulphur Springs and Waterloo in order to drive back the Confederates who had crossed at those points. Though the bridge had fallen, it was still imperative that rebel engineers not have the opportunity to rebuild it with any supplies of wood nearby. The task of destroying any remaining structures fell to Tower's rear-guard brigade in general and to the Twenty-Sixth in particular. Christian chose Companies C and G for the unpopular task, with Capt. Edmund Shurly in command. Those companies were quickly detailed for the purpose of putting the torch to the station building and surrounding houses. Anything that might be usable to the rebels was considered fair game. Tower supervised all of this in person, but when all was ready, the rain kicked up again, making the process of firing the buildings extremely difficult. Success was soon obtained; however, the blazing fires soon brought numerous Confederate batteries into action in an attempt to halt the New Yorkers' actions any further. Federal artillery quickly joined in, giving one last artillery duel to the skirmishes along the Rappahannock.[1]

Tower's other order that had been relayed by his adjutant general was that after destroying the buildings those same two companies were to hold the earthwork at the crossing until the army had successfully crossed the bluffs in their rear. The outlook for their survival appeared grim since only one gun from the Second U.S. Artillery would be accompanying Shurly's men. Their orders were simple and straightforward: abandon the gun if you must, but keep Lee on the far side of the river until it subsides. Once the Union army had passed the bluffs on the north side of the Rappahannock, they could abandon the earthwork and rejoin the regiment.

The New Yorkers kept up a methodical fire with their piece, well protected by the earthen walls. Scores of Confederate shells slammed into the redoubt but the agile New Yorkers suffered no injuries. Once the tail end of the army was seen descending the bluffs, they prepared to rejoin their command. Unfortunately, the only way out was to follow the riverbank for about a quarter of a mile, directly at a point where rebel artillery was kicking up plenty of earth and rock. With some effort, the bluecoats finally reached their comrades, suffering the loss of only one man who was captured by Confederate cavalry. Shurly soon reported to Colonel Christian, who was as shocked as delighted to see his subordinate officer. "I doubted whether you would get of that scrape," remarked Christian, "but I am glad you did. You generally land on your feet, which is why I left you behind."[2]

With the bridge and its attendant buildings successfully destroyed, Tower's brigade began a march back toward Warrenton,

1st Lt. John Jennings, Company G (Don Wisnoski Collection, USAMHI).

the place from where it had started over a month prior. The regiment trekked all night, halting only to rest their weary legs for several hours. The forced march then resumed, amid rumors that the rebels were closing in on the column's rear, which would precipitate a fight for possession of the army's trains. The rumor proved a false one, though, and by late afternoon of August 25 the Twenty-Sixth dropped their knapsacks at their new Warrenton campsite, which was only a mile from their earlier locations. The rest was not nearly as long as the men would have liked, for the following morning more rumors of Confederate troops nearby prompted a westward march back toward Waterloo, where Gen. Franz Sigel's corps at Sulphur Springs was said to be in need of reinforcements. There the Second Oneida was drawn up in a line of battle to await their foe. The arrangement of their fellow troops led the New Yorkers to think that a large-scale battle was imminent, for they could see and smell the smoke of the rebel guns. Any action, ultimately, was not coming their way. It was an excruciatingly hot day, with no offer of rest for the weary in the offing. By the time Ricketts' division was able to help, it was learned that they were no longer needed. Tempers, legs, and stomachs were all starting to significantly weaken by this point. The about-face order was given for the division to go back to their early morning position near Waterloo Bridge. That evening, the supperless, exhausted, and confused men of Ricketts' division went to sleep wondering what they had supposedly accomplished.[3]

The next day brought the disturbing news that a large part of the rebel army under Jackson had already succeeded in getting behind Pope, and to further aggravate the situation, the rest of the army under James Longstreet was rapidly marching toward Thoroughfare Gap, where the two wings would apparently join up. The New Yorkers received orders to quickly move out as part of a forced march to intercept the rebels. Tower's brigade was in the rear again with the Twenty-Sixth and some cavalry screening off to the left. Rations had been scarce and many of the men were weak from lack of food and the constant marching. Straggling was epidemic, with hundreds of men lying down in fields along the road or nestled against trees or fences along the way. Threats and pleas from officers to get back in line often produced few results. Colonel Christian later wrote that when the sleeping men were aroused, "the reply was to the effect that they could not march and did not care if they were taken by the enemy." To prevent just such an occurrence, Charles McClenthen noted that in some instances, his rear-guard company was compelled to "drive the men before it at the point of the bayonet." In addition to the obvious fatigue, General Tower was beside himself over the lack of rations for his men, and was seen riding from one company to another attempting to beg or borrow some hardtack to keep his troops from total starvation. He knew he had his hands full with his bedraggled brigade, and only through his resolve and force of will was he able to keep his men together as a cohesive unit.[4]

On the 28th, Ricketts' entire division was hastened toward Thoroughfare Gap with the new intelligence that Longstreet's wing was approaching the narrow passage. Holding the gap was crucial so that Pope could concentrate all of his forces, and throw them between the two wings of the rebel army. It would certainly be no easy task for Ricketts' roughly 5,000-man division to suppress Longstreet's 25,000, yet both generals knew that the terrain of the gap would probably give a decisive advantage to whoever got there first. At Haymarket, those men who still had knapsacks were ordered to discard them so as to gain a fast track to the gap.

For eight hours Ricketts' men held Longstreet at bay, essentially by Gen. George Hartsuff's Third Brigade. Ricketts' First and Fourth Brigades were moved forward in support, but Tower's Second brigade, which included the Twenty-Sixth, was initially held in reserve. Tower's brigade formed a line of battle but was still close enough to be under fire of the enemy's guns. Colonel Christian and his men had marched all over the Virginia countryside since Pope's campaign began in earnest almost a month before, with almost no combat to show for it.[5]

Ricketts' division engaged their enemy at the gap until dusk, in the process doing an admirable job of holding the rebels in check. It was soon learned, in spite of this success, that Longstreet's men were also streaming through Hopewell Gap, above and to the right of the bluecoats, a move that placed Ricketts' division in danger of being cut off. When at last after dark the division was obliged to yield, it began to fall back in good order toward Gainesville. They arrived footsore and hungry at that small village around 2:00 in the morning, made coffee, and tried to get some much-needed rest. At dawn, Tower's men broke camp and continued their haggard march to Manassas, stopping briefly to rest at Bristoe Station.[6]

Again, as with practically every other march during the campaign, the Twenty-Sixth brought up the rear of Tower's brigade, which was likewise bringing up the rear of Ricketts' division. It appeared at the time that the New Yorkers were forever destined to be "the rear of the rear." The New Yorkers were formed in line of battle several times during the eastward march from Thoroughfare Gap to Bristoe Station, in anticipation of facing Longstreet's men, but clearly, "Ol' Pete" was more concerned with catching up to Jackson.[7]

> **Volunteers Wanted for the 26th Regiment N. Y. Volunteers.**
> **THE BEST CHANCE YET.**
> THIS splendid Regiment needs more men, and offers a fine chance for young men to assist in giving the death blow to this infamous rebellion. The regiment is an old one, having been in service
> **FOURTEEN MONTHS,**
> and in point of efficiency is
> SECOND TO NONE IN THE SERVICE.
> The inducements now offered by the General Government, to those desirous of entering the service, are much better than heretofore; merit is sure to meet rapid promotion.
> **So Come Along and Volunteer.**
> This war will be crushed out by the immense mass of men to be sent to the field, so the term of service will be short. Pay and bounty the same as received in any other corps.
> For full particulars inquire at the rendezvous, 28 Catharine street.
> Col. WM. H. CHRISTIAN, Commanding.
> Dr. COVENTRY, Surgeon.
> Dr. BRISTOL, Chaplain.
> 1y10dtf   Lieut. C. H. SCHMIDT, Recruiting Officer.

Newspaper recruiting ad for the Twenty-Sixth New York Volunteers, August 1862 (*Utica Morning Herald and Daily Gazette*).

Second Bull Run

Ricketts' worn-out division continued its eastward trek toward Manassas Junction, then upon reaching that place, turned north up the Manassas-Sudley Road. They finally caught up to the rest of the Third Corps on the evening of August 29, bivouacking on the old First Bull Run battlefield near the Warrenton Pike and Sudley Road intersection, which placed them well within the range of the enemy's guns. Again, as with so many other times in the recent days, Tower's brigade formed the division's rear guard during the march. After days of forced marches and constant skirmishing, the New Yorkers and their brigade comrades must have appeared little better than their Confederate adversaries. "The men at this time were in a destitute condition, nearly all being barefooted and to say nothing of dirt and vermin," recalled one man from the Ninetieth Pennsylvania. Another Keystoner, from the Eighty-Eighth Infantry, added that they had "no decent chance to wash or a square meal since August 18th." Since both of those Pennsylvania regiments were companions of the Second Oneida within Tower's brigade, it is reasonable to assume that the Twenty-Sixth New York suffered similar privations. What rest and food could be found would be desperately needed for the following day.[8]

The Twenty-Sixth learned soon enough just how deadly the day's fighting had been. Lead elements of Pope's army had clashed with Stonewall Jackson late in the afternoon of the August 28 near the small village of Groveton, setting the stage for the next day's battle. Throughout the 29th, Pope had launched one attack after another against Jackson and his men, who were dug in along an unfinished railroad bed, but a lack of Union coordination failed to dislodge the rebels. Pope was still pleased, believing that he had the rebels right where he wanted them, and that he would destroy them the next day.

At sunrise on the 30th, Ricketts was ordered to send two of his brigades to Gen. Philip Kearny on the Union's right flank to assist with the planned attack. Gen. Abram Duryea's First Brigade and Col. Joseph Thoburn's Fourth Brigade were quickly picked for the task and soon thereafter began their march. Gen. George Hartsuff's Third Brigade, now commanded by Col. John W. Stiles due to a severe stomach illness that sent Hartsuff to Alexandria, was placed under General Tower's command as it was also depleted of its staff officers. Four batteries were assigned to Tower to occupy the left in reserve. By this time, Tower had ultimately succeeded in getting adequate rations for his brigade, giving his bedraggled Pennsylvanians and New Yorkers their first real meal in days.

While making these dispositions, Ricketts received orders shortly after midday to report to General Heintzelman, and to advance his division on the road leading from "Sudley Springs to New Market," directions which were probably an error in dictation since Haymarket was Ricketts' destination. The Union high command had believed that Lee's Confederates were in full retreat, so Ricketts was given the order to follow along that road "in pursuit of the enemy." It soon became apparent that the rebels had no intention of abandoning the field, and that James Longstreet's entire wing had arrived and was now massing on the Confederate right. Longstreet's wing had, in fact, arrived the previous day, a point that John Pope was only recently aware of. It now dawned on Union commanders that their left flank was sparsely defended and in grave danger. Any major Confederate thrust in that sector could roll up the entire federal army. Ricketts' advance was promptly called off.[9]

Unfortunately for General Pope and his army, John Reynolds' division, which had been positioned on the far left of the Union line at Chinn Ridge, had been called away to help with Union activities further to the right. That crucial piece of high ground on the Union far left was now unoccupied and open for the taking. Longstreet had his entire wing, totaling five divisions, on an east-northeasterly trek, converging in a perfect pincer movement with Jackson's wing at the north end of the field.

Realizing the crisis at hand, Tower's and Stiles' brigades, which had marched toward the army's far right in the morning along with Hall's and Leppien's Maine batteries, were now rushed at the double-quick back to the extreme left of the endangered Union line along Chinn Ridge. The Twenty-Sixth New Yorkers all realized that a maelstrom of smoke and lead lay straight ahead.

★ ★ ★

But where was Colonel Christian? Some men now realized that their colonel was no longer at the head of the column and word of the circumstance filtered back through the ranks. Earlier, he had been seen by a number of the men sitting under a tree with a blanket pulled up over his body and being attended to by a physician and orderlies. The colonel was plainly not feeling well with an ailment real or imagined.

Theodore Ashley, hospital steward for the Twenty-Sixth, testified decades later on behalf of a pension application for Christian's then-widowed wife that, "Dr. Coventry was with him when I saw him. [Coventry] diagnosed it as a case of sunstroke."

Several other comrades voiced similar recollections years later during depositions that were part of Mary Christian's widow's pension application process. Others being deposed at that time remembered the colonel as merely having a bad cold. In either case, that Second Bull Run incident raised the first public suspicions over Christian's ability to command. A journalist for the *New York Daily Tribune* reported on September 6, 1862 that "much feeling is expressed against the colonel" for sitting out the crucial battle with nothing more severe than a cold. An anonymous retort from the Twenty-Sixth's camp printed in the September 15, 1862, *Utica Morning Herald* came strongly to the colonel's, and by extension, the regiment's defense, claiming that Christian had been very ill and hoarse in the days prior to the Second Bull Run battle, his throat being so inflamed that he was unable to speak loud enough to be heard along the line. Christian therefore judiciously transferred command to Lieutenant Colonel Richardson the night of the 29th.

All those veterans deposed many years later, including the regiment's surviving officers, all agreed on one point: regardless of the exact cause of their colonel's troubles, absolutely nothing had seemed wrong with Christian the morning of the battle. History provides no answers as to what, if anything, Christian did at the time to explain himself. In a letter, though, written 13 years after the war ended to Union Gen. James McQuade, the then-mentally ailing Christian gave an account of why he was not in the engagement: "I was not considered to be on duty. The day previous the brigade surgeon had said that I had better go to Washington and the privilege had been granted by Gen. Tower. This was because of having been badly poisoned with oak or ivy down near the Rappahannock which had now caused a bad swelling of hands and face, which with constant exposure for many days and nights had now brought on severe pains in the head. [My] hands were so swollen and stiff that I could only guide my horse by having the bridle wound around my wrists." Regardless of the reasons, it was now clear to all that William Christian was not going to lead his New Yorkers into their first significant fight. That task would be left up to Lt. Col. Richard Richardson.[10]

★ ★ ★

After completing their lengthy run at the double-quick, the brigade was given a rest of about 45 minutes at their new position astride the Sudley Road, just south of the Warrenton Turnpike. Having caught its collective breath, Tower's brigade went into the fight again at the double-quick around 4:30 P.M. with the Eighty-Eighth Pennsylvania in the lead position. They marched from their position just off the Sudley Road and headed down a small slope, skipping over a stream before beginning their ascent up the ridge. All soon saw a portent of what was to come. Capt. Samuel Fessenden, staff aide to General Tower and well-respected by all, lay mortally wounded under the shade of a tree. He had been shot while delivering orders regarding the needed support up on the ridge. McClean's brigade of Ohio troops had been getting pummeled on the crest top and was now in dire need of reinforcements. Tendering that support and holding the ridge was Tower's intention, though at this stage he had no idea what he was up against. The Eighty-Eighth was followed in line by the Ninetieth Pennsylvania, then the Ninety-Fourth New York, with the Twenty-Sixth New York bringing up the rear. The regiments were to quickly form a line of battle in that same marching order from left to right. Echoing back to the Cedar Mountain battle formation, the Twenty-Sixth's initial objective was the far right of the brigade line in support of Capt. George Leppien's Fifth Maine Battery. Scores of men in such a small area, intense battle smoke, and the screams and shouts of orders momentarily confused the Oneidans as to which way they should face. The New Yorkers tried to sort out the melee as best they could, filing left in rear of Leppien's artillery, which was now actively engaged.

Once into a semblance of a line, it became ominously clear to every man in blue what was coming toward him. A fellow brigade comrade in the Eighty-Eighth Pennsylvania later described the Confederate legions as advancing in "many lines of battle, extending as far as could be seen; they came on in thousands, with battle flags well to the front and their officers urging them on." Tower's four regiments were getting shot apart before they even crested the hill. "[We] received a volley before we even thought of firing a gun," wrote Pvt. Warren Firman. "A part of them rallied but to no affect for the numbers were much greater than ours." Two companies on the left of the regiment—at the moment the only ones in proper position—able to open fire. The rebel reply was again furious, staggering the entire line of New Yorkers. "We were now under as heavy and as galling a fire as ever has been poured upon any body of troops during this war," recalled McClenthen. "Shot, shell, grape and cannister with a heavy enfilading fire of musketry, it seemed as if every arm and all the projectiles known in modern warfare had been let loose upon us at once." By the time the right of the regiment had almost worked its way into proper position, the left of the line was already starting to falter. This was due to a withering crossfire being delivered from the front and right, which would prevent the Twenty-Sixth from ever properly forming a full battle line. The New Yorkers quickly realized that there was a devil to pay on Chinn Ridge. Men in blue were

Modern panoramic view looking toward the west-southwest from the Twenty-Sixth's position atop Chinn Ridge during the climax of Second Bull Run. The entire background would have been filled with Longstreet's on-coming gray-clad legions.

falling every few seconds, the whiz and dull thud of the Minié ball indicating that rebel riflemen were finding their marks. "No troops in the world could stand it, and we commenced falling back," observed McClenthen. Adjutant William Bacon did his best to rally his men on the far right of the line, to no avail. They were also retreating, the colors retiring with them. "You can imagine my feelings at this moment," lamented the young officer. "Mortification, shame, indignation, were all commingled."[11]

The oncoming rebels were likewise sucked up into the din of battle. A Virginian firing his Enfield rifle at the disintegrating New Yorkers' shared their deadly perspective: "[F]or a space of about fifteen minutes the commotion was terrible. Bursts of sound surpassed everything that was ever heard or could be conceived. The baleful flashes of the cannon, darting out against the dusky horizon, played on the surface of the evening clouds like sharp, vivid lightning. Long lines of musketry vomited through the plain their furious volleys of pestilential lead, sweeping scores of brave soldiers into the valley of the Shadow of Death."[12]

Even greater troubles were developing on the far left of the brigade's line. The entire brigade was quickly being outflanked. General Tower hastily ordered Lieutenant Colonel Richardson to face his men to the left and move on the double-quick to the relief of the hard pressed Ninety-Fourth New York, whose tenuous hold on the extreme left flank was quickly weakening.

Richardson moved his men to their new front and rapidly opened fire with the left of his line while advancing the right of the regiment to the rise of Chinn Ridge. Through the cauldron of smoke and lead, the Twenty-Sixth kept up its fire as fast as possible. Unfortunately, McClean's brigade, which had been positioned in front of Tower's men, fell apart as the New Yorkers began their work. Sensing the impending collapse, one of the batteries situated at the crest of the hill quickly limbered up and pulled back in haste, crashing through the center of the Twenty-Sixth and creating chaos within the regiment. Simultaneously, hundreds of men from McClean's panic-stricken brigade now joined in on the rout, effectively cutting the Twenty-Sixth in two. Numerous bluecoats within the Twenty-Sixth were swept up in the retreat. Cpl. John Williams of the Twenty-Sixth recalled that horrible moment: "Before we had time to look around us, the first thing we saw was one of the regiments on top of the hill coming to an about face, and tearing down the hill a little faster than the regulation allows for a double-quick, running right into our left wing and breaking it, and a battery ran right into our right wing and broke that also." The line of New Yorkers that remained was slowly breaking, unable to stand the maelstrom of lead delivered by the advancing gray wall. Their predicament was not helped by the order to cease firing, given under the mistaken belief that they were actually firing into their own troops. So who were those blue-clad troops now rushing toward them? Through the smoke and dust, the Palmetto flag of South Carolina could be discerned, which quickly told the New Yorkers that it was rebel troops clad in Union uniforms. They had probably acquired them several days prior during their sacking of Manassas Junction.[13]

Tower's entire brigade was now caught in a rebel crossfire coming from three directions. The general was fervent with his pleas, urging his men to stay and crying out, "For God's sake, reform the line!" In the next instant, General Tower himself became a costly casualty, taking a rebel bullet in the left knee. Tower later wrote that he was wounded "so seriously that I was compelled to retire from the field of action on my worn out and wounded horse." His shattered knee ultimately rendered him unable to perform further field duty for the remainder of the war. Years later during congressional testimony, John Pope heaped high praise on Zealous Tower both for his efforts at Second Bull Run and the manner in which his men had conducted their lengthy marches during the weeks leading up to that battle.[14]

★ ★ ★

Not seeing any of his comrades around him, Private McClenthen decided that discretion was the better part of valor and fell back as well. Nor did he see his regiment's colors anywhere nearby, prompting him to recall in a letter to a friend that, "I can assure you I did not stay long to hunt them up, but made the best of my way toward the rear."

Just down the hill were spied the fluttering colors of the Twenty-Sixth, then being born by Capt. James Caryl of Company K. McClenthen and rest of the retreating New Yorkers were rallied at this point near the brigade's extreme left flank at the edge of some woods to await the surging Confederates, now within 200 yards of the Twenty-Sixth's flank. The wait was not long. The regiment was able to fire only two or three volleys before a rebel battery began to pour grape and canister into the New Yorkers, once again causing their thin line to again melt and give way. The oncoming graybacks, with their "rebel yell" piercing through the air, were virtually on top of the Twenty-Sixth. For a few brief moments, Companies F and H, located at the far left of the regiment, were engaged in hand-to-hand fighting with the advancing Confederates. Muskets became clubs in the confusion. Capt. Ezra Wetmore of Company F had to be carried off the field by his retreating men after

Rout of the federal troops by Longstreet's Corps at Second Manassas. The fleeing bluecoats would have been those from McClean's and Tower's brigades (Longstreet—"From Manassas to Appomattox").

he was knocked senseless in the melee. He would not fully recover until the battle was over. Those who did not leave fast enough were caught in a box. "As the long gray line closed in on each flank they threw down their arms and surrendered with but few exceptions; those few, as they ran, turned and fired," recalled one gray-clad "Johnny."[15]

The Twenty-Sixth formed its last line of the day some 250 yards in rear of Chinn Ridge, at nearly right angles with the brigade. By now, Tower's entire brigade as well as the whole left of the Union army was in full flight. The regiment had given the fight all they had during the 20 to 25 minutes they were under fire, firing during the time an average of, as nearly as can be ascertained, 30 rounds per man.[16]

With the line broken, all of Tower's regiments quickly turned and streamed down the ridge toward Sudley Road, where they reformed on Henry Hill for a feared last-ditch stand. By that time, troops from Gen. Franz Sigel's First Corps had also arrived at Henry Hill to provide a line of defense sufficient to stop the Union rout. Exhausted by their offensive efforts, the Confederate juggernaut now ran out of steam. The federal success in stopping Longstreet's advance at Henry Hill was due in large measure to the precious time that had been bought for John Pope's army by the sacrifices of Tower's men on Chinn Ridge. Pope acknowledged their efforts by writing in his official report that Tower's brigade "was pushed forward into action in support of Reynolds' division, and was led forward in person by General Tower with conspicuous skill and gallantry. The conduct of that brigade, in plain view of all the forces on our left, was especially distinguished, and drew forth hearty and enthusiastic cheers. The example of this brigade was of great service, and infused new spirit into all the troops who witnessed their intrepid conduct."[17]

With dusk at hand and the day's battle seemingly over, Lieutenant Colonel Richardson led the shot-up Twenty-Sixth off the deadly field, soon joining in on the army's somber retreat toward the Centreville fortifications. Scores were left behind, including Capt. Thomas Davis of Company H and Montgomery Cossleman of Company A, both dead on the field after being hit with numerous balls in the torso and limbs. The battered northerners knew they had fought bravely, but even the dullest private construed that they had been caught completely unaware on their entire left flank. Once again, their proud army had simply been outgeneraled by the rebels. John Pope and the corps commander, Irvin McDowell, received the most venomous commentary from the privates. Two weeks later, Pvt. Samuel Rightmire of Company K lay dying of his wounds at a Washington hospital. In a final letter home to his parents, the private revealed his beliefs on the matter: "Now I die one of the victims of McDowal's [sic] treachery ... our men were sold their blood for gold." Such recriminations against Pope and McDowell would last for years.[18]

Sweaty, bloodied men clogged the dirt road along with teamsters, artillery, and wagons of all sorts. Cries of "This way for Tower's brigade" filled the night, as scores of separated men tried to find and rejoin their regiments. Despite the confusion and the oncoming darkness, Colonel Christian was able to find and rejoin the Twenty-Sixth for the first time since the battle started, his ailments seeming to have passed. He urged his battered men on, pleading with them to take good care of the regiment's flags. Private McClenthen, among others, sarcastically noted that the banner did not seem in much danger at *that* point. In a letter home written a few days later, McClenthen remarked that Christian was not on the field and then diplomatically commented, "I shall say nothing of our field officers except Gen. Tower than whom a better or braver [man] does not exist." A good number of the surviving officers, however, were not content to satisfy their anger with acerbic commentary on their colonel's absence from the battle. Lt. Jabez Miller of Company A recalled years later that shortly after Christian's reappearance "a meeting of the officers was held for the purpose of presenting [Christian's] name to the general for removal. But I protested so hard, and told of having heard him excused by the surgeon, that nothing was done about it then." After about one-half hour, Christian rode away, ostensibly to find the rest of the brigade, while Capt. Norman Palmer was sent on to Alexandria in hopes of finding more of the regiment's men who might be on their way there in the ambulances. Since Gen. Zealous Tower was down with a serious wound, obtained while leading his men in battle, command of the brigade ironically passed to Christian since he was the senior colonel. Christian eventually gathered the four badly cut-up regiments and led them on their solemn retreat. With the brigade flag safely in his hand, he had them stop and camp just outside of Centreville.[19]

★ ★ ★

For the first time in the war, a large number of bluecoats from the Twenty-Sixth New York Infantry found themselves with their hands in the air, perhaps staring down the business end of a rebel musket or feeling the sharp jab of a bayonet in their back if they did not move quickly enough. That was the case for over 30 of the New Yorkers, who were reported captured or missing after their gallant, but ill-fated stand on Chinn Ridge. Among them were Cpl. Francis Crigier and Capt. Charles Jennings. Jennings was also severely wounded, having suffered a bullet through the foot. He lay on the dry, bloodstained field for over six hours before the Confederate orderlies were able to remove him to a field hospital. Though a prisoner, Jennings wrote highly of his captors in a letter he penned from the field hospital on September 2. "Their surgeons make no distinction between our men and their own, but treat all with the same kindness. I must say that the Southerner is a brave, generous, and magnanimous enemy, and so deeply regret that this war exists." Though he was optimistic for a full recovery, Captain Jennings' wound became

Cpl. George W. Clark died December 21, 1862, from wounds suffered at Second Bull Run (New York State Military Museum).

infected in the Washington hospitals, leading to his demise a little over a month later.[20]

Crigier escaped any type of wounding, but was nevertheless captured by the Confederates during the melee. Marched swiftly off the field, Crigier, like Jennings and most of the prisoners for that matter, was paroled by the rebels on the Bull Run battlefield several days after the fight. During the first two years of the war, both sides agreed to the "parole" system of exchanging their respective prisoners of war. Having originated in Europe, the agreement called for the prisoners to give a pledge that they would not take up arms against their captors until officially exchanged for an enemy soldier of equal rank.

In Crigier's case, it meant that his war was essentially over. He was sent to the army camp in Annapolis, Maryland, known as "Camp Parole," and then to the camp in Elmira, where, like so many of his comrades, he spent the rest of his enlistment whiling away the days.[21]

Those who were captured faced the prospect of at least some rudimentary attention to their wounds, and perhaps a few hard crackers and coffee for their stomachs. Such was not the case for those unfortunate wounded who were left behind on the battlefield. Shortages of everything from ambulances to food to medical supplies would ensure, in some cases, days of nightmarish hell for many who were abandoned at Manassas. A number of the Twenty-Sixth's men were included in that miserable lot. A correspondent of the *New York Herald* reported that he was given a page torn from a diary by one of nine men from the Twenty-Sixth who had managed to crawl together on a small plot of grass near Chinn Ridge. The nine had hastily scribbled their names along with the fervent plea: "We have laid here ever since August 30, two o'clock P.M.—some seventy-two hours. Please get us off before night." No ambulances were to be had but some food and stimulants were found to bring to the injured group.[22]

The final casualty tallies proved that the battle of Second Bull Run was a devastating blow to the fighting strength of the regiment. The casualty numbers attest to the bravery and gallantry they displayed in attempting to stop the Confederate juggernaut. 169 men were either killed, wounded, or reported missing after the battle, a horrific number that placed the Twenty-Sixth New York Infantry among the top 12 Union infantry regiments with the highest casualty figures out of over 150 taking part in this three-day engagement. By extension, General Tower's brigade had the highest casualty figures for any Union brigade engaged during the Second Bull Run battle.[23]

Both sides seemed to pause and catch their collective breaths on August 31. A chilling rain in the morning added a bleak exclamation point to the sound whipping that the dejected Yankees had endured the previous day. Stragglers and the walking wounded slowly wandered into the Twenty-Sixth's camp throughout the day, which had been set up along the Warrenton Pike *(modern Route 29)* along with the rest of the Third Corps about two miles east of Centreville. Since the Union army still faced west against their Confederate foe, that position placed them, by design, well in the reserve. Nevertheless, Confederate demonstrations across a small stream known as Cub Run prompted Union officers to expect another rebel attack, causing Tower's brigade, among others, to be formed in line of battle to await the strike. By nightfall, it was concluded that no attack would occur, allowing the exhausted men to return to their camps for some badly needed rest. For the wounded and others who had not been able to take part in the day's maneuvering, that Sunday was a day of woeful countenance. The injured New Yorkers who could not walk, as well as the rest of the army's injured, were laid out everywhere—in yards, on sidewalks, and in the homes and outsheds of the dilapidated little village.[24]

In spite of huge losses to both sides, the campaign was not yet over. Lee had decided to once again attempt to flank Pope by sending Stonewall Jackson's wing on a wide flanking maneuver around Pope's right, in the hope of getting in his rear and cutting off the Union army. Leaving around midday on August 31, Jackson marched his wing north from the Manassas battlefield through a muddy, dismal back road, finally emerging on the Little River Turnpike after dusk and camping at a point known as Pleasant Valley for the night. His goal was to march in an east-southeast direction down the pike on September 1, hopefully cutting off Pope's dispirited army somewhere near the small, all-but-ruined village called Germantown. Pope's reconnaissance discovered the rebel movement, which prompted a large and quick Union buildup at Germantown. By late afternoon on September 1, Jackson's Confederate columns had halted on the Little River Turnpike at an eminence known locally as Ox Hill, about one mile in front of the federal defensive works. While Jackson was waiting for Longstreet to come up, two Union divisions under Gens. Isaac Stevens and Philip Kearny surprised the Confederates by marching north from their ongoing eastward retreat on the Warrenton Pike in an attempt to cut off Jackson's advance. Fearing that he might be attacked now on his right flank as well as his front, Jackson threw practically his entire corps into the fight, which started just before dusk and briefly continued into the night. Both Stevens and Kearny would subsequently lose their lives in the battle. The short but vicious engagement was alternately known as the battle of Ox Hill to the Confederates, or Chantilly to the Union, and occurred in some of the worst weather conditions of any battle in the war. Near gale-force winds,

Pvt. Philip Winchell was wounded August 30, 1862, at the battle of Second Bull Run (New York State Military Museum).

crackling thunder, and a torrential thunderstorm provided a backdrop for a fight that none of its participants ever forgot.

Having marched in the early afternoon of September 1 from their camp toward Fairfax along the Warrenton Pike, the New Yorkers ended up missing out on the main engagement at Ox Hill, but were among the Union's well-entrenched defenders a mile away to the east along the Germantown defense line. Mother Nature's tempest, though, stretched to the Twenty-Sixth as well, and provided them with a most depressing, wet, and uncomfortable evening. Like practically every man who was there, Charles McClenthen never forgot the night of September 1, 1862: "I have witnessed what falls to the lot of few men; a hard battle in a thunderstorm, and seen lightning and a thirty-two pound shell strike trees within thirty yards of each other. [It is] A poor place for nervous people."[25]

The stress of conflict proved too much for Capt. Ezra Wetmore of Company F while sitting in line at Germantown during the Battle of Chantilly. Perhaps it was the memory of his physical beating and the carnage at Chinn Ridge just two days prior, coupled with the fearful expectation of repeating the butchery. In any event, Wetmore was forced to leave his position due to a severe intestinal disorder. The captain later alleged that the condition stayed with him throughout the remainder of his term of service, and in similar attempt as William Christian's alleged sunstroke, the captain attempted to parlay his newly acquired chronic diarrhea into a postwar pension.[26]

Following the brief but deadly engagement at Chantilly, the thoroughly beaten and demoralized Union army streamed eastward into its Washington fortifications. In a span of less than two months, Robert E. Lee had soundly whipped two Union armies and moved the theater of operations from the outskirts of Richmond to the gates of the federal capitol over 100 miles away. An exasperated Lincoln knew a change in leadership had to occur yet again. McClellan was given control of all defensive positions with Washington, though Pope was still in command of the retreating bluecoats. Both men enjoyed little in the way of trust or confidence with Lincoln and a good part of his cabinet. Advice poured in from all fronts to the president.

The Twenty-Sixth and their comrades throughout Ricketts' division trudged wearily through Fairfax Court House and into the Washington defenses. By the night of September 2, they found themselves camped at Hall's Hill, near Arlington Heights just opposite Georgetown.[27] To no one's surprise, the Twenty-Sixth, along with the rest of Tower's brigade, were reported as temporarily unfit for further duty after having been decimated at Second Bull Run.

The next week would provide a time of badly needed rest and recuperation. Uniforms, shoes, and accoutrements were in dire need of replenishment. The soldiers in the Twenty-Sixth, not to mention the entire army, needed emotional rejuvenation as well as physical. They knew they had been thoroughly whipped on the field of battle due to questionable leadership decisions, had marched to hell and back, yet the army was in the same position it had been months before. "Within the last few weeks," wrote Charles McClenthen, "I have seen soldiers give a gold dollar for a five cent loaf of bread and that at a point when we had railroad connections with Alexandria & Washington. I have slept on the ground without tent, blanket or overcoat or oilcloth since the 9th of Aug and have had no change of underclothes since then. We have been on the march for three or four days and nights together some of us barefooted others sick, and there are plenty of men who were wounded last Sat. [Second Bull Run] whose wounds have not been dressed yet."[28]

Fortunately for what remained of the regiment, they were able to procure new tents, clothing, and blankets, unlike many others. Though grateful for the rest, the next four days of leisure caused an expected emotional letdown and constant feeling of fatigue, what with adrenaline no longer surging through the New Yorkers' trim bodies. So by the time they resumed the march on September 6, the restocked, heavy knapsacks were causing the regiment much difficulty. That extra weight would soon be the least of their concerns.[29]

6

Maryland, My Maryland

The days following Second Bull Run brought more change to the Union high command. Ambrose Burnside was proffered command of the entire army, but in full realization of his ambitions and limitations, declined the offer. Meanwhile, John Pope was relieved of command of the Army of Virginia, per his request, and sent west to deal with Indian uprisings, effectively ending his Civil War career. George McClellan, despite Lincoln's misgivings and to the dismay of many in the cabinet, was given command of the Washington defenses. Organization and preparing men to fight had always been "Little Mac's" strong suit and he set about streamlining the various commands. Lincoln's administration viewed his assignment as strictly related to the area defenses with no pretense of a field command, but McClellan all but disregarded such nuances.

The Confederates had no time to concern themselves with such machinations in Washington. Following the just-concluded and highly successful campaign, Lee was now faced with a major strategic decision. Where to go next? Heading south back toward Richmond would mean giving up the initiative and smacked of retreat. A strike eastward toward Washington was likewise ruled out. Its defenses were too formidable, and besides, Lee's rebels were in dire need of food and rest every bit as much as their Yankee counterparts. Staying put near Manassas offered no chance for the famished army to feed itself. After more than a year of constant fighting, the northern Virginia landscape had been picked clean and now presented a vista of extreme poverty and desolation. Heading west would probably be to Washington's liking as it would take the pressure off the capital, but as with moving south, would mean Lee was surrendering the hard-won initiative. Moving north into Maryland and Pennsylvania seemed the only viable option. The lush farmlands of central Maryland were untouched by war and would provide ample provisions for his hungry army. Virginia could thereby gain a much-needed reprieve. In addition, Lee felt that many Marylanders would eagerly join his Confederates in the announced "liberation" of the state. By Lee's own admission, the Army of Northern Virginia was hardly in condition to begin a new campaign. His animals were worn out and many, if not most, of his men were without shoes. Nevertheless, he had the initiative and intended to keep it. North it would be. After several days of rest near Leesburg, Virginia, the rebel army splashed across the Potomac River and into Maryland, singing the popular *Maryland, My Maryland* as they marched.[1]

Now realizing that the rebels were closing in on Frederick, Maryland, in force, "Little Mac" wasted no time in moving the reorganized Army of the Potomac out of Washington and into the field. According to McClellan, "The disappearance of the enemy from the front of Washington and their passage into Maryland enlarged the sphere of operations, and made an active campaign necessary to cover Baltimore, prevent the invasion of Pennsylvania, and drive them out of Maryland."[2]

McClellan had his army divided into three wings, or columns, as they headed out of Washington. Ambrose Burnside had overall command of the two corps making up the right wing, which included Joseph Hooker's First Corps. Hooker had replaced Irvin McDowell as commander of that corps. Jesse Reno's Ninth Corps was also in the right column and initially advanced due north. James Ricketts still had command of his division within the First Corps. Due to Gen. Zealous Tower's war-ending injury, Colonel Christian was now formally in command of Tower's old brigade, with Lieutenant Colonel Richardson officially leading the Twenty-Sixth.

General-in-Chief Henry Halleck's main worry was still the safety of Washington, and he urged McClellan that, regardless of his plans, he must make sure that the Confederate army did not get between the Union army and the capital. The new campaign began on September 6, when orders came for the Twenty-Sixth New York to pack up and move out. Abandoning their camp at Hall's Hill, they marched through Georgetown and Washington, and then along with their comrades in Hooker's division, moved out from the capital via Seventh Street during the night. It was a forced night march, reminiscent of the Rappahannock marches of two weeks past. Straggling was again problematic for the entire division. One of Ricketts' men wrote of that night in his journal: "General Ricketts must have been either mad or crazy for he marched us over six miles without a halt.... I heard many Officers say that they thought Gen Ricketts must be crazy to march the men the way he did. It is not always the distance that tires the men the most. It is the manner in which we are made to march it. If we don't march but six miles, if the Gen marches us that distance without a halt he will have very few men come in with him." By dawn they had reached Leesborough, some 15 miles away.[3]

Sunday, September 7, dawned bright and clear for the reenergized bluecoats. The well-kept dwellings and highly cultivated fields of Maryland provided stark contrast to the desolation and poverty left behind in Virginia. The smiling citizens added much welcome relief, causing morale to soar from the depths of despair where it had resided over the past week. To the pleasant surprise of many, it was not uncommon for a sympathetic farmer to have buckets and barrels of cool water by the road for the thirsty men to dip their tin cups into as they marched by. Those tin cups, though, were still relatively few in number. To one man in the Ninetieth Pennsylvania, it seemed that there were no more than 300 men in Christian's entire brigade, while Pvt. Warren Firman of the Twenty-Sixth noted with tongue-in-cheek that his entire regiment was able to rest under the shade of *one* large tree! Any of the vigorous recruiting and enlistments that had transpired over the previous month had not yet filtered down to the older regiments such as the Twenty-Sixth.

The marches often seemed to proceed in a piecemeal fashion, consisting of short excursions followed by long periods of rest. Wagon trains often blocked a good part of the road, and during the periods of rest, other units were consistently marching past. It appeared that a type of leapfrog pattern was playing out, with McClellan's army again proceeding in an agonizingly slow fashion. The young foot soldiers, however, seemed not to mind. The weather was beautiful, the cornfields were full of roasting ears, and the fruit trees hung heavy with their bounty. To add to the feast, on September 8 the New Yorkers enjoyed soft bread for the first time since July 4. By the 11th, the regiment had reached Mechanicsville, another 12 miles away. The men knew that "Johnny Reb" was in the Old Line state, but any specific plan of engagement was still unknown.[4]

At Cookesville, the army stopped its northward trek, stepped onto the Old National Road *(modern Route 40)* and turned to the west, marching through the villages of Coopersville and Poplar Springs before crossing over the Monocacy River. The residents of the various villages seemed amazed at the quantity of men marching past, many remarking that they thought there were not that many people in the whole country. Union sentiment was strong, with almost every house displaying "Old Glory." Late in the evening of September 13, the Second Oneida and their corps comrades arrived on the outskirts of Frederick, Maryland, after days of hard marching. A journey of some 44 miles had been traversed in the week since they had left Washington. Lee's army was gone, having marched to the west.[5]

The Battle of South Mountain

On the morning of September 14, Ricketts' division was ordered to march at daylight from its encampment near the Monocacy River, and proceed toward South Mountain, about 18 miles to the west. The men in Christian's brigade were given an early reveille at 3:00 A.M., and by 6:00 were well on their way. The scene when they reached Frederick around 9:00 A.M. stood in stark contrast to the indifference that their Confederate adversaries had experienced. For the Yankees, it was one of adulation and triumph. With flags flying and drums beating, the Twenty-Sixth and their brigade companions marched through the town amidst the wild cheers for "Matellan." Numerous citizens offered bread, water, and apples to the passing bluecoats. By midafternoon the brigade had passed over the southern tip of the Catoctin Mountains and then reached Middletown, which seemed almost deserted by its appearance. The sound of cannonading and the sight of smoke in the distance told all that battle was not far off. The men rested along the side of the National Road to let Reno's division pass, and shortly thereafter, General McClellan with his staff and bodyguards rode by as well.

Ricketts' division arrived at the east side of South Mountain, about a mile north of the National Road, late in the afternoon around 5:00 P.M. The sound of combat raged near the top of the peak. A battle line was formed with Brig. Gen. Abram Duryea's First Brigade on the extreme right. Brig. Gen. George Hartsuff's Third Brigade took their place in the center, with Christian's Second Brigade on the left. Christian's initial orders were simply to provide support for Hartsuff's brigade.

The march of the First and Third Brigades extended over very rough ground to the top of the mountain. Fighting virtually every step of the way, Duryea's and Hartsuff's men succeeded in taking the crest. Meanwhile, off to Ricketts' left, Gen. Abner Doubleday's division had been hard pressed and was nearly out of ammunition. Christian's Second Brigade, which was still unengaged, was ordered to aid Doubleday.[6]

A rested Twenty-Sixth New York heads north out of Washington (1) on September 7, 1862, as part of Joseph Hooker's First Corps. Lee's Confederates are in Maryland and it is the army of the Potomac's intent to intercept them. The regiment arrives in Frederick (2) on September 13 and the next day, September 14, takes part in the battle of South Mountain (3). They are also heavily engaged three days later at the battle of Antietam (4). Lee's army retreats back into Virginia, but George McClellan decides to keep his army in and around Sharpsburg through the end of October.

Christian promptly ordered his brigade into battle line formation. The Twenty-Sixth took its prescribed place on the far right of the line and advanced up the slope toward Colonel Joseph Walker's South Carolinians, who occupied a cornfield and thick brush at the top of the hill. Walker's goal was to slow down the Union advance and to prevent the bluecoats from pouring through Turner's Gap, one of three natural passages at the mountain's crest being defended by the Confederates. While advancing up the mountain, the New Yorkers received orders to march by the left flank, for the purpose of gaining ground to the left and assisting the regiments then engaged. On reaching the fence along the timber at the hilltop, the Twenty-Sixth halted and quickly began returning firing. The barrage was heaviest from the left of the regiment, the right initially reserving its fire, as it was not yet in range of the enemy until some moments later. During this movement, the New Yorkers relieved elements of the Fourteenth Brooklyn, who had exhausted their ammunition and whose right was about 100 feet in the rear of the Eightieth New York Infantry. Unfortunately, none of the officers of the Twenty-Sixth had the slightest inkling that their fellow bluecoats were in their front, due to the darkness that had quickly descended over the field. In front of the regiment, some shadowy movement was detected through the smoke-filled haze. Thinking it to be the enemy, the New Yorkers let loose with a volley that was in fact aimed directly into the left of the Eightieth New York. Miraculously, the exposed New Yorkers suffered no injury, and before the Twenty-Sixth could repeat the mistake, the Eightieth's colonel sternly advised Lieutenant Colonel Richardson of his position as well as that of the enemy.[7]

The night firing continued for only about 20 minutes with little damage apparently done to either side. Christian's brigade was, for the most part, now firing into an empty field, for unbeknownst to most, the Confederates had mostly withdrawn from the battleground. A few rounds did occasionally come back in response, one of which almost made a casualty of Lieutenant Colonel Richardson. A spent ball hit him in the forehead, knocking him from his horse and leaving an ugly mark for days. Compared to Second Bull Run, the engagement had been a minor skirmish for the Twenty-Sixth. Not one man was killed, and other than the regiment's commanding officer, only one other man in the regiment suffered any type of wound.

The number of rounds fired had also been comparatively light. The left wing of the regiment fired some 20 rounds and the right wing only about four rounds when the order was finally given to cease firing. The Turner's Gap section of the battle of South Mountain was over. Orders were given for the men to hold the ground they lay on. Most slept on their arms in the same position until morning, no doubt pleased that they had savored their first taste of victory. In retrospect, the battle of South Mountain would prove to be the largest engagement the Twenty-Sixth was involved in, in which the Union army could claim a decisive victory. For those men on skirmish duty, rehashing their involvement would have to wait until tomorrow as they dutifully waited to sound the alarm.[8]

The specter that greeted Christian's brigade when they awoke on the foggy morning of September 15 was far different than what they could make out the preceding evening. Nothing but dead and wounded men clad in tattered gray cloth lay in piles in front of their lines, some in the most unimaginable positions. In walking over the rebel lines, some of the Union soldiers discovered, to their surprise, that the dead rebels' haversacks were actually well stocked with biscuits and cold ham that must have been obtained in Frederick. Usually, it was a hungry rebel that was to be found rifling through an abandoned Yankee haversack. To the victor went the spoils, which this morning consisted of a fine breakfast for the northern patrols.[9]

The time for investigation soon passed with the order to fall in. The Twenty-Sixth moved off to their left, down the western face of the mountain until they reached the National Pike once again. All the houses they passed within Turner's Gap and vicinity were filled with the cries of wounded men. By 2:00 P.M. on the 15th, the outskirts of Boonsboro was reached, at which time the men were allowed to stop and rest. Some cooked while others slept for no danger was apparent. Late in the afternoon came the order to fall in and continue the march. The men were now heading toward the village of Keedysville. Along the way, many buildings and tents were passed that were still in use as rebel hospitals. The surgeons could still be seen inside employing their bloody work. In many cases, the rebel flag still flew above these dwellings; nevertheless, no one seemed to care about removing the offending banners. The exhausted troops reached the fields surrounding Keedysville late in the afternoon, happily stacked their arms and lay down to rest for several hours. During this down time, scores of men in blue continued to march past the New Yorkers and to many of the young men it seemed that the entire army was marching past them. The consensus was building that another battle seemed to be in the offing. Soon McClellan and his entourage came thundering past to the roar of approval from each regiment that they passed.[10]

Most of the men in the Twenty-Sixth were fast asleep when the order to fall in was given around 10:00 P.M. Wearily anticipating a night march of unknown distance, the soldiers trudged out of camp and through the village of Keedysville. They soon found themselves splashing across a small creek known as the Antietam, and then halted in a large clover field. It turned out to be a short march of only a mile or so; nevertheless, the New Yorkers were grateful when it became apparent that they were stopping for good. This was their campsite for about the next 15 hours.[11]

The time was whiled away with the men cleaning their arms or napping. Another major battle was soon expected by everyone from officers down to the youngest privates. That belief, coupled with the rumored surrender of the garrison at Harper's Ferry, Virginia, left the northern men in an apprehensive mood.[12] Around 3:00 P.M. on September 16, the call to fall in once again sounded, and this time was carried out with unusual speed. The regiment marched westward from its camp near Keedysville toward the small village of Sharpsburg, in the direction of what was rapidly becoming the Confederate's left flank. All indications were that the next engagement would be somewhere in the vicinity of Sharpsburg. King's and Meade's divisions soon joined Ricketts' division as they all marched northwesterly in a roughly parallel manner. Ricketts' division crossed over winding Antietam Creek at both its upper bridge and via the ford near Pray's Mill. By nightfall, the lead elements had reached the Hagerstown Pike just north of Sharpsburg and encamped as far west as Hoffman's Farm. After passing through all manners of plowed fields, stone walls, and rail fences, the Twenty-Sixth took its position in the growing line at the edge of some woods near the Samuel Poffenberger farm around 8:30 P.M. Rebel and Union batteries lobbed a few shells in each other's direction, but no damage was suffered. The brief cannonading and accompanying infantry

Hooker's corps crossing Antietam Creek (E. Forbes sketch—*Century Magazine*).

fire, however, did alert Robert E. Lee where the Union army would begin the next morning's attack. After posting their pickets as ordered, the Second Oneida kept their arms close by and went to sleep as best they could, knowing that death awaited many with the new dawn. The restless night brought heavy rain, which many took as a bad omen.[13]

The Twenty-Sixth at the Battle of Antietam Creek

The Twenty-Sixth arose around 4:00 A.M. on September 17 and moved out of camp with an urgency and haste born of anticipation. The trek was relatively easy across the unbroken fields, but when the forests were reached it became a different story. The woods were so dark in the predawn hour that finding one's way was virtually impossible. Every man was compelled to grab onto the clothing or scabbard of his comrade in front of him just to keep the units together. The march continued through the dawn when the orders came to cross the final fields and to form in a line of battle. Ricketts' division, consisting of Duryea's, Hartsuff's, and Christian's brigades, was poised on the left side of the attacking Union forces, which Hooker had assembled in two broad columns just north of Sharpsburg.[14]

Christian's brigade was positioned on the far left of Ricketts' division, therefore, the extreme left of Hooker's entire First Corps. The Twenty-Sixth occupied the far left of the battle line with the Ninety-Fourth New York to its immediate right. The bluecoats continued to slowly advance in a south-southwesterly fashion just west of the Smoketown Road until they were halted some 400 or 500 yards from the East Woods, beyond which the rebels lay awaiting the Union assault. Lt. Col. Richard Richardson was directed to deploy his men in column, and he advanced his regiment obliquely toward the woods under a heavy fire of shot and shell. Private McClenthen later wrote: "The heavier report of the field pieces convinced us that the ball was about to open in earnest."

Rebel shells began to come in thick and fast, many of them from J.E.B. Stuart's rebel horse artillery, which was favorably posted on a slight eminence just west of the Hagerstown Pike known as "Nicodemus Heights." From there, his guns could control the entire field of battle. Col. Stephen D. Lee's guns just to the south added to the misery by placing Christian's men in an artillery crossfire. Despite the shower of lead, the New Yorkers marched bravely on, ducking their heads and hunching their shoulders, doing all they could to ignore the deadly missiles. Colonel Christian, on the other hand, positioned about 10 rods behind his old regiment on his black charger, was starting to lose whatever mettle he may have possessed at one time. On that cool early morning, there was no sunstroke to be had or head cold to fall back on. The man simply could not stand the scream and explosion of the shells and each step took him deeper into his personal abyss. To delay the inevitable reckoning, Christian directed his brigade as if they were still on the parade ground, which was the place where he was most comfortable. The excessive martial maneuvering prompted one of his Pennsylvanian's to recollect that, "If the brigade had been taken into [Second] Bull Run like a mob, it was evident that the error was not to be repeated here." First the cries of "Forward, guide center!" then "By the right flank!" concluding with "Forward!" again. With no let up from the shrieking missiles in sight, Christian finally cracked. Jumping off his mount, Christian grabbed the horse's reins and broke for the rear, leading the poor animal along. Ducking and dodging his head with every step, his men saw all and were aghast at the cowardly spectacle. Word later reached his men after the battle that Christian had almost started a panic among the reserve troops in the rear by shouting that the battle was lost and the army in full flight. With no commander to lead them, the entire brigade seemed to pause, unsure of where to go next.[15]

With no further instructions, the Twenty-Sixth New York was ordered to come to a halt, about 100 yards in the rear of General Duryea's brigade as it was now moving off to the right. In the meantime, Hartsuff's command, which had preceded Christian's brigade into the fight, was slugging it out with the Confederates within the Miller family's cornfield. Hartsuff had gone down with a serious wound early on, which initially produced some command confusion. Once the issue was resolved, command of the brigade passed to Col. Richard Coulter of the Eleventh Pennsylvania. Coulter had pounded his horse up to the head of the just-arriving Ninetieth Pennsylvania and begged for assistance. The request had been quickly relayed to Christian prior to his abandoning the field; paralyzed with fear, he did nothing. A leading officer of the Ninetieth Pennsylvania recalled the situation: "We received no orders what to do and the balance of the brigade was at a standstill in the hollow of the woods...."[16]

Meanwhile, Ricketts and his aides saw from the rear that Christian's Second Brigade was stalled and with no word as to why, Ricketts sent his assistant adjutant general to find out just what his new brigade commander was doing. Capt. Norman Palmer, originally from the Twenty-Sixth New York, but now Christian's chief-of-staff since the colonel's elevation to brigade command, frantically explained what had transpired and where he thought the colonel had headed. When word ultimately got back to Ricketts as to what occurred, a courier was quickly dispatched to Gen. Truman Seymour to inform him that Christian's troops were leaderless and to promptly take command of the Second Brigade. Seymour was a tough army regular who commanded a brigade in George Meade's First Division and had led Hooker's left column into the battle. The general raced back to bring Christian's men forward for badly needed support. Once there, Seymour wasted no time in putting the idle New Yorkers and Pennsylvanians into action. He ordered Richardson to advance to the support of General Hartsuff and to begin forming a battle line so that when completed, the far right of the brigade would connect with Hartsuff's left flank. Richardson set the Second Oneida in motion by moving them through the small forest and then deploying along a snakerail fence just past the southern edge of the East Woods, where the New Yorkers now represented the extreme left of Hooker's corps. The right of the Twenty-Sixth connected with the left of the Ninety-Fourth New York Volunteers, whose right flank, in turn, rested upon the Smoketown Road. The new line then continued toward Hartsuff's beleaguered brigade with the Eighty-Eighth and Ninetieth Pennsylvania to the right of the Ninety-Fourth New York.[17]

By the time the Twenty-Sixth was in line, the gray- and butternut-clad enemy soldiers were clearly in sight about 350 yards away, where they were still hotly engaged with Hartsuff's regiments. These were men from Gen. Isaac Trimble's brigade, who were briefly the closest rebels to the New Yorkers. In particular was the Twenty-First Georgia, whose men were precariously positioned along a fence bordering the Smoketown Road, in effect presenting only their right flank to the advancing New Yorkers. Further in front of the Second Oneida lay a plowed field and on an upward slope just beyond that, a burning house and barn that belonged to the Samuel Mumma family. The Confederates had put the torch to the house and barn when the battle got underway to prevent it from being used by the Yankees as a sharpshooter's hideout. They would prove to be the only civilian properties purposely destroyed during the entire battle. Slightly off to the right of the New Yorkers' front lay a low fence that bordered the Mumma family cemetery. With the appearance of Christian's brigade, the rebels shifted their line and began forming a new one to confront the advancing New Yorkers and their comrades. Quickly advancing to assist Trimble were the Georgians and North Carolinians of Gen. Roswell Ripley's brigade who took a position along the Mumma property.[18]

Realizing they had been spotted, Richardson gave the command to commence firing. The battalion opened with everything they had and continued discharging their muskets evenly and carefully for some 30 rounds. The Confederates sent volley after volley in return, delivering their fire with "promptness and spirit," according to Charles McClenthen.

When the regiment's color bearer fell with a bullet wound, Pvt. Charles Cleveland of Company C voluntarily picked up the flag and continued holding it aloft, still slowly moving the men forward. In the process, Cleveland suffered gunshot wounds in the left forearm, left breast, and left foot. His wounds at Antietam cost

Modern view from where the Twenty-Sixth fought at Antietam looking toward the Confederate position at the Mumma Farm. The low cemetery wall at the right background was built in the 1870s but is in the same spot as the low fence from which the Confederates fought. A farm building is in the center background.

him a two-month stay in a Baltimore hospital, but would later earn him what would be the first of three Medal of Honor awards for soldiers in the Twenty-Sixth New York.

It was essentially a stand-up fight and though the New Yorkers' volleys were having the desired effect, their ranks were being nominally thinned from the rebels' return fire. With ammunition running low, Richardson was forced to tell his men to slow their fire, and twice sent an aide to look for Christian and plead for ammunition or relief. Apparently unbeknownst to Richardson, Christian was still nowhere to be found. He was last seen running for the rear in a zigzag pattern.[19]

When it became apparent that help was still a ways off, Richardson ordered the command to cease firing in an attempt to stall for time, hoping that at least fresh rounds would be delivered. This cessation brought the rebels out from behind their fence and more plainly into view on the open ground, prompting the New Yorkers' to again open fire. This had the effect of driving Ripley's men back behind the fence and under partial cover of the cornfield. Knowing that his men could safely retire into the East Woods if the need arose, Richardson decided his New Yorkers would stay to the last ball and ordered his men to resume their firing until every cartridge was expended. The rebel forces engaged with the Twenty-Sixth were also hoping for reinforcements and the sight of Alfred Colquitt's brigade from Gen. D. H. Hill's division advancing onto the right of Ripley's brigade brought welcome

A modern view of the Twenty-sixth's position at Antetam taken from the Confederate perspective at the cemetery next to the Mumma Farm. Extant East Woods is in the background.

relief. All of these Confederate veterans enjoyed a hard-won reputation for fierceness that Christian's brigade had not yet earned. With his ammunition virtually exhausted and Confederate reinforcements looming in his front, Richardson, as well the Eighty-Eighth Pennsylvania and the Ninety-Fourth New York regiments, decided that it was time to withdraw from the field. Besides, Richardson saw that Gen. Joseph K. Mansfield's Twelfth Corps was now arriving, which would allow his men an opportunity to be resupplied. Seeing Mansfield's troops, Richardson ordered his men to withdraw through the woods to the nearest supply post. Gaining fresh rounds, the regiment marched back to the front where they quickly learned that the entire line had advanced. Moving forward, the regiment reached a high knoll and saw that the battle had practically ceased on the right.[20]

By 7:30 A.M., the Twenty-Sixth's day was essentially over. With an apparent lull in the fighting, they were sent to the rear along the far right of the federal line, where the regiment rested across the Hagerstown Turnpike. There they stayed for the remainder of the day and evening. Other than having to dodge some rebel artillery, the Twenty-Sixth, as well as Ricketts' entire division, would face no further action. That night, Companies H, A, and C performed some solitary picket duty.[21]

Total casualties for the Twenty-Sixth were nowhere near what they had been at Manassas two and a half weeks earlier, but were still significant when based as a percentage of the regiment's fighting strength. Approximately two hours of battle cost them five killed, 41 wounded, and 20 missing for a total of 66 casualties from their already thinned ranks. With little more than 200 men going into the fight, this number represented about one-third of the unit.[22]

By 9:00 A.M. it was essentially over at the northern edge of the battlefield. History would later record that the soldiers of Joseph Hooker's First Corps had fought bravely and well. Support for the initial attack had been piecemeal, and coupled with dogged Confederate resistance, the battle had spelled death and destruction on a scale not previously known in the war. Men with blackened faces and sweat-stained and torn uniforms looked glazed and stunned as they wandered off the bloody field. Those that were still able to fight could not be found in many instances, such had been the confusion. In reality, Hooker's First Corps had temporarily dissolved. Gen. Edwin Sumner later quoted Ricketts as saying that he could not locate more than 300 men from his entire *division* once their fighting had ceased.[23] That included the Second Oneida, who were clearly done for the day. Though their withdrawal from the field was far more orderly than the rout at Second Bull Run, like that battle they had gallantly advanced as ordered, but eventually failed to hold the ground they had fought upon. The battle of Antietam would continue on throughout the day, concluding with the grisly title of the bloodiest single day in American military history.

The End for William Christian

After abandoning his men on the field, Christian was later found cowering behind a tree. Gen. Truman Seymour rode up to the shaken New Yorker, and like Gen. Henry Slocum almost a year before, Seymour ascertained the measure of the man in front of him in a single glance. Seymour relieved Christian of command on the spot, and later that night when the rage of battle died down, James Ricketts summoned the shell-shocked colonel to his tent. Ricketts had two horses shot out from under him during the day's fight and had been seriously injured when the second one fell on him.[24] Despite his obvious pain, the division commander knew what justice called for. Ricketts demanded Christian's immediate resignation. If Christian refused, charges of gross cowardice in battle would be brought against him in a court-martial. Christian obviously saw the handwriting on the wall. The next morning, September 18, writing from Union headquarters near Keedysville, Maryland, Col. William Henry Christian penned his letter of resignation:

> I most respectfully offer my resignation as Colonel of the 26th Regiment N.Y. Volunteers. Business of importance requires my presence with my family and regiment being reduced in numbers to less than two hundred men, and it having able officers, therefore I ask that I may be permitted to retire from the service and ask that I may be honorably discharged there from.

Ricketts wasted no time in forwarding the letter on to Maj. Gen. George Meade, who had been placed in command of the First Corps by McClellan following Joseph Hooker's and James Ricketts' serious injuries of the previous day. Hurriedly scribbling on the back of Christian's letter, Ricketts urged that Christian's offer be accepted and that he be relieved at once, citing "a general want of confidence in him." Acceptance of Christian's resignation was granted by Meade without delay, who then placed Col. Peter Lyle of the Eighty-Eighth Pennsylvania Infantry in command of the brigade.[25]

The folks back home in Oneida County were wholly perplexed when they learned of their colonel's resignation, in large part because they were told none of the sordid details by the newspapers. In reality, the local newspapers seemed to have been as in the dark as their readers were. The *Utica Morning Herald and Daily Gazette* reported in its September 23 issue that it had no information on the rumored resignation of Christian. Nor did the colonel mention the matter in a letter of the 18th to his brother. Thomas Christian shared the letter with the *Utica Morning Herald*, which published it in the September 23 issue. In it, William Christian wrote only of his brigade's actions, and how its fighting force was reduced from around 2,000 to *350*. No official announcement was ever made in any of the local papers, nor did Christian ever publicly speak of his actions on that fateful September day.[26]

Personal thoughts within the brigade about the Christian incident seemed to be as scarce as public comment. One of Christian's Pennsylvanians wrote in his diary on September 19 that Christian's dismissal from command "gives general satisfaction." The 14-year-old drummer boy for the Ninetieth Pennsylvania tried his best to be a bit more evocative, describing in a letter to his parents how, as the battle began, Christian simply "stood behind a tree and said forward men forward." The lad concluded by remarking how the regiment's officers stated after the fight that none would continue to serve under Christian. Warren Firman of the Twenty-Sixth did not even bother to mention the sad affair in his journal. Overall, this lack of written commentary can be partly explained: In essence, nineteenth-century decorum dictated that such affairs were not discussed in polite society. Illustrative of that fact was the Twenty-Sixth's Charles McClenthen, who was on the field when Christian broke. He would not reveal specifics, though he would push the envelope somewhat in his slender 1863 *Narrative of the Fall and Winter Campaign* by only revealing that, "Our Col. has proven himself to be afflicted with a constitutional timidity under fire, that even his pride and ambition for military distinction could not overcome, and which at last forced him to resign under unfavorable circumstances." Over 30 years later, Victorian sensibilities still reigned. Ezra Ayers Carman, the Antietam battlefield's first official historian and one who would have certainly been aware of Christian's actions, still delicately danced around the affair in his unpublished 1890s history of the battle. He wrote of how Christian's men "did an unnecessary amount of drilling" and were subjected to a "wicked artillery fire," but with regards to the colonel himself, Carman would only state that the barrage "demoralized one or two of the most prominent officers."[27] Maintaining proper etiquette was no different for the Twenty-Sixth's aged veterans, either. In a series of private letters written in 1893 telling of the regiment's Antietam positions, an elderly William Holstead still felt it essential to clarify his motives about revealing Christian's collapse. "I repeat this not to tell tales out of school," stressed Holstead, "so much as to have you know what I know about our camping in the rear of the woods."

Christian's assertion of the regiment being reduced to less than 200 men was accurate. Repeated casualties, the inevitable desertions, coupled with a lack of new recruits had now depleted it to the size of a handful of companies. This was a situation that was far from unique to the Twenty-Sixth New York. Statistically, its manpower dilemma had been shared across the entire brigade and even extended well into the First Corps. Daniel Jones, the brigade's assistant quartermaster, explained after Antietam how the brigade had numbered about 2,800 men back in late May. He then noted that on September 19, two days after the battle, he had issued rations to only 861 men. Col. Charles S. Wainwright, artillery commander of the First Corps, reported prior to the battle that "the last return shows forty-six regiments of infantry in the corps, with about 28,000 men on their rolls, or only some 600 men to a regiment; yet of these 16,000 are absent and only 12,000 are present. Our regiments average 260 officers and men in the field. This is a horrible state of affairs...." The numbers after the battle were even worse. The evening of the 17th found the First Corps able to muster only 7,000 men, a far cry from the tens of thousands that existed on paper.[28]

The brief Civil War career of Col. William Henry Christian was comparable in some respects to that of his Army of the Potomac commanding general, George McClellan. Both men were considered to be of fine stock and countenance, whose bearing commanded the utmost respect from their men in camp and on the parade ground. Their military reputations in the early months of the war were unquestioned. To their credit, achieving military readiness and instilling martial discipline were their strong suits, but in the end, aggressive engagement in the art of combat was shown to be both men's Achilles' heel.

Despite these similarities, Christian's speed and decisiveness in submitting his resignation on that 18th of September stood in sharp contrast to George McClellan's military strategies of the same day. To everyone in the army on the night of the 17th, it seemed a certainty that the attack would continue with the dawn. McClellan even wired Halleck at 8:00 A.M. on the 18th "the battle will probably be renewed today." By the end of the day, though, no attacks had been made, giving Lee the opportunity to remove his weakened Confederates across the Potomac and to relative safety on the southern side. Though the rebels were gone from Yankee eyes, the stench of death and decay from the battlefield would fill their nostrils for days to come, in some cases causing burial parties to leave the field for their personal health.[29]

The 19th saw the Twenty-Sixth engaged in picket duty that extended from their Sharpsburg camp to the northern bank of the Potomac. In the course of their duty, the regiment rounded up numerous stragglers and deserters from Lee's army, the quantity of rebels providing ample proof that the rumors were true. The Confederates had indeed crossed back into Virginia.[30] Maryland was now free of the rebels and back in federal control, though the battle had been far from a decisive Union victory. From McClellan's perspective, it was a glorious triumph, even though he believed his army had been badly bruised and now needed ample time to recuperate. For the remainder of the month and then some, "Little Mac" would have his army encamped in and around the battlefield area.

★ ★ ★

After the battle at Antietam, many of the wounded were sent north to hospitals in New York and around the Washington, D.C., area. Despite their removal from the front lines, many of the injured looked forward to returning to their friends and comrades back at camp. To the unpleasant surprise of some, the care and food in the hospitals left much to be desired. "A sick or wounded man is here like a convict," wrote the Twenty-Sixth's Pvt. Frank Ingersoll, from Carver Hospital, within the D.C. area. Injured at Antietam with a severe shell wound of the scalp and skull, Ingersoll was soon able to transfer into quarters that offered a quicker chance to recover. "We have a comfortable house, like the Elmira long sheds, though; and comfortable beds enough, and better food than when I first came; we have now 2 slices of bread and a piece of meat and a pint of coffee. I'd rather be at a private house, but they won't allow it." Despite his optimistic outlook, Private Ingersoll was discharged due to his debility on January 12, 1863.[31]

Not all soldiers were fortunate enough to see a hospital that purportedly offered a higher level of care. Numerous men unable to be moved ended up in field hospitals established near the battleground and camps. Pvt. Hugh Collins of Company I took a rebel ball right above his right eye which ended up lodging four inches below his left ear. His wound was typical of those that required immediate attention on the field and did not allow further movement. The man miraculously survived, but nevertheless was sent back to the Smoketown, Maryland, field hospital on October 8. Though a survivor, Collins was permanently affected with a partial blindness in both eyes that caused his discharge from the service on December 20, and permanent disability for the rest of his life.[32]

★ ★ ★

The New Yorkers' activities in October proved to be little different from those in the latter half of September. Like the rest of the army, the weeks following the battle of Antietam were spent whiling away at the usual routines of drill practice and picket duty. Their only movements were twice moving their camp somewhat closer to the Potomac. When off duty, the men passed the time writing letters, rehashing the just-fought battle, or predicting the future course of the war. Reading was also a popular pastime, with Chaplain Bristol making sure that ample quantities of the Soldier's Prayer Book were on hand for his young men. Unfortunately for the chaplain, Major Jennings seemed not to know what to do with the 300 copies in their camp and happily gave 100 of them to Col. Adrian Root of the brigade's Ninety-Fourth New York when that officer came calling seeking the title. The demand in that regiment was apparently stronger than in the Twenty-Sixth, for Root later returned seeking more. Derisively referring to the Twenty-Sixth as a body of "ruthless invaders," the colonel became quite vexed when an allegedly drunken Jennings denied his request, now realizing, according to Root, "that a demand existed in the market." Root sarcastically informed Jennings how the major's spur-of-the-moment decision "reflected great credit upon his anxiety for the 'moral welfare' of his regiment" before angrily retiring back to his camp. It would not be Root's last unpleasant exchange with an officer of the Second Oneida.[33]

The early fall weather was generally pleasant and food was now available in ample quantities, with one favorite of the New Yorkers being baked corn cakes. Charles McClenthen had a popular recipe in which the corn meal was grated on an old canteen that had been punctured with the point of a bayonet. The weeks were relatively comfortable for the average private since new uniforms, blankets, and other accoutrements had also arrived. For the Twenty-Sixth New York, those Maryland days of October, 1862 harkened back to the months in Washington just after the first battle at Bull Run, when the two great armies could eye each other from across the Potomac, but both were too weakened and tired to make an attack.[34]

Despite McClellan's protestations that his army was in no condition to move, Abraham Lincoln was growing ever more impatient at what he saw as a lack of urgency on the part of his commanding general. The president decided to visit the battlefield for himself, arriving on October 2 in order to see the status of the army firsthand. Four days later, Lincoln had satisfied himself that the army was in fighting shape and ordered McClellan to cross the Potomac and pursue Lee's battered army. Yet more time was frittered away with no advance apparent.

On October 13, an exasperated Lincoln wrote again to McClellan. Since the president could not reason with "Little Mac" via military logic, he subtly appealed to McClellan's unbridled pride by asking, "Are you not overcautious when you assume that you cannot do what the enemy is constantly doing? Should you not claim to be at least his equal in prowess, and act upon the claim?" and "Why can you not reach [Richmond] before him, unless you admit that he is more than your equal on a march? His route is the arc of a circle, while yours is the chord. The roads are as good on yours as on his." Such back and forth would continue for two more weeks.

Pontoon bridge across the Potomac River at Berlin, Maryland, seen from the Virginia shore. Here the Twenty-Sixth and the rest of the Union army crossed back into Virginia in early November 1862 (*Gardner's Photographic Sketchbook*).

By late October, McClellan finally decided that the army was ready to again take up the advance. On October 26 the lead elements of the Union army finally began crossing the long pontoon bridges over the Potomac into Virginia. It was slow going and was not until the 28th that the First Corps even reached the Potomac at Berlin, Maryland *(known today as Brunswick)*. Berlin was situated under a hill on the north bank of the river and consisted of only a few ramshackle houses. It also sat next to the Baltimore and Ohio Railroad, a few miles east of Harpers Ferry and was therefore used as a federal supply depot.[35] Moving the entire Army of the Potomac across the river was slow, but by the 30th the Twenty-Sixth and the rest of the First Corps had crossed at Berlin and were encamped three miles away near Lovettsville. The next campaign was underway.

7

The Fredericksburg Campaign

November 1 found the regiment, now commanded by the field-promoted Col. Richard H. Richardson, at long last marching south back through Virginia. As second in command since the regiment's formation, Richardson had been the obvious choice to lead the unit and so his name had been submitted for promotion to the governor of New York following William Christian's forced resignation. It was not, however, a foregone conclusion that Richardson would become the regiment's next colonel. Letters of recommendation had to be written, including one by Dr. Coventry. In the end, Richardson was formally promoted to colonel on November 24, retroactive to September 19. On the same day, Maj. Gilbert S. Jennings was promoted to lieutenant colonel, with Capt. Ezra Wetmore of Company F moving up to major.[1]

By early November, the next campaign was well in progress, and the marching weather was as glorious to the boys in blue as any they had ever seen. Lee's Confederates were on the move and it was the Union army's intent to stay with them, but at the same time, the bluecoats had to make sure that they stayed between the rebels and Washington. On the 3rd of November, the regiment turned off the Leesburg and Winchester Pike at Purcellville, and headed south toward Fillemont. In the days to follow, the roads heading south were so filled with troops and wagon trains that it was no uncommon event to come across men or officers who had been unable to locate their regiments for days. The New Yorkers ultimately found themselves back in the familiar village of Warrenton on November 7. Unfortunately, the beautiful Indian summer weather they had enjoyed quickly ended and then took an abrupt turn, for the army now found itself in the midst of an early winter snowstorm with temperatures so cold that water froze in canteens. To some, it was an eerie portent of things to come. One letter writer from the Second Oneida tried to convey to the readers back home a sense of the trying conditions his unit was facing. "Let our friends at home imagine themselves called forth from their warm beds and refreshing slumbers at one in the morning and be required to take down their homes, pack up their furniture and sit up till noon in a cold, searching wind; they would then have our experience just a week ago."[2]

In addition to officially having a new colonel for their regiment, the Twenty-Sixth also now had new corps, division, and brigade commanders. Despite his serious injuries and therefore his temporary unfitness for field command, James Ricketts had protested only days after Antietam that George Meade had been given command of the corps over him, in light of the fact that Meade was his junior. This perceived slight, coupled with the fact that the injuries he had suffered during the battle had never healed thoroughly, prompted Ricketts in late October to request reassignment. The request was quickly granted on November 2, with orders following for Ricketts to report to the garrison at Harpers Ferry, Virginia, and await further instructions. He would spend the next year and a half serving on court-martial boards, not returning to the field until March 1864. Ricketts' replacement as division commander was Gen. John Gibbon, a 35-year-old Pennsylvanian by birth who had graduated from West Point in 1847, alongside fellow Union general Ambrose Burnside and Confederate A. P. Hill. Gibbon's reputation was that of a hard-nosed disciplinarian and tough fighter who tolerated no nonsense from his subordinates. His division was still in the First Corps, now commanded by a fellow Pennsylvanian, Maj. Gen. John Reynolds.[3]

The Twenty-Sixth's new brigade was now formally commanded by Col. Peter Lyle of the Ninetieth Pennsylvania, who had led the unit in the field since Antietam. Despite Lyle's gallantry at Antietam, Gibbon somehow viewed Lyle as a weak link in his chain of command. First, Gibbon informed Lyle on November 12 that he was dissatisfied with the sanitary conditions within Lyle's brigade. Several weeks later, Lyle came in for a second rebuke from Gibbon, due to similar issues. A few days later, after reinspecting the camps for the third time, Gibbon had apparently seen enough and sought Lyle's dismissal. Writing to corps commander John Reynolds, Gibbon flatly stated, "I am much in want of a commander for my Second Brigade." In spite of Gibbon's misgivings, nothing happened, since Lyle had proven himself a hard and reliable fighter on the battlefield.[4]

Not all of the regiments stayed the same within the Twenty-Sixth's revamped brigade. Gone were the Eighty-Eighth Pennsylvania and the Ninety-Fourth New York. Their replacements would be the fairly small Twelfth Massachusetts, whose ranks had been decimated at Second Bull Run, and the heavily-manned One Hundred-Thirty-Sixth Pennsylvania Infantry, which had just been recruited in August of that year.

Col. Richard H. Richardson (Massachusetts MOLLUS—USAMHI).

All of this restructuring came about because changes in command were also occurring at the highest level of the Army of the Potomac. Lincoln had clearly had enough of George McClellan. For over six weeks, "Little Mac" and his Army of the Potomac had essentially not moved, despite Lincoln's repeated pleas that the army do something in the way of pressing the Confederates. McClellan always had an excuse as to why his army was in no shape to move, despite the president's assertions that the Union army was in far better shape than its enemy. Lincoln ended the debate in early November, informing McClellan that he was relieved of duty and that his replacement was Gen. Ambrose P. Burnside, who, unbeknownst to McClellan, had reluctantly accepted Lincoln's offer. McClellan accepted the announcement with grace and immediately announced the change via a farewell address on November 7. On November 10, the Twenty-Sixth and the entire Army of the Potomac witnessed the ceremonial review during which McClellan handed over command to Burnside, much to that affable general's internal hesitation. The self-effacing Burnside was a man who knew his limitations. Although Burnside had a good reputation in the army, a disheartening feeling, and perhaps premonition, was displayed by many of the rank and file at "Little Mac's" dismissal.[5]

Lt. Col. Gilbert S. Jennings (Don Wisnoski Collection—USAMHI).

At the regimental level, Colonel Richardson's new command was not getting off to the start he had probably hoped for. Fever had stricken the colonel during the march from Maryland, to the point that he had been granted a 15-day leave of absence to recuperate, which was scheduled to end on November 30th. Near the end of this period, it was still evident that the colonel was too weak to travel, so a request for an additional 10 days was requested and granted. Upon his recovery and perhaps sensing what lay before him, the new colonel wisely took out a life insurance policy prior to his return to the field. With their new commander absent, it would be up to Lieutenant Colonel Jennings to lead the New Yorkers into battle. By the time Richardson returned to the regiment, the forthcoming clash at Fredericksburg would be over.[6]

The regiment's march from Maryland continued, and by November 27th, the Twenty-Sixth found themselves encamped within six miles of Fredericksburg. For at least a week, the Twenty-Sixth and the rest of Gibbon's division had known that colonial town lay in the path of their general march. Edwin Sumner's corps had reached the outskirts of Fredericksburg by the 17th and was now encamped awaiting the rest of the army. Though a large force was with them, most soldiers still did not know their final objective.[7]

By December 1, both the Union and Confederate forces faced each other across the Rappahannock River at Fredericksburg. Gibbon's division occupied positions near Stafford Court House and Brooks Station on the Richmond, Fredericksburg, and Potomac Railroad. Sensing that they were going into winter quarters, Gibbon's men began preparing rudimentary shanties to protect themselves from the elements. Here they stayed through December 10 in weather that was brutally cold. The area had been stripped clean of firewood to the point that the men attempted to burn green wood and any loose railroad ties they could find.[8]

The Battle of Fredericksburg

At dawn on the morning of December 11, John Reynolds' three First Corps divisions broke their camps and began to march toward the Rappahannock River. Reynolds corps, along with William F. Smith's Sixth Corps, formed the newly designated Left Grand Division of the Army of the Potomac, under the command of Maj. Gen. William Franklin. The bridges over the river had yet to be completed, however Yankee engineers were feverishly working to finish the task. It was anticipated that they would be finished by the end of the day to allow the crossing. By the morning of the 12th, the Twenty-Sixth and all the other regiments in Reynolds' First Corps, at last crossed the Rappahannock under cover of a very heavy fog. Smith's corps preceded the First, which slowly crossed throughout the cold and clammy morning. Gibbon's division formed and deployed on the left of Smith's in two lines of brigades. Maj. Gen. George Meade's division, composed of the Pennsylvania Reserves, was also deployed in two lines of brigades with his left resting on the Rappahannock while his right joined nearly at right angles with the left of Gibbon. Reynolds kept Doubleday's division in reserve on the riverbank to the left rear of Meade's. Soon the artillery came up and was it was quickly dispatched to command the approach by the Bowling Green road. It took the better part of the day for the Union soldiers to complete their dispositions. Throughout it all, there seemed to be little fire from their Confederate enemy across the plain. Those forces opposing them were commanded by Stonewall Jackson, and they had secured excellent elevated defensive positions on Prospect Hill, a heavily wooded ridge line that faced the wide-open plains the Yankees would be marching across. Near the base of the hill ran the Richmond, Fredericksburg and Potomac Railroad, whose elevated embankment provided perfect defensive cover for Confederate skirmishers. Throughout the day, just enough skirmish fire came in to advise the Federals that the Confederates knew they were there. Any hope for surprise had been clearly dashed. With little to cheer him, the average Union private settled in as best he could for a long, cold night.[9]

About 7:30 on the morning of the 13th, Brig. Gen. James Hardie arrived from Burnside's headquarters, and informed Left Grand Division commander William

Two of the pontoon bridges used by the Army as part of Franklin's Left Grand Division. Here they crossed the Rappahannock River just below Fredericksburg. Prospect Hill can be seen in the far background (*Gardner's Photographic Sketchbook*).

Franklin verbally of Burnside's plans for the coming attack, and that written orders would soon arrive by an aide-de-camp. These orders arrived shortly before 8:00 A.M. In the meantime, Franklin informed General Reynolds that his corps was to make the attack indicated by General Hardie. Reynolds immediately ordered Meade to form his division for the attack, informing him that he would have ample support on the right with Gibbon's division and to cover his left with Doubleday's.[10]

That morning of December 13, 1862, was bitterly cold with the ground now in a semifrozen state. A thick fog was everywhere, which seemed to hang before the army like an impenetrable veil. The previous night had been just as miserable as the northern men had feared. Fires and smoking had been strictly forbidden, so the various regiments within Lyle's brigade had been forced to lay on their arms and shiver throughout the night as they gloomily watched the bright fires of the Confederate pickets. With the coming of dawn, all soldiers within the Second Oneida knew that some type of attack was imminent. Worse, even the most obtuse man could look across the wide, open plain and know the rebels would be well-entrenched with plenty of artillery judiciously placed to sweep the entire ground. The corn fields of yesterday would surely become the killing fields of tomorrow.

For the officers, the night had been particularly restless, with each man questioning within himself as to whether he would live to see the next night. For Adjutant William Bacon, recently returned to duty following his Bull Run wounding, a portent of his imminent demise was resolutely painted in his mind. The young man voiced his premonition to Gilbert Jennings, who was Bacon's senior by almost 25 years. The older Jennings calmly reassured the youthful adjutant, claiming that he was merely homesick. "Colonel" remarked Bacon, "no man on earth has a dearer home than I have, but if a wish could place me there now, I would not go. My place is here, and here I remain." The time for battle was at hand. Around 9:00 A.M., orders were received to form battle lines, though no specifics were yet forthcoming. Reynolds had personally gone to Gibbon with orders for the pending advance, yet the brigadier's actions prior to this call had been unusually hesitant.[11]

The New Yorkers leapt to their feet and immediately obeyed the order, taking their prescribed place in line. To get to the point of attack, the brigade had to cross a ravine and a small rise where it then arrived at the Bowling Green Road. A ditch ran parallel to each side of the muddied road with the displaced earth piled high on each side of the ditch to form an embankment. All fences had been torn down in order to make bridges across the ditch for the artillery to pass. Beyond the ditch lay a plowed field across which the bluecoats would make their advance. The Twenty-Sixth was second in line of the brigade, the Twelfth Massachusetts on their right and the Ninetieth Pennsylvania Volunteers on their left. The One Hundred Thirty-Sixth Pennsylvania rounded out the line with the extreme left position. The Second Brigade formed the second line, taking a position about 100 yards to the rear of the Third Brigade. The advance had yet to begin and they were already within range of rebel artillery.[12]

All hearts were beating rapidly as Gibbon's men stepped off smartly in support of George Meade's Third Division, which had already initiated the federal attack and was having some initial success. Meade was under the impression that Gibbon's assault would coincide with his, though it soon became apparent that, initially at least, Meade was on his own. Nevertheless, due to an unprotected opening in the Confederate lines, Meade's Pennsylvanians successfully carried the woods in their front. The charging Yankees soon crossed the railroad

Adj. William Bacon (Bacon—"Memorial of William Kirkland Bacon").

embankment and charged up the slope of Prospect Hill, driving the rebels from their fortified positions in the ditches and railroad cut with every step. Meade's bluecoats captured two regimental flags and about 200 prisoners during their advance.[13]

* * *

The Twenty-Sixth moved forward by the right of companies to the front, across the Bowling Green Road running south from Fredericksburg. No sooner than its advance across the fields had begun was the brigade's battle line subjected to a severe barrage of canister from the rebel batteries posted on a slight elevation beyond the railroad toward the line's right front. Men in blue staggered and fell with every blast from the Confederate guns, especially along the far right of the division's battle line. The gray-clad artillerist in charge of a portion of those batteries, Capt. Greenlee Davidson, was keenly aware of the effect his gunners were having on the Yankee enemy. "My guns were double shotted with canister and we let them have it low," wrote Davidson. "The head of the column went down like wheat before the reaper. Another and another volley in quick succession completed the work. The Yankees broke, took to their heels and you never saw such a stampede in your life."[14]

Taking a securer position in what was once a corn field, the Twenty-Sixth was ordered to lie down in hopes that the Confederate shells would pass over. The surface of the ground had frozen hard earlier in the morning but the trampling of a

Open field at Fredericksburg across which the Twenty-Sixth and Gibbon's division advanced. The ridgeline of Prospect Hill is in the background and the railroad embankment from which the Confederates fought runs along the foot of the hill. The picture was taken from the Bowling Green Road (modern Route 2).

thousand feet was now slowly turning it into mud and water several inches deep. "The warmth of our bodies drew the frost from the newly plowed ground, and the soil stuck to our clothes," recalled Maj. Ezra Wetmore. Due to the intensity of the rebel artillery in their front and on the flank, the Twenty-Sixth was forced to remain prone on the cold ground until about 1:00 P.M. The lying down proved successful, for the New Yorkers suffered only one man killed and six wounded during the interim.[15]

Col. Peter Lyle of the Ninetieth Pennsylvania, still commanding the brigade despite Gibbon's reservations, at last gave the order to renew the advance. The Second Oneida and their comrades formed a long blue line and with bayonets gleaming began their second advance at about 1:00 P.M. When about 80 yards from the enemy, they halted and opened fire upon their partly concealed foe. The Confederates at this spot were Gen. James Lane's North Carolinians, who had the defensive advantage of firing from behind the railroad embankment. This stand-up fight continued for about one-half hour, though Lane's Tar Heels suffered little due to their superior defensive position. By then, ammunition was now running precariously low for several of the Union regiments. Major Wetmore, as well as Lt. Col. William Leech of the Ninetieth Pennsylvania, notified Lyle of their mutual predicament. Knowing that the First Brigade was quickly coming to their support, Lyle ordered the Twenty-Sixth and the Ninetieth to stay where they were. They were to simply lie down as Col. Adrian Root's First Brigade arrived and to then allow Root's men to pass through the two beleaguered regiments. Root's men quickly marched over the prone New Yorkers with little effort. Unfortunately, once they were past, confusion existed as to exactly what role the Twenty-Sixth was to play. Despite being almost out of ammunition, Root assumed that all four regiments in Lyle's brigade would stand firm and assist his brigade with the pending charge, using only the bayonet if necessary. Without them, Root rightfully saw that his own men would make little headway into the teeth of the rebel defenses. He pleaded with Lyle's regimental commanders to stay and fight, but only the colonels of the Twelfth Massachusetts, and far off to the left, the One Hundred Thirty-Sixth Pennsylvania, agreed to help. The Ninetieth Pennsylvania and the Second Oneida refused his appeal, opting to retire per Colonel Lyle's previous set of orders, which were for the two regiments to immediately withdraw and salvage much-needed ammunition. Whether he was aware of Lyle's previous orders or not, Root considered their withdrawal so despicable that he was compelled to mention it in his post-battle report. With the First Brigade having passed by, Wetmore led his shaken New Yorkers to a ravine roughly 160 yards from the spot they had occupied in the morning and slowly began to collect ammunition from the cartridge boxes of the killed and wounded. While the New Yorkers were withdrawing, General Gibbon was riding from the left of his line toward the right when he was struck in the hand by a shell fragment, delivering an injury serious enough to send him to a field hospital. Gibbon sent word to Brig. Gen. Nelson Taylor to take command of the division so that he could seek medical attention.[16]

As the New Yorkers and the Pennsylvanians were scrounging for ammunition in the rear, Capt. Edward Lee, the acting inspector general on General Gibbon's staff, hastily rode up to both regiments. He and Taylor had angrily watched the regiments withdraw, clearly unaware that they had been given orders to do so by

Colonel Lyle. Like Adrian Root before him, Lee viewed these men as little more than shirkers, drew his pistol upon the men, and threatened its use if they did not immediately return to the fray. Colonel Leech of the Ninetieth Pennsylvania was so incensed by Lee's behavior that he dressed down the captain on the spot. Leech later called attention to the incident in his post-battle report, saying in part: "As these men had withdrawn in good order, and with a perfect consciousness of what they were about, and as it was not the first time they had been in action, I consider it my duty, as commanding officer of the regiment, to call attention to it. The men that he threatened were, to say the least, much cooler than he appeared to be. Dismissing Captain Lee, we formed here without time to collect any ammunition. We received various orders from different aides-de-camp, and were finally ordered to advance and charge bayonets upon the enemy in the wood."[17]

Soon thereafter Lyle received orders from Taylor to get the Pennsylvanians and New Yorkers back into the action. The command was immediately relayed to the two regiments to reform and attack without delay. With an average of only two rounds per man, the Twenty-Sixth turned around, fixed bayonets and charged back into the maelstrom along with the Ninetieth Pennsylvania.[18]

A hornet's nest of Confederate lead greeted the single-minded New Yorkers. The Twenty-Sixth lost heavily during this charge, as well as the initial advance, including Lieutenant Colonel Jennings, who suffered a broken leg in the early part of the action after a bullet tore through his fibula. In addition, a rebel ball ricocheted off the forehead of Capt. William Neil of Company D, resulting in a wound that was insufficient to draw blood but which rendered him totally blind for weeks to come.

Casualties among the privates were also piling up from the disorganized attack. Lead officers and those men carrying the regimental flags, known as color bearers, were always prime targets for the enemy. The regimental and national flags were not only great sources of inspiration, but served as the rallying point as well as a

Franklin's men charging across the railroad (*Century Magazine*).

visual reminder of where each man was supposed to be within the attacking column. To bring down the color bearer often brought about a certain level of uncertainty and confusion within the smoke-filled lines. Therefore, an abundant number of soldiers were often assigned the duty in an descending order should the man in front of him be brought down. Into this tempest of bayonets, lead, and confusion at Fredericksburg, gallantry and honor conspicuously arose within two privates of the Twenty-Sixth.

With the regimental colors on the ground, Pvt. Joseph Keene, a 5' 4½", 20-year-old English immigrant farmer, voluntarily rescued them from the earth, held them aloft and led his unit onward. Surviving the charge, Keene would receive the Medal of Honor almost 30 years later for his valor.[19]

The second of the Twenty-Sixth's two Medal of Honor recipients from the Fredericksburg battle was German-born Pvt. Martin Schubert of Company E, a butcher by trade, whose gallantry at Fredericksburg was noted not for any single

Medal of Honor winner—Private Martin Schubert (*Utica Saturday Globe*).

action, but for simply showing up to fight. Seriously wounded three months earlier at Antietam, Schubert had been granted a medical furlough to return home and recuperate. Deciding he would be of more use to his comrades on the field than at home by the fire, Schubert voluntarily returned to his command on December 10, joining them at Brook Station, Virginia. Years later, Schubert recalled his decision: "My old wound, not yet healed, gave me considerable trouble. I went into the battle [Fredericksburg] with the regiment, however, against the protests of my colonel and captain, who insisted that I should use the furlough. I thought the Government needed me on the battlefield rather than at home." While carrying the regimental colors, Schubert took another bullet, which he carried in his body for decades to come. After the battle, Gen. Ambrose Burnside learned of Schubert's bravery and promised him the Medal of Honor on the spot.[20]

★ ★ ★

With Jennings down, command of the regiment now officially passed to Major Wetmore. He too was struck by a rebel bullet, high on the left breast. Fortunately for the major, he had tied together a piece of tent and thick blanket which was thrown over his shoulder and under his arm. The Confederate ball whizzed into the cloth, the density of which stalled the bullet from going further. Though staggered, Major Wetmore continued to lead his men during the attack. This final assault took the New Yorkers and the Ninetieth Pennsylvania as far as the railroad where they found the One Hundred and Seventh Pennsylvania of the First Brigade attempting to form a defensive line at the embankment. Lyle planned to slide the three regiments along the railroad to support Root's brigade, further off to the right.[21]

Despite those intentions, it was evident that the attack was stalled. Major Wetmore noticed that both the troops of the First and Third brigades were retiring, and soon enough Lyle ordered the Twenty-Sixth to withdraw. As at Antietam, the regiment executed the movement in good order, falling back to virtually the same position it had occupied earlier that morning. Each step of the withdrawal brought ample opportunity for the New Yorkers to replenish their cartridge boxes and to assist their scores of wounded to the rear. One casualty in particular being carried toward the rear would end up as being among the regiment's most painful. William Bacon, the diminutive adjutant who had always been popular among the privates, had predicted his death the previous day. His ominous portent came to pass as he suffered a gunshot wound in the upper left leg during the final assault. One private later wrote to Bacon's parents, informing them that their son "was in the thickest of the battle, and was seen to step in front of our line with a rifle, and shoot at the rebels when he was struck." Despite the many casualties, the regiment had been under strict orders that during the advance no soldier was to stop and attend to a wounded comrade, lest the charge be slowed down. A good number of the New Yorkers saw Bacon fall and in spite of the command rushed to his aid. Major Wetmore, the man responsible for enforcing the order, saw the commotion. Knowing the sentiment that existed toward the adjutant, Wetmore kindly turned his back on the scene, in effect giving Bacon's aides de facto permission to carry him to the rear.[22]

Bacon and the other casualties went to the Second Division's field hospital, which was located just north of the Rappahannock at the William Pollock house. The large tents that were pitched on the lawn in the rear of the house, which were reserved for the more serious cases, were quickly filled. The scene there was a crimson horror with the cries of the wounded piercing the air. "Men lying on the ground mortally wounded without so much as a blanket under or over them & with no attendance at all," wrote a man from the One Hundred and Thirty-Sixth Pennsylvania,

Maj. Ezra Wetmore (USAMHI).

who had himself taken a bullet through the hand during the second line's assault. A wound in the hand, however, was far preferable to a wound in the knee. Such was the sad case for Cpl. Jerome Frazier of the Twenty-Sixth's Company F, who took a rebel ball just above the knee. So shattered were his bones that an amputation had to be performed later that night.[23]

No rest was to come to the healthy but exhausted soldiers of the Twenty-Sixth. Word came during the night that Union pickets on the army's extreme left were being driven in and that the Second Division was to go to their support. The men fell into columns and marched off to the far left of the federal position where they would remain in support for the next several days.[24] It was another dreadfully cold evening, and the shivering survivors could easily hear the cries of their wounded up and down the line. Near midnight, Major Wetmore decided that simply sitting and listening to the pitiful pleas was intolerable. Something had to be done for his wounded friends and

Pvt. William Evans was wounded at the battle of Fredericksburg (New York State Military Museum).

comrades. Taking a small squad of men, Wetmore and his band went back to the battle ground and removed as many injured men as possible, working until the rising moon rendered them visible, moving targets for the rebel sharpshooters. Similar acts took place the next two nights; though by this time, survivors were no longer rescuing the wounded, but simply removing the nearly frozen bodies of the dead. Members of the Twenty-Sixth located their fallen comrades and moved the bodies nearer the Rappahannock, where a brief burial was conducted with headboards obtained from broken cracker boxes. The soldiers' name and companies were inscribed on the cracker box lids, which concluded the ceremony.[25]

Fredericksburg turned out to be the Twenty-Sixth's most deadly engagement, and one of the most statistically devastating for any Union regiment during the entire war. With Major Wetmore now the commanding officer of the regiment pending the return of Lieutenant Colonel Jennings and Colonel Richardson, it was therefore up to the major to write the unit's official post-battle report. According to his account, the fighting strength of the regiment at the start of the battle was only 280 rifles. Its total losses amounted to 170 casualties, initially breaking down as 23 killed, 136 wounded, and 11 missing. Reports show that an additional 28 men would later die of their wounds bringing the total killed to 51, or approximately one in five. Those numbers included eleven commissioned officers and statistically worked out to 61 percent of the regiment's soldiers sent into the fight. With the exception of the Sixteenth Maine, the Twenty-Sixth New York suffered more casualties in the Second Division than any of Gibbon's 14 infantry regiments. In fact, like Second Bull Run, the Twenty-Sixth suffered more casualties than over 90 percent of all Union regiments engaged at Fredericksburg. By the end of the battle, the regiment's fighting strength had dwindled to that of one good-sized company. That night, Wetmore wrote that barely 50 men and officers answered the regimental roll call.[26]

Pvt. Buel Munson died January 2, 1863 (New York State Military Museum).

Ministering to the regiment's injured after the battle proved a mountainous task for Chaplain Bristol. "Nearly all our officers are wounded," wrote the chaplain the day after the fight. Lt. Col. Gilbert Jennings had been severely wounded in the leg. Capt. Norman Palmer of Company E had also taken a rebel ball just above the left knee, an injury that would hamper his walking for the rest of his life, and prompt a reenlistment two years later into the cavalry instead of the infantry. Adjutant William Bacon was mortally wounded and would be dead by the morning of the 16th. Bristol continued, "I am surrounded by suffering men. The scene is terrible ... our line of battle could not have been less than five miles in length. I stood upon an eminence which overlooked nearly the whole line. It was a fearful but grand sight. I never wish to look upon the like again. But I cannot describe the scene now. We are surrounded by hundreds of wounded men who are suffering, many of them with intense pain. They have paid a high price

Chaplain Daniel Bristol (USAMHI).

A camp near Fletcher Chapel (Locke—"Story of the Regiment").

for the integrity of the government. Our surgeons are doing everything that can be done for the sufferers."[27]

Both armies spent the 14th and 15th in their respective positions, though some batteries were ultimately redeployed. As part of that artillery maneuvering, the decimated Twenty-Sixth was ordered to the front to support a battery during the late morning of the 15th. The skirmishers on both sides kept up a desultory fire, with rebel cannons occasionally opening upon the Union left from long-range guns posted beyond the Massapomax Creek. Most of the infantry, however, spent their time employed under flags of truce in burying the dead and caring for the scores of wounded. As a final point, around 7:00 P.M. on the night of the 15th, an order came to withdraw the army to the left bank of the river. The movement commenced beginning on the far left of the Union line. The Second Oneida's involvement in the Fredericksburg debacle came to an end around 10:00 P.M. when they crossed the Rappahannock and returned to a point near where their ill-fated adventure had begun days before.[28]

The morning of the 16th found Gibbon's Second Division, now commanded by Nelson Taylor, encamped in a large open field left of the road which ran from Fredericksburg to Belle Plain. Although the battle of Fredericksburg was over, rebel batteries still occasionally sent some solid shot into the camp, though no damage was reported.

The final two weeks of 1862 thankfully passed with little action for the New Yorkers. On the 20th the regiment along with their brigade comrades marched toward Fletcher's Chapel. They would remain there for the rest of the year, spending their time building winter huts and engaged in the always-constant drill, which resulted in a year-ending review by Gen. Nelson Taylor on the last day of the year.[29]

8

Into the Mud: January 1863

The opening of the new year was punctuated by Abraham Lincoln's signing of the Emancipation Proclamation, announced months earlier but to go into effect at the first of the year. It stated that all slaves held in states in revolt against the federal government were now and forever free. Ongoing reaction to the announcement was far from positive even though news of the proclamation and its effects had been predicted for some time. What was of greater concern to the administration was the sinking morale of the Army of the Potomac. After the Union fiasco at Fredericksburg, confidence was at its lowest point. Ambrose Burnside seemed especially lost and angry, convinced that his underlings were nonsupportive and conspiring against him. After meeting with Lincoln, Burnside wrote an open letter, laying out his position and threatening to retire in order to promote the public good. With no clear replacement available, Lincoln urged the commanding general to reconsider.

Sad news ushered in the new year when it was learned that old Chaplain Daniel Bristol, who had faithfully delivered the Word to his regimental flock, had resigned as of January 3 to return to New York due to poor health. Additional disappointing events were apparent within the Twenty-Sixth, as the opening of 1863 brought unpleasant court-martial proceedings to the regiment's encampment. With little else going on, disciplinary issues that been festering all year were finally dealt with. In one case, Pvt. Nathan B. Cowen was charged with being absent without leave during the crucial week of December 11–17 when the battle of Fredericksburg was fought. During the proceeding, Lt. Albert Lynch alleged that Cowan had asked for permission to fall out of the marching column so that he could "answer a call of nature." Permission was granted, with the stipulation that Cowen leave his musket with another soldier and then return immediately. According to Lieutenant Lynch, Cowen was not seen for the next week. Capt. James Caryl of Company K further stated for the prosecution that he had never known Cowen to be in any fight other than South Mountain. At both Second Bull Run and Antietam, Cowen was purportedly out sick. Cowen sheepishly pleaded not guilty, arguing that he was as good a soldier as any, but in the end was found guilty. The sentence handed down on January 8 was a forfeiture of one months pay, plus the private would be forced to march two hours a day for the next 10 days, wearing a large sign on his back with the word "straggler" written on it in large letters.[1]

Private Cowen had been one of the regiment's few soldiers to abandon the ranks without proper authority to do so following Fredericksburg. At least he had returned to his comrades. The desertion exodus that seemed to exist within the

8. Into the Mud

The Twenty-Sixth and the Union Army of the Potomac crossed back into Virginia on November 1 at its Berlin, Maryland, crossing point (1). By the 7th, the regiment had reached Warrenton (2). It was camped outside of Fredericksburg in early December and took part in the forthcoming debacle at that town. The entire army then retired into its winter quarters at Belle Plain (3) until late April 1863. May 1–6 brought the massive battle of Chancellorsville in which the Twenty-Sixth was present but not engaged (4). On May 7 the Twenty-Sixth New York marched to Falmouth (5) and there boarded trains to begin the final journey home.

Twenty-Sixth during the summer months had now fortunately slowed to a trickle. Unlike the Second Oneida, the bloody defeat at Fredericksburg coupled with the brutal winter brought about scores of desertions within the Army of the Potomac as a whole. By mid–February, it was estimated the army was losing over 200 men per day and that a total of approximately 85,000 men were absent from their posts, though the Twenty-Sixth reported losing only four men to desertion from November 1862 through February 1863.[2] By that stage of their enlistment, the usual justifications for desertion had vanished. No campaign was imminent and with their heading home to their families only a few months away, very few Oneidans saw the need to risk the stockade or even a firing squad.

★ ★ ★

The new year quickly brought more change in the command structure. With John Gibbon still out of action due to his hand wound, a division commander needed to be formally named. Gen. Nelson Taylor had held the position since Fredericksburg and expected to retain that command. It was, therefore, a tremendous surprise when Gen. John C. Robinson was given the command in early January, to the total consternation of Taylor. Not willing to take the rebuff, Taylor sent in his resignation the same day.

General Robinson immediately set out to familiarize himself with his new division. He reviewed the Twenty-Sixth and the rest of the division for the first time on January 12. Formerly a brigade commander in the Third Corps, Robinson was a fiery, old army regular who was as well known to the men for his extensive facial hair as for his military prowess. Col. Peter Lyle of the Ninetieth Pennsylvania remained in command of the brigade for the time being.[3]

Frequent light rain and snow were the New Yorkers' camp companions throughout mid–January. The ever-present picket duty was resumed, and now, new rumors began to surface of an impending move of the army. Orders were given that the troops were to be ready to move at any moment.

Ultimately, the rumors proved true, and would give the ill-fated Burnside one more egg to lay. Though both armies were in the midst of their winter camps, the federal government demanded action. Deciding once again to attack the Confederates and seize Fredericksburg, Burnside decided to cross the Rappahannock further to the north and hit Lee in his left flank, thereby avoiding another frontal assault into the heavily fortified town. "The auspicious moment seems to have arrived to strike a great and mortal blow to the rebellion, and to gain that decisive victory which is due to the country," announced Ambrose Burnside to his army on the morning of January 20, 1863.

Reluctantly taking apart their comfortable winter huts, the Second Oneida made preparations for another march. The frosty morning had yet to deliver rain or snow, but the foreboding of a coming storm was intertwined with gray skies and a damp, chilly wind. The men slowly fell in line and proceeded as far as White Oak Church, at which point their march turned to the southwest, crossing roads and fields till they reached a point just above Falmouth. By the time the tired warriors were ready to camp for the night, nature's full fury erupted over them. Biting wind, rain, snow, and sleet conspired to render campfires impossible. No poles or pins were available to erect the small tents, so the New Yorkers had to make due with their bayonets, muskets and ramrods. Inevitably, they were blown over by the wind creating the most miserable experience many of the men endured in their entire two years of service. Such was certainly the case for Charles McClenthen, who lamented the Twenty-Sixth's predicament: "Sick, wounded, and dying men have neither strength nor energy to swell their lugubrious chorus of woe to such a pitch as mingled with the howling of the winds, and the merciless pelting of the rains, sleet and snow rose on the air like a chant of despair from the infernal regions. Let no one think that I exaggerate in this description; that would be impossible. Danger, disaster, defeat, and the fear of instant death could hardly render us more miserable than we were for the time being...." Men who had amazingly been able to fall asleep now found their shelters blowing down around them, awaking confused and perplexed as they thrashed about in their soaked tents.[4]

All men suffered the same, officers and privates alike. The months of hard marches, desperate battles, and now blistering cold conditions once again got the better of Colonel Richardson. The colonel had been back with the regiment less than a month when the wintry January caused the colonel to contract a severe cold. The simple illness degenerated into pneumonia, weakening the man to the point that during the advance, he had to be helped off his horse and carried nearly unconscious to an ambulance. He would not be able to leave the wagon until his regiment returned back to camp. With Lieutenant Colonel Jennings away from camp and recuperating from his Fredericksburg leg wound, temporary command of the Twenty-Sixth was handed to Major Wetmore.[5]

Morning came at last, but with no abatement in the weather. The entire countryside seemed to be a vast sea of mud, with the occasional hill jutting out on the horizon. Burnside ordered the army to continue the planned march, but it was soon obvious to every bluecoat private that they were going nowhere. Roads had become quagmires, and any attempt to move artillery, wagons, or supply trains was futile. McClenthen continued, "I [saw] twenty horses hitched to one piece of artillery, where it had sank in the mud until the axles and even the piece itself rested upon the surface. Our own trains never came up with us during the four days, and although they had not proceeded as far as ourselves, did not succeed in returning to camp until two days afterward." Finally, on January 22, Burnside called off the advance and ordered a return to their Belle Plain camps. What would become known as "Burnside's Mud March" was over, and it was simply the latest embarrassment to the Union high command.[6]

Rebel pickets watched the entire farce with great amusement on the south side of the river. Openly taunting their beleaguered enemy and often laughing beyond control in plain view, the Confederates even erected large signs on their riverbank that read "Burnside's army stuck in the mud," "This way to Richmond," as well as "Yanks, if you cant place your pontoons, we will send help."

Upon their return to camp, the Twenty-Sixth New York refitted their old winter cabins and log huts as best they could. A fellow New Yorker within General Robinson's division described the standard dwelling as "six feet square three logs high and our tent on top a fire place and sod chimney in one end." Despite the winter season, food was apparently in sufficient supply, which stood in stark contrast to their Confederate enemy. "[We] draw beans rice crackers meat coffee sugar and today we have a little flour so we live some better than we did when on campaign," continued the New Yorker.[7]

To accomplish the daily camp requirements, the brigade was divided into two units, each doing its share of picket duty at the supply base at Belle Plain, known within the ranks simply as the "landings." The Twenty-Sixth was joined with the Twelfth Massachusetts and a portion of the One Hundred and Thirty-Sixth Pennsylvania, while the remainder of that once-huge regiment joined with the Ninetieth Pennsylvania. Like the Twenty-Sixth New York, death, injuries, disease, and desertion had whittled away at the once-massive One Hundred Thirty-Sixth by around 30 percent, leaving it now at around 700 men. The shortage of soldiers that befell the New Yorkers was also now clearly evident. Casualties from Second Bull Run, Fredericksburg and Antietam of the previous year, coupled with current illnesses and desertions, rendered the Twenty-Sixth a regiment in name only. Every hand, including officers, cooks, and waiters was needed to fulfill their picket duty.[8]

Burnside's final, desperate act after the "Mud March" fiasco was to make it clear to Lincoln that he believed a cadre of his generals had conspired to undermine his command. Through his General Order No. 8, a total of eight generals would either be cashiered from the service or dismissed from their respective commands. His letter to Lincoln on the 25th stated that unless these generals were replaced, he would immediately resign his command. Lincoln was nonplussed, and was more than willing to see a successor named. Thus, on January 26, 1863, Gen. Joseph Hooker became the latest commanding general of the Union Army of the Potomac. Burnside was probably relieved that his emotional burden had ended. His placement at the head of the nation's primary army in the field was a role that he had neither sought nor especially wanted. The general tendered his resignation to Lincoln and then calmly announced, "If Hooker can gain a victory, neither you nor he will be a happier man than I shall be." Instead of accepting Burnside's resignation, Lincoln respectfully placed the general on an extended leave of absence.[9]

Hooker had been one of the generals on Burnside's hit list, and his distaste for Burnside was no secret: "His moral degradation is unfathomable," wrote Hooker to Secretary of War Edwin Stanton regarding Burnside several months after assuming his new command. Command of the Army of the Potomac was a role for which Hooker had practically campaigned for and accepted with relish. Lincoln believed that his new man possessed all the necessary characteristics for a leader of an army, but also felt compelled to caution Hooker. Writing from the White House on January 26th, Lincoln wrote one of his most memorable letters, stating to Hooker, in part: "You are ambitious, which, within reasonable bounds, does good rather than harm; but I think that during Gen. Burnside's command of the army, you have taken counsel of your ambition, and thwarted him as much as you could, in which you did a great wrong to the country and to a most meritorious and honorable brother-officer. I have heard, in such a way as to believe it, of your recently saying that both the army and the Government needed a dictator. Of course, it was not for this, but in spite of it, that I have given you the command. Only those generals who gain success can set up dictators. What I now ask of you is military success, and I will risk the dictatorship."[10]

Forty-eight-year-old Joe Hooker was a member of the West Point class of 1837. He served as a staff officer during the Mexican War but resigned soon after to settle in California. He obtained a commission in the army following the debacle at First Bull Run and quickly gained a reputation as a hard fighter and equally hard drinker. Hooker also publicly spoke ill of his superiors far too often, but was generally thought well of by his front-line men. By the time of his appointment by Lincoln as the Army of the Potomac's commander, he had been given the moniker "Fighting Joe Hooker" due primarily to a newspaper copy mistake.

The first week of February 1863 was ushered in with wintry snows and biting cold. Sadly for the privates, the dreary winter camp routines were well underway. Like the previous winter, these long days brought an opportunity for court-martial boards to perform their functions. Only this time, the situations were far more grievous. February 9 brought about the final and most contentious court-martial proceedings yet within the regiment. Capt. James Caryl of Company K, who had served honorably on previous court-martial boards, now found himself as the accused. In the process he became the highest-ranking soldier within the regiment to face such an action. Having served bravely and in the thick of all the regiment's battles, Caryl had apparently seen enough of the regiment's commanding officers. In an emotional outburst in early January, Caryl allegedly derided Major Wetmore and Lieutenant Colonel Jennings in front of the other line officers. He was accused of referring to Wetmore as a "damned, cowardly dog" who was unfit for his position and then boasted that he would "ride him into the ground." He was even willing to wager $20 with Dr. Coventry that he would have Wetmore cashiered from the service. On January 18th, Caryl took the matter a huge step further by sending a list of his accusations to brigade and division headquarters, *signed by 10 other officers within the regiment*. This finger-pointing included the allegations that Colonel Richardson, Lieutenant Colonel Jennings, and Major Wetmore had all displayed "cowardice in the face of the enemy and general incompetence." Obviously, these letters were not sent via Colonel Richardson which therefore constituted a serious breach of the chain of command. Caryl then capped off the episode by purportedly sending in his resignation during the "Mud March" fiasco.

Division commander Gen. John Robinson did not suffer fools gladly and was incensed when he read Caryl's allegations, not so much that they had been made but rather the manner in which they were presented. He noted in a reply letter of January 30 regarding the Twenty-Sixth that "there is evidently a want of discipline and it is feared great insubordination exists. If necessary, all the officers of this regiment will be brought before a board for examination." Casting his own stern eye toward army procedure and discipline, Robinson was forced to acknowledge that "no application of this kind from a junior officer can be entertained. There is evidently in this regiment a combination against its commanding officers which must be put down." All of Caryl's demands that Wetmore and Jennings be examined were therefore denied. Robinson ordered brigade commander Peter Lyle to look into the soldiers' grievances while ensuring that regulatory offenders be presented for punishment by general court-martial. Caryl ended up facing three charges: (1) Conduct subversive of good order and military discipline; (2) Positive disobedience of general orders and disregard of army regulations; (3) Misbehavior in the face of the enemy. The captain was the only officer formally charged, despite the fact that three officers testified that the accusations about Wetmore had originated with other officers and *not* with Caryl. They acknowledged that Caryl had sent the papers in, but that was because he had been a lawyer prior to the war and that he would have a better understanding of the proper language.

Caryl vigorously pleaded not guilty on all counts. Nevertheless, the three-day trial ended with his conviction on all charges. He was dismissed from the service on March 11, 1863. The number of officers who had willingly signed Caryl's initial letter of protest was indicative of just how far respect and discipline had sunk within the regiment. Second Lt. Albert Lynch had even gone on record as testifying that he had long sought a transfer out of the Twenty-Sixth due to the "dissatisfaction prevailing in the regiment." In determining Caryl's fate, the court correctly pointed out that a very distasteful state of affairs existed within the Twenty-Sixth and hoped that the captain's dishonorable discharge would serve as a warning to any other troublemakers. It was becoming fast apparent that the war could not end soon enough for the Twenty-Sixth.[11]

Despite such legal proceedings, the day-to-day picket and guard duties had to continue. Due to a shortage of manpower, February 13 saw practically the entire regiment manning their turn at the picket positions on the north side of the Rappahannock River. In fact, the Second Oneida spent most of February doing little more than wading through snow while performing picket and fatigue duty at Belle Plain. In the process, keeping warm seemed the primary, if not the sole goal of every private. Occasionally, if the opportunity presented itself, a little trading and conversing with like-minded rebel pickets was not out of the question, either. In their free time, the New Yorkers contented themselves with reading, writing letters, or enjoying a few hours of a new outdoor game called "baseball." The last week of the month brought yet another snowstorm, prompting Lt. William Holstead to note that it dropped "more snow on the ground than I ever saw in the South at one time."[12]

★ ★ ★

As part of his new strategy for revitalizing the army, Hooker instituted a new reorganization of the Army of the Potomac. Gone were Burnside's grand divisions, to be replaced by the more traditional corps and division format. This latest reorganization found the Twenty-Sixth still serving in the First Corps, Second Division. Hooker also wasted no time in addressing the ills that he believed ailed the Army of the Potomac. New tents, shoes, and supplies were ordered. To the delight of the troops, soft bread was to be issued at least four times per week. Fresh potatoes or onions, if practicable, were issued twice a week and desiccated vegetables or potatoes at least once a week.[13]

The results of Hooker's improvements were immediate. Morale improved and due to offers of amnesty, men absent without leave returned to their regiments and desertions practically ceased. Hooker knew that restoring soldierly pride was crucial to his army. He took another step in that direction when on February 2 he ordered that all regiments should inscribe "upon the colors of all regiments and batteries in the service of the United States the names of the battles in which they have borne a meritorious part." To further instill unit pride and recognition, and to "prevent injustice by reports of straggling and misconduct through mistake," Hooker ordered on March 21, that badges identifying each corps and division would be used hereafter. The First Corps utilized a sphere as its symbol, with the three divisions utilizing the colors of red, white, and blue respectively. These woolen insignias would henceforth be fastened to the top center of each enlisted man's cap. With little to no action under way, the Twenty-Sixth had ample time to properly sew on their new, white circular patch.[14]

Despite Hooker's ideas, monotony, miserable weather, and poor camp conditions were still getting the better of some soldiers. Another act of defiance and the subsequent court-martial proceeding took place within the camp of the Twenty-Sixth. Pvt. Henry Kilburn was accused of obeying a direct order and then threatening his superior officer with the bayonet.[15]

By late March, the improvement in morale and discipline within the ranks made Joseph Hooker a happy man. He invited Lincoln down to Falmouth to review the troops and the president accepted, arriving on April 5. On the 9th, the entire First Corps was reviewed by President Lincoln, Secretary of War Edwin Stanton, and several other dignitaries. A Pennsylvanian in the New Yorkers' Second Brigade described the martial pomp and circumstance that was witnessed on that spring day by the Twenty-Sixth New York and their First Corps comrades: "President Lincoln was down here yesterday and he reviewed the four Army corps, him and his wife and son. Well, the First [Corps] was to get our breakfast in the morning at five o'clock , and then clean our brass and muskets, and have our boots blackened, and then go out. We had to walk about four miles to go where it was. The review was to be at six o'clock in the morning, but it didn't come off until the afternoon. We was the first brigade on the ground and we had to wait till they was all there. They fired a dozen cannons when he appeared on the field. After he was there it did not last long, for he was to ride in front of the rest of them, and after we passed in review, march by companies front. After we got past him we was done...."[16]

In addition to John Robinson as the new Second Division commander, a new brigade commander was forthcoming. Brig. Gen. Henry Baxter, formerly a lieutenant colonel in the Seventh Michigan, was back in service after recovering from a shoulder wound received at Fredericksburg. He was given command of the Twenty-Sixth's Second Brigade on April 18. The previous commander, Col. Peter Lyle, resumed his command of the Ninetieth Pennsylvania. The match would be a fitting one, for like the depleted Twenty-Sixth, its final brigadier had been seriously wounded in every campaign he had been involved with.[17]

Clearly, every man in the regiment was more than ready to go home and it showed in the lack of spit and polish within the Twenty-Sixth's camp. Upon taking over command of the brigade, Baxter directed his staff to inspect his four regiments. The results from the Twenty-Sixth were not impressive. Baxter's acting assistant inspector general, Lt. Francis Thomas, reported to the regiment that "the inspector of this brigade regrets to learn the results of his first inspection of the 26th NY." A date was set for the follow-up with the expectation that all demerits would be corrected. A war was still being waged and such sloppiness from his oldest regiment no doubt raised a red flag to Baxter. Since the Virginia weather had cleared and the mud-laden roads had dried, one more campaign remained for the regiment: westward toward a one-time tavern called "Chancellorsville" located in the brambles of Virginia's Wilderness.[18]

9

A Less-Than-Glorious Finale: Chancellorsville and Home

As the hard winter gave way to spring, federal authorities made plans for a new offensive against rebel positions. Commanding general Joseph Hooker agonized over plans that were impressive on paper, calling for a multipronged attack against Confederate positions on the south side of the Rappahannock. Every possible Union soldier would be needed, and on this end, Hooker was in trouble. The Union's initial two-year enlistments from the spring of 1861 as well as the nine-month enlistments of the previous summer were all set to expire. All of these expiring enlistments added up to close to one-third of Hooker's entire army.

The two-year term of federal service for 38 of his New York regiments was set to expire in May, including the Twenty-Sixth New York's. Rumors were rampant throughout the camps that terms of enlistment would be arbitrarily extended until the men were no longer needed, prompting a groundswell of mutinous rumblings. The rumor and innuendo swept across the home front as well, with soldiers and families nervously quizzing each other for any news within their letters. Many of the bluecoats felt that their patriotic duty had been more than fulfilled and were quite anxious to return to their loved ones back home. The possibility, and even likelihood, of being on the receiving end of a rebel Minié ball, only days from their departure, did not sit well with many.

The imminent departure for home, whether it be April or May, was also reflected by a lack of coverage in the regiment's hometown newspapers. Since Fredericksburg, the army had been hunkered down in its winter encampment at Belle Plain. The subsequent lack of noteworthy news resulted in almost no dispatches or letters being published from the camp of the Twenty-Sixth. This probably had little to due with the quantity of letters sent home, for the lack of action brought about by the winter weather afforded the troops ample opportunity to write. The apparent loss of public and media interest in the regiment's movements and actions was not lost on some of its few remaining, battle-hardened survivors. Evening camp fire conversations throughout the brigade turned toward the current politics of the war, especially Lincoln's Emancipation Proclamation, and as to whether or not the Negro should be armed. One man from the Twenty-Sixth calling himself "Jackson" opined in a letter to the *Utica Daily Gazette* that "if the people of the North have lost their enthusiasm" and "will use no endeavors to keep the army up to an efficient standard, but allow those now in the field to remain inactive for want for want of men and means to successfully prosecute the war"—a clear reference to the skeletal state of the Twenty-Sixth—"then I think the sooner the slave population is armed, the better the prospect of our first success." Not all agreed with those sentiments, of course. Across the field, a brigade comrade in the camp of the One Hundred and Thirty-Sixth Pennsylvania opined, "Give this powerful body of men the assurance that they are fighting for the preservation of our old Union, the Constitution of our Fathers, and not for the freedom of negroes, and a happier more brave and cheerful army never was reared."[1]

During these late-night discussions, the cynicism of the remaining soldiers became apparent on another issue: those civilian gentlemen of leisure who were condemning the war's progress and strategy but were refusing to join in. Instead of enlisting, these men opted to hire others to take their places in the ranks. Jackson addressed that issue as well: "I would not wish to be inferred that I doubt the *courage* of these men, by any means. A man that is benevolent enough to subscribe two or three hundred dollars to *encourage* another to be *patriotic,* and then in his comfortable Northern home displays *his* patriotism by censuring every move of not only those he has been instrumental in sending here, but the very Government he has sworn to uphold, *must* be a very patriotic and courageous man."[2]

★ ★ ★

Though many in the Union high command believed that a sizeable portion of the two-year New York men would ultimately reenlist, it was also a forgone conclusion that would not occur until the boys had returned home, visited with their families, and then collected the sizeable bounty that was being offered to all new volunteers. From all angles, these indispensable men would not be available for the upcoming spring campaign.

The essential point of contention was when those two-year terms of service had rightfully begun. The New Yorkers felt that their service began when their original companies had officially formed for state service, which for many was mid- to late–April 1861. Federal authorities concluded that the two-year term began with the regiment's transfer into government duty, which placed the end of the term at mid- to late–May. Despite their case, many New Yorkers were not optimistic that their version of justice would come to pass. Charles McClenthen wrote home on April 19, believing that: "We have as yet no definite information as to when we will be discharged, but it is my opinion they will endeavor to hold us to open the Spring Campaign as they are taking no steps to raise troops to replace us."[3]

Hooker had attempted to deal with the matter before it blew up in his face. On March 19, Hooker met with the authorities in Washington on this matter and returned to the field satisfied that his men would not be discharged until the end of their two years in the government's service. To further strengthen his position, Hooker reported to the War Department on the vast quantity of New Yorkers he felt he would lose. He showed the Twenty-Sixth as having 393 two-year men and 138 three-year men under arms for a grand total of 531 men in the service of the U. S. government. That paper number was clearly a fanciful figure that must have included all those on furlough or in the hospitals and parole camps, considering that the unit had gone into the Fredericksburg fight with little more than 280 able-bodied men, suffered 51 deaths from that battle, and had no recruiting since then. One month later on April 19, Hooker entertained Lincoln and General-in-Chief Henry Halleck at Aquia Creek to revisit this issue, and to speak along with Lincoln to any soldiers who may have been displeased with the government's interpretation. The next day, Hooker issued General Order 44 which stated what he believed was the government's position. The order was read to the head of each company of the two-year regiments. The announcement did not go over well with many of the New Yorkers, who in some cases vowed not to pick up their rifles again.[4]

The matter was apparently settled by the U.S. solicitor general on April 24 with a ruling that seemed to favor the New Yorkers. The ruling cited as precedent a decree dating back to July 24, 1861, that said 90-day Ohio volunteers were entitled to federal compensation from the date of their organization and acceptance into state service. The opinion never reached the New Yorkers, but it is clear that Hooker was aware of it.

This tempest of controversy only worsened as the April days went past and before long the Twenty-Sixth New York was fully caught up in the whirlwind. Tempers on this issue were short and near the breaking point as the spring campaign loomed. Trying to get to the bottom of the matter, Lieutenant Colonel Jennings issued an order to all of his company commanders on April 26 requesting an immediate, written statement from them as to when their respective companies were accepted into *state* service. The whole matter came to a head on a rainy and dreary April 28, when the regiment received orders to march at noon. About a third of the Twenty-Sixth remained adamant that their time of enlistment was up. Believing that they had served their country honorably for two years, they were more than ready to go home and therefore decided to test the authority of those in command by refusing to march. Division commander Gen. John Robinson and Brig. Gen. Henry Baxter were in no mood for such refusals. Robinson had been forced to deal with a near-revolt of the regiment's junior officers only three months prior and now was faced with a mutiny from its privates. Both men proceeded to explain the reality of the situation to the New Yorkers. The generals ordered the regiment to the parade ground, where Robinson requested all those who refused to march to step to the front. Over 100 men from the Second Oneida instantly obliged the general by stepping forward. Robinson immediately placed the mutineers of the Twenty-Sixth under armed guard, stripped them of all weaponry, and then forced them to march in the rear of the brigade toward Falmouth, about four miles away. During a conference later in the afternoon with the regiment's officers, a stern Robinson offered advice about the future of the young men's military careers if any such actions occurred again, whether it be from officers or enlisted men. Robinson gave the prisoners a second opportunity to rejoin the regiment; nevertheless very few agreed to take up their arms. The mutineers were then handed over to Provost Marshal Gen. Marsena Patrick for safekeeping. Patrick, in turn, assigned the New Yorkers to Col. William Rogers' Twenty-First New York Infantry with the orders that they be put to work strengthening the redoubts, with a further musing from the general that burying dead horses might be a more appropriate task for the mutineers if the army stayed put just a bit longer. Being forced to inhale the foul stench emitted by the decaying animals would be ample punishment for the New Yorkers. Rogers was less than pleased with his new assignment as his main concern, as well as that of his men, was when *they* would be heading home to Buffalo. The revolt continued into the next day as well, when another 20 to 30 men from the Twenty-Sixth refused to fight.[5]

The Second Oneida was far from alone in its obstinance. Up and down the line, two-year men were making known their anger and their unwillingness to fight. Brig. Gens. George Meade and Dan Sickles endured similar acts of defiance; they placed the refractory men under armed guard, and warned all insurgents that further insubordination would be carried out at their own peril. In Sickles' case, the First New York Infantry was ordered to have nothing to eat for 24 hours except bread and water, while being forced to build corduroy roads near camp. If the men carried out those duties properly, no further punishments would be forthcoming. If not, drumhead court-martials would be arranged. Meade's actions were similar, also going so far as to threaten the humiliation of having the men's chevrons publicly pulled off their uniforms.

The boys in blue who were forced to perform the unpopular guard duty were torn with their emotions. Describing his ambivalence, a Pennsylvanian remarked, "This is a sad affair. Candidly, I feel that the New Yorkers are in the right and that justice should be done them. They are brave men who have served their country faithfully and well, and their case should be promptly looked into. However much I or members of the regiment sympathize with them, our duty is plain." That duty included obeying orders from a superior officer without question, and if said orders included leveling a musket at your own comrades, then so be it.[6]

* * *

The Chancellorsville campaign finally began with Reynolds' First Corps encamped on the far end of the Union line several miles east of Fredericksburg near Belle Plain, an army supply depot on Potomac Creek. Hooker's overall scheme called for three corps to march upstream, cross the Rappahannock and then swing back down behind Lee's army. Three other corps, including the First, were to remain below Fredericksburg to act as a diversionary force against Lee's entrenched army.

For its final campaign, the Twenty-Sixth New York would again have a new acting regimental commander, the fourth change in the past eight months. Colonel Richardson's ailments of the past five months had never really gone away, and by early March his illnesses had deteriorated into pneumonia, complicated with pericarditis. Richardson had been convalescing in Washington since April 2, where he probably was aware of the rumored campaign, but not its specifics. Apparently still physically unable to lead, on April 29 Richardson was formally granted his request by surgeon Charles L. Allen for an extended 30-day leave of absence. As with the battle of Fredericksburg four months earlier, Richardson would miss the upcoming action due to illness. Since Lt. Col. Gilbert Jennings had sufficiently recovered from his leg wound at Fredericksburg and was back in the field, he took command of the regiment.[7]

The New Yorkers were well aware that a major campaign was underway. They had been expecting such an announcement for at least two weeks, which probably contributed in part to their poor dispositions. McClenthen had written home over a week earlier and declared, "We have already received orders to hold ourselves in readiness to march at a moment's notice and keep eight days rations constantly packed in our knapsacks and haversacks. How we are to carry them God only knows." With backpacks bulging, the regiment moved out from its encampment near Fletcher Chapel about 1:00 P.M. on the 28th. Marching steadily, the Twenty-

Sixth bivouacked that night near the woods in the rear of the old Fitzhugh mansion, a 1000-acre estate which had been the home of Maj. Norman Fitzhugh, now serving with the Confederates. That night at Fitzhugh's, with a view from the veranda described as " a scene of rare landscape lovliness," would be a final night of peace. The next morning would be the start of a holding and diversionary action along the army's left flank.[8]

April 29 dawned gray and misty, and the dismal weather seemed to match the gloom of the Union soldiers. Everyone could tell another battle was in the offing. The New Yorkers broke camp around noon and marched with the rest of Baxter's brigade to the pontoon bridges which were laid at the mouth of Pollock's Mill Creek, roughly three miles south of Fredericksburg. During the afternoon of the 30th, enemy shells unexpectedly came whistling into their positions. The Twenty-Sixth was spared, but the shells landed close enough to kill and wound several officers and enlisted men in the brigade's Ninetieth Pennsylvania. More shells landed close to Robinson's division headquarters while his men were striking their tents. The unexpected barrage prompted General Robinson to move the entire Second Division back to the protection of the ditches and hedges bordering the River Road, where it rested in relative safety for the next two and a half days. April 30 had been designated by President Lincoln the month before as a national day of fasting, so not only did the New Yorkers have little to do but also nothing to eat. No infantry skirmishing occurred but cannonading back and forth across the Rappahannock was plainly visible and audible to all.[9]

The Main Battle Begins—May 1

"Fighting Joe" Hooker's entire plan of campaign was based on the assumption that Lee would withdraw southward once he realized what he was up against. "Our enemy must either ingloriously fly," proclaimed Hooker, "or come out from behind his defenses and give us battle on our own ground, where certain destruction awaits him."

Although heavily outnumbered almost two to one, and blatantly ignoring the opinion of the man he contemptuously referred to as "Mr. F. J. Hooker," Lee clearly had no intention of going anywhere. Once again, a Union commander completely misread Robert E. Lee's aggressive mindset. Defying accepted military logic, Lee divided his smaller army into two parts: the smaller section under Jubal Early remained in place to guard Fredericksburg, while the larger part hurried west to meet the new Union threat. When the advance guard of Hooker's column collided with the Confederates on May 1, Hooker pulled his troops back to Chancellorsville, a lone one-time tavern at a crossroads clearing in a dense wood known locally as the Wilderness. Hooker now abandoned the offense and took up a defensive position, believing that any rebel attack through the tangled undergrowth would leave enemy forces confused and exposed.

One of the war's most legendary images occurred on the night of May 1 in the Confederate camp. Sitting on cracker boxes around a small campfire, Robert E. Lee and Stonewall Jackson mapped out their plans for the next day. Lee had received reconnaissance reports from cavalry Gen. J.E.B. Stuart that the Union right was "up in the air," or without any type of firm defensive position. Sensing an opportunity to keep the initiative, Lee risked dividing his smaller force even further, opting to keep two divisions in place as a diversion to keep Hooker's attention, while sending Stonewall Jackson and the bulk of the army on what would become a legendary westward flank march through the tangled woods of the Wilderness, ultimately reappearing in force on the Union army's exposed right flank. Jackson's men set out on the morning on May 2 and reached their objective late in the afternoon. Union forces, in fact, observed their march on several occasions, but mistakenly reported that the rebel forces were retreating to the south instead of actually redeploying to the west. Later that day, unsuspecting federal soldiers of the Eleventh Corps on the far right of the federal line were peaceably preparing their evening meals when scores of frightened deer and rabbits bounded out of the woods in the predusk hours. The amusing sight was soon followed by the terrifying, high-pitched shriek of the rebel yell as Jackson's legions stormed from the forest to completely surprise and rout the terrified bluecoats. The Union line collapsed in on itself, almost to the Chancellor house, but nightfall and confusion in the Confederate ranks conspired to stop the rebel advance. With darkness rendering visibility negligible within the dense Wilderness, the surging Confederate line paused about 9:00 P.M. to reform. Still wanting to press the attack, Stonewall and his staff rode well in front of their own lines to reconnoiter. Upon their return, Jackson was accidentally shot by some of his own men, who mistakenly thought the general and his staff were Union cavalry. Later that night, Jackson's left arm was amputated just below the shoulder.

Movements of the Twenty-Sixth New York Infantry

May entered in the same fashion that April had left, with the Twenty-Sixth sitting in their muddy positions along the Rappahannock, occasionally ducking rebel artillery fire. Smiles replaced the sullen stares of many, though, when in the afternoon the troops learned that they were each going to be given a ration of liquor by order of General Robinson.[10]

Early Saturday morning on May 2, while Jackson's Confederates were gearing up for their stealthy march toward the Union far right, a Union rider came pounding up to Reynolds' headquarters with orders from Hooker. The orders stated that the First Corps was to leave its Rappahannock position and to march quickly to the United States Ford. Strangely, the orders stipulated that Reynolds' corps was to be at the ford at the very hour Reynolds actually received it. Due to a bureaucratic error, it had taken close to 24 hours for the crucial instructions to reach Reynolds. A fever-pitched fight was underway and all possible reinforcements were needed with haste. Having been at the extreme left of the Union line, a 22 mile march was now in the works that would put the First Corps on the extreme right of the new line. The weather intensified as the march progressed, prompting numerous Union soldiers to abandon their coats by the side of the road. The sun, heat, and humidity were all out in full force, signifying the fury of what lay in front. It was apparent from the growing sounds of battle in the distance that Hooker's army was getting the fight he had wanted.[11]

The First Corps finally reached United States Ford and crossed about sunset. Robinson's division advanced along the Mineral Springs Road with Baxter's brigade bringing up the rear. They then prepared to bivouac for the night on the south side of the United States Ford.[12] Reynolds hastily rode off in the direction of the Chancellorsville house to seek further orders, leaving Gen. Abner Doubleday of Reynolds' Third Division in temporary command of the corps. The Twenty-Sixth New York, however, did not reach the main line until about 11:00 P.M. due in large part to the thick, tangled forest that they had to work their way through once the roads had been abandoned. The fresh bluecoats were confident that no further action would occur that night, but upon seeing the reddened skies of battle in the distance, fully expected their advance into the fight on the morrow. To everyone's dismay, panic-stricken fugitives from the routed Eleventh Corps were now reaching Robinson's lines with stories of mayhem from the far side of the Union line. To ensure that they ran no farther, the Ninety-Fourth New York was deployed across the front of the corps to keep the routed troops from fleeing back across the river. Orders at this point dictated that the division was to take up a position on and covering the Ely's Ford Road. Union forces were now tightly compacted in a "V"-shaped position, with Robinson's division from Reynolds' Corps occupying the far right of the line. They were the anchor that rested against the Rapidan River along the Ely's Ford Road, just east of Hunting Run.[13]

Arriving at his division's advance positions around 1:00 A.M. on Sunday, May 3, Robinson immediately pushed forward one regiment of each brigade, two in front and one on the right, to feel the enemy and establish them as pickets. The road was choked with men and teamsters, and it took every man on Reynolds' staff just to keep the road clear for the column to advance. Baxter's Second Brigade along with Col. Samuel Leonard's Third Brigade were then established in the line of battle to the left of the road. Col. Adrian Root's First Brigade was formed with its left on the road and extending its right down Hunting Run. Not yet knowing that Stonewall Jackson had been seriously wounded, Hooker feared that another effort would be made by the Confederates to flank the Union right and cut off the bluecoats from their route of retreat at the various fords on the Rappahannock. With orders in hand, General Robinson directed breastworks and trenches to be quickly built to meet the expected rebel assault. Even though they had just endured a daylong 20-mile march, the Twenty-Sixth and their comrades went forcefully to work. Due to the forced march, digging tools were in exceedingly short supply, so bayonets became picks and tin plates substituted for shovels. All through the night and throughout the course of May 3, the New Yorkers and their comrades completed a formidable line of rifle pits and earthworks, as they were first in the battle line. The tired privates no longer seemed to mind this type of work for by this stage of the war they were well aware of the advantages of fighting from being behind a bank of dirt. The division's artillery, which consisted of Ransom's Fifth U.S. Artillery and Hall's Second Maine Battery, arrived soon after. Both of these batteries covered the right to sweep the sloping ground and the heights beyond. Robinson was now quite confident his men could defeat any attack that might be thrown at them. The foot soldiers shared their general's confidence, though to everyone's amazement, it remained quiet on their front through midday. South of their lines, it was another matter. "Just ought to hear the firing and the roaring with cannons and muskets," wrote a private whose Ninetieth Pennsylvania Infantry was in Robinson's trenches alongside the Twenty-Sixth New York. "I thought the whole world was coming to an end." Hooker himself rode by the breastworks around 1:00 P.M., to the thunderous cheers of all, wanting to ensure that all was ready. Later in the afternoon, and with no obvious sign of a Confederate attack coming their way, the Twenty-Sixth went out on picket duty just to ensure that was the case.[14]

The Main Battle—May 3

Though things were relatively quiet on May 3 at the Twenty-Sixth's end of the line, the battle of Chancellorsville was raging with full fury at the other end. J.E.B. Stuart, now in command of Jackson's wing following serious wounds to both Stonewall and then Gen. A. P. Hill, issued a series of bloody, frontal assaults in an effort to drive Hooker from his Chancellorsville defense. Carnage was everywhere and despite a strong resistance from his men, Hooker ordered a withdrawal to a position north of the Chancellor house. Couriers soon notified Lee that the remaining Union troops at Fredericksburg had broken through Gen. Jubal Early's meager defenses and were now quickly advancing to Hooker's aid. At a small house of worship east of Chancellorsville known as Salem Church, Lee threw most of his remaining men against these Federals, blocking their advance and forcing them back across the Rappahannock.

★ ★ ★

The right of the Union line remained in a heightened state of alert throughout May 3. Pickets and reconnaissance patrols were a constant within the First Corps. The day seemed to go with little excitement for the Twenty-Sixth, but later that night after hearing a strange noise, Major Wetmore called for officers to reconnoiter yet again. Finding no volunteers, he took three men himself to explore the woods where the noises had come from. They promptly captured a lone rebel scout, and while Wetmore and his men were returning with their prisoner to camp, they came across four others whom the major promptly marched into the Union lines. However small, it was still a "victory."

Monday, May 4, dawned cool and cloudy, giving all a welcome respite from the previous day's heavy heat of battle. Hooker and his staff were still concerned about a possible Confederate flanking movement toward the Union right, so he ordered General Robinson to make a reconnaissance-in-force along the Ely's Ford Road. Personally leading the expedition, Robinson selected the Twelfth and Thirteenth Massachusetts Infantry and a section of Hall's battery to accompany him. After proceeding about three miles, they ran into Confederate skirmishers to the left of the road. A sharp firefight ensued that resulted in casualties to both sides. Proceeding cautiously to the forks of the road, Robinson became convinced that the enemy was in significant force on his left. Thinking himself outgunned and with orders not to bring on a general engagement, he directed his command to return to camp. In reality, Robinson's men confronted nothing more than a squadron of Confederate cavalry with one horse battery who happened to pull a noticeable bluff on the unknowing Yankees.[15] Closer to the lines, scouting parties from the Twenty-Sixth were sent out beyond the pickets several times throughout the day. In part, this was due to Major Wetmore's minor success of the previous night, but primarily to see if the expected rebel thrust was imminent. In one of the rare, undeniable victories for the regiment, one of the parties surprised and captured 15 Confederates without ever firing a gun. Around 4:00 P.M., the pickets were relieved by the One Hundred and Thirty-Sixth Pennsylvania and happily returned to their earthworks.[16]

The remainder of the Twenty-Sixth as well as the rest of Baxter's brigade had to content themselves with strengthening and refining their already formidable line of breastworks. Pioneers in front cleared the ground for the artillery. Though ready to go into the fight, no call to action was forthcoming. With plenty of time to relax, the men passed the time playing cards or reading in the trenches.

Late on the night of the 4th, and for the first time in the campaign, Hooker sought out the opinion of his generals as to whether the army should continue to fight or fall back. John Reynolds was of the opinion that even though his 20,000-man First Corps had been virtually unengaged, the army should retain its position south of the river. After all, the bluecoats still enjoyed a huge numerical superiority and were entrenched in strong defensive positions. Though the majority of those generals present voted in favor of attacking, Hooker ultimately felt otherwise, and gave the order that the army would retreat across the Rappahannock by way of the same fords it had crossed less than a week earlier. Reynolds was wholly perplexed. Within earshot of Hooker, he muttered, "What was the use of calling us together at this time of night when he intended to retreat anyhow?" Hooker would finally answer that question decades later by stating that he considered Reynolds his ablest officer and that he knew the First Corps was ready and eager to be brought into the action. Nevertheless, he was fully convinced of the futility of attacking Lee's fortified positions, not to mention that his soldiers' eight-day supply of rations had been exhausted. One may debate the merits of his former reason, but on the latter, Hooker was being disingenuous. Though Union haversacks may have been running low, supply wagons brimming with rations and forage stood at the ready on the other side of the Rappahannock at U. S. Ford.[17] With the decision made, it was again clear that bridges had to be built by the engineers and roads had to be corduroyed for retreat that was soon to follow. Much of the manual labor fell to the soldiers in Reynolds' corps, including the Twenty-Sixth New York. Finally, during an appropriately morose, torrential rain and dense fog on the night of May 5, the First Corps was withdrawn from its position and crossed the Rappahannock in good order. As with the "Mud March" back in January, rebel pickets on the south side of the Rappahannock could not contain their glee as the downtrodden bluecoats withdrew. "Hey Yank, how do you like Hooker now?" was typical of the shouts and hollers. Col. Charles Wainright, First Corps chief of artillery, overheard enough of his soldiers' angry discussions to have unknowingly answered those Confederate jeers within his journal: "All appeared to feel that our retreat was a disgrace, and none could understand it, but each conversation concluded the same: 'If Little Mac had been here we would never have gone off this way.'" The privates' love for George McClellan still burned brightly.[18]

The dreary and wet march continued throughout the night until the regiment finally stopped around 8:00 A.M. on the 6th for a mere 20-minute rest. The night of May 6 found all of Reynolds' corps encamped near the Wallace house, on the

Retreat of the Union Army across the Rappahannock at United States Ford (*Century Magazine*).

Falmouth and Belle Plain road. That day's lonesome march added a final, dismal exclamation point to the entire campaign, as it was conducted in a rain and hailstorm that rivaled the rebel Minié balls. One divisional artillerist observed that, "The hailstones being in some instances, actually larger than hen's eggs, and knocking men off their horses." The next day the corps assembled in rear of the place where they had practically started out from five days earlier, near Pollock's Mill.[19]

In the end, the Twenty-Sixth New York's final campaign ended with nary a shot being fired either by or at them. They were so removed from the action that not a single soldier from the regiment was killed or wounded during the five-day battle.[20] Their impending dismissal from service, their decimated ranks, as well as the impetuous mutiny of April 28 had clearly labeled the Twenty-Sixth as unreliable in key quarters. Robinson and Baxter made sure that fatigue duty would be the extent of the Second Oneida's involvement at the battle of Chancellorsville. It was virtually a moot point, for Reynolds' corps as a whole was, for the most part, out of the fight. The surgeon of the Twelfth Massachusetts, which was joined with the Twenty-Sixth New York within Baxter's brigade, succinctly summed up the brigade's lack of action: "Our position on the right at Chancellorsville was almost invulnerable, but it was no object to hold it after we had lost the left, so a retreat was accomplished without the loss of a man." First Corps commander John Reynolds, equally disgusted, had his own opinion regarding his corps' lack of action: "We did not effect much more by our crossing than to be slaughtered and to slaughter the rebels. I think it will turn out that they got more of the spoils than did we. My corps was very little in action and has of course suffered very little, tho' I do not consider its morale improved by the operations."[21]

The end of the road was at hand for the Twenty-Sixth New York Volunteers. The evening of May 7 brought the orders that most of the exhausted New Yorkers had dreamed of for months. They were to return to Falmouth and turn in all public property other than muskets, then take the train north to Aquia Landing. Since darkness was at hand, they camped for the night where they were. Early the next morning, they fell into line without much coaxing and marched to Falmouth. Once at the landing, they boarded a Washington-bound steamboat to begin their final homebound journey. Upon their arrival around 9:00 P.M., many of the tired men dispersed, some staying at Soldier's Retreat, others taking better rooms at local inns.

The tired men of the Twenty-Sixth reached Elmira, New York on May 11, almost two years to the day from the time and place where they officially started as a Federal regiment. Gone were the freshly scrubbed faces of the boy volunteers and young men who clamored for glory. Instead, the returning warriors were now battle-scarred veterans with weatherworn, hardened faces. The circle was almost complete. But there was still army business to be taken care of and final administrative matters to be dealt with. A final parade drill was to be held at 5:00 P.M. on May 12 with all soldiers in full uniform and weaponry. The following week, William Holstead wrapped up his matters by settling the regiment's clothing book on May 18.[22]

Pvt. Albert Loveland mustered out of Company D, May 1863, at Utica, New York. (New York State Military Museum).

The formal welcome that awaited the regiment on its arrival back home in Utica was that of the conquering hero. Weeks of planning had gone on that would entail a May 20 parade, decorating the town, and providing plenty of home cooking for the returning warriors. Plans had been set forth so that the Twenty-Sixth and their fellow Uticans from the Fourteenth New York Infantry would arrive back home by train at approximately the same time. In a case of near perfect timing, the Fourteenth arrived from Albany at noon on May 20 while the Twenty-Sixth arrived from Elmira a mere five minutes later. Thunderous ovations and the booming of cannon greeted the Oneida men as they exited their cars. It appeared as if the town had never been so full of people. Streets, sidewalks, even trees and rooftops were all covered with the citizenry. The mayor of the town, Charles S. Wilson, gave a short speech and then Col. Richard Richardson, still recovering from his ailments, paused to say a few words to the gathered throng, expressing his gratitude. Then the Honorable C. H. Doolittle arose and gave a much longer speech praising the Twenty-Sixth. After the remarks, the parade weaved its way through the town, passing through three triumphal arches that had been built for the occasion. Joining the parade were numerous members of fraternal organizations, with the men of the Twenty-Sixth and their comrades from the Fourteenth New York Infantry, bringing up the rear. All of the men who had been honorably discharged days before had their place in the line. The sight of the Twenty-Sixth's bullet-riddled banner at the head of the column reminded everyone of the young men who had not returned home. There were plenty of those. Of the approximately 1,200 men who had

Pvt. Thomas A. Jones mustered out of Company F, May 1863, at Utica, New York (New York State Military Museum).

filled the ranks of the Twenty-Sixth at one time or another, only 350 were left to officially muster out. After two years of hard service, their national flag had taken over 50 bullet holes. The eagle had been shot from the staff and a gaping hole existed in the field of stars where a rebel shell had gone through. They also carried their Second Division brigade flag and it was deemed to be little more than shreds clinging to the staff. Perhaps balls that had shortened the life of a young New Yorker made some of the holes in those banners as well. An additional poignant reminder was the riderless horse of William Kirkland Bacon, the young and popular adjutant who had fallen at Fredericksburg. Although the wearied New Yorkers were glad to be home, they were proud of the two years they had served their country. William Holstead, who had now received a commission as a first lieutenant, ended his time of service by commenting that he had the grandest time on record.[23]

Home from the war (*Harpers Weekly*).

Not all of the Twenty-Sixth's soldiers came home. Those men who had enlisted for a period of three years were consolidated into the Ninety-Seventh New York Infantry, also from Oneida County, who had the moniker Third Oneida. Others were sent into the Eighty-Third New York. For them, a lavish homecoming would have to await another day. Duty still called as the war showed no sign of abatement.

10

1863–1865 and the Postwar Years

With their two-year tour of duty over, many men returned home to enjoy the warmth of family and to return to their prewar vocations. Those few soldiers who had three-year enlistments were reassigned to the hometown Ninety-Seventh New York Infantry, which had been christened the Third Oneida Regiment. Others who still felt the call to patriotic duty, or simply needed a paying job, reenlisted with other regiments. An ample bounty was being offered by the government, and many saw no reason not to collect it.

Popular reenlistment destinations for many of the returning New Yorkers from the central part of the state were the Third New York Light Artillery and the Sixteenth New York Heavy Artillery. Others chose the cavalry, including the Twelfth and Twenty-Fourth New York Cavalry, believing that riding a horse was easier duty than marching across muddy fields all day. In either case, perhaps as a testament to the sorrows they had endured, very few privates who mustered out from the Twenty-Sixth New York Infantry opted to reenlist into another infantry regiment. It was a similar story for the regiment's remaining officers.

Richard Richardson was approved to recruit men into the Sixteenth New York Heavy Artillery, but only after having showed that his health had sufficiently improved even for that type of light administrative duty. Further work back in the field was rejected.[1]

Gilbert Jennings, still recovering from his shattered leg, reenlisted into the Eleventh U.S. Veterans Reserve Corps. He had been offered the colonelcy of a cavalry regiment, but declined the offer due to his leg wound. The Veterans Reserve Corps, originally known as the Invalid Corps, was started in 1863 and its intent was to provide military tasks for those soldiers too weak or wounded to assume normal frontline duty. Guard or provost duty, cooks, and orderly work were common roles. Garrison duty at the forts in and around Washington was also customary and into this role Jennings was finally placed, serving as commander of the Eleventh Veteran Reserve Corps in the District of St. Mary's, Maryland. His men also served as guards for prisoners-of-war at Elmira, New York; Camp Douglas at Chicago; Camp Briggs in Alexandria; and at Point Lookout, Maryland.[2]

William Christian tried repeatedly after Antietam to offer his military services to any who would have him. He did not attend the regiment's coming-home ceremonies, being in Pennsylvania at the time to tender his service in any capacity, offering to decline any compensation, and even to pay his own expenses. "The colonel is anxious to get an opportunity to repel by acts the imputations cast on his courage," wrote the *Utica Morning Herald*. It was the first indication given by any paper that Christian's actions at Antietam had been questionable. In the end, however, all of his requests for a post were rebuffed. It was thought for a while close to the end of the war that he would obtain a commission as major in a newly formed colored regiment, however that too came to naught. A local paper summed up the opinion of many when it learned of the then-pending rumor by editorializing, "We have heard that his [Christian's] reputation for courage and military capacity did not stand high in the army while he commanded the 26th, and if so, his new appointment is a very unfortunate one."[3]

Despite the opportunity to reenlist, many men felt satisfied that they had answered their nation's call and chose to retire from any further military duty. Due to poor health acquired during the regiment's arduous months in service, Maj. Ezra F. Wetmore became the highest ranking veteran of the Twenty-Sixth New York who voluntarily declined any further service. The major spent his postwar years peaceably engaged in carpentry and farming while trying to regain his lost vigor. Wetmore was also the most active of the regiment's senior officers in post-war reunions and veterans affairs. He served as the first president of the Twenty-Sixth New York Veteran's Association and also served as vice president of the Oneida County Veteran's Association. He was a fixture at virtually every reunion and in the process became one of Oneida County's most-revered Civil War veterans. He passed away on July 25, 1905. [4]

Retirement was also in order for the Twenty-Sixth's bullet-riddled banners, one of which was officially retired on April 20, 1864, during a ceremony at the state legislature. From that point, the flags were ultimately destined for the New York

Reunion invitation.

10. 1863–1865 and the Postwar Years

State Archives. Col. Richard Richardson, in a letter accompanying the colors, wrote, "I have the honor to return to the custody of the state of New York, the colors by this regiment since June, 1861. They have been borne through every battle of Eastern Virginia, and under their folds have fallen five good and true men. We return them to the State from which we received them, well knowing that they will be cherished as mementoes of the living and the dead. They bear the marks of bullets, and of the blood of those who defended them, and, as such, will always be regarded with respect and veneration by those who are left to mourn of their comrades on the field of battle."[5]

When the war was fully over, the weathered veterans returned to their prewar trades with the hope and expectations that the bloody struggle was now relegated to history. Veterans from every state turned to the pen to tell their tales of battle and marches, though for the Twenty-Sixth, that tale would never be officially told by any surviving members.

Certainly not by Colonel Christian, who, despite his forced resignation at Antietam and subsequent inability to obtain a commission in any regiment anywhere, was brevetted brigadier general of volunteers on March 13, 1865, for "meritorious

Reunion of the Twenty-Sixth's veterans, May 28, 1885. This photograph was taken on the courthouse steps in Utica, New York (Clinton Historical Society—Clinton, New York).

Pvt. Edwin Kane later in life.

and gallant services during the war." For the most part, his fellow soldiers in the Twenty-Sixth always treated him with respect and courtesy when they saw him after the war. Other Oneida County regiments did likewise, such as inviting him to their reunion banquets. Nevertheless, Christian could never overcome the horror of that fateful September day and became more and more despondent in the decades to follow. His behavior became so moody and unpredictable that ultimately it landed him in the state insane asylum at Utica. He died there on May 8, 1887. In the local obituaries, no mentions were made of the man's shortcomings, only of his bravery and that the cause of death was due to the effects of a sunstroke received at Second Bull Run.[6]

Also honored after the war was Gilbert Jennings, who, after his enlistment in the Veterans Reserve Corps and subsequent mustering out in September 1866, was brevetted colonel of volunteers for his service during the war. Prior to his leaving the volunteer ranks, Jennings sought a position in the regular army, appealing on several occasions during the summer of 1866 to the secretary of state and former governor of New York, W. H. Seward, to help secure an "honorable position" for him. Ultimately, Jennings succeeded in obtaining a commission in January 1867 and served respectably until his retirement from the military in 1878. Along the way, he was brevetted a captain in the U.S. regular army for his meritorious service at the battles of Second Bull Run and Fredericksburg. Upon his retirement, Jennings settled in Michigan. Jennings died in his sleep at his home in Detroit on November 1, 1893, the accidental victim of natural gas poisoning in his bedroom.[7]

Richard H. Richardson never fully recovered from the pneumonia which had beset him in January 1863. A thin man all of his life, numerous acquaintances later recalled that he was a far more gaunt and emaciated man in his postwar years than they remembered him prior to the conflict. His few remaining years were spent dealing with a persistent cough and labored breathing which, for the most part, rendered him house-bound. He died in Oneida County on March 18, 1869.[8]

Those veterans who returned from the war with disabilities or missing limbs from their time in service had the right to seek an invalid pension from the federal government. Scores of returning veterans, from those obvious cases such as Jerome Frazier with his amputated leg to those of a more dubious nature, applied for pensions in the decades to follow, and the Twenty-Sixth New York was no different. A researcher delving today into the Civil War's dusty pension records at the National Archives would be surprised to learn just how often diarrhea and "consumption," allegedly acquired during the war years, produced lifelong disabilities in the decades to follow.

Veterans associations popped up everywhere, as well as various posts and chapters of the Grand Army of the Republic (G.A.R.), which served as the preeminent mouthpiece of Union veterans in the last half of the nineteenth century.

The 12th formal meeting of the regiment's survivors was in December 1897, when the remaining regimental flag was presented by survivors to the Oneida Historical Society. Veterans from all units who came from Oneida County were present, as well as some of the ladies who had originally sewn the banners. Though the day was rainy, the large meeting hall was overflowing with a standing-room-only crowd. Maj. Ezra Wetmore was present, and spoke to the gathered throng, as Medal of Honor winners Joseph Keene and Charles Cleveland carried the torn flag. Tears of memory were prevalent, as many of the old veterans knew they were nearing "the eternal campground." By the late 1880s (see picture), only a few dozen of the old veterans were left to tell their tales of beating drums and booming cannons.

The Twenty-Sixth's veteran association officers from the year 1901. Clockwise from top left: Charles F. Cleveland, president; Federick Graff, secretary; Jabez L. Miller, treasurer; and John H. Jones, vice president.

Ultimately, nature took from the old Twenty-Sixth what many rebel bullets could not. The men passed on from this earth, most of whom realized that the late, great Civil War was *the* adventure of their lives. Most recalled their travails and comradeship fondly. Memory was a powerful instrument. Near the end of the 19th century, William Sanford, who had been a first lieutenant in Company F, put in words the emotions that their tattered banner had held in the hearts of many: "I can see it now as it waved on the many bloody battlefields of the regiment during its two years service. I can see it gracefully waved in regulation as Little Mac and our martyred president, the noble Abraham Lincoln, reviewed the army, soon after the battle of Antietam. After two years of faithful service, we returned as a regiment, brought back the old flag unsullied, but badly torn and shredded by shot and shell. After our discharge, many of us re-entered the service, and served till the close of the war, but I venture to say there is nothing that will quicken the pulse and brighten the eye of the comrades of the 26th Regiment like the mention of that old flag."[9]

11

Author's Afterword

As research on this book progressed, one of the most compelling questions in my mind was trying to theorize *why* the story of this regiment had never been *fully* told by any of its veterans. Not an irrelevant question, since four other infantry regiments recruited primarily from New York's Oneida County marched off to war and every one of them had a book-length regimental history written in the late nineteenth century or the early years of the twentieth century.[1] In addition to full-length histories, some of them have had collections of soldiers letters published, as well. I concluded that it couldn't have been that since the Twenty-Sixth was "only" a two-year regiment, no one deemed their story to be of sufficient length. Numerous New York regiments of two-year enlistments have had their story told, some of them quite famously. Perhaps some veterans felt that the Bacon memorial volume and the two exceedingly slim Charles McClenthen pamphlets told their story adequately, or maybe, some well-intentioned survivor started the task but never got around to finishing it. Regardless of why pen was never put to paper, it seems fair to say that from information I gleaned from G.A.R. records and regimental reunions, the Twenty-Sixth's veterans displayed an *outward* pride in their unit every bit as much as others.

I pondered which veteran might have been able to write that history. Certainly not their founding colonel. William Christian's stain at Antietam, coupled with his postwar depression and slow slide into lunacy rendered him an impossible candidate. Richard Richardson was not even with the regiment for most of its final six months of enlistment, including the battles of Fredericksburg and Chancellorsville, therefore, his version of the history would have had some significant holes in it. Plus, Richardson died a mere four years after the war ended, a victim of ever-declining health. Surgeon Walter Coventry died even before Richardson, passing away shortly after the war's end. Of all the senior officers, only Maj. Ezra Wetmore, an Oneida County farmer after the war, seems to have maintained any type of active role or even interest in the regiment's postwar reunions. I know the major gave speeches and addresses on the regiment's history; unfortunately, his notes and any memoir he may have penned seem lost to history.

The theory that slowly began to form in my mind over the years of examination as to why no formal history existed became somewhat distressing. I came to realize that not once during their entire two-year term of service did the Twenty-Sixth experience the exhilaration of carrying the enemy's works or seizing its colors. Victory was usually absent and glory was not their companion. To be fair, more often than not the regiment was placed in difficult, often impossible-to-maintain tactical situations, which inevitably resulted in the New Yorkers being forced to leave the field in disorder. In that regard, Second Bull Run and perhaps Fredericksburg come readily to mind. In their defense, it could be argued that virtually every Union regiment in the eastern theater experienced similar results during the timeframe of First Bull Run in July 1861 through Chancellorsville in May of 1863. History shows that though fate often seemed to place the Twenty-Sixth in a less-than-desirable military position, the average private fought courageously and honorably. The extreme casualties that the unit suffered at Second Bull Run, Antietam, and Fredericksburg bear solemn witness to the New Yorkers' fortitude, as do their three Medal of Honor winners who arose from those same bloody fields.

Not all of the privates stayed to fight, however. An analysis of the regiment's roster (Appendix B) reveals that roughly 13 percent of the regiment's enlistees were reported as deserting from the ranks. This is significantly higher statistically than the 8.9 percent desertion rate average for the New York regiments. Why desertions or bounty jumping within the Twenty-Sixth were higher than the typical New York regiment is a topic that can be endlessly debated. The late nineteenth century compilers of the Civil War's *Official Records* seem to have already given us their ready explanation: "It is a notorious circumstance that the great mass of the professional bounty jumpers were Europeans. In general, the manufacturing States, as, for instance, Massachusetts, Connecticut, Rhode Island, *New York*, and New Jersey, rank high in the column of desertion; and this result is to be attributed not only to the fact that such States are dotted with towns and cities, but to the secondary fact that these towns and cities are crowded with foreigners. The respectable and industrious part of this population did, indeed, produce a mass of faithful troops; but with these were mixed a vast number of adventurers, unworthy of any country, who had no affection for the Republic, and who only enlisted for money." As previously put forth, the Twenty-Sixth had a higher-than-average number of Europeans within its ranks.[2]

It is probable that the resignation-in-disgrace of their founding colonel also did not lend itself to veterans glorifying the regiment with pen and paper. Though William Christian's actions on September 17, 1862, certainly in no way reflected negatively on the Twenty-Sixth since he was now leading the brigade instead of their regiment, any reliable postwar history of the unit would have had to publicly discuss the man and this embarrassing event. As previously discussed in this book, such an expose would have been socially unacceptable in late nineteenth-century American culture. Closer to the end of their enlistment, it appeared that some in the regiment viewed their unit as largely forgotten by the hometown papers, prompting some bitterness from the survivors. Examination of the various Oneida papers showed that in the late winter and early spring of 1863, virtually all of the press coverage was devoted to the newer regiments, such as the One Hundred-Seventeenth Infantry. Perhaps those letters home from the Twenty-Sixth spoke of the foul atmosphere that permeated the camp in those early months of 1863. That was, without doubt, not the type of copy that the hometown papers would have been looking for. Certainly, the near-revolt of some officers led by Captain Caryl in January 1863 and the privates' mutiny just prior to the Chancellorsville campaign did not lend itself to self-congratulatory memory.

Despite all of these adverse circumstances, the fact remains that the Twenty-

Sixth New York Volunteer Infantry, a hard-luck regiment if there ever was one, was in the thick of some of the Civil War's most legendary battles. Its veterans marched long and hard, slept in rain and snow, stopped Confederate bullets, and bled for their state and country as well as any number of more famous regiments. The battalion's beautiful, silken flags that were proudly carried high into battle came home as little more than shredded pieces of cloth attached to splintered poles. Like those young men from central New York state, the banners had a story worth telling. I hope I have done them all justice.

Appendix A: Command Within Campaigns and Post Assignments

Defenses of Washington:
Col. John McCunn's Brigade, Army of Northeast Virginia, July 21, 1861, to August 3, 1861
    Fifteenth New York Infantry
    Twenty-Fifth New York Infantry
    Twenty-Sixth New York Infantry
    Thirty-Seventh New York Infantry

Gen. Samuel Heintzelman's Brigade, Division of the Potomac, Washington, D.C., August 4, 1861, to October 14, 1861
    Fifth Maine Infantry
    Sixteenth New York Infantry
    Twenty-Sixth New York Infantry
    Twenty-Seventh New York Infantry
    Second U.S. Artillery, Tidbali's battery (A)

Brig. Gen. Henry W. Slocum's Brigade, Franklin's Division, Army of the Potomac, October 15, 1861, to November 1861
    Fifth Maine Infantry
    Sixteenth New York Infantry
    Twenty-Sixth New York Infantry
    Twenty-Seventh New York Infantry
    Ninety-Sixth Pennsylvania Infantry

Defenses of Washington: Brig. Gen. James Wadsworth, Commanding
    Assigned to Fort Lyon, Alexandria, Virginia, November 1861 to May 1862

Marches to Fredericksburg and the Shenandoah Valley, May 16, 1862, to June 26, 1862
    Department of the Rappahannock:
    Gen. E. O. C. Ord's Division
    Brig. Gen. James Rickett's Brigade
    Twenty-Sixth New York Infantry
    Ninety-Fourth New York Infantry
    Eighty-Eighth Pennsylvania Infantry
    Ninetieth Pennsylvania Infantry

Second Bull Run Campaign and Battle, June 26, 1862, to September 7, 1862
    Army of Virginia: Maj. Gen. John Pope
    Third Army Corps: Maj. Gen. Irvin McDowell
    Second Division: Brig. Gen. James B. Ricketts
    Second Brigade: Brig. Gen. Zealous B. Tower
    Twenty-Sixth New York Infantry
    Ninety-Fourth New York Infantry
    Eighty-Eighth Pennsylvania Infantry
    Ninetieth Pennsylvania Infantry

The Maryland Campaign: Battles of South Mountain and Antietam, September 7, 1862, to November 10, 1862
    Army of the Potomac: Maj. Gen. George McClellan
    First Army Corps: Maj. Gen. Joseph Hooker
    Second Division: Brig. Gen. James B. Ricketts
    Second Brigade: Col. William H. Christian
    Twenty-Sixth New York Infantry
    Ninety-Fourth New York Infantry
    Eighty-Eighth Pennsylvania Infantry
    Ninetieth Pennsylvania Infantry

Appendix A

The Fredericksburg Campaign and Battle, November 11, 1862, to February 1863
    Army of the Potomac: Maj. Gen. Ambrose E. Burnside
    Left Grand Division: Maj. Gen. William B. Franklin
    First Army Corps: Maj. Gen. John F. Reynolds
    Second Division: Brig. Gen. John Gibbon
    Second Brigade: Col. Peter Lyle
    Twenty-Sixth New York Infantry
    Ninetieth Pennsylvania Infantry
    Twelfth Massachusetts Infantry
    One Hundred, Thirty-Sixth Pennsylvania Infantry

The Chancellorsville Campaign and Battle, February 1863 to May 28, 1863
    Army of the Potomac: Maj. Gen. Joseph Hooker
    First Army Corps: Maj. Gen. John F. Reynolds
    Second Division: Brig. Gen. John Robinson
    Second Brigade: Brig. Gen. Henry Baxter
    Twenty-Sixth New York Infantry
    Ninetieth Pennsylvania Infantry
    Twelfth Massachusetts Infantry
    One Hundred, Thirty-Sixth Pennsylvania Infantry

Appendix B: Regimental Roster[1]

1. ABERCROMBY, WILLIAM H.—Age, 21 years. Enlisted, May 2, 1861, at Rochester, to serve two years; mustered in as private, Company G, May 21, 1861; deserted, June 13, 1862, at Front Royal, Va.; also listed as William H. Abercorombie.

2. ABRAHAM, ANTONE—Age, 21 years. Enlisted, May 8, 1861, at Utica, to serve two years; mustered in as private, Company D, May 21, 1861; mustered out with company, May 28, 1863, at Utica, N.Y.

3. ACKERMAN, CHARLES—Age, 24 years. Enlisted, May 7, 1861, at Utica, to serve two years; mustered in as private, Company E, May 21, 1861; second lieutenant, January 11, 1862; first lieutenant and adjutant, April 1, 1863; mustered out with regiment, May 28, 1863, at Utica, N.Y.; commissioned second lieutenant, January 17, 1862, with rank from January 11, 1862, vice Chas. Smith, promoted; adjutant (first lieutenant), February 11, 1863, with rank from December 15, 1862, vice Bacon, died of wounds.

4. ACKERMAN, JOHN—Age, 43 years. Enlisted, May 3, 1861, at Utica, to serve two years; mustered in as private, Company F, May 21, 1861; promoted corporal, August 19, 1861; sergeant, June 19, 1862; mustered out with company, May 28, 1863, at Utica, N.Y.; subsequent service in Third Artillery.

5. ADAMS, AARON—Age, 19 years. Enlisted, May 14, 1861, at Camden, to serve two years; mustered in as sergeant, Company K, May 21, 1861; promoted first sergeant, August 1, 1862; mustered out with company, May 28, 1863, at Utica, N.Y.; commissioned second lieutenant, May 13, 1863, with rank from October 19, 1862, vice Lynch, promoted; not mustered.

6. ALBERT, JAY M. C.—Age, 24 years. Enlisted, May 7, 1861, at Utica, to serve three months; mustered in as private, Company D, May 21, 1861; deserted, June 5, 1861, at Elmira, N.Y.

7. ALBRO, CHARLES—Age, 19 years. Enlisted, May 2, 1861, at Rochester, to serve two years; mustered in as private, Company G, May 21, 1861; captured, August 30, 1862, at Bull Run, Va.; paroled, date not stated, at Gainesville, Va.; mustered out with company, May 28, 1863, at Utica, N.Y.; also listed as Charles H. Albro.

8. ALLEN, EDGAR C.—Age, 32 years. Enlisted, May 2, 1861, at Rochester, to serve two years; mustered in as private, Company G, May 21, 1861; promoted corporal, date not stated; wounded, December 13, 1862, at battle of Fredericksburg, Va.; died of such wounds, same date.

9. ALLEN, JOHN—Age, 25 years. Enlisted, September 4, 1861, at Rochester, to serve three years; mustered in as private, Company H, September 5, 1861; discharged for disability, November 15, 1861, at Camp Franklin, Va.

10. ALLEN, LEANDER—Age, 26 years. Enlisted, May 7, 1861, at Utica to serve three months; mustered in as private, Company B, May 21, 1861; deserted, July 10, 1861, at Camp Van Valkenburgh, Washington, D.C.

11. ANDERSON, EDWARD—Age, 20 years. Enlisted, May 7, 1861, at Utica, to serve three mouths; mustered in as private, Company B, May 21, 1861; transferred to Company B, date not stated; discharged for disability, September 4, 1861, near Alexandria, Va.

12. ANDERSON, JOHN—Age, 35 years. Enlisted, May 21, 1861, at Elmira, to serve three months; mustered in as private, Company E, May 21, 1861; no further record.

13. ANNIS, JOSEPH—Age, 29 years. Enlisted, May 1, 1861, at Utica, to serve two years; mustered in as private, Company A, May 21, 1861; killed, October 13, 1862, at battle of Fredericksburg, Va.

14. ANTHONY, SAMUEL—Age, 24 years. Enlisted, May 7, 1861, at Elmira, to serve three months; mustered in as private, Company C, May 21, 1861; deserted, May 31, 1861, at Elmira, N.Y.

15. ANTHONY, WILLIAM C.—Age, 21 years. Enlisted, May 8, 1861, at Utica, to serve two years; mustered in as private, Company B, May 21, 1861; deserted, June 29, 1861, at Washington, D.C.

16. ANTONE, JOSEPH—Age, 24 years. Enlisted, May 7, 1861, at Utica, to serve two years; mustered in as private, Company D, May 21, 1861; wounded, August 30, 1862, at battle of Second Bull Run, Va.; died of wounds, October 29, 1862, at Washington, D.C.

17. ARNOLD, FRANK—Age, 19 years. Enlisted, August 14, 1861, at Rome, to serve three years; mustered in as private, Company I, August 20, 1861; discharged for disability, February 4, 1863, at Convalescent Camp, Va.

18. ARROWSMITH, GEORGE—Age, 22 years. Enrolled, May 7, 1861, at Utica, to serve two years; mustered in as captain, Company D, May 21, 1861; mustered out, to date, September 9, 1862, to accept promotion of assistant adjutant general of volunteers; commissioned captain, July 4, 1861, with rank from May 7, 1861, original.

19. ASHLEY, THEODORE—Age 24 years. Enlisted, May 3, 1861, at Utica, to serve two years; mustered in as private, Company F, May 21, 1861; promoted, June 1, 1861, to hospital steward; mustered out with regiment, May 28, 1863, at Utica, N.Y.; subsequent service in Twenty-Fourth Cavalry; also listed as Theodore J. Ashley.

20. ATWELL, OSCAR M.—Age, 20 years. Enlisted, May 13, 1861, at Utica, to serve two years; mustered in as private, Company I, May 21, 1861; wounded, date not stated, at battle of Fredericksburg, Va.; died, January 9, 1863, at Lincoln Military Hospital, Washington, D.C.

21. BABCOCK, CHESTER L.—Age, 20 years. Enlisted, September 9, 1861, at Utica, to serve two years; mustered in as private, Company B, September 17, 1861; mustered out with company, May 28, 1863, at Utica, N.Y.

22. BACHMAN, PHILIP—Age, 42 years. Enlisted, September 15, 1862, at Utica, to serve three years; mustered in as private, unassigned, same date; discharged for disability, November 20, 1862, at Albany, N.Y.

23. BACON, CHARLES E.—Age, 20 years. Enlisted, October 19, 1861, at Rochester, to serve—years; mustered in as private, unassigned, October 24, 1861; no further record.

24. BACON, WILLIAM K.—Private, Company A, Fourteenth Infantry; transferred, July 1861, to Company F, this regiment; mustered in as adjutant, August 7, 1861; wounded in action, August 31, 1862, at Bull Run, Va., and December 13, 1862, at battle of Fredericksburg, Va.; died, December 15, 1862, of such wounds; commissioned adjutant August 14, 1861, with rank from August 7, 1861, original.

25. BAKER, AMDON—Age, 28 years. Enlisted, May 2, 1861, at Elmira, to serve two years; mustered in as private, Company G, May 21, 1861; mustered out with company, May 28, 1863, at Utica, N.Y.; also listed as Amandon Baker.

26. BAKER, THOMAS H.—Age, 18 years. Enlisted, May 3, 1861, at Utica, to serve two years; mustered in as private, Company F, May 21, 1861; deserted, June 19, 1862, at Manassas, Va.; executed by firing squad for desertion August 13, 1862.

27. BALCH, HIRAM—Age, 23 years. Enlisted, May 7, 1861, at Elmira, to serve three months; mustered in as private, Company C, May 21, 1861; deserted, May 21, 1861, at Elmira, N.Y.; also listed as Hiram Black.

28. BALL, CHARLES—Age, 23 years. Enlisted, May 21, 1861, at Elmira, to serve three months; mustered In as private, Company E, May 21, 1861; no further record.

29. BALL, DANIEL—Age, 21 years. Enlisted, May 1, 1861, at Utica, to serve two

years; mustered in as private, Company A, September 2, 1861; discharged for disability, November 11, 1861.

30. BALL, JOSEPH—Age, 28 years. Enlisted, August 30, 1861, at Utica, to serve two years; mustered in as private, Company C, May 21, 1861; killed, August 30, 1862, at battle of Second Bull Run, Va.

31. BARAGER, CHARLES F.—Age, 23 years. Enrolled, May 14, 1861, at Camden, to serve three months; mustered in as first lieutenant, Company K, May 21, 1861; resigned, August 7, 1861; commissioned first lieutenant, July 4, 1861, with rank from May 14, 1861, original.

32. BARBER, GEORGE W.—Age, 20 years. Enlisted, May 14, 1861, at Camden, to serve two years; mustered in as private, Company K, May 21, 1861; deserted, November 21, 1861, at Elmira, N.Y.

33. BARD, ISAAC—Age, 21 years. Enlisted, May 3, 1861, at Utica, to serve two years; mustered in as private, Company C, May 21, 1861; promoted corporal, January 1, 1862; wounded and captured at Bull Run, Va., August 30, 1862; deserted, December 3, 1862, at Brook's Station, Va., and enlisted in the Eighteenth Regular Infantry.

34. BARDEN, EZRA—Age, 19 years. Enlisted, December 2, 1861, at Taberg, to serve unexpired term of two years; mustered in as private, Company A, December 11, 1861; mustered out with company, May 28, 1863, at Utica, N.Y.

35. BARDEN, NELSON—Age, 25 years. Enlisted, December 2, 1861, at Taberg, to serve unexpired term of two years; mustered in as private, Company A, December 11, 1861; transferred to Company I, February 11, 1862; mustered out with company, May 28, 1863, at Utica, N.Y.; also listed as Nelson A. Barden.

BARKER, ANTHONY—see Berger, Anthony.

36. BARLOW, ABAGER—Age, 43 years. Enlisted, August 26, 1862, at Utica, to serve three years; mustered in as private, unassigned, same date; reported deserted, date not stated.

37. BARNETT, HENRY D.—Age, 21 years. Enrolled, May 1, 1861, at Utica, to serve two years; mustered in as second lieutenant, Company B, May 21, 1861; as first lieutenant, August 7, 1861; resigned, October 28, 1861; commissioned second lieutenant, July 4, 1861, with rank from May 1, 1861, original; first lieutenant, August 14, 1861, with rank from August 7, 1861, original.

38. BARNHARDT, PETER—Age, 32 years. Enlisted, August 4, 1862, at Verona, to serve three years; mustered in as private, Company E, September 4, 1862; killed, December 13, 1862, at the battle of Fredericksburg, Va.; also listed as Peter Bernhard.

39. BARNHOST GEORGE H.—Age, 21 years. Enlisted, May 7, 1861, at Utica, to serve, two years; mustered in as private, Company E, May 21, 1861; promoted corporal in May 1862; discharged for disability, October 30, 1862, at Hammond General Hospital, Point Lookout, Md.

40. BARNS, GEORGE H.—Age, 21 years. Enlisted, May 7, 1861, at Utica, to serve two years; mustered in as private, Company E, May 21, 1861; mustered out with company, May 28, 1863, at Utica, N.Y.; also listed as George Barnes.

41. BARNUM, EDWARD—Age, 21 years. Enlisted, November 12, 1861, at Buffalo, to serve two years; mustered in as private, Company D, November 20, 1861; deserted, May 7, 1862, place not stated.

42. BARRELL, JOSEPH R.—Age, 21 years. Enlisted, September 27, 1861, at Buffalo, to serve two years; mustered in as private, Company K, same date; deserted, August 13, 1862, at Culpeper, Va.; also listed as Joseph M. Barrell.

43. BARRETT, ELVIN A.—Age, 19 years. Enlisted, October 19, 1861, at Rochester, to serve three years; mustered in as private, Company G, same date; mustered out with company, May 28, 1863, at Utica, N.Y.

44. BARRETT, JAMES M.—Age, 19 years. Enlisted, May 14, 1861, at Camden, to serve two years; mustered in as private, Company K, May 21, 1861; wounded at battle of Second Bull Run, Va.; August 30, 1862; discharged on account of such wounds, December 11, 1862, at Washington, D.C.

45. BARTON, JOSHUA—Age, 18 years. Enlisted, May 7, 1861, at Utica, to serve two years; mustered in as private, Company E, May 21, 1861; mustered out with company, May 28, 1863; at Utica, N.Y.; subsequent service in Company C, Fourteenth Artillery.

46. BASCOM, CHARLES—Age, 20 years. Enlisted, October 19, 1861, at Rochester, to serve two years; mustered in as private, Company C, October 24, 1861; wounded, August 30, 1862, at battle of Second Bull Run, Va.; mustered out with company, May 28, 1863, at Utica, N.Y.

47. BASHORK, JACOB—Age, 22 years. Enlisted, May 7, 1861, at Utica, to serve two years; mustered in as private, Company E, May 21, 1861; promoted corporal, November 1, 1861; mustered out with company May 28, 1863, at Utica, N.Y.; also listed as Jacob Barnhart and Bernhard.

48. BASS, HANFORD—Age, 22 years. Enlisted, October 19, 1861, at Rochester, to serve two years; mustered in as private, Company C, October 21, 1861; mustered out with company, May 28, 1863, at Utica, N.Y.; also listed as Sanford Bass.

49. BATCHELOR, JAMES—Age, 18 years. Enlisted, February 18, 1862, at Utica, to serve three years; mustered in as private, Company F, March 27, 1862; died of disease, December 15, 1862, at Stanton Hospital, Washington, D.C.

50. BATES, SABIN T.—Age, 30 years. Enlisted, May 7, 1861, at Utica, to serve two years; mustered in as private, Company D, May 21, 1861; promoted corporal, date not stated reduced, November 11, 1861; wounded, December 13, 1862, at battle of Fredericksburg, Va.; mustered out with company May 28, 1863, at Utica, N.Y.

51. BAUER, FREDERICK—Age, 20 years. Enlisted, May 2, 1861, at Rochester, to serve two years; mustered in as private, Company G, May 21, 1861; mustered out with company, May 28, 1863, at Utica, N.Y.

52. BAUN, CHARLES—Age, 36 years. Enlisted August 3, 1861, at Rochester, to serve three years; mustered in as private, Company I, August 9, 1861; wounded, December 11, 1862, at battle of Fredericksburg, Va.; died, January 6, 1863 at Lincoln Military Hospital, Washington, D.C.

53. BEECH, CHARLES E.—Age, 22 years. Enlisted, May 7, 1861, at Utica, to serve two years; mustered in as private, Company E, May 21, 1861; promoted corporal, January 11, 1862; mustered out with company, May 28, 1863, at Utica, N.Y.; also listed as Charles Beach.

54. BEEMAN, WILLIAM H.—Age, 27 years. Enlisted, May 7, 1861, at Utica, to serve two years; mustered in as private, Company E, May 21, 1861; mustered out with company May 28, 1863, at Utica, N.Y.; also listed as William Beeman.

55. BEERS, BENJAMIN B.—Age, 40 years. Enlisted, July 29, 1861, at Rochester, to serve three years; mustered in as private, unassigned August 9, 1861; deserted, August 11, 1861, place not stated.

56. BELL, FREDERICK—Age, 21 years. Enlisted, May 3, 1861, at Utica, to serve two years; mustered in as private, Co, F, May 21, 1861; deserted, November 8, 1861, at Camp Franklin, Va.

57. BELL, GEORGE—Age, 18 years. Enlisted, September 30, 1861, at Rochester, to serve three years; mustered in as private, Company F, same date; wounded, December 11, 1862, at battle of Fredericksburg, Va.; mustered out with company May 28, 1863, at Utica, N.Y.; subsequent service in Company H, Twenty-Fourth Cavalry.

58. BENEDICT, SAMUEL B.—Age, — years. Enlisted, May 2, 1861, at Elmira, to serve two years; mustered in as principal musician, May 21, 1861; discharged; November 2, 1862, at Purcellville, Va.

59. BENJAMIN, DAVID W.—Age, 27 years. Enlisted, May 2, 1861, at Rochester, to serve two years; mustered in as private, Company G, May 21, 1861; wounded, December 13, 1862, at battle of Fredericksburg, Va., and died same day, of such wounds.

60. BENJAMIN, JOHN—Age, 21 years. Enlisted, May 13, 1861, at Utica, to serve two years; mustered in as private, Company I, May 21, 1861; captured, August 29, 1862, at Manassas, Va.; paroled, September 8, 1862, at Manassas or Charlestown; mustered out with company, May 28, 1863, at Utica, N.Y.

61. BENJAMIN, OLIVER D.—Age, 20 years. Enlisted, May 3, 1861, at Utica, to serve two years; mustered in as sergeant, Company F, May 21, 1861; reduced, June 1, 1862; deserted, September 16, 1862, at Antietam, Md.

62. BENNETT, PATRICK—Age, 30 years. Enlisted, May 2, 1861, at Rochester, to serve two years; mustered in as private, Company O, May 21, 1861; discharged, July

16, 1863, at Albany, N.Y.; subsequent service in Company C, Twenty-First Cavalry.

63. BENSCHOTEN, HIRAM—Age, 21 years. Enlisted, September 24, 1861, at Utica, to serve three years; mustered in as private, unassigned, same date; no further record.

64. BENSON, JOHN J.—Age, 23 years. Enlisted, May 13, 1861, at Utica, to serve two years; mustered in as private, Company I, May 21, 1861; mustered out with company, May 28, 1863, at Utica, N.Y.

65. BERGER, ANTHONY—Age, 39 years. Enlisted, May 16, 1861, at Utica, to serve two years; mustered in as private, Company E, May 21, 1861; mustered out with company, May 28, 1863, at Utica, N.Y.; also listed as Anthony Barker.

BERNHARD—see Barnhard, Barnhort and Barhork.

66. BERTON, STEPHEN—Age, 19 years. Enlisted, May 1, 1861, at Utica, to serve two years; mustered in as private, Company B, May 21, 1861; mustered out with company, May 28, 1863, at Utica, N.Y. Also listed as Stephen Burton.

67. BESWICK, JOHN D.—Age, 18 years. Enlisted, August 14, 1861, at Rome, to serve three years; mustered in as private, Company I, August 20, 1861; mustered out with company, May 28, 1863, at Utica, N.Y.

68. BESWICK, THOMAS—Age, 19 years. Enlisted, May 1, 1861, at Utica, to serve two years; mustered in as corporal, Company A, May 21, 1861; reduced, September 16, 1861; discharged for disability, February 1, 1862, at Fort Lyon, Va.

69. BEVERGE, THOMAS—Age, 20 years. Enlisted, May 3, 1861, at Utica, to serve two years; mustered in as corporal, Company F, May 21, 1861; promoted sergeant, November 9, 1861; wounded, date not stated, at battle of Second Bull Run, Va.; discharged for disability, October 7, 1862, at Philadelphia, Pa.; also listed as Thomas Beveridge.

70. BEVINES, JOHN—Age, 27 years. Enrolled, August 30, 1862, at Utica, to serve three years; mustered in as second lieutenant, Company A, November 24, 1862; mustered out with company, May 28, 1863, at Utica, N.Y.; commissioned second lieutenant, November 24, 1862, with rank from August 30, 1862, vice Jones, promoted.

71. BEVINS, JOHN—Age, 25 years. Enrolled, May 3, 1861, at Utica, to serve three months; mustered in as second lieutenant, Company F, May 21, 1861; resigned, August 8, 1861; also listed as John Bevine; commissioned second lieutenant July 4, 1861, with rank from May 3, 1861, original.

72. BINDER, FRANK L.—Age, 22 years. Enrolled, May 2, 1861, at Rochester, to serve—years; mustered in as second lieutenant, Company G, May 21, 1861 as first lieutenant, August 7, 1861; as captain, to date, October 1, 1862; mustered out with company, May 28, 1863, at Utica, N.Y.; commissioned second lieutenant, July 4, 1861, with rank from May 18, 1861; original; first lieutenant, August 14, 1861, with rank from August 7, 1861; original; captain, November 7, 1862, with rank from October 1, 1862, vice C. E. Jennings, resigned.

BINGHAM, L. M.—Acted as paymaster in the state service from May 1861, to July 1861. Not commissioned and not mustered in.

73. BIXLER, MARTIN—Age, 27 years. Enlisted, July 31, 1861, at Rochester, to serve three years; mustered in as private, Company I, August 7, 1861; discharged for disability, August 6, 1862, at General Hospital, Fairfax Seminary; also listed as Martin V. Bixier.

BLACK, HIRAM—see Balch, Hiram.

74. BLACK, JOHN—Age, 33 years. Enlisted May 1, 1861, at Utica, to serve two years; mustered in as private, Company A, May 21, 1861; died, September 8, 1862, at Trinity Hospital, of gunshot wound in thigh.

75. BLACKMAN, ANDREW W.—Age, 27 years. Enlisted, May 1, 1861, at Utica, to serve two years; mustered in as private, Company A, May 21, 1861; discharged for disability, November 14, 1862, at Utica, N.Y.

76. BLACKWELL, GEORGE A.—Age, 22 years. Enrolled, May 1, 1861, at Utica, to serve two years; mustered in as captain, Company B, May 21, 1861; resigned, April 2, 1862; again enlisted, February 10, 1863, as captain, Company F, at Albany, N.Y.; mustered out with company, May 28, 1863, at Utica, N.Y.; commissioned captain, July 4, 1861, with rank from May 1, 1861, original; again commissioned captain, December 26, 1862, with rank of same date, vice Wetmore, promoted.

77. BLACKWELL, WILLIAM B.—Age, 23 years. Enrolled, May 17, 1861, at Utica, to serve two years; mustered in as quartermaster, May 21, 1861; resigned, October 30, 1862; commissioned quartermaster, August 27, 1861, with rank from May 17, 1861, original.

78. BLAIR, ALEXANDER—Age, 21 years. Enlisted, May 2, 1861, at Rochester, to serve two years; mustered in as private, Company H, May 21, 1861; mustered out with company, May 28, 1863, at Utica, N.Y.

79. BLAKENEY, ISAAC—Age, 22 years. Enlisted, October 22, 1861, at Rochester, to serve unexpired term; mustered in as second-class musician, same date; mustered out with band, September 4, 1862, at Upton's Hill, Va.

80. BLAKENEY, SAMUEL—Age, 25 years. Enlisted, May 21, 1861, at Rochester, to serve three months; mustered in as second-class musician, same date; mustered out with band, September 10, 1861, at Fort Ellsworth, Va.; again enlisted as first-class musician, October 14, 1861, for three years, at Rochester, N.Y.; mustered out with band, September 4, 1862, at Upton's Hill, Va.

81. BLANCHARD, SIMON Jr.—Age, 25 years. Enlisted, May 14, 1861, at Camden, to serve two years; mustered in as private, Company K, May 21, 1861; deserted, April 30, 1862, at Fort Lyon, Va.

82. BLATT, JOHN—Age, 40 years. Enlisted, August 22, 1862, at Utica, to serve three years; mustered in as private, Company E, same date; transferred, May 7, 1863, to Company B, Eighty-Third Infantry; also listed as John Platt.

83. BLISS, WILLIAM H.—Age, 19 years. Enlisted, May 3, 1861, at Utica, to serve two years; mustered in as private, Company F, May 21, 1861; promoted corporal, July 3, 1862; mustered out with company, May 28, 1863, at Utica, N.Y.

84. BOLAND, JOHN—Age, 23 years. Enlisted, July 29, 1861, at Rochester, to serve three years; mustered in as private, unassigned, August 9, 1861; deserted, August 16, 1861, place not stated.

85. BOOTH, WAKEFIELD—Age, 23 years. Enlisted, May 14, 1861, at Camden, to serve two years; mustered in as corporal, Company K, May 21, 1861; promoted sergeant, August 7, 1861; mustered out with company, May 28, 1863, Utica, N.Y.

86. BOSS, JEREMIAH—Age, 18 years. Enlisted, May 13, 1861, at Utica, to serve two years; mustered in as private, Company I, May 21, 1861; wounded at battle of Fredericksburg, Va., December 13, 1862; mustered out with company, May 28, 1863, at Utica, N.Y.

87. BOWEN, WILLIAM E.—Age, 20 years. Enlisted, May 7, 1861, at Utica, to serve two years; mustered in as private, Company E, May 21, 1861; mustered out with company, May 28, 1863, at, Utica, N.Y.; subsequent service in Company C, Fourteenth Artillery.

88. BRACE, CHARLES—Age, 19 years. Enlisted, May 14, 1861, at Camden, to serve two years; mustered in as private, Company K, May 21, 1861; killed, August 30, 1862, at battle of Second Bull Run, Va.

89. BRADFORD, JOSEPH—Age, 31 years. Enlisted, September 3, 1861, at Utica, to serve two years; mustered in as private, Company C, September 5, 1861; deserted, May 7, 1862, at Brook's Station, Va.

90. BRADLEY, GEORGE S.—Age, 20 years. Enlisted, May 7, 1861, at Utica, to serve two years; mustered in as private, Company D, May 21, 1861; promoted corporal, August 30, 1862; mustered out with company, May 28, 1863, at Utica, N.Y.; subsequent service in Third Artillery.

91. BRADLEY, MORTIMER—Age, 22 years. Enlisted, August 3, 1861, at Rochester, to serve three years; mustered in as private, Company F, August 9, 1861; wounded, date and place not stated; mustered out with company, May 28, 1863, at Utica, N.Y.; also listed as Mortimer L. Bradley.

92. BRADY, JAMES—Age, 24 years. Enlisted, August 22, 1861, at Rochester, to serve three years; mustered in as private Company H, September 5, 1861; mustered out with company, May 28, 1863, at Utica, N.Y.; subsequent service in Company G, First Veteran Cavalry.

93. BRANCH, EDWIN A.—Age, 31 years. Enlisted, July 7, 1861, at Elmira, to serve two years; mustered in as private, Company I, same date; discharged for disability, December 15, 1861, at Fort Lyon, Va.

94. BRESTEL, WILLIAM HENRY—

Age, 22 years. Enlisted, May 8, 1861, at Elmira, to serve two years; mustered in as private, Company E, May 21, 1861; mustered out with company, May 28, 1863, at Utica, N.Y.; also listed as William H. Prestele.

95. BREVOURT, NAPOLEON—Age, 21 years. Enlisted, May 3, 1861, at Utica, to serve two years; mustered in as private, Company F, May 21, 1861; promoted corporal, December 14, 1862; mustered out with company, May 28, 1863, at Utica, N.Y.

96. BREWER, NICHOLAS—Age, 21 years. Enlisted, May 3, 1861, at Utica, to serve two years; mustered in as private Company C, May 21, 1861; mustered out with company, May 28, 1863, Utica, N.Y.; also listed as Nicholas E. Brewer

97. BREWER, OLIVER—Age, 26 years. Enlisted, September 16, 1861, at Buffalo, to serve three years; mustered in as private, Company C, September 16, 1861; mustered out with company, May 28, 1863, at Utica N.Y.; also listed as Oliva Brewer.

98. BRIGGS, JAMES—Age, 35 years. Enlisted, May 1, 1861, at Utica, to serve two years; mustered in as private, Company A, May 21, 1861; wounded, December 13, 1862, at battle of Fredericksburg, Va.; died, December 26, 1862, at Armory Square Hospital.

99. BRIGGS, LEMUEL—Age, 23 years. Enlisted, September 16, 1861, at Buffalo, to serve three years; mustered in as private, Company D, September 16, 1861; transferred to Company B, November 1, 1861; deserted, November 7, 1861, at Camp Franklin, Va.

100. BRIGHAM, GEORGE H.—Age, 18 years. Enlisted, May 1, 1861, at Utica, to serve two years; mustered in as private, Company A, May 21, 1861; promoted corporal, February 20, 1862; sergeant, October 2, 1862; mustered out with company, May 28, 1863, at Utica, N.Y.

101. BRINDLE, ANTON—Age, 50 years. Enrolled, May 7, 1861, at Utica, to serve three months; mustered in as captain, Company E, May 21, 1861; discharged, August 7, 1861; commissioned captain, July 4, 1861, with rank from May 7, 1861, original.

102. BRINK, JOSHUA—Age, 28 years. Enlisted, May 14, 1861, at Camden, to serve three months; mustered in as private, Company K, May 21, 1861; deserted, June 1, 1861, at Elmira, N.Y.

103. BRISTOL, ADOLPHUS—Age, 40 years. Enlisted, August 13, 1861, at Rochester, to serve three years; mustered in as private, Company C, September 5, 1861; mustered out with company, May 28, 1863, at Utica, N.Y.

104. BRISTOL, DANIEL W.—Age, — years. Enrolled, September 27, 1861, at Utica, to serve two years; mustered in as chaplain, September 27, 1861; resigned, January 3, 1863; commissioned chaplain, October 18, 1861, with rank from September 27, 1861, vice Ira Smith, resigned.

105. BRITTON, ADAM—Age, 24 years. Enlisted, May 2, 1861, at Rochester, to serve two years; mustered in as private, Company H, May 21, 1861; killed, December 13, 1862, at battle of Fredericksburg, Va.

106. BROOKS, BENJAMIN J.—Age, 23 years. Enlisted, May 14, 1861, at Camden, to serve two years; mustered in as first sergeant, Company K, May 21, 1861; reduced, July 31, 1861; wounded, August 30, 1862, at battle of Second Bull Run; discharged for disability, December 28, 1862, at Fort Lyon, Va.

107. BROWN, CHARLES B.—Age, 23 years. Enlisted, December 22, 1861, at Geneva, to serve unexpired term of two years; mustered in as private, unassigned, January 3, 1862; no further record.

108. BROWN, EDWIN T.—Age, 24 years. Enlisted, May 1, 1861, at Utica, to serve two years; mustered in as sergeant, Company B, May 21, 1861; reduced, September 29, 1861; discharged for disability, February 16, 1863, at Armory Square Hospital, Washington, D.C.

109. BROWN, EUGENE—Age, 23 years. Enlisted, May 1, 1861, at Utica, to serve two years; mustered in as private, Company A, May 2, 1861; promoted corporal, February 20, 1862; reduced, date not stated; mustered out with company, May 28, 1863, at Utica, N.Y.; also listed as Eugene H. Brown; subsequent service in Twenty-Fourth Cavalry.

110. BROWN, HENRY—Age, 21 years. Enlisted, May 28, 1861, at Elmira, to serve two years; mustered in as private, Company B, May 2, 1861; deserted, June 1, 1862, on the march.

111. BROWN, JOHN K.—Age, 19 years. Enlisted, October 24, 1861, at Rochester, to

serve three years; mustered in as private, Company C, October 24, 1861; mustered out with company, May 28, 1863, at Utica, N.Y.; also listed as John R. Brown.

112. BROWN, MELVIN—Age, 27 years. Enrolled, May 2, 1861, at Rochester, to serve two years; mustered in as first lieutenant, Company H, May 21, 1861; as captain, Company B, April 2, 1862; resigned, July 24, 1862; also listed as W. Melvin Brown; commissioned first lieutenant, July 4, 1861, with rank from May 2, 1861, original; captain, April 9, 1862, with rank from April 2, 1862, vice George A. Blackwell, resigned.

113. BROWN, MORRIS A.—Age, 21 years. Enlisted, May 7, 1861, at Utica, to serve two years; mustered in as private, Company D, May 21, 1861; mustered out with company May 28, 1863, at Utica, N.Y.

114. BROWN, ROBERT—Age, 27 years. Enlisted, May 2, 1861, at Rochester, to serve two years; mustered in as private, Company H, May 21, 1861; mustered out, May 24, 1863, at Utica, N.Y.

115. BROWN, WILLIAM—Age, 23 years. Enlisted, May 3, 1861, at Elmira, to serve two years; mustered in as private, Company B, May 21, 1861; promoted sergeant, September 29, 1861; transferred to Company A, February 10, 1862; back to Company B, November 23, 1862; no further record; also listed as William T. Brown; subsequent service, in Company C, Sixteenth Artillery.

116. BRYDEN, MATHEW—Age, 22 years. Enlisted, May 3, 1861, at Utica, to serve two years; mustered in as corporal, Company F, May 21, 1861; reduced, date not stated; deserted, June 19, 1862, Manassas, Va.; subsequently enlisted (May 11, 1864) in Company C, Nineteenth United States Infantry.

117. BUDDLE, WILLIAM T.—Age, 38 years. Enlisted, May 1, 1861, at Utica, to serve two years; mustered in as sergeant, Company A, May 21, 1861; discharged for disability, June 21, 1862, at Washington, D.C.

118. BURCH, PHILO H.—Age, 29 years. Enlisted, December 5, 1861, at Rome, to serve unexpired term of two years; mustered in as private, Company A, December 11, 1861; discharged for disability, February 23, 1863, at Emory Hospital; also listed as Philo Burch; subsequent service in Third Artillery.

119. BURDICK, OSCAR—Age, 20 years. Enlisted, May 13, 1861, at Utica, to serve two years; mustered in as private, Company I, May 21, 1861; wounded, December 1862, at battle of Fredericksburg, Va.; mustered out with company, May 28, 1863, at Utica, N.Y.

120. BURGAN, JAMES—Age, 22 years. Enlisted, May 21, 1861, at Elmira, to serve three months; mustered in as private, Company K, May 21, 1861; no further record.

121. BURNES, PETER—Age, 22 years. Enlisted, November 12, 1861, at Utica, to serve unexpired term of two years; mustered in as private, Company I, November 22, 1861; wounded, December 13, 1862, at battle of Fredericksburg, Va.; discharged for disability, December 23, 1862, at Smoke House Hospital, Md.

122. BURNHAM, EDWARD—Age, 19 years. Enlisted, May 14, 1861, at Elmira, to serve two years; mustered in as corporal, Company I, May 21, 1861; promoted sergeant, date not stated; mustered out with company, May 28, 1863, at Utica, N.Y.; subsequent service, Company F, Eighth Artillery.

123. BURNIE, WILLIAM—Age, 21 years. Enlisted, May 28, 1861, at Elmira, to serve two years; mustered in as private, Company B, same date; promoted corporal, March 1, 1862; wounded at battle of Fredericksburg, Va., December 13, 1862; mustered out with company, May 28, 1863, at Utica, N.Y.

124. BURNS, MICHAEL C.—Age, 20 years. Enlisted, May 3, 1861, at Utica, to serve two years; mustered in as private, Company F, May 21, 1861; promoted corporal, July 3, 1862; sergeant, May 1, 1863; mustered out with company, May 28, 1863, at Utica, N.Y.; also listed as Michael Burns.

125. BURR, WALTER H.—Age, 21 years. Enlisted, August 28, 1861, at Utica, to serve two years; mustered in as private Company K, September 2, 1861; promoted corporal, April 22, 1863; mustered out with company, May 28, 1863, at Utica, N.Y.

126. BURROWS, JABEZ T.—Age, 29 years. Enlisted, May 13, 1861, at Utica, to serve two years; mustered in as private, Company I, May 21, 1861; deserted, January 29, 1862, at Fort Lyon, Va.

127. BURTON, GEORGE—Age, — years. Enlisted, August 28, 1861, place not stated, to serve—years; mustered. in as private, Company K, date not stated; dropped; no further record.

128. BURTON, HEBRON—Age, 19 years. Enlisted, October 1, 1861, at Rome, to serve three years; mustered in as private, Company K, same date; mustered out with company, May 28, 1863, at Utica, N.Y.; subsequent service, Third Artillery.

BURTON, STEPHEN—see Berton, Stephen.

129. BURTON, WILLIAM—Age, 36 years. Enlisted, September 20, 1861, at Rome, to serve 19 months; mustered in as private, Company K, September 20, 1861; wounded at battle of Second Bull Run, Va., August 30, 1862; mustered out with company, May 28, 1863, at Utica, N.Y.

130. BUSHNELL, JOHN—Age, 29 years. Enlisted, December 10, 1861, at Rochester, to serve two years; mustered in as private, Company H, December 12, 1861; mustered out with company, May 28, 1863, at Utica, N.Y.; subsequent service, Company K, Fourth Artillery.

131. BUSKERK, GEORGE—Age, 21 years. Enlisted, August 3, 1861, at Utica, to serve two years; mustered in as private, Company C, September 2, 1861; discharged for disability, November 10, 1862, at Alexandria, Va.; subsequent service, Third Artillery.

132. BUTLER, JONAS—Age, 24 years. Enlisted, May 2, 1861, at Rochester, to serve two years; mustered in as private, Company H, May 21, 1861; dropped, September 14, 1862, since the battle of South Mountain.

133. BYSHIM, JUSTUS—Age, 26 years. Enlisted, October 18, 1861, at Rochester, to serve unexpired term of two years; mustered in as first-class musician, same date; mustered out with band, September 4, 1862, at Upton's Hill, Va.

134. CACKETT, THOMAS—Age, 22 years. Enlisted, May 13, 1861, at Utica, to serve two years; mustered in as corporal, Company I, May 21, 1861; promoted color sergeant, date not stated; captured, August 30, 1862, at Bull Run, Va.; paroled, August 31, 1862, at Gainesville, Va.; mustered out with regiment, May 28, 1863, at Utica, N.Y.

135. CADWELL, EGBERT D.—Age, 20 years. Enlisted, May 14, 1861, at Camden, to serve two years; mustered in as private, Company K, May 21, 1861; wounded, date not stated; mustered out with company, May 28, 1863, at Utica, N.Y.

136. CAISY, PHILLIP—Age, 27 years. Enlisted, May 2, 1861, at Rochester, to serve three months; mustered in as private, Company H, May 21, 1861; deserted, August 20, 1861, at Alexandria, Va.; also listed as Phillip Casey.

137. CALAGIN, JAMES—Age, 33 years. Enlisted, November 9, 1861, at Rochester, to serve three years; mustered in as private, Company H, November 12, 1861; mustered out with company, May 28, 1863, at Utica, N.Y.; also listed as James Callahan.

138. CALMAN, TIMOTHY—Age, 22 years. Enlisted, May 2, 1861, at Rochester, to serve two years; mustered in as private, Company H, May 21, 1861; discharged for disability, March 27, 1863, caused by a pistol shot in knee, received by the accidental discharge of a pistol while in the hands of a comrade; also listed as Timothy Calnan.

139. CAMERON, ALEXANDER—Age, 18 years. Enlisted, May 7, 1861, at Utica, to serve two years; mustered in as private, Company E, May 21, 1861; killed, August 30, 1862, at battle of Second Bull Run, Va.

140. CAMERON, LEWIS B.—Age, 34 years. Enlisted, July 30, 1861, at Rochester, to serve three years; mustered in as private, Company I, August 9, 1861; died, February 19, 1862, at Regimental Hospital, Fort Lyon, Va.; also listed as Lewis Cameron.

141. CAMPBELL, ALEXANDRIA—Age, 24 years. Enlisted, May 8, 1861, at Elmira, to serve two years; mustered in as private, Company E, May 21, 1861; mustered out with company, May 28, 1863, at Utica, N.Y.; subsequent service, Twenty-Fourth Cavalry.

142. CAMPBELL, ALEXANDER—Age, 32 years. Enlisted, July 3, 1861, at Rochester, to serve three years; mustered in as private, Company G, August 9, 1861; promoted corporal, date not stated; wounded, December 13, 1862, at battle of Fredericksburg, Va.; mustered out with company, May 28, 1863, at Utica, N.Y.

143. CAMPBELL, JAMES W.—Age, 29 years. Enlisted, September 30, 1861, at

Buffalo, to serve 19 months; mustered in as private, Company K, same date; wounded, August 30, 1862, at battle of Second Bull Run, Va.; also at Bull Run, Va.; discharged for disability, February 10, 1863, at Philadelphia, Pa.

144. CAMPION, WILLIAM—Age, 18 years. Enlisted, May 1, 1861, at Utica, to serve two years; mustered in as private, Company A, May 21, 1861; wounded, date not stated; mustered out with company, May 28, 1863, at Utica, N.Y.; subsequent service in Company A, Tenth Artillery; also listed as William J. Campion.

145. CANNON, JOHN—Age, 28 years. Enlisted, May 2, 1861, at Rochester, to serve two years; mustered in as private, Company G, May 21, 1861; mustered out with company, May 28, 1863, at Utica, N.Y.; also listed as John Canay.

146. CAPRON, AUGUSTUS—Age, 35 years. Enlisted, June 1, 1861, at Elmira, to serve two years; mustered in as private, Company G, same date; discharged, June 1, 1863, at Utica, N.Y.

147. CAREY, MORRIS A.—Age, 21 years. Enlisted, November 16, 1861, at Utica, to serve two years; mustered in as private, Company B, November 20, 1861; discharged, January 7, 1864, at Convalescent Camp, Va.

148. CARMAN, JOHN S.—Age, 22 years. Enlisted, June 2, 1861, at Elmira, to serve two years; mustered in as private, Company D, same date; deserted, August 9, 1861, at Alexandria, Va.

149. CARNEY, JOHN—Age, 20 years. Enlisted, May 3, 1861, at Utica, to serve two years; mustered in as private, Company C, May 21, 1861; promoted corporal, September 4, 1861; sergeant, April 4, 1862; reduced, January 10, 1863; mustered out with company, May 28, 1863, at Utica, N.Y.; also listed as John Kainey.

150. CARPENTER, HENRY—Age, 28 years. Enlisted, May 2, 1861, at Rochester, to serve two years; mustered in as private, Company G, May 21, 1861; mustered out with company, May 28, 1863, at Utica, N.Y.; also listed as Henry B. Carpenter; subsequent service in Company H, Twenty-First Cavalry.

151. CARRALL, JOSEPH—Age, 18 years. Enlisted, May 1, 1861, at Utica, to serve two years; mustered in as private, Company A, May 2, 1861; discharged for disability, November 11, 1861, at Camp Franklin, Va.

152. CARRIGAN, JOHN—Age, 22 years. Enlisted, May 7, 1861, at Utica, to serve two years; mustered in as private; Company D, May 21, 1861; mustered out with company, May 28, 1863, at Utica, N.Y.; also listed as John Corrigan.

153. CARRIGAN, MICHAEL—Age, 22 years. Enlisted, May 7, 1861, at Utica, to serve two years; mustered in as private, Company D, May 21, 1861; mustered out with company, May 28, 1863, at Utica, N.Y.; subsequent service in Seventh Independent Battery as Corrigan.

154. CARROLL, TORRENCE—Age, 24 years. Enlisted, December 20, 1861, at Geneseo, to serve two years; mustered in as private, unassigned, January 3, 1861; no further record.

155. CARTER, AMOS—Age, 18 years. Enlisted, May 3, 1861, at Utica, to serve two years; mustered in as private, Company F, May 21, 1861; mustered out with company, May 28, 1863, at Utica, N.Y.; subsequent service in Company A, Sixteenth Artillery.

156. CARTER, LUTHER—Age, 23 years. Enlisted, May 1, 1861, at Utica, to serve two years; mustered in as private, Company B, May 21, 1861; discharged for disability, July 16, 1862, at Warrenton, Va.

157. CARYL, JAMES B.—Age, 31 years. Enrolled, May 14, 1861, at Camden, to serve two years; mustered in as captain, Company K, May 21, 1861; dismissed, March 11, 1863, by sentence of general court-martial; subsequent service in Sixteenth Artillery; commissioned captain, July 4, 1861, with rank from May 14, 1861, original.

CASEY, PHILLIP—*see* Caisy, Phillip.

158. CASSETY, SHERMAN P.—Age, 39 years. Enlisted, May 3, 1861, at Utica, to serve two years; mustered in as private, Company F, May 21, 1861; mustered out with company, May 28, 1863, at Utica, N.Y.; also listed as Sherman Caserty; subsequent service in Company A, Sixteenth Artillery.

159. CHANDLER, SILAS—Age, 45 years. Enlisted, September 23, 1861, at Utica, to serve three years; mustered in as private, Company F, same date; discharged

for disability, March 20, 1863, at Baltimore, Md.

160. CHANDLER, SILAS E.—Age, 18 years. Enlisted, May 3, 1861, at Utica, to serve two years; mustered in as private, Company F, May 21, 1861, killed, August 30, 1862, at battle of Second Bull Run, Va.

161. CHAPMAN, EDWARD—Age, 35 years. Enlisted, May 1, 1861, at Utica, to serve two years; mustered in as private, Company B, June 19, 1861; promoted corporal, August 24, 1861; sergeant, date not stated; sergeant major, August 30, 1862; discharged, June 9, 1863, at Albany, N.Y.; subsequent service in Forty-Second Infantry; commissioned second lieutenant, May 13, 1863, with rank from April 20, 1863, vice W. H. Halstead, promoted; not mustered.

162. CHAPMAN, SAMUEL—Age, 20 years. Enlisted, May 3, 1861, at Utica, to serve two years; mustered in as private, Company F, May 21, 1861, transferred to Company D, July 30, 1861; discharged, June 26, 1862.

163. CHAPMAN, WILLIAM—Age, 35 years. Enlisted, date not stated, at Utica, to serve three years; mustered in as private, Company I, August 7, 1861; discharged for disability, January 31, 1862, at Fort Lyon, Va.

164. CHARLES, EDWARD F.—Age, 27 years. Enlisted, May 2, 1861, at Rochester, to serve two years; mustered in as private, Company H, May 21, 1861; discharged for disability, October 12, 1862, at Carver Hospital, Washington, D.C.; subsequent service in Company L, Fourth Artillery.

165. CHATTERDON, EDWIN F.—Age, 22 years. Enlisted, January 11, 1862, at Rochester, to serve two years; mustered in as private, unassigned, same date; discharged, January 27, 1862.

166. CHERNY, GEORGE—Age, 19 years. Enlisted, July 24, 1861, at Rochester, to serve three years; mustered in as private, Company G, August 9, 1861; deserted, June 19, 1862, at Manassas, Va.

167. CHICHESTER, JOHN—Age, 23 years. Enlisted, September 13, 1861, at Buffalo, to serve three years; mustered in as private, unassigned, same date; no further record.

168. CHILDS, GEORGE F.—Age, 32 years. Enlisted, May 2, 1861, at Rochester, to serve two years; mustered in as private, Company H, May 21, 1861; transferred to Company A, February 24, 1862; discharged, August 6, 1862, by court-martial.

169. CHILLAID, BENEDICT—Age, 43 years. Enlisted, August 5, 1861, at Rochester, to serve three years; mustered in as private, unassigned, same date; no further record.

170. CHRISTIAN, WILLIAM H.—Age, 36 years. Enrolled, May 17, 1861, at Elmira, to serve three months; mustered in as colonel, May 21, 1861; resigned, September 19, 1862, at Sharpsburg, Md.; commissioned colonel, June 20, 1861, with rank from May 17, 1861, original. Died May 8, 1887, at New York State Lunatic Asylum.

171. CHURCH, WILLIAM H.—Age, 31 years. Enlisted, May 3, 1861, at Utica, to serve—years; mustered in as corporal, Company C, May 21, 1861, promoted sergeant, July 20, 1861; first sergeant, November 7, 1861; mustered as captain, Company B, July 24, 1862; resigned, November 14, 1862; commissioned captain, August 30, 1862, with rank from July 24, 1862, vice Brown, resigned while under charges.

172. CINAMON, PETER—Age, 41 years. Enlisted, May 14, 1861, at Camden, to serve two years; mustered in as private, Company K, May 21, 1861; mustered out with company, May 28, 1863, at Utica, N.Y.

173. CLANCY, JOHN—Age, 32 years. Enlisted, May 3, 1861, at Utica, to serve two years; mustered in as private, Company A, May 21, 1861; killed, August 30, 1862, at Bull Run, Va.

174. CLANCY, JOHN—Age, 22 years. Enlisted, May 4, 1861, at Elmira, to serve two years; mustered in as private, Company H, May 21, 1861; discharged for disability, October 14, 1861, at Camp Franklin, Va.

175. CLANCY, JOHN B.—Age, 20 years. Enlisted, May 2, 1861, at Rochester, to serve two years; mustered in as corporal, Company H, May 21, 1861; discharged for disability, July 3, 1862, at Manassas, Va.

176. CLARK, ADAM—Age, 41 years. Enlisted, October 22, 1861, at Rochester, to serve three years; mustered in as private, Company B, October 22, 1861; mustered out with company, May 28, 1863, at Utica, N.Y.

177. CLARK, GEORGE—Age, 22 years. Enlisted, May 7, 1861, at Utica, to serve three months; mustered in as private, Company

D, May 21, 1861; deserted, June 20, 1861, at Elmira, N.Y.

178. CLARK, GEORGE W.—Age, 22 years; Enlisted, May 13, 1861, at Utica, to serve two years; mustered in as private, Company D , May 21, 1861; wounded, August 30, 1862; promoted corporal, November 1, 1862; died, December 21, 1862, at General Hospital, Alexandria, Va.

179. CLARK, HENRY A.—Age, 27 years. Enlisted, September 9, 1861, at Utica, to serve two years; mustered in as private, Company F, September 17, 1861; mustered out with company, May 28, 1863, at Utica, N.Y.; also listed as Henry Clark.

180. CLARK, HENRY C.—Age, 19 years. Enlisted, May 13, 1861, at Utica, to serve three months; mustered in as private, Company I, May 21, 1861; deserted, July 21, 1861, at Washington, D.C.

181. CLARK, JOHN W.—Age, 19 years. Enlisted, May 1, 1861, at Utica, to serve two years; mustered in as private, Company A, May 21, 1861; promoted, corporal, August 1, 1861; discharged February 20, 1862.

182. CLARKE, CHARLES H.—Age, 21 years. Enlisted, May 3, 1861, at Utica, to serve two years; mustered in as private, Company F, May 21, 1861; killed, September 17, 1862, at Antietam, Md.; also listed as Charles A. Clark.

183. CLEARY, JAMES—Age, 26 years. Enlisted, February 20, 1862, at Rochester, to serve three years; mustered in as private, Company F, March 27, 1862; deserted, August 9, 1862, at Cedar Mountain, Va.

184. CLEARY, PATRICK—Age, 21 years. Enlisted, September 22, 1862, at Utica, to serve three years; mustered in as private, unassigned, September 22, 1862; discharged for disability, September 26, 1862.

185. CLEVELAND, ANSON D.—Age, 18 years. Enlisted, May 14, 1861, at Elmira, to serve two years; mustered in as fifer, Company I, May 21, 1861; mustered out with company, May 28, 1863, at Utica, N.Y.

186. CLEVELAND, CHARLES B.—Age, 18 years. Enlisted, June 1, 1861, at Elmira, to serve two years; mustered in as private, Company C, June 1, 1861; mustered out with company, May 28, 1863, at Utica, N.Y.; also listed as Charles F. Cleveland; awarded a Medal of honor by act of Congress for most distinguished gallantry in action at Antietam, Md., Sept. 17, 1862. Died February 29, 1908.

187. CLEVELAND, JAMES W.—Age, 19 years. Enlisted, May 3, 1861, at Utica, to serve two years; mustered in as private, Company C, May 21, 1861; promoted corporal, January 1, 1862; mustered out with company, May 28, 1863, at Utica, N.Y.; also listed as James Cleveland.

188. CLEMINGER, WILLIAM—Age, 20 years. Enlisted, May 3, 1861, at Elmira, to serve two years; mustered in as private, Company A, May 21, 1861; discharged, date not stated, for disability; also listed as William Clomminger.

189. CLEMMINGER, WILLIAM—Age, 20 years. Enlisted, May 1, 1861, at Utica, to serve two years; mustered in as musician, Company B, May 21, 1861; mustered out with company, May 28, 1863, at Utica, N.Y.; also listed as William Clommingle; subsequent service as first sergeant in Company L, Fourteenth Artillery.

CLOMMINGER, WILLIAM—see Cleminger, William.

190. CLUNAN, THOMAS—Age, 28 years. Enlisted, May 3, 1861, Utica, to serve two years; mustered in as private, Company F, May 21, 1861; mustered out with company, May 28, 1863, at Utica, N.Y.

191. COAN, WILLIAM—Age, 29 years. Enlisted, May 3, 1861, Utica, to serve three months; mustered in as private, Company F, May 21, 1861; promoted corporal, August 6, 1861; mustered in as first lieutenant, August 13, 1861; resigned, November 7, 1861; also listed as William Cone; commissioned first lieutenant, August 14, 1861, with rank from August 7, 1861, original.

192. COBLIN, OBEDIAH—Age, 43 years. Enlisted, December 1, 1861, at Rome, to serve unexpired term of two years; mustered in as private, Company A, December 11, 1861; discharged for disability, September 19, 1862, at Providence, R.I.; also listed as Obediah Collins.

193. COFFEE, JOHN—Age, 20 years. Enlisted, May 21, 1861, Elmira, to serve three mouths; mustered in as private, Company May 21, 1861; no further record.

194. COFLIN, JOHN—Age, 23 years. Enlisted, May 1, 1861, at Utica to serve two

years; mustered in as private, Company B, May 21, 1861; mustered out with company, May 28, 1863, at Utica, N.Y.

195. COGSWELL, SAMUEL B.—Age, 40 years. Enlisted, May 2, 1861, at Rochester, to serve two years; mustered in as private Company G, May 21, 1861; died of disease, May 14, 1863.

196. COLBERT, JOHN—Age, 19 years. Enlisted, May 2, 1861, at Rochester, to serve two years; mustered in as private, Company H, May 21, 1861; mustered out, May 28, 1863, at Utica, N.Y.

COLE, MUNROE—*see* Monroe, Cowles.

197. COLEMAN, REDMOND—Age, 19 years. Enlisted, May 15, 1861, at Rochester, to serve three years; mustered in as private, Company K, August 2, 1861; deserted, June 26, 1862, at Manassas, Va.

198. COLLIER, ALBERT A.—Age, 19 years. Enlisted, May 7, 1861, at Utica, to serve two years; mustered in as private, Company D, May 21, 1861; mustered out with company, May 28. 1863, at Utica, N.Y.

199. COLLINS, HUGH—Age, 19 years. Enlisted, May 13, 1861, at Utica, to serve two years; mustered in as private, Company I, May 21, 1861; wounded, date not stated, at Antietam, Md.; discharged for disability, December 20, 1862, at Smoketown Hospital, Md.

200. COLLINS, JAMES—Age, 28 years. Enlisted, September 4, 1861, at Rochester, to serve three years; mustered in as private, Company H, September 5, 1861; mustered out with company, May 28, 1863, at Utica, N.Y.

COLLINS, OBEDIAH—*see* Coblin, Obediah.

201. COMPTON, AMOS—Age, 29 years. Enlisted, May 14, 1861, at Camden, to serve three years; mustered in as private, Company K, May 21, 1861; promoted sergeant, date not stated; discharged for disability, December 20, 1861, at Fort Lyon, Va.

CONE, WILLIAM—*see* Coan, William.

202. CONEY, CHARLES—Age, 24 years. Enlisted, May 14, 1861, at Camden, to serve two years; mustered in as private, Company K, May 21, 1861; deserted, June 12, 1861, at Elmira, N.Y.

203. CONEY, STEPHEN—Age, 20 years. Enlisted, May 14, 1861, at Camden, to serve two years; mustered in as private, Company K, May 21, 1861; deserted, June 4, 1861, at Elmira, N.Y.

204. CONGAR, EDWARD W.—Age, 24 years. Enlisted, May 7, 1861, at Utica, to serve two years; mustered in as private, Company D, May 21, 1861; mustered out with company, May 28, 1863, at Utica, N.Y.

205. CONGDON, JOEL M.—Age, 23 years. Enlisted, May 13, 1861, at Utica, to serve two years; mustered in as private, Company I, May 21, 1861; deserted, April 27, 1862, at Fort Lyon, Va.

206. CONKLIN, EDGAR—Age, 18 years. Enlisted, November 23, 1861, at Rome, to serve unexpired term of two years; mustered in as private, Company D, December 11, 1861; wounded, September 14, 1862, at South Mountain, Md.; transferred, September 3, 1863, to Forty-Seventh Company, Second Battalion, Veteran Reserve Corps; no further record.

207. CONKLIN, GEORGE M.—Age, 25 years. Enlisted, May 22, 1861, at Elmira, to serve two years; mustered in as private, Company K, May 22, 1861; promoted corporal, January 1, 1862; mustered out with company, May 28, 1863, at Utica, N.Y.

208. CONLAN, JOHN E.—Age, 19 years. Enlisted, August 14, 1861, at Rome, to serve three years; mustered in as private, Company I, August 20, 1861; died, March 18, 1862, at Fort Lyon, Va.

209. CONLEY, PETER—Age, 32 years. Enlisted, August 19, 1862, at Utica, to serve three years; mustered in as private. Company A, same date; killed, December 13, 1862, at battle of Fredericksburg, Va.

210. CONNOR, THOMAS—Age, 20 years. Enlisted, May 2, 1861, at Rochester, to serve three years; mustered in as private, Company H, May 21, 1861; promoted sergeant, date not stated; mustered out May 24, 1863, at Utica, N.Y.; subsequent service in First Veteran Cavalry.

211. CONOVER, DANIEL S.—Age, 26 years. Enlisted, May 21, 1861, at Elmira, to serve three months; mustered in as private, Company B, same date; no further record.

212. COOK, CHARLES—Age, 18 years. Enlisted, May 1, 1861, at Utica, to serve two

years; mustered in as private, Company A, May 21, 1861; mustered out with company, May 28, 1863, at Utica, N.Y.; subsequent service in Third Artillery.

213. COOK, GEORGE—Age, 33 years. Enlisted, May 7, 1861, at Utica, to serve two years; mustered in as private, Company D, May 21, 1861; mustered out with company, May 28, 1863, at Utica, N.Y.; also listed as Geo. Cooke.

214. COOK, ROBERT—Age, 23 years. Enlisted, May 3, 1861, at Utica, to serve two years; mustered in as private, Company C, May 21, 1861; transferred to Company D, July or August 1861; promoted corporal, date not stated; reduced, September 9, 1862; wounded, at battle of Fredericksburg, Va., December 1862; died of such wounds, December 24, 1862, at Armory Square Hospital.

215. COOLEY, FORBES—Age, 38 years. Enlisted, May 14, 1861, at Camden, to serve three months; mustered in as private, Company K, May 21, 1861; deserted, June 3, 1861, at Elmira, N.Y.

216. COOLEY, OLIVER B.—Age, 23 years. Enlisted, May 3, 1861, at Utica, to serve two years; mustered in as sergeant, Company F, May 21, 1861; promoted first sergeant, November 7, 1861; transferred to Company D, May 15, 1863; mustered in as second lieutenant, May 16, 1863; mustered out, to date, May 28, 1863; commissioned second lieutenant, May 13, 1863, with rank from March 11, 1863, vice W. G. Halstead, promoted.

217. COONROD, PHILIP—Age, 21 years. Enlisted, May 7, 1861, at Utica, to serve two years; mustered in as corporal, Company E, May 21, 1861; reduced, September 1, 1862; mustered out with company, May 28, 1863, at Utica, N.Y.; also listed as Philip Conrad.

218. COONS, RUSSELL—Age, 19 years. Enlisted, May 2, 1861, at Rochester, to serve two years; mustered in as private, Company G, May 21, 1861; mustered out with company, May 28, 1863, at Utica, N.Y.; subsequent service in Company C, Twenty-First Cavalry.

COONSADT, FREDERICK— *see* Howard, Frederick.

219. COOPER, JOHN H. Jr.—Age, 19 years. Enlisted, May 14, 1861, at Camden, to serve two years; mustered in as private, Company K, May 21, 1861; deserted, September 15, 1861, at Alexandria, Va.

220. COOPER, HENRY—Age, 27 years. Enlisted, May 2, 1861, at Rochester, to serve two years; mustered in as private, Company G, May 21, 1861; discharged for disability, February 17, 1863, at Convalescent Camp, Va.; also listed as James H. Cooper.

221. CORCORAN, THOMAS—Age, 29 years. Enlisted, August 5, 1862, at Utica, to serve three years; mustered in as private, unassigned, August 21, 1862; reported deserted, date not stated.

222. CORNER, CHARLES L.—Age, 23 years. Enlisted, December 28, 1861, at Genesco, to serve two years; mustered in as private, unassigned, January 3, 1862; no further record.

CORRIGAN, JOHN—*see* Carrigan, John.

223. CORRIGAN, JOSEPH—Age, 28 years. Enlisted, August 17, 1861, at Utica, to serve two years; mustered in as private, Company I, same date; wounded, September 17, 1862, at Antietam, Md.; mustered out with company, May 28, 1863, at Utica, N.Y.

224. CORTWRIGHT, AUGUSTUS—Age, 24 years. Enlisted, November 6, 1861, at Rochester, to serve two years; mustered in as private, Company K, November 20, 1861; promoted corporal, January 1, 1862; discharged, July 8, 1863, at Utica, N.Y.; also listed as Augustus Cortright.

225. COSGROVE, WILLIAM F.—Age, 22 years. Enlisted, May 3, 1861, at Utica, to serve two years; mustered in as private, Company F, May 21, 1861; promoted corporal, June 19, 1862; wounded, December 1862, at battle of Fredericksburg, Va.; mustered out with company, May 28, 1863, at Utica, N.Y.

226. COSSLEMAN, MONTGOMERY—Age, 25 years. Enrolled, May 1, 1861, at Utica, to serve two years; mustered in as captain, Company A, May 21, 1861; killed, August 30, 1862, at battle of Second Bull Run, Va.; commissioned captain, July 4, 1861, with rank from May 1, 1861, original.

227. COSTELLO, PETER—Age, 26 years. Enlisted, February 20, 1862, at Rochester, to serve three years; mustered in

as private, Company C, March 27, 1862; killed, August 30, 1862, at Bull Run, Va.

228. COURTRIGHT, JOHN—Age, 29 years. Enlisted, May 21, 1861, at Elmira, to serve two years; mustered in as private, Company H, same date; mustered out, May 24, 1863, at Utica, N.Y.; subsequent service in Company C, Fourteenth Artillery, and Company L, Fourth Artillery.

229. COVENTRY, CHARLES B.—Age, 26 years. Enlisted, May 7, 1861, at Utica, to serve two years; mustered in as private, Company E, May 21, 1861; promoted commissary sergeant, date not stated; mustered in as first lieutenant, Company E, August 6, 1861; captain, Company I, January 11, 1862; resigned, October 19, 1862; commissioned first lieutenant, August 14, 1861, with rank from August 7, 1861, original; captain, January 17, 1862, with rank from January 11, 1862, vice West, resigned.

230. COVENTRY, WALTER B.—Age, 28 years. Enrolled, May 17, 1861, at Camden, to serve two years; mustered in as surgeon, May 21, 1861; mustered out with regiment, May 28, 1863, at Utica, N.Y.; commissioned surgeon, August 14, 1861, with rank from May 17, 1861, original.

231. COWEN, NATHAN C.—Age, 19 years. Enlisted, May 14, 1861, at Camden, to serve two years; mustered in as private, Company K, May 21, 1861; mustered out with company, May 28, 1863, at Utica, N.Y.

232. COWLES, MONROE—Age, 18 years. Enlisted, May 13, 1861, at Utica, to serve two years; mustered in as private, Company I, May 21, 1861; mustered out with company, May 28, 1863, at Utica, N.Y.; also listed as Munroe Cole.

233. COX, JAMES—Age, 20 years. Enlisted, May 13, 1861, at Utica, to serve two years; mustered in as private, Company I, May 21, 1861; mustered out with company, May 28, 1863, at Utica, N.Y.

234. COX, JOSEPH T. Jr.—Age, 17 years. Enlisted, October 16, 1861, at Rochester, to serve unexpired term of two years; mustered in as musician, band, same date; mustered out with band, September 4, 1862, at Upton's Hill, Va.

235. COX, WALTER—Age, 30 years. Enlisted, May 7, 1861, at Utica, to serve two years; mustered in as private, Company D, May 21, 1861; promoted corporal, August 8, 1862; wounded, December 13, 1862, at battle of Fredericksburg, Va.; mustered out with company, May 28, 1863, at Utica, N.Y., as Waller E. Cox.

236. CRANE, SAMUEL H.—Age, 35 years. Enlisted, May 1, 1861, at Utica, to serve two years; mustered in as private, Company A, May 21, 1861; died, February 11, 1863, at Windmill Point, Va.

237. CRASK, JAMES—Age, 25 years. Enlisted, May 1, 1861, at Utica, to serve two years; mustered in as private Company A, May 21, 1861; promoted corporal, February 20, 1862; mustered out with company, May 28, 1863, at Utica, N.Y.

238. CRAVEN, MATHEW—Age, 31 years. Enlisted, May 1, 1861, at Utica, to serve two years; mustered in as private, Company B, May 21, 1861; mustered out with company, May 28, 1863, at Utica, N.Y.; subsequent service in unassigned Sixteenth Artillery.

CRIGIER, FRANCIS—*see* Grigier, Francis.

239. CRONKHITE, HENRY M.—Age, 27 years Enlisted, July 29, 1861, at Utica, to serve three years; mustered in as private, Company C, August 7, 1861; mustered out with company, May 28, 1863, at Utica, N.Y.

240. CROSS, BENJAMIN—Age, 20 years. Enlisted, May 3, 1861, at Utica, to serve two years; mustered in as private, Company C, May 21, 1861; promoted corporal, January 1, 1862; mustered out with company, May 28, 1863, at Utica, N.Y.; subsequent service in Company G, Second Artillery.

241. GROSS, GEORGE W.—Age, 19 years. Enlisted, August 28, 1861, at Utica, to serve two years; mustered in as private, Company A, September 2, 1862; wounded, date and place not stated; mustered out with company, May 28, 1863, at Utica, N.Y.

242. CROW, JOHN—Age, 18 years. Enlisted, June 10, 1861, at Elmira, to serve two years; mustered in as private, Company I, May 21, 1861; killed, August 30, 1862, at battle of Second Bull Run, Va.

243. CUNNINGHAM, FRANK—Age, 22 years. Enlisted, May 1, 1861, at Utica, to serve two years; mustered in as corporal, Company B, May 21, 1861; reduced, August 24, 1861; discharged for disability, June 21, 1862.

244. CURLY, JAMES—Age, 21 years. Enlisted, May 2, 1861, at Rochester, to serve two years; mustered in as private, Company H, May 21, 1861; killed, August 30, 1862, at Bull Run, Va.

245. CURRY, ABRAM W.—Age, 19 years. Enlisted, May 1, 1861, at Utica, to serve two years; mustered in as private, Company B, May 21, 1861; promoted corporal, May 21, 1861; sergeant, February 13, 1862; wounded, August 30, 1862; mustered out with company, May 28, 1863, at Utica, N.Y.

246. DABLER, CHARLES—Age, 28 years. Enlisted, October 22, 1861, at Rochester, to serve unexpired term of two years; mustered in as third class musician, band, same date; discharged, June 16, 1862, at Front Royal, Va.; subsequent service in Twenty-Fourth Cavalry.

247. DAILY, CHARLES H.—Age, 21 years. Enlisted, November 19, 1861, at Utica, to serve unexpired term of two years; mustered in as private, Company I, November 25, 1861; mustered out with company, May 28, 1863, at Utica, N.Y.; also listed as Charles Daily.

248. DALEY, THOMAS—Age, 21 years. Enlisted, May 13, 1861, at Utica, to serve two years; mustered in as private, Company I, May 21, 1861; mustered out with company, May 28, 1863, at Utica, N.Y.; also listed as Thomas Daily.

249. DALTON, WILLIAM—Age, 22 years. Enlisted, October 24, 1861, at Rochester, to serve three years; mustered in as private, Company C, same date; discharged for disability, November 5, 1862, at Baltimore, Md.

250. DARLA, CHARLES—Age, 28 years. Enlisted, May 2, 1861, at Rochester, to serve three months; mustered in as private, Company H, May 21, 1861; drowned, June 9, 1861, while in bathing at Elmira.

251. DAVIDSON, WILLIAM—Age, 23 years. Enlisted, May 1, 1861, at Utica, to serve two years; mustered in as private, Company B, May 21, 1861; discharged for disability, February 12, 1863.

252. DAVIS, BENJAMIN W.—Age, 21 years. Enlisted, September 20, 1861, at Utica, to serve three years; mustered in as private, Company F, September 28, 1861; transferred to Company K, date not stated; back to Company F, January 1, 1862; mustered out with company, May 28, 1863, at Utica, N.Y.; also listed as Benjamin B. Davis; subsequent service in Twenty-Fourth Cavalry.

253. DAVIS, CORNELIUS—Age, 33 years. Enlisted, December 5, 1861, at Buffalo, to serve two years; mustered in as private, Company I, same date; promoted sergeant, date not stated; killed, December 13, 1862, at battle of Fredericksburg, Va.

254. DAVIS, DEWITT—Age, 18 years. Enlisted, May 3, 1861, at Utica, to serve two years; mustered in as private, Company C, May 21, 1861; wounded, December 13, 1862, at battle of Fredericksburg, Va.; mustered out with company, May 28, 1863, at Utica, N.Y.

255. DAVIS, HENRY A.—Age, 35 years. Enlisted, October 28, 1861, at Utica, to serve three years; mustered in as private, Company E, same date; mustered out with company, May 28, 1863, at Utica, N.Y.; also listed as Henry H. Davis.

256. DAVIS, JOHN C.—Age, 27 years. Enlisted, December 12, 1861, at Utica, to serve two years; mustered in as private, Company A, December 29, 1861; killed, September 17, 1862, at Antietam, Md.

257. DAVIS, JOSEPH W.—Age, 27 years. Enlisted, May 2, 1861, at Rochester, to serve two years; mustered in as sergeant, Company H, May 21, 1861; wounded, August 30, 1862, at Bull Run, Va.; promoted first sergeant, date not stated; discharged on account of wounds, March 26, 1863, at General Hospital, Philadelphia, Pa.

258. DAVIS, OSCAR C.—Age, 18 years. Enlisted, May 1, 1861, at Utica, to serve two years; mustered in as private, Company B, May 21, 1861; promoted corporal, August 24, 1861; sergeant, October 28, 1861; mustered out with company, May 28, 1863, at Utica, N.Y.

259. DAVIS, THOMAS—Age, 28 years. Enrolled, May 2, 1861, at Rochester, to serve two years; mustered in as captain, Company H, May 21, 1861; wounded, August 30, 1862, at battle of Bull Run, Va., left on the field supposed to be dead; no further record; commissioned captain, July 4, 1861, with rank from May 2, 1861, original.

260. DEAN, ANTHONY—Age, 21 years. Enlisted, May 1, 1861, at Utica, to serve two

years; mustered in as private, Company A, May 21, 1861; wounded, December 13, 1862; mustered out with company, May 28, 1863, at Utica, N.Y.

261. DEAN, HENRY H.—Age, 22 years. Enlisted, November 25, 1861, at Rome, to serve unexpired term of two years; mustered in as private, Company E, December 11, 1861; discharged for disability, June 26, 1862, at Carver Hospital; also listed as Henry C. Dean.

262. DEARBORN, OSCAR—Age, 19 years. Enlisted, May 14, 1861, at Camden, to serve two years; mustered in as private, Company K, May 21, 1861; mustered out with company, May 28, 1863, at Utica, N.Y.; also listed as Oscar N. Dearborn.

263. DEARBORN, ROBERT—Age, 21 years. Enlisted, May 14, 1861, at Camden, to serve two years; mustered in as private, Company K, May 21, 1861; mustered out with company, May 28, 1863, at Utica, N.Y.; also listed as Robert T. Dearborn.

264. DEGROAT, NELSON—Age, 19 years. Enlisted, May 14, 1861, at Camden, to serve two years; mustered in as private, Company K, May 21, 1861; mustered out with company, May 28, 1863, at Utica, N.Y.; also listed as Nelson H. Degroat; subsequent service in Company M, Fourth Artillery.

265. DEITZ, HENRY—Age, 19 years. Enlisted, May 13, 1861, at Utica, to serve two years; mustered in as private, Company I, May 21, 1861; captured, August 30, 1862; paroled in September 1862; mustered out with company, May 28, 1863, at Utica, N.Y.

266. DEITZ, MICHAEL—Age, 22 years. Enlisted, May 13, 1861, at Utica, to serve two years; mustered in as private, Company I, May 21, 1861; mustered out with company, May 28, 1863, at Utica, N.Y.

267. DELANEY, MICHAEL—Age, 42 years. Enlisted, July 23, 1861, at Utica, to serve three years; mustered in as private, Company F, August 19, 1861; transferred to Company D, May 8, 1863; no further record.

268. DELEHART, JAMES—Age, 23 years. Enlisted, May 4, 1861, at Utica, to serve two years; mustered in as private, Company A, May 21, 1861; killed, August 30, 1862, at battle of Second Bull Run, Va.

269. DELONG, JACOB—Age, 20 years. Enlisted, May 14, 1861, at Camden, to serve two years; mustered in as private, Company K, May 21, 1861; deserted, June 12, 1861, at Elmira, N.Y.

270. DELONG, WILLIAM—Age, 18 years. Enlisted, May 14, 1861, at Camden, to serve two years; mustered in as private, Company K, May 21, 1861; deserted, June 13, 1862, at Front Royal, Va.

271. DEMONT, JOHN—Age, 22 years. Enlisted, May 2, 1861, at Rochester, to serve three months; mustered in as private, Company H, May 21, 1861; deserted, June 21, 1861, at Rochester, N.Y.

272. DENNIS, CHARLES—Age, 18 years. Enlisted, May 3, 1861, at Utica to serve two years; mustered in as private, Company C, May 21, 1861; promoted corporal, December 15, 1862; mustered out with company, May 28, 1863, at Utica, N.Y.; subsequent service in Company C, Twenty-First Cavalry.

273. DENNIS, HENRY L.—Age, 33 years. Enlisted, May 14, 1861, at Camden, to serve two years; mustered in as private, Company K, May 21, 1861; deserted, June 13, 1862, at Front Royal, Va.

274. DERRICK, AUSTIN—Age, 35 years. Enlisted, May 3, 1861, at Utica, to serve two years; mustered in as private, Company C, May 21, 1861; deserted, September 3, 1862, at Hall's Hill, Va.

275. DERX, MICHAEL—Age, 18 years. Enlisted, August 2, 1861, at Elmira, to serve three years; mustered in as private, Company G, August 9, 1861; mustered out with company, May 28, 1863, at Utica, N.Y.; subsequent service in Company K, Fiftieth Engineers.

276. DEVINE, DANIEL—Age, 21 years. Enlisted, November 14, 1861, at Utica, to serve unexpired term of two years; mustered in as private, Company F, November 22, 1861; mustered out with company, May 28, 1863, at Utica, N.Y.; subsequent service in Third Artillery.

277. DEVINE, JAMES—Age, 19 years. Enlisted, May 1, 1861, at Utica, to serve two years; mustered in as private, Company B, May 21, 1861; mustered out with company, May 28, 1863, at Utica, N.Y.

278. DEWEY, ALFRED—Age, 22 years. Enlisted, November 4, 1861, at Oswego, to serve two years; mustered in as private,

unassigned, November 20, 1861; no further record.

279. DEXON, CHARLES—Age, 22 years. Enlisted, May 1, 1861, at Utica, to serve two years; mustered in as private, Company B, May 21, 1861; mustered out with company, May 28, 1863, at Utica, N.Y.; also listed as Charles Dickinson.

280. DICKINSON, MOSES—Age, 24 years. Enlisted, May 3, 1861, at Utica, to serve two years; mustered in as private, Company F, May 21, 1861; mustered out with company, May 28, 1863, at Utica, N.Y.; also listed as Moses Dickenson; subsequent service in Third Artillery.

281. DICKINSON, WILLIAM H.—Age, 27 years. Enlisted, August 15, 1862, at Utica, to serve three years; mustered in as private, unassigned, August 15, 1862; mustered out, May 16, 1864, at New York city; subsequent service in Company L, Twenty-Fourth Cavalry.

282. DILLMAN, CHARLES—Age, 18 years. Enlisted, September 30, 1861, at Rochester, to serve three years; mustered in as private, Company C, same date; wounded, December 13, 1862, at battle of Fredericksburg, Va.; mustered out with company, May 28, 1863, at Utica, N.Y.

283. DILLON, WILLIAM—Age, 22 years. Enlisted, May 14, 1861, at Elmira, to serve three months; mustered in as private, Company I, May 21, 1861; deserted, June 15, 1861, at Elmira, N.Y.

DINSMAN, CONRAD—*see* Tinsman, Conrad.

284. DIPLEY, GEORGE—Age, 18 years. Enlisted, May 8, 1861, at Elmira, to serve two years; mustered in as private, Company D, May 21, 1861; promoted corporal, November 11, 1861; mustered out with company, May 28, 1863, at Utica, N.Y.

285. DIPLEY, JOHN—Age, 20 years. Enlisted, May 7, 1861, at Utica, to serve two years; mustered in as private, Company D, May 21, 1861; mustered out with company, May 28, 1863, at Utica, N.Y.

286. DISCHLER, ANDREW—Age, 39 years; Enlisted, May 1, 1861, at Utica, to serve two years; mustered in as corporal, Company A, May 21, 1861; promoted sergeant, August 21, 1861; mustered out with company, May 28, 1863, at Utica, N.Y.

287. DOCKERTY, ROBERT—Age, 19 years. Enlisted, May 14, 1861, at Camden, to serve two years; mustered in as private, Company K, May 21, 1861; promoted corporal, September 1, 1861; sergeant, January 18, 1862; mustered out with company, May 28, 1863, at Utica, N.Y.

288. DOERHERTY, JAMES—Age, 20 years. Enlisted, May 2, 1861, at Rochester, to serve two years; mustered in as private, Company G, May 21, 1861; mustered out with company, May 28, 1863, at Utica, N.Y.; also listed as James Doherty; subsequent service in Company M, First Veteran Cavalry.

289. DONNELLY, JAMES—Age, 19 years. Enlisted, May 3, 1861, at Utica, to serve two years; mustered in as private, Company C, May 21, 1861; mustered out with company, May 28, 1863, at Utica, N.Y.; also listed as James Donely.

290. DONOHUE, MICHAEL—Age, 20 years. Enlisted, May 7, 1861, at Utica, to serve two years; mustered in as private, Company D, May 1861; discharged for disability, October 16, 1861, at Camp Franklin.

291. DOODG, JOSEPH—Age, 25 years. Enlisted, May 1, 1861, at Utica, to serve two years; mustered in as private, Company A, May 21, 1861; promoted corporal, date not stated; sergeant, November 5, 1861; killed, August 30, 1862, at battle of Second Bull Run, Va.

292. DORELL, HENRY—Age, 18 years. Enlisted, May 1, 1861, at Utica, to serve two years; mustered in as private, Company B, May 21, 1861; died of disease, February 5, 1863, at Annapolis, Md.; also listed as Henry Dorrell.

293. DOTY, CHAUNCEY E.—Age, 21 years. Enlisted, May 7, 1861, at Utica, to serve three months; mustered in as private, Company D, May 21, 1861; discharged for disability, September 4, 1861, at Camp Vernon, Va.

294. DOWD, JAMES E.—Age, 23 years. Enlisted, May 2, 1861, at Rochester, to serve two years; mustered in as private, Company G, May 21, 1861; discharged, March 18, 1863, at General Hospital, Fort Schuyler, N.Y.

295. DOWD, JOHN—Age, 33 years. Enlisted, September 8, 1862, at Utica, to serve three years; mustered in as private, unassigned, same date; no further record.

296. DOWNS, JAMES—Age, 28 years. Enlisted, August 2, 1861, at Buffalo, to serve three years; mustered in as private, Company B, August 9, 1861; mustered out with company, May 28, 1863, at Utica, N.Y.

297. DOX, WILLIAM H.—Age, 18 years. Enlisted, December 17, 1861, at Geneva, to serve unexpired term of two years; mustered in as private, unassigned, January 3, 1862; no further record.

298. DOYLE, THOMAS—Age, 30 years. Enlisted, December 23, 1861, at Buffalo, to serve two years; mustered in as private, Company G, same date; promoted commissary sergeant, March 1, 1863; discharged, June 22, 1863, at Utica, N.Y.

299. DRAKE, AMOS—Age, 19 years. Enlisted, May 7, 1861, at Utica, to serve two years; mustered in as private, Company E, May 21, 1861; mustered out with company, May 28, 1863, at Utica, N.Y.

300. DUELL, NICHOLAS R.—Age, 27 years. Enlisted, May 3, 1861, at Utica, to serve two years; mustered in as private,. Company C, May 21, 1861; captured, August 30, 1862, at Bull Run, Va.; paroled, date not stated; deserted in April 1863, at Camp Parole, Md. Company C descriptive roll states, "Taken prisoner, exchanged and never reported to the regiment."

301. DUFFY, STEPHEN—Age, 19 years. Enlisted, May 13, 1861, at Utica, to serve two years; mustered in as private, Company I, May 21, 1861; mustered out with company, May 28, 1863, at Utica, N.Y.

302. DUNHAM, MARTIN N.—Age, 23 years. Enlisted, May 1, 1861, at Utica, to serve two years; mustered in as sergeant, Company B, May 21, 1861; promoted first sergeant, date not stated; mustered as first lieutenant, Company B, November 20, 1862; mustered out with company, May 28, 1863, at Utica, N.Y.; commissioned first lieutenant, February 11, 1863, with rank from November 20, 1862, vice Harlow, promoted.

303. DUNN, PATRICK—Age, 23 years. Enlisted, July 27, 1861, at Utica, to serve three years; mustered in as private, Company F, same date; mustered out with company, May 28, 1863, at Utica, N.Y.

304. DURAND, ADOLPHOS S. V.—Age, 21 years. Enlisted, May 2, 1861, at Rochester, to serve two years; mustered in as private, Company G, May 21, 1861; discharged for disability, April 16, 1862, at Fort Lyon, Va.; also listed as Adolphus St. Durand.

305. DYER, DAVID J.—Age, 19 years. Enlisted, May 2, 1861, at Rochester, to serve two years; mustered in as private, Company G, May 21, 1861; promoted corporal, date not stated; mustered out with company, May 28, 1863, at Utica, N.Y. Died, November 1909.

306. DYSNEY, THOMAS S.—Age, 36 years. Enlisted, May 1, 1861, at Utica, to serve two years; mustered in as private, Company A, May 21, 1861; killed, December 13, 1862, at battle of Fredericksburg, Va.

307. EAGER, WORDEN L.—Age, 37 years. Enlisted, September 2, 1861, at Rochester, to serve three years; mustered in as private, Company H, September 5, 1861; discharged for disability, November 12, 1861, at Camp Franklin, near Alexandria, Va.

308. EARL, STEPHEN D.—Age, 41 years. Enlisted, December 1, 1861, at McConnellsville, to serve two years; mustered in as private, Company C, December 21, 1861; transferred to Company I, May 1, 1862; discharged for disability, October 23, 1862, at Albany, N.Y.; also listed as Stephen A. Earle.

309. EASTMAN, ANDREW J.—Age, 24 years. Enlisted, May 2, 1861, at Rochester, to serve three months; mustered in as private, Company G, May 21, 1861; discharged for disability, June 21, 1861, at Elmira, N.Y.

310. EASTMAN, ROYAL—Age, 20 years. Enlisted, May 3, 1861, at Utica, to serve two years; mustered in as private, Company F, May 21, 1861; mustered out with company, May 28, 1863, at Utica, N.Y.

311. EBERHART, CHRISTIAN—Age, 42 years. Enlisted, October 2, 1862, at Utica, to serve three years; mustered in as private, unassigned, October 7, 1862; reported deserted, October 18, 1862, from rendezvous at Utica.

312. EBNER, JOSEPH—Age, 21 years. Enlisted, May 7, 1861, at Utica, to serve two years; mustered in as private, Company E, May 21, 1861; mustered out with company, May 28, 1863, at Utica,. N.Y.

313. ECCLES, FISH—Age, 21 years.

Enlisted, May 1, 1861, at Utica, to serve two years; mustered in as private, Company B, May 21, 1861; promoted corporal, March 1, 1862; mustered out with company, May 28, 1863, at Utica, N.Y.

314. EDIC, JOHN J.—Age, 31 years. Enlisted, May 3, 1861, at Utica, to serve two years; mustered in as private, Company C, May 21, 1861; mustered out with company, May 28, 1863, at Utica, N.Y.; also listed as John Edie; subsequent service in Company G, Second Artillery.

315. EDSON, CHARLES—Age, 22 years. Enlisted, May 8, 1861, at Elmira, to serve two years; mustered in as private, Company D, May 21, 1861; deserted, August 25, 1862, while on the march near Warrenton, Va.; also listed as Charles M. Etson.

316. EGAN, JOHN—Age, 26 years. Enlisted, May 2, 1861, at Rochester, to serve two years; mustered in as private, Company H, May 21, 1861; mustered out, May 24, 1863, at Utica, N.Y.

317. EGAN, WILLIAM—Age, 28 years. Enlisted, May 2, 1861, at Rochester, to serve two years; mustered in as private, Company H, May 21, 1861; wounded, August 30, 1862, at Bull Run, Va.; discharged for disability, December 26, 1862, at Hammond General Hospital, Point Lookout, Md.

318. EINHOLZ, ANTHONY—Age, 43 years. Enlisted, October 9, 1861, at Utica, to serve unexpired term of two years; mustered in as private, Company E, October 14, 1861; discharged for disability, October 30, 1862, at Washington, D.C.

319. ELLIS, WILLIAM—Age, 19 years. Enlisted, May 3, 1861, at Utica, to serve two years; mustered in as private, Company C, May 21, 1861; discharged for disability, March 6, 1862, at Fort Lyon, Va.

320. ELMS, FRANKLIN—Age, 19 years. Enlisted, December 23, 1861, at Utica, to serve two years; mustered in as private, Company I, December 24, 1861; deserted, April 29, 1863, at Falmouth, Va.

321. ENGERSOLL, FRANK D.—Age, 27 years. Enlisted, May 1, 1861, at Utica, to serve two years; mustered in as private, Company B, May 21, 1861; transferred to Company E, November 1, 1861; wounded at the battle of Antietam, Md.; discharged for disability, January 12, 1863, at Carver Hospital; also listed as Frank D. Ingersoll.

322. ERHARDT, JOHN P.—Age, 42 years. Enlisted, August 22, 1862, at Utica, to serve three years; mustered in as private, Company E, same date; discharged for disability, December 29, 1862.

323. ERNEST, JACOB—Age, 20 years. Enlisted, May 7, 1861, at Utica, to serve two years; mustered in as private, Company E, May 21, 1861; deserted, June 6, 1862, at Front Royal, Va.

324. ETHERIDGE, WILLIAM—Age, 20 years. Enlisted, September 26, 1861, at Utica, to serve three years; mustered in as private, Company D, same date; mustered out with company, May 28, Utica, N.Y.

325. ETTS, MORRIS—Age, 24 years. Enlisted, May 2, 1861, at Rochester, to serve two years; mustered in as private, Company G, May 21, 1861; mustered out with company, May 28, 1863, at Utica, N.Y.

326. EUPER, FLORIAN—Age, 23 years. Enlisted, September 26, 1861. at Rome, to serve three years; mustered in as private Company C, same date; mustered out with company, May 28, 1863, at Utica, N.Y.; also listed as Florins Euper.

327. EVANS, EDWIN M.—Age, 22 years. Enlisted, March 24, 1862, at Utica, to serve three years; mustered in as private, Company D, April 25, 1862; wounded, August 30, 1862, at battle of Second Bull Run, Va.; transferred, May 7, 1863, to Eighty-Third Infantry; also listed as Edward M. Evans.

328. EVANS, GEORGE—Age, 19 years. Enlisted, May 7, 1861, at Utica, to serve two years; mustered in as private, Company E, May 21, 1861; killed, August 30, 1862, at battle of Second Bull Run, Va.

329. EVANS, JUSTIS—Age, 23 years. Enlisted, May 14, 1861, at Camden, to serve two years; mustered in as private, Company K, May 21, 1861; wounded, August 30, 1862, at battle of Second Bull Run, Va.; died, September 14, 1862, at Washington, D.C., of such wounds; also listed as Judson Evans.

330. EVANS, THOMAS R.—Age, 40 years. Enlisted, May 1, 1861, at Utica, to serve two years; mustered in as private, Company A, May 21, 1861; wounded at battle of Fredericksburg, Va.; died, December 18, 1862, of such wounds.

331. EVANS, THOMAS S.—Age, 22

years. Enlisted, May 1, 1861, at Utica, to serve two years; mustered in as private, Company A, May 21, 1861; mustered out with company, May 28, 1863, at Utica, N.Y.; also listed as Thomas T. Evans.

332. EVANS, WILLIAM—Age, 21 years. Enlisted, May 1, 1861, at Utica, to serve two years; mustered in as private, Company B, May 28, 1861; wounded, December 13, 1862; mustered out with company, May 28, 1863, at Utica, N.Y.; subsequent service in Twenty-Fourth Cavalry.

333. EVANS, WILLIAM H.—Age, 18 years. Enlisted, August 30, 1861, at Utica, to serve three years; mustered in as private, Company B, same date; killed, September 17, 1862, at Antietam, Md.

334. EVANS, WILLIAM J.—Age, 20 years. Enlisted, May 1, 1861, at Utica, to serve two years; mustered in as private, Company A, May 21, 1861; appointed musician, date not stated; discharged for disability, August 27, 1861, at Alexandria, Va.

335. EVERETT, WILLIAM W.—Age, 21 years. Enlisted, July 22, 1861, at Utica, to serve three years; mustered in as private, Company C, August 7, 1861; mustered out with company, May 28, 1863, at Utica, N.Y.; subsequent service in Company K, Second Artillery.

336. EWALD, FREDERICK—Age, 44 years. Enlisted, December 19, 1861, at Elmira, to serve unexpired term of two years; mustered in as private, unassigned, January 3, 1862; no further record.

337. EWALD, HENRY—Age, 18 years. Enlisted, December 19, 1861, at Elmira, to serve unexpired term of two years; mustered in as private, unassigned, January 3, 1862; no further record.

338. EXELL, JAMES—Age, 18 years. Enlisted, May 3, 1861, at Utica, to serve two years; mustered in as private, Company F, May 21, 1861; mustered out with company, May 28, 1863, at Utica, N.Y.; also listed as James Excell.

339. FAIRBANKS, JOHN H.—Age, 43 years. Enrolled, May 3, 1861, at Utica, to serve three months; mustered in as captain, Company C, May 21, 1861; resigned, August 7, 1861; commissioned captain, July 4, 1861, with rank from May 18, 1861, original. Reenlisted, August 1862 in the 117th New York Infantry.

340. FALK, JOHN—Age, 43 years. Enlisted, August 16, 1862, at Utica, to serve three years; mustered in as private, Company E, August 18, 1862; killed, December 13, 1862, at battle of Fredericksburg, Va.

341. FARMER, DAVID A.—Age, 26 years. Enlisted, May 7, 1861, at Utica, to serve two years; mustered in as corporal, Company D, May 21, 1861; reduced, November 19, 1861; discharged for disability, January 25, 1862, at Alexandria, Va.

342. PENNER, CHARLES—Age, 26 years. Enlisted, October 14, 1861, at Rochester, to serve unexpired term of two years; mustered in as third-class musician, same date; mustered out with band September 4, 1862, at Upton's Hill, Va.

FERGUSON, ALLEN J.—*see* Furguson, Allen J.

343. FERGUSON, HENRY—Age, 21 years. Enlisted, October 4, 1861, at Utica, to serve three years; mustered in as private, Company C, October 28, 1861; died of disease, February 11, 1862, at hospital, at Alexandria, Va.

344. FERRY, JAMES—Age, 27 years. Enlisted, May 3, 1861, at Utica, to serve two years; mustered in as private, Company C; May 21, 1861; mustered out with company, May 28, 1863, at Utica, N.Y.

345. FIGGAR, TRUMAN G.—Age, 30 years. Enlisted, August 21, 1861, at Rochester, to serve three years; mustered in as private, Company C, September 5, 1861; discharged for disability, August 23, 1862, at Cliffburn Hospital, Washington, D.C.

346. FINIEN, EDWARD—Age, 18 years. Enlisted, May 2, 1861, at Rochester, to serve two years; mustered in as private, Company G, May 21, 1861; deserted, November 1, 1861, at Alexandria, Va.; also listed as Edward Tinien.

347. FINKLE, HENRY J.—Age, 21 years. Enlisted, January 25, 1862, at Utica, to serve three years; mustered in as private, Company F, March 27, 1862; transferred to Company A, May 1, 1862; deserted, February 3, 1863, at Belle Plain, Va.; also listed as Henry G. Finkle.

348. FINN, MICHAEL—Age, 19 years. Enlisted, May 7, 1861, at Utica, to serve two years; mustered in as private, Company E,

May 21, 1861; mustered out with company, May 28, 1863, at Utica, N.Y.

349. FINN, RICHARD—Age, 24 years. Enlisted, May 13, 1861, at Utica, to serve two years; mustered in as private, Company I, May 21, 1861; appointed wagoner, date not stated; mustered out with company, May 28, 1863, at Utica, N.Y.

350. FIRMAN, WARREN S.—Age, 21 years. Enlisted, October 19, 1861, at Rochester, to serve two years; mustered in as private, Company C, October 21, 1861; promoted sergeant, January 10, 1863; mustered out with company, May 28, 1863, at Utica, N.Y.

351. FISCHER, JOSEPH—Age, 35 years. Enlisted, July 22, 1862, at Rochester, to serve three years; mustered in as private, unassigned, same date; rejected, August 16, 1862.

352. FISHER, WILLIAM—Age, 22 years. Enlisted, May 7, 1861, at Utica, to serve two years; mustered in as private, Company D, May 21, 1861; killed, December 13, 1862, at battle of Fredericksburg, Va.

353. FITZGERALD, JOHN—Age, 21 years. Enlisted, May 2, 1861, at Rochester, to serve two years; mustered in as private, Company H, May 21, 1861; mustered out, May 24, 1863, at Utica, N.Y.; subsequent service in Company M, First Veteran Cavalry.

354. FITZMORRIS, JOHN—Age, 25 years. Enlisted, July 30, 1861, at Rochester, to serve three years; mustered in as private, Company F, August 9, 1861; deserted, September 24, 1862, at Sharpsburg, Md.

355. FLINT, HENRY J.—Age, 28 years. Enrolled, May 14, 1861, at Elmira, to serve three months; mustered in as first lieutenant, Company I, May 21, 1861; resigned, August 7, 1861; commissioned first lieutenant, July 4, 1861, with rank from May 13, 1861, original.

356. FLINT, HENRY J.—Age, 35 years. Enlisted, December 11, 1861, at Utica, to serve two years; mustered in as private, Company I, December 11, 1861; promoted sergeant, date not stated; wounded, at battle of Fredericksburg, Va., December 13, 1862; mustered out with company, May 28, 1863, at Utica, N.Y.

357. FOBLEY, JACOB—Age, 41 years. Enlisted, December 5, 1861, at Rome, to serve unexpired term of two years; mustered in as private, Company D, December 11, 1861; mustered out with company, May 28, 1863, at Utica, N.Y., as Jacob Fogle; subsequent service in Company A, Sixteenth Artillery.

358. FORBES, AMOS—Age, 24 years. Enlisted, June 27, 1861, at Rochester, to serve three years; mustered in as private, Company K, August 9, 1861; discharged for disability, October 16, 1861, at Camp Franklin.

359. FORD, DANIEL—Age, date of enlistment, muster-in and term, not stated; mustered in as private, Company B; deserted, November 7, 1861, at Camp Franklin, Va.

360. FORD, ISAAC S.—Age, 23 years. Enlisted, June 10, 1861, at Elmira, to serve three years; mustered in as private, Company I, same date; mustered out with company, May 28, 1863, at Utica, N.Y.; subsequent service in Company E, Twenty-Second Cavalry.

361. FORT, JOHN—Age, 18 years. Enlisted, May 1, 1861, at Utica, to serve three years; mustered in as private, Company A, May 21, 1861; promoted quartermaster sergeant, November 1, 1862; mustered out with regiment, May 28, 1863, at Utica, N.Y.; also listed as John B. Fort.

362. FOSBECK, JOHN—Age, 24 years. Enlisted, September 9, 1861, at Utica, to serve two years; mustered in as private, Company H, September 17, 1861; deserted, June 16, 1862, at Front Royal, Va.

363. FOSTER, MARTIN—Age, 21 years. Enlisted, May 7, 1861, at Utica, to serve two years; mustered in as private, Company E, May 21, 1861; mustered out with company, May 28, 1863, at Utica, N.Y.

364. FOX, PETER—Age, 20 years. Enlisted, September 23, 1861, at Utica, to serve three years; mustered in as private, Company F, September 28, 1861; discharged, August 20, 1862.

365. FRANCIS, CHARLES—Age, 24 years. Enlisted, September 4, 1861, at Utica, to serve two years; mustered in as private, unassigned, September 5, 1861; no further record.

366. FRANCIS, THOMAS—Age, 19 years. Enlisted, May 3, 1861, at Utica, to serve two years; mustered in as private, Company C, May 21, 1861; promoted corporal, April 3, 1862; sergeant, December 1, 1862; mustered out with company, May 28,

1863, at Utica, N.Y.; also listed as Thomas E. Francis.

367. FRANCIS, THOMAS—Age, 25 years. Enlisted, November 12, 1861, at Utica, to serve unexpired term of two years; mustered in as private, Company B, November 22, 1861; mustered out with company, May 28, 1863, at Utica, N.Y.

368. FRANK, HENRY—Age, 19 years. Enlisted, May 1, 1861, at Utica, to serve two years; mustered in as private, Company B, May 21, 1861; captured, December 13, 1862, at battle of Fredericksburg, Va.; paroled, date not stated; mustered out with company, May 28, 1863, at Utica, N.Y.

369. FRANKLIN, JACOB H.—Age, 32 years. Enlisted, May 14, 1861, at Camden, to serve three months; mustered in as private, Company K, May 21, 1861; deserted, August 22, 1861, at Alexandria, Va.

370. FRAZIER, JEROME B.—Age, 25 years. Enlisted, May 3, 1861, at Utica, to serve two years; mustered in as private, Company F, May 21, 1861; promoted corporal, February 28, 1862; severely wounded at battle of Fredericksburg, Va., December 13, 1862; mustered out, May 21, 1863, at Utica, N.Y. Died September 4, 1887.

371. FRAZIER, SAMUEL J.—Age, 20 years. Enlisted, May 15, 1861, at Elmira, to serve two years; mustered in as private, Company K, June 15, 1861; killed, August 30, 1862, at battle of Second Bull Run, Va.; also listed as Samuel Frazier Jr.

372. FRENCH, ISAAC W.—Age, 23 years. Enlisted, June 9, 1861, at Elmira, to serve two years; mustered in as private, Company D, same date; wounded, August 30, 1862; discharged, June 9, 1863, at Albany, N.Y.; also listed as Isaac French.

373. FRENCH, JAMES—Age, 18 years. Enlisted, May 1, 1861, at Utica, to serve two years; mustered in as private, Company B, May 28, 1861; mustered out with company, May 28, 1863, at Utica, N.Y.; subsequent service, Company G, Twenty-Second Cavalry.

374. FRESHOUS, HENRY—Age, 26 years. Enlisted, December 22, 1861, at Geneva, to serve two years; mustered in as private, unassigned, January 3, 1862; no further record.

375. FRICK, ANTHONY—Age, 32 years. Enlisted, May 7, 1861, at Utica, to serve two years; mustered in as private, Company E, May 21, 1861; mustered out with company, May 28, 1863, at Utica, N.Y.

376. FROST, EDWARD—Age, 25 years. Enlisted, May 7, 1861, at Utica, to serve two years; mustered in as private, Company D, May 21, 1861; deserted, July 17, 1862, near Warrenton, Va.; also listed as Edward L. Frost.

377. FULLER, ROBERT C.—Age, 23 years. Enlisted, May 14, 1861, at Camden, to serve two years; mustered in as private, Company K, May 21, 1861; wounded at battle of Second Bull Run, Va., August 30, 1862; promoted corporal, May 1, 1863; mustered out with company, May 28, 1863, at Utica, N.Y.; subsequent service in Company A, Sixteenth Artillery.

378. FURGUSON, ALLEN J.—Age, 33 years. Enlisted, May 1, 1861, at Utica, to serve two years; mustered in as private, Company B, May 21, 1861; transferred to Company E, June 30, 1861; discharged for disability, July 8, 1862, at Philadelphia, Pa.; also listed as Allen J. Ferguson.

379. GAFFNEY, TIMOTHY—Age, 20 years. Enlisted, May 3, 1861, at Utica, to serve two years; mustered in as private, Company F, May 21, 1861; died, January 7, 1862, at Fort Lyon, Va., from injuries received while at work on fortifications.

380. GALLER, MICHAEL—Age, 18 years. Enlisted, May 14, 1861, at Elmira, to serve two years; mustered in as private, Company E, May 21, 1861; deserted, June 21, 1861, at Elmira, N.Y.; also listed as Michael Gallaher.

381. GALVIN, MARTIN—Age, 21 years. Enlisted, May 7, 1861, at Utica, to serve two years; mustered in as private, Company D, May 21, 1861; transferred to Company H, February 21, 1862; deserted, May 14, 1862, at Fredericksburg, Va.

382. GANAN, JOHN—Age, 18 years. Enlisted, May 2, 1861, at Rochester, to serve two years; mustered in as private, Company G, May 21, 1861; wounded at battle of Second Bull Run, Va.; died, August 30, 1862, of such wounds.

383. GARDINER, WILLIAM C.—Age, 19 years. Enlisted, May 7, 1861, at Utica, to serve two years; mustered in as first sergeant, Company D, May 21, 1861; first

lieutenant, August 9, 1861; resigned, January 10, 1863; also listed as William C. Gardner; commissioned first lieutenant, August 14, 1861, with rank from August 7, 1861, original.

384. GARDNER, HENRY—Age, 25 years. Enlisted, May 2, 1861, at Rochester, to serve two years; mustered in as private, Company G, May 21, 1861; discharged for disability, July 27, 1862, at Alexandria, Va.

385. GARREL, GEORGE—Age, 33 years. Enlisted, August 1, 1861, at Rochester, to serve three years; mustered in as private, unassigned, date not stated; deserted, August 5, 1861, place not stated.

386. GARVEY, JOHN—Age, 19 years. Enlisted, May 13, 1861, at Utica, to serve two years; mustered in as private, Company I, May 21, 1861; mustered out with company, May 28, 1863, at Utica, N.Y.

387. GEIR, FRANK—Age, 25 years. Enlisted, May 7, 1861, at Utica, to serve two years; mustered in as private, Company E, September 2, 1861; deserted, April 29, 1862, at Fort Lyon, Va.

388. GHERES, JOHN—Age, 25 years. Enlisted, August 6, 1861, at Utica, to serve three years; mustered in as private, Company D, August 9, 1861; mustered out with company, May 28, 1863, at Utica, N.Y.

389. GHILARDI, BENEDICT—Age, 43 years. Enlisted, August 6, 1861, at Rochester, to serve three years; mustered in as private, Company A, August 6, 1861; killed, December 13, 1862, at battle of Fredericksburg, Va.; also listed as Benedict Ghirardi.

390. GIBBS, BENJAMIN—Age, 41 years. Enlisted, May 3, 1861, at Utica, to serve two years; mustered in as private, Company C, May 21, 1861; promoted corporal, July 24, 1862; mustered out with company, May 28, 1863, at Utica, N.Y.

391. GIDDINGS, GEORGE H.—Age, 23 years. Enlisted, September 2, 1861, at Buffalo, to serve three years; mustered in as private, Company C, same date; mustered out with company, May 28, 1863, at Utica, N.Y.

392. GIFFORD, WILLIAM P.—Age, 24 years. Enlisted, May 13, 1861, at Utica, to serve two years; mustered in as sergeant, Company I, May 21, 1861; second lieutenant, to date January 29, 1862; first lieutenant, to date February 26, 1863; mustered out with company, May 28, 1863, at Utica, N.Y.; commissioned, second lieutenant, February 12, 1862, with rank from January 28, 1862, vice Johnson, resigned; first lieutenant, May 13, 1863, with rank from February 26, 1863, vice Gardner, resigned.

393. GILBOY, JAMES—Age, 20 years. Enlisted, May 7, 1861, at Utica, to serve two years; mustered in as private, Company D, May 21, 1861; mustered out with company, May 28, 1863, at Utica, N.Y.; subsequent service, Company A, Fifteenth Cavalry.

394. GILLET, SAMUEL—Age, 19 years. Enlisted, May 3, 1861, at Utica, to serve two years; mustered in as private, Company C, May 21, 1861; killed at Bull Run, Va., August 30, 1862; also listed as Samuel R. Gillott.

395. GIST, JOHN—Age, 19 years. Enlisted, May 3, 1861, at Utica, to serve two years; mustered in as private, Company F, May 21, 1861; wounded at battle of Fredericksburg, Va., December 13, 1862; discharged, February 20, 1863, at Philadelphia, Pa., on account of wounds.

396. GLAZIER, JULIUS M.—Age, 22 years. Enlisted, May 13, 1861, at Utica, to serve two years; mustered in as private, Company I, May 21, 1861; mustered out with company, May 28, 1863, at Utica, N.Y.; subsequent service, Company C, Sixteenth Artillery.

397. GLEASON, GEORGE W.—Age, 23 years. Enlisted, May 14, 1861, at Camden, to serve two years; mustered in as private, Company K, May 21, 1861; transferred to Company H and promoted corporal, May 21, 1861; wounded, August 30, 1862, at Bull Run, Va.; discharged for disability, December 25, 1862, at Point Lookout Hospital.

398. GLEASON, LEROY—Age, 18 years. Enlisted, September 1, 1862, at Utica, to serve three years; mustered in as private, Company K, September 18, 1862; transferred, May 9, 1863, to Eighty-Third Infantry; also listed as LeRoy Gleason.

399. GODFREY, JAMES—Age, 21 years. Enlisted, May 1, 1861, at Utica, to serve two years; mustered in as private, Company A, May 21, 1861; died, July 24, 1861, at Fort Ellsworth, Va., of accidental gunshot wound.

400. GODWIN, HENRY B.—Age, 24 years. Enlisted, May 2, 1861, at Rochester, to serve three months; mustered in as fifer, Company G, May 21, 1861; discharged for disability, June 12, 1861, at Elmira, N.Y.

401. GOODNOW, CHARLES W.—Age, 19 years. Enlisted, May 1, 1861, at Utica, to serve two years; mustered in as private, Company A, May 21, 1861; wounded, August 30, 1862; mustered out with company, May 28, 1863, at Utica, N.Y.; subsequent service, Company I, Third Artillery.

402. GOODWIN, ISAAC—Age, 23 years. Enlisted, May 13, 1861, at Utica, to serve two years; mustered in as private, Company I, May 21, 1861; died, June 1, 1862, at Carver General Hospital, Washington, D.C.

403. GORDON, GEORGE—Age, 22 years. Enlisted, May 7, 1861, at Utica, to serve two years; mustered in as private, Company E, May 21, 1861; mustered out with company, May 28, 1863, at Utica, N.Y.

404. GORTON, VERNON—Age, 22 years. Enlisted, May 13, 1861, at Utica, to serve three months; mustered in as private, Company I, May 21, 1861; deserted, July 10, 1861, at Elmira, N.Y.

405. GOULD, ALMEROND D.—Age, 40 years. Enlisted, March 13, 1862, at Utica, to serve three years; mustered in as private, Company D, April 25, 1862; deserted, June 13, 1862, at Front Royal, Va.; also listed as Allen Gould.

406. GRACE, CHARLES—Age, 24 years. Enlisted, May 2, 1861, at Rochester, to serve two years; mustered in as corporal, Company H, May 21, 1861; wounded, August 30, 1862, at battle of Second Bull Run, Va.; died, November 21, 1862, on account of wounds.

407. GRAFF, FREDERICK—Age, 18 years. Enlisted, August 19, 1862, at Utica, to serve three years; mustered in as private, Company E, September 18, 1862; transferred, May 7, 1863, to Company B, Eighty-Third Infantry.

408. GRAHAM, DAVID—Age, 23 years. Enlisted, date not stated at Utica, to serve three years; mustered in as private, Company F, August 7, 1861; discharged for disability, November 13, 1861, at Camp Franklin.

409. GRAHAM, MICHAEL—Age, 27 years. Enlisted, July 30, 1861, at Buffalo, to serve three years; mustered in as private, Company F, August 9, 1861; mustered out with company, May 28, 1863, at Utica, N.Y.; subsequent service, Company B, Thirteenth Artillery.

410. GRANTS, DELA F.—Age, 19 years. Enlisted, September 16, 1861, at Utica, to serve two years; mustered in as private, Company B, September 17, 1861; mustered out with company, May 28, 1863, at Utica, N.Y.; also listed as Dela F. Grands.

411. GRAY, JOSEPH C.—Age, 18 years. Enlisted, May 13, 1861, at Utica, to serve two years; mustered in as private, Company I, May 21, 1861; wounded, August 30, 1862; died of wounds, October 5, 1862, at Carver Hospital, Washington, D.C.

412. GRAYHAM, OWEN—Age, 20 years. Enlisted, May 13, 1861, at Utica; to serve two years; mustered in as private, Company I, May 21, 1861; mustered out with company, May 28, 1863, at Utica, N.Y.

413. GREEN, AMBROSE—Age, 25 years. Enlisted, May 3, 1861, at Utica, to serve two years; mustered in as private, Company F, May 21, 1861; deserted, September 14, 1861, at Alexandria, Va.; subsequent service in Company F, One Hundred and Fourteenth Infantry.

414. GREEN, CLARK W.—Age, 25 years. Enlisted, August 12, 1862, at Utica, to serve three years; mustered in as private, Company F, same date; transferred, May 8, 1863, to Eighty-Third Infantry.

415. GREEN, HENRY—Age, 35 years. Enlisted, May 21, 1861, at Elmira, to serve three months; mustered in as private, Company E, same date; no further record.

416. GREEN, HENRY—Age, 39 years. Enlisted, December 2, 1861, at Rome, to serve three years; mustered in as private, Company C, December 21, 1861; mustered out with company, May 28, 1863, at Utica, N.Y.

417. GREEN, JASPER D.—Age, 18 years. Enlisted, May 3, 1861, at Utica, to serve two years; mustered in as private, Company F, May 21, 1861; wounded, December 13, 1862, at Fredericksburg, Va.; died, January 2, 1863, at Douglas Hospital, Washington, D.C.; also listed as Jasper L. N. Green.

418. GREENE, JEROME—Age, 20 years. Enlisted, May 3, 1861, at Utica, to serve two years; mustered in as private, Company F, May 21, 1861; mustered out with company, May 28, 1863, at Utica, N.Y.; also listed as Jerome A. Green.

419. GREENMAN, JABEZ—Age, 37 years. Enlisted, May 13, 1861, at Utica, to serve two years; mustered in as private, Company I, May 21, 1861; mustered out with company, May 28, 1863, at Utica, N.Y.; subsequent service in Company A, Sixteenth Artillery, as Job Greenman.

420. GRIFFIN, GEORGE—Age, 21 years. Enlisted, December 20, 1861, at Buffalo, to serve two years; mustered in as private, Company I, same date; discharged, July 1, 1865.

421. GRIGGS, WILLIAM E.—Age, 19 years. Enlisted, May 2, 1861, at Rochester, to serve two years; mustered in as private, Company G, May 21, 1861; discharged for disability, December 3, 1862, at Brook's Station, Va.

422. GRIGIER, FRANCIS—Age, 21 years. Enlisted, November 1, 1861, at Utica, to serve two years; mustered in as private, Company B, November 22, 1861; promoted corporal, March 1, 1862; captured at battle of Second Bull Run, August 30, 1862, paroled, sent to Camp Parole, Md.; mustered out with company, May 28, 1863, at Utica, N.Y.; also listed as Francis Crigier; subsequent service in Third New York Light Artillery.

423. GROSS, ANTHONY—Age, 26 years. Enlisted, May 7, 1861, at Utica, to serve two years; mustered in as private, Company E, May 21, 1861; wounded, date and place not stated; mustered out with company, May 28, 1863, at Utica, N.Y.; subsequent service in Twenty-Fourth Cavalry.

424. GROSS, CHARLES—Age, 27 years. Enlisted, May 8, 1861, at Elmira, to serve two years; mustered in as private, Company E, May 21, 1861; killed, December 13, 1862, at Fredericksburg, Va.

425. GUENTHER, CHARLES—Age, 21 years. Enlisted, May 2, 1861, at Rochester, to serve two years; mustered in as private, Company G, May 21, 1861; mustered out with company, May 28, 1863, at Utica, N.Y.

426. GUNN, BENJAMIN H.—Age, 23 years. Enlisted, November 16, 1861, at Utica, to serve two years; mustered in as private, Company B, November 20, 1861; deserted, September 1, 1862, at camp near Centreville, Va.; also listed as Benjamin Gun.

427. GUNNING, BERNARD—Age, 25 years. Enlisted, May 1, 1861, at Utica, to serve two years; mustered in as private, Company B, May 21, 1861; discharged for disability, July 3, 1862, at DeKalb, Va.

428. GUTCHESES, EUGENE—Age, 18 years. Enlisted, May 14, 1861, at Camden, to serve two years; mustered in as private, Company K, May 21, 1861; rejected, May 26, 1861, at Elmira, N.Y.

429. HABLET, PHILIP—Age, 36 years. Enlisted, May 7, 1861, at Utica, to serve two years; mustered in as corporal, Company E, May 21, 1861; promoted sergeant, date not stated; died of disease, June 11, 1862, in Military Hospital, Alexandria, Va.

430. HAIG, THOMAS—Age, 19 years. Enlisted, May 8, 1861, at Utica, to serve two years; mustered in as private, Company C, May 21, 1861; deserted, April 18, 1863, at Belle Plain Landing, Va.

431. HAINS, GEORGE—Age, 21 years. Enlisted, July 27, 1861, at Buffalo, to serve three years; mustered in as private, Company D, August 9, 1861; promoted corporal and reduced, dates not stated; mustered out with company, May 28, 1863, at Utica, N.Y., as George Haines.

432. HALL, ANDREW—Age, 21 years. Enlisted, June 18, 1861, at Elmira, to serve two years; mustered in as private, Company K, same date; discharged for disability, September 24, 1861, at Camp May, Va.

433. HALL, CHARLES—Age, 34 years. Enlisted, May 2, 1861, at Rochester, to serve two years; mustered in as private, Company H, same date; promoted sergeant, date not stated; first sergeant, March 26, 1863; mustered out, May 24, 1863, at Utica, N.Y.; subsequent service in First Veteran Cavalry and Fourteenth Artillery; commissioned second lieutenant, May 13, 1863, with rank from February 24, 1863, vice Wampole, resigned; not mustered.

434. HALL, MORRIS P.—Age, 20 years. Enlisted, May 1, 1861, at Utica, to serve two years; mustered in as private, Company B, May 21, 1861; discharged for disability, Jan-

uary 12, 1863, at Alexandria, Va.; subsequent service in Fifteenth Cavalry.

435. HALL, PARMER—Age, 21 years. Enlisted, January 31, 1862, at Utica, to serve three years; mustered in as private, Company C, March 27, 1862; mustered out with company, May 28, 1863, at Utica, N.Y.; also listed as Parma Hall.

436. HALL, RICHARD C.—Age, 25 years. Enrolled, March 7. 1861, at Utica, to serve three months; mustered in as second lieutenant, Company D, May 21, 1861; resigned, August 7, 1861; also listed as Richard L. Hall; commissioned second lieutenant, July 4, 1861, with rank from May 7, 1861, original.

437. HALSTEAD, CHARLES—Age, 21 years. Enlisted, November 26, 1861, at Buffalo, to serve unexpired term of two years; mustered in as private, Company D, November 26, 1861; captured, August 30, 1862, at battle of Second Bull Run, Va.; paroled, September 13, 1862, at Aiken's Landing, Va.; mustered out with company, May 28, 1863, at Utica, N.Y.; subsequent service in Thirty-Third Independent Battery.

438. HALSTEAD, WILLARD G.—Age, 19 years. Enlisted, May 3, 1861, at Utica, to serve two years; mustered in as private, Company C, May 21 1861; promoted corporal, September 4, 1861; sergeant, November 7, 1861; sergeant major, April 2, 1862; mustered in as second lieutenant, Company D, August 30, 1862; as first lieutenant, Company K, May 15, 1863; mustered out with company, May 28, 1863, at Utica, N.Y.; commissioned second lieutenant, November 7, 1862, with rank from August 30, 1862, vice Miller, promoted; first lieutenant, May 13, 1863, with rank from, March 11, 1863, vice Harden, promoted.

439. HALSTEAD, WILLIAM H.—Age, 20 years. Enlisted, May 3, 1861, at Utica, to serve two years; mustered in as sergeant, Company C, May 21, 1861; promoted first sergeant, September 4, 1861; mustered in as second lieutenant, November 7, 1861; wounded, December 13, 1862, at battle of Fredericksburg, Va.; mustered out with company, May 28, 1863, at Utica, N.Y.; also listed as William H. Holstead; commissioned second lieutenant, November 18, 1861, with rank from November 7, 1861, vice Neill promoted; first lieutenant, not mustered, May 13, 1863, with rank from April 20, 1863, vice Jones, promoted.

440. HALSY, MICHAEL—Age, 33 years. Enlisted, May 2, 1861, at Rochester, to serve two years; mustered in as private, Company H, May 21, 1861; mustered out, May 24, 1863, at Utica, N.Y.; subsequent service in Company G, Sixteenth Cavalry.

441. HAMMOND, GILBERT—Age, 21 years. Enlisted, May 13, 1861, at Utica, to serve three months; mustered in as private, Company I, May 21, 1861; deserted, June 15, 1861, at Elmira, N.Y.

442. HANANER, FREDERICK—Age, 28 years. Enlisted, May 7, 1861, at Utica, to serve two years; mustered in as private, Company E, May 21, 1861; mustered out with company, May 28, 1863, at Utica, N.Y.; subsequent service in Twenty-Fourth Cavalry.

443. HANDLY, JOHN—Age, 22 years Enlisted, May 1, 1861, at Utica, to serve two years; mustered in as private, Company A, May 21, 1861; killed, August 30, 1862, at Groveton, Va.; also listed as John Handley.

444. HANES, ALLEN—Age, 23 years. Enlisted, September 20, 1861, at Buffalo, to serve three years; mustered in as private, Company K, September 20, 1861; deserted, August 13, 1862, at Culpeper, Va.; also listed as Allen Humes.

445. HANNSFELDER, JOSEPH—Age, 22 years. Enlisted, May 1, 1861 at Utica to serve two years; mustered in as corporal, Company A, May 21, 1861; promoted sergeant, August 1, 1861; reduced, April 26, 1862; mustered out with company, May 28, 1863, at Utica, N.Y.

446. HANONS, JAMES—Age, 21 years. Enlisted, July 30, 1861, at Rochester, to serve three years; mustered in as private, unassigned, August 9, 1861; no further record.

447. HANSCOMB, ALBY—Age, 37 years. Enlisted, July 30, 1861, at Rochester, to serve three years; mustered in as private, Company I, August 9, 1861; wounded, at battle of Antietam; mustered out with company, May 28, 1863, at Utica, N.Y.; also listed as Alvah Hanscomb.

448. HARDER, EMMETT—Age, 24 years. Enrolled, May 14, 1861, at Camden, to serve two years; mustered in as second lieutenant, Company K, May 21, 1861; as

first lieutenant, to date, August 8, 1861; as captain, to date, March 12, 1863; mustered out with company, May 28, 1863, at Utica, N.Y.; commissioned second lieutenant, July 4, 1861, with rank from May 14, 1861, original, first lieutenant, August 14, 1861, with rank from August 7, 1861, original; captain, May 13, 1863, with rank from March 11, 1863, vice Caryl, dismissed.

449. HARGRAVES, WILLIAM—Age, 40 years. Enlisted, July 27, 1861, at Rochester, to serve three years; mustered in as private, Company B, August 9, 1861; killed, December 13, 1862, at battle of Fredericksburg, Va.; also listed as William Hargrave.

450. HARLON, WILLIAM—Age, 19 years. Enlisted, May 3, 1861, at Utica, to serve two years; mustered in as sergeant, Company B, May 21, 1861; mustered in as second lieutenant, August 7, 1861; as first lieutenant, April 7, 1862; as captain, November 20, 1862; wounded, December 13, 1862, at battle of Fredericksburg, Va.; mustered out with company, May 28, 1863, at Utica, N.Y.; also listed as William J. Harlon; commissioned second lieutenant, August 14, 1861, with rank from August 7, 1861, original; first lieutenant, April 14, 1862, with rank from April 7, 1862, vice C. E. Lasher, resigned; captain, December 20, 1862, with rank from November 20, 1862, vice Church, resigned.

451. HARNEY, JOSEPH—Age, 21 years. Enlisted, May 2, 1861, at Rochester, to serve two years; mustered in as private, Company G, May 21, 1861; mustered out with company, May 28, 1863, at Utica, N.Y.; also listed as Joseph J. Harney.

452. HARPER, JOHN—Age, 20 years. Enlisted, May 2, 1861, at Rochester, to serve two years; mustered in as private, Company G, May 21, 1861; deserted, May 7, 1862, at Brook's Station, Va.

453. HARRINGTON, EDWIN—Age, 24 years. Enrolled, May 3, 1861, at Utica, to serve three months; mustered in as second lieutenant, Company C, May 21, 1861; resigned, July 20, 1861; commissioned second lieutenant, July 4, 1861, with rank from May 3, 1861, original.

454. HARRINGTON, MICHAEL—Age, 44 years. Enlisted, May 2, 1861, at Rochester, to serve two years; mustered in as private, Company B, May 21, 1861; discharged for disability, October 7, 1861, at Fort Lyon, Va.

455. HARRINGTON, MOSES—Age, 24 years. Enlisted, May 7, 1861, at Utica, to serve two years; mustered in as private, Company E, May 21, 1861; mustered out with company, May 28, 1863, at Utica, N.Y.

456. HARRIS, NELSON J.—Age, 18 years. Enlisted, May 8, 1861, at Elmira, to serve two years; mustered in as sergeant, Company D, May 21, 1861; wounded, August 30, 1862, at Groveton, Va.; discharged for disability, May 13, 1863, at Albany, N.Y.

457. HARRIS, WILLIAM—Age, 18 years. Enlisted, December 8, 1861, at Rome, to serve unexpired term of two years; mustered in as private, Company F, December 8, 1861; wounded, date and place not stated; mustered out with company, May 28, 1863, at Utica, N.Y.

458. HARRISON, WILLIAM B.—Age, 18 years. Enlisted, May 1, 1861, at Utica, to serve two years; mustered in as private, Company B, May 21, 1861; wounded, August 31, 1862, at Groveton, Va.; mustered out with company, May 28, 1863, at Utica, N.Y.; also listed as William Harrison; subsequent service in Twenty-Fourth New York Cavalry.

459. HARTHORN, ROBERT B.—Age, 27 years. Enlisted, May 2, 1861, at Rochester, to serve two years; mustered in as sergeant, Company B, May 21, 1861; reduced to ranks, date not stated; mustered out, May 24, 1863, at Utica, N.Y.; subsequent service in First Veteran Cavalry.

460. HARTMAN, JOHN—Age, 27 years. Enlisted, May 8, 1861, at Elmira, to serve two years; mustered in as private, Company E, May 21, 1861; mustered out with company, May 28, 1863, at Utica, N.Y.

461. HARTMAN, LOUIS—Age, 20 years. Enlisted, September 2, 1861, at Rochester, to serve two years; mustered in as private, Company E, September 5, 1861; transferred to Company I, July 1, 1862; killed, September 17, 1862, at battle of Antietam, Md.; also listed as Lewis Bartiman.

462. HARVEY, WILLIAM—Age, 24 years. Enlisted, September 2, 1861, at Rochester, to serve three years; mustered in as private, Company B, September 5, 1861; deserted, August 8, 1862, at Culpeper, Va.

463. HARWICK, HAMILTON M.—Age, 21 years. Enlisted, August 14, 1861, at

Rome, to serve three years; mustered in as private, Company I, August 20, 1861; deserted, January 25, 1862, at Fort Lyon, Va.; also listed as Hamilton Harwick.

464. HASKIN, ELEAZER—Age, 21 years. Enlisted, May 14, 1861, at Camden, to serve two years; mustered in as private, Company K, May 21, 1861; mustered out with company, May 28, 1863, at Utica, N.Y.

HASKINS, HENRY D.—*see* Hoskins, Henry D.

465. HAY, GILBERT—Age, 42 years. Enlisted, June 1, 1861, at Utica, to serve two years; mustered in as private, Company A, June 1, 1861; promoted sergeant, July 1, 1861; mustered in as second lieutenant, July 21, 1861; as first lieutenant, August 7, 1861; resigned, November 5, 1861; commissioned second lieutenant, August 14, 1861, with rank from July 30, 1861, original; first lieutenant, August 14, 1861, with rank from August 7, 1861, original.

466. HAYES, EDWARD—Age, 21 years. Enlisted, May 7, 1861, at Utica, to serve two years; mustered in as private, Company E, May 21, 1861; mustered out with company, May 28, 1863, at Utica, N.Y.

467. HAYES, JOHN—Age, 31 years. Enlisted, May 22, 1861, at Elmira, to serve two years; mustered in as private, Company K, May 22, 1861; transferred, to Company G, date not stated; deserted, November 1, 1861, at Alexandria, Va.

468. HAYES, SEYMOUR—Age, 20 years. Enlisted, May 13, 1861, at Utica, to serve two years; mustered in as private, Company I, May 21, 1861; wounded at Antietam, Md.; promoted corporal, date not stated; mustered out with company, May 28, 1863, at Utica, N.Y.

469. HAZLEHURST, THEODORE—Age, 19 years. Enlisted, February 9, 1862, at Utica, to serve three years; mustered in as private, Company F, March 27, 1862; killed, August 30, 1862, at Groveton, Va.

470. HEAD, HAMILTON—Age, 25 years. Enlisted, December 13, 1861, at Rochester, to serve two years; mustered in as private, Company K, December 13, 1861; deserted, May 15, 1862, at Brook's Station; also listed as Hamilton M. Head.

471. HEALEY, MORRIS—Age, 24 years. Enlisted, May 2, 1861, at Rochester, to serve two years; mustered in as private, Company G, May 21, 1861; mustered out with company, May 28, 1863, at Utica, N.Y.; also listed as Maurice Healey.

472. HEGNANOR, HENRY—Age, 25 years. Enlisted, May 1, 1861, at Utica, to serve two years; mustered in as private, Company A, May 21, 1861; wounded, August 30, 1862, at battle of Second Bull Run; mustered out with company, May 28, 1863, at Utica, N.Y.

473. HELPLER, WALTER D.—Age, unknown. Enlisted,—, 1861, at Buffalo, to serve two years; mustered in as private, Company F, September 17, 1861; deserted, February 15, 1862, at Fort Lyon, Va.; also listed as Wagman D. Hepler.

474. HEMMINGWAY, HENRY—Age, 20 years. Enlisted, May 3, 1861, at Utica, to serve two years; mustered in as private, Company C, May 21, 1861; captured, August 30, 1862, at battle of Second Bull Run, Va.; paroled and rejoined company, December 5, 1862; mustered out with company, May 28, 1863, at Utica, N.Y.

475. HERRICK, ELBRIDGE B.—Age, 18 years. Enlisted, May 2, 1861, at Rochester, to serve two years; mustered in as private, Company G, May 21, 1861; died of disease, January 3, 1862, at Alexandria, Va.; also listed as Elbridge G. Herrick.

476. HEWITT, WILLIAM A.—Age, 18 years. Enlisted, May 2, 1861, at Rochester, to serve two years; mustered in as private, Company G, May 21, 1861; transferred to Company D, June 1, 1861; deserted, June 1, 1862, at Front Royal, Va.

477. HIBBARD, CLARK C.—Age, 22 years. Enlisted, May 7, 1861, at Utica, to serve two years; mustered in as corporal, Company D, May 21, 1861; promoted sergeant, August 9, 1861; discharged for disability, February 20, 1862.

478. HICKEY, MATTHEW—Age, 28 years. Enlisted, May 1, 1861, at Utica, to serve two years; mustered in as private, Company A, May 21, 1861; promoted corporal, September 16, 1861; sergeant, December 15, 1862; mustered out with company, May 28, 1863, at Utica, N.Y.; subsequent service in Twenty-Fourth Cavalry.

479. HICKEY, THOMAS—Age, 19 years. Enlisted, May 4, 1861, at Elmira, to

serve three months; mustered in as private, Company G, May 21, 1861; deserted, June 1, 1861, at Elmira, N.Y.

480. HICKOX, PERRY D.—Age, 25 years. Enrolled, May 1, 1861, at Utica, to serve three months; mustered in as second lieutenant, Company A, May 21, 1861; resigned, July 30, 1861; commissioned second lieutenant, July 4, 1861, with rank from May 1, 1861, original.

481. HICKS, WILLIAM—Age, 18 years. Enlisted, May 2, 1861, at Rochester, to serve two years; mustered in as private, Company G, May 21, 1861; mustered out with company, May 28, 1863, at Utica, N.Y.; subsequent service in Company C, Twenty-First Cavalry.

482. HIGGINS, JOHN—Age, 29 years. Enlisted, November 11, 1861, at Rochester, to serve two years; mustered in as private, Company H, November 20, 1861; promoted corporal, February 20, 1862; deserted, June 24, 1862, at Manassas, Va.

483. HIGGS, ISAAC W.—Age, 19 years. Enlisted, May 14, 1861, at Camden, to serve two years; mustered in as private, Company K, May 21, 1861; mustered out with company, May 28, 1863, at Utica, N.Y.

484. HILL, JAMES—Age, 18 years. Enlisted, May 2, 1861, at Rochester, to serve two years; mustered in as private, Company G, May 21, 1861; transferred to Company C, November 1, 1861; deserted, August 31, 1862, at Centerville, Va.

485. HILLS, GEORGE—Age, 24 years. Enlisted, May 21, 1861, at Utica, to serve three years; mustered in as private, Company F, same date; transferred to band, date not stated; mustered out with band, September 10, 1861, at Fort Ellsworth, Va.; again enlisted and mustered in, as second-class musician, October 21, 1861; promoted leader, April 3, 1862; mustered out with band, September 4, 1862, at Upton's Hill, Va.; subsequent service, as second lieutenant in Sixteenth Cavalry; also listed as George Hill.

486. HIMMELL, JOSEPH—Age, 22 years. Enlisted, May 2, 1861, at Rochester, to serve two years; mustered in as private, Company G, May 21, 1861; mustered out with company, May 28, 1863.

487. HINES, MICHAEL—Age, 18 years. Enlisted, July 26, 1861, at Buffalo, to serve three years; mustered in as private, Company D, August 7, 1861; promoted corporal and reduced, dates not stated; killed, August 30, 1862, at battle of Second Bull Run, Va.; also listed as Michael Hiney.

488. HOBERT, JOHN A.—Age, 22 years. Enlisted, May 2, 1861, at Rochester, to serve two years; mustered in as private, Company H, May 21, 1861; discharged for disability, November 5, 1862.

489. HOELZER, MICHAEL—Age, 41 years. Enlisted, December 18, 1861, at Rochester, to serve two years; mustered in as private, Company E, same date; wounded at Fredericksburg; discharged for disability, February 26, 1863, at Mount Pleasant Hospital, Washington, D.C.; also listed as Michael Halser.

490. HOGAN, PATRICK—Age, 22 years. Enlisted, May 2, 1861, at Rochester, to serve two years; mustered in as private, Company H, May 21, 1861; mustered out, May 24, 1863, at Utica, N.Y.; subsequent service in First Veteran Cavalry.

491. HOLENBACH, RENSLER—Age, 19 years. Enlisted, May 1, 1861, at Utica, to serve two years; mustered in as private Company B, May 21, 1861; promoted corporal, date not stated; discharged for disability, April 7, 1863, at Baltimore, Md.; also listed as Ranslaer Hollenback.

492. HOLMES, AMERICUS—Age, 23 years. Enlisted, May 7, 1861, at Utica, to serve two years; mustered in as private, Company D, May 21, 1861; mustered out with company, May 28, 1863, at Utica, N.Y.; subsequent service as sergeant in Company H, Fourteenth Artillery.

493. HOLMES, CHARLES—Age, 23 years. Enlisted, August 14, 1861, at Utica, to serve three years; mustered in as private unassigned, August 20, 1861; no further record.

494. HOLMES, CHARLES RAY—Age, 24 years. Enlisted, May 14, 1861, at Elmira, to serve two years; mustered in as sergeant, Company I, May 21, 1861; promoted first sergeant, date not stated; wounded, August 30, 1862, at Bull Run; mustered out with company, May 28, 1863, at Utica, N.Y.

495. HOLMES, ELORN G.—Age, 19 years. Enlisted, May 1, 1861, at Utica, to serve two years; mustered in as private, Company B, May 21, 1861; captured, August

29, 1862, at Manassas, Va.; paroled, date not stated; mustered out with company, May 28, 1863, at Utica, N.Y.

496. HOLMES, JOHN W.—Age, 22 years. Enlisted, May 1, 1861, at Utica, to serve two years; mustered in as private, Company B, May 21, 1861; captured, September 17, 1862; paroled, date not stated; mustered out with company, May 28, 1863, at Utica, N.Y.

HOLSTEAD, WILLIAM H.—see Halstead, William H.

497. HOPKINS, DANIEL A.—Age, 20 years. Enlisted, May 7, 1861, at Utica, to serve two years; mustered in as private, Company D, May 21, 1861; mustered out with company, May 28, 1863, at Utica, N.Y.

498. HOPKINS, PATRICK—Age, 19 years. Enlisted, May 3, 1861, at Utica, to serve two years; mustered in as corporal, Company C, May 21, 1861; promoted sergeant, October 16, 1861; killed, December 13, 1862, at battle of Fredericksburg, Va.

499. HOSKINS, HENRY D.—Age, 18 years. Enlisted, May 13, 1861, at Utica, to serve two years; mustered in as private, Company I, May 21, 1861; killed, August 30, 1862, at the battle of Second Bull Run, Va.; also listed as Henry D. Haskins.

500. HOTCHKIN, GEORGE—Age, 22 years. Enlisted, May 14, 1861, at Elmira, to serve two years; mustered in as corporal, Company I, May 21, 1861; promoted sergeant, date not stated; mustered out with company, May 28, 1863, at Utica, N.Y.; also listed as George A. Hotchkin; subsequent service in Third Artillery.

501. HOUDER, HENRY—Age, 22 years. Enlisted, August 18, 1861, at Rochester, to serve three years; mustered in as private, Company C, September 5, 1861; killed, December 13, 1862, at battle of Fredericksburg, Va.

502. HOUGHTON, CHARLES—Age, 19 years. Enlisted, September 4, 1861, at Utica, to serve two years; mustered in as private, Company A, September 5, 1861; discharged for disability, October 14, 1862, at Philadelphia, Pa.

503. HOUNSON, JOHN H.—Age, 21 years. Enlisted, November 14, 1861, at Rochester, to serve two years; mustered in as private, Company B, November 20, 1861; deserted, March 26, 1862, at Aquia Creek, Va.

504. HOUSTON, CARTER—Age, 22 years. Enlisted, December 13, 1861, at Rochester, to serve two years; mustered in as private, Company I, same date; wounded at battle of Antietam, Md.; mustered out with company, May 28, 1863, at Utica, N.Y.

505. HOVER, ALONZO—Age, 27 years. Enlisted, May 14, 1861, at Camden, to serve two years; mustered in as private, Company K, May 21, 1861; mustered out with company, May 28, 1863, at Utica, N.Y.

506. HOWARD, ABRAHAM—Age, 21 years. Enlisted, December 5, 1861, at Buffalo, to serve three years; mustered in as private, Company D, same date; deserted, June 13, 1862, at Front Royal, Va.

507. HOWARD, ERASTUS—Age, 18 years. Enlisted, May 7, 1861, at Utica, to serve three months; mustered in as private, Company D, May 21, 1861; deserted, June 11, 1861, at Elmira, N.Y.

508. HOWARD, FREDERICK.—Age, 28 years. Enlisted, , 1861, at Utica, to serve three years; mustered in as private, Company E, August 7, 1861; wounded, at Fredericksburg, Va.; died, January 12, 1863, at Harewood Hospital, Washington, D.C.; also listed as Frederick Coonsadt.

509. HOWARD, GEORGE—Age, 28 years. Enlisted, September 17, 1861, at Buffalo, to serve three years; mustered in as private, Company K, same date; deserted, May 26, 1862, at Alexandria, Va.

510. HUGHES, FRANK—Age, 43 years. Enlisted, August 10, 1861, at Rochester, to serve three years; mustered in as private, Company K, same date; mustered out with company, May 28, 1863, at Utica, N.Y.

511. HUGHES, JOHN—Age, 20 years. Enlisted, May 7, 1861, at Utica, to serve two years; mustered in as private, Company D, May 21, 1861; deserted, June 11, 1862, at Front Royal, Va.

512. HUGHES, JOHN H.—Age, 23 years. Enlisted, May 3, 1861, at Utica, to serve two years; mustered in as private, Company C, May 21, 1861; promoted corporal, September 4, 1861; reduced, August 27, 1862; wounded, August 30, 1862, at battle of Second Bull Run, Va.; mustered out with company, May 28, 1863, at Utica, N.Y.;

subsequent service in Twenty-Fourth Cavalry.

513. HUGHES, THOMAS—Age, 18 years. Enlisted, October 12, 1861, at Utica, to serve three years; mustered in as private, Company C, October 14, 1861; mustered out with company, May 28, 1863, at Utica, N.Y.; also listed as Thomas J. Hughes.

514. HUGHS, CYRUS L.—Age, 22 years. Enlisted, May 1, 1861, at Utica, to serve three months; mustered in as private, Company A, May 21, 1861; deserted, June 11, 1861, at Elmira, N.Y.

HUMES, ALLEN—see Hanes, Allen.

515. HUNT, THOMAS—Age, 38 years. Enlisted, May 2, 1861, at Rochester, to serve two years; mustered in as private, Company H, May 21, 1861; promoted corporal, February 20, 1862; wounded, September 17, 1862, at Antietam, Md.; discharged, October 31, 1862, by reason of enlistment in Company B, Second United States Cavalry.

516. HUNTLY, THOMAS—Age, 28 years. Enlisted, May 3, 1861, at Utica, to serve two years; mustered in as private, Company F, May 21, 1861; mustered out with company, May 28, 1863, at Utica, N.Y.

517. HURLBURT, JOHN S.—Age, 25 years. Enlisted, May 3, 1861, at Utica, to serve two years; mustered in as first sergeant, Company C, May 21, 1861; discharged for disability, September 4, 1861, near Alexandria, Va.

518. HUTTON, JAMES—Age, 28 years. Enlisted, May 2, 1861, at Rochester, to serve two years; mustered in as private, Company H, May 21, 1861; transferred, April 1, 1862, to Company I; mustered out with company, May 28, 1863, at Utica, N.Y.; subsequent service in First Veteran Cavalry.

519. INGERSOLL, FRANCIS M.—Age, 28 years. Enlisted, May 1, 1861, at Utica, to serve two years; mustered in as private, Company A, May 21, 1861; appointed wagoner, August 8, 1861; deserted, January 27, 1862, at Fort Ellsworth, Va.

INGERSOLL, FRANK D.—see Engersoll, Frank D.

520. ITTINGER, STEPHEN—Age, 22 years. Enlisted, September 10, 1861, at Buffalo, to serve three years; mustered in as private, Company C, same date; mustered out with company, May 28, 1863, at Utica, N.Y.

521. JACKSON, WILLIAM—Age, 18 years. Enlisted, May 3, 1861, at Utica, to serve two years; mustered in as private, Company C, May 21, 1861; died of disease, November 27, 1861, in Seventh New York Brigade Hospital, Alexandria, Va.

522. JAMES, EDWARD—Age, date and place of enlistment not stated; commissioned second lieutenant, date not stated, with rank from May 1, 1861, original; not mustered.

523. JAMISON, WILLIAM—Age, 34 years. Enlisted, August 4, 1861, at Rochester, to serve three years; mustered in as private, Company A, August 9, 1861; wounded, August 31, 1862, at Bull Run, Va.; discharged for disability, December 14, 1862, at Baltimore, Md.

524. JENNINGS, CHARLES E.—Age, 34 years. Enrolled, May 2, 1861, at Rochester, to serve two years; mustered in as captain, in Company G, May 21, 1861; wounded, August 30, 1862, at Groveton, Va.; died of wounds, October 1, 1862, at Washington, D.C.; commissioned captain, July 4, 1861, with rank from May 18, 1861, original.

525. JENNINGS, GILBERT S.—Age, 44 years. Enrolled, May 2, 1861, at Elmira, to serve two years; mustered in as captain, Company G, May 21, 1861; as major, May 21, 1861; as lieutenant colonel, September 20, 1862; wounded, December 16–17, 1862, at Fredericksburg, Va.; mustered out with regiment, May 28, 1863, at Utica, N.Y.; commissioned captain, date not stated, with rank from May 2, 1861, original; major, June 20, 1861, with rank from May 17, 1861. original; lieutenant colonel, November 25, 1862, with rank from September 19, 1862, vice Richardson, promoted.

526. JENNINGS, JOHN S.—Transferred from Battery I, First Ohio Veteran Artillery as first lieutenant, Company G, this regiment; mustered out with company, May 28, 1863, at Utica, N.Y.; commissioned first lieutenant, November 7, 1862, with rank from October 1, 1862, vice Binder, promoted.

527. JOHNS, FRANKLIN—Age, 27 years. Enlisted, May 2, 1861, at Rochester, to serve two years; mustered in as private, Company G, May 21, 1861; mustered out with company, May 28, 1863, at Utica, N.Y.

528. JOHNSON, ARCHIBALD—Age,

19 years. Enlisted, May 21, 1861, at Elmira, to serve three months; mustered in as private, Company E, same date; no further record.

529. JOHNSON, CHARLES R.—Age, 22 years. Enlisted, May 3, 1861, at Utica, to serve two years; mustered in as private, Company C, May 21, 1861; second lieutenant, Company I, August 7, 1861; resigned, January 28, 1862; commissioned second lieutenant, August 14, 1861, with rank from August 7, 1861, original.

530. JOHNSTON, EDWARD A.—Age, 42 years. Enlisted, May 14, 1861, at Camden, to serve two years; mustered in as private, Company K, May 21, 1861; killed at Groveton, Va., August 30, 1862.

531. JONES, DAVID R.—Age, 26 years. Enlisted, May 3, 1861, at Utica, to serve two years; mustered in as private, Company C, May 21, 1861; captured at Mount Vernon, September 6, 1861; paroled at Salisbury, N.C., May 28, 1862; mustered out with company, May 28, 1863, at Utica, N.Y.; subsequent service in Fourteenth Artillery and Twenty-Fourth Cavalry.

532. JONES, ENOCH—Age, 23 years. Enlisted, June 1, 1861, at Utica, to serve two years; mustered in as private, Company A, same date; promoted. first sergeant, August 7, 1861; mustered as second lieutenant, November 5, 1861; first lieutenant, August 30, 1862; mustered out with company, May 28, 1863, at Utica, N.Y.; commissioned second lieutenant, November 18, 1861, with rank from November 6, 1861, vice Kingsbury, promoted; first lieutenant, November 7, 1862, with rank from August 30, 1862, vice Kingsbury, promoted; captain, May 13, 1863, with rank from April 20, 1863, vice Shirley, discharged.

533. JONES, JOHN H.—Age, 18 years. Enlisted, May 3, 1861, at Utica, to serve two years; mustered in as private, Company C, June 1, 1861; appointed musician, date not stated; mustered out with company, May 28, 1863, at Utica, N.Y.

534. JONES, JOHN M.—Age, 24 years. Enlisted, November 8, 1861, at Utica, to serve unexpired term of two years; mustered in as private, Company C, November 22, 1861; wounded, December 13, 1862, at Fredericksburg, Va.; mustered out with company, May 28, 1863, at Utica, N.Y.

535. JONES, NATHAN G.—Age, 34 years. Enlisted, May 2, 1861, at Rochester, to serve two years; mustered in as private, Company G, May 21, 1861; discharged for disability, October 7, 1861, at Fort Lyon, Va.

536. JONES, RALPH G.—Age, 18 years. Enlisted, May 3, 1861, at Utica, to serve two years; mustered in as private, Company C, May 21, 1861; discharged for disability, October 30, 1862, at Carver Hospital.

537. JONES, REUBEN M.—Age, 35 years. Enlisted, June 1, 1861, at Elmira, to serve two years; mustered in as private, Company K, same date; wounded at Fredericksburg, Va.; discharged, January 7, 1863, at Washington, D.C.

538. JONES, SMITH—Age, 28 years. Enlisted, May 21, 1861, at Rochester, to serve two years; mustered in as second-class musician, band, same date; mustered out, September 10, 1861, with band, at Fort Ellsworth, Va.

539. JONES, THOMAS—Age, 20 years. Enlisted, May 3, 1861, at Utica, to serve two years; mustered in as private, Company F, May 21, 1861; mustered out with company, May 28, 1863, at Utica, N.Y.; subsequent service in Twenty-Fourth Cavalry.

540. JONES, THOMAS—Age, 40 years. Enlisted, October 7, 1861, at Utica, to serve three years; mustered in as private, Company I, October 14, 1861; discharged for disability, January 3, 1862, at Fort Lyon, Va.

541. JONES, WILLIAM—Age, 28 years. Enlisted, May 3, 1861, at Utica, to serve two years; mustered in as private, Company F, May 21, 1861; wounded, August 30, 1862, at Groveton, Va.; discharged for disability, December 1, 1862, at United States General Hospital, Alexandria, Va.; subsequent service in Company D, Fifty-Second Infantry.

542. JONES, WILLIAM E.—Age, 19 years. Enlisted, May 2, 1861, at Rochester, to serve two years; mustered in as private, Company G, May 21, 1861; mustered out with company, May 28, 1863, at Utica, N.Y.

543. JONES, WILLIAM O.—Age, 25 years. Enlisted, May 1, 1861, at Utica, to serve two years; mustered in as private, Company A, May 21, 1861; wounded, August 30, 1862; died of disease, January

13, 1863, at Columbia College Hospital; also listed as William Jones.

544. JOSLIN, JAMES—Age, 19 years Enlisted, May 13, 1861, at Utica, to serve two years; mustered in as private, Company I, May 21, 1861; deserted, January 25, 1862, at Fort Lyon, Va.

545. JOY, LEWIS—Age, 20 years. Enlisted, May 1, 1861, at Utica to serve two years; mustered in as private, Company B, May 21, 1861 promoted corporal, March 1, 1862; wounded, August 30, 1862, at Bull Run, Va.; discharged, August 20, 1863, at Utica, N.Y. also listed as Louis Joy.

546. JUDSON, DE JAY—Age, 22 years. Enlisted, May 13, 1861, at Utica, to serve two years; mustered in as private, Company I, May 21, 1861; mustered out with company, May 28, 1863, at Utica N.Y.

547. KAIN, PATRIC—Age, 22 years. Enlisted, May 1, 1861, at Utica to serve two years; mustered in as private, Company B, May 21, 1861 wounded, August 30, 1862, at Bull Run, Va.; mustered out with company, May 28, 1863, at Utica, N.Y.; also listed as Patrick Kaine; subsequent service in Company B, Fifteenth Cavalry.

KAINEY, JOHN—see Carney, John.

548. KANE, EDGAR—Age, 19 years. Enlisted, May 1, 1861, at Utica to serve two years; mustered in as private, Company B, May 21, 1861, mustered out with company, May 28, 1863, at Utica, N.Y.; subsequent service in Third Artillery.

549. KANE, EDWIN—Age, 19 years. Enlisted, May 1, 1861, at Elmira, to serve two years; mustered in as private, Company B, May 21, 1861; mustered out with company, May 28, 1863, at Utica N.Y.; subsequent service in Third Artillery.

550. KANE, JOHN—Age, 24 years. Enlisted, September 30, 1861, at Rochester, to serve three years; mustered in as private, Company K, September 30, 1861; wounded, August 31, 1862, at Bull Run, Va.; mustered out with company, May 28, 1863, at Utica, N.Y.

551. KATHARAN, CHARLES—Age, 23 years. Enlisted, September 13, 1861, at Buffalo, to serve three years; mustered in as private, Company D, same date; deserted, January 30, 1862, at Fort Lyon, Va.; also listed as Charles Kathlan.

552. KEARNS, NICHOLAS—Age, 33 years. Enlisted, May 2, 1861, at Rochester, to serve two years; mustered in as private, Company H, May 21, 1861; died, January 1, 1863, at York, Pa.

553. KECK, HARRISON—Age, 21 years. Enlisted, May 3, 1861, at Utica, to serve two years; mustered in as private, Company F, May 21, 1861; deserted, November 8, 1861, at Camp Franklin, Va.

554. KECK, TRUMAN—Age, 24 years. Enlisted, May 5, 1861, at Utica, to serve two years; mustered in as private, Company F, May 21, 1861; deserted, September 1, 1862, at Manassas, Va.; returned to Company, date not stated; assigned to the Second United States Artillery, to serve out time lost by desertion.

555. KEELER, HARRY H.—Age, 21 years. Enlisted, May 7, 1861, at Utica, to serve three months; mustered in as private, Company D, May 21, 1861; discharged for disability, June 20, 1861, at Elmira, N.Y.

556. KEELER, JOHN—Age, 20 years. Enlisted, October 26, 1861, at Rochester, to serve unexpired term of two years; mustered in as private, Company B, October 27, 1861; mustered out with company, May 28, 1863, at Utica, N.Y.

557. KEENE, CHARLES—Age, 21 years. Enlisted, May 1, 1861, at Utica, to serve two years; mustered in as private, Company A, May 21, 1861; discharged for disability, October 9, 1861, at Alexandria, Va.

558. KEENE, JOSEPH—Age, 20 years. Enlisted, May 1, 1861, at Utica, to serve two years; mustered in as private, Company B, May 21, 1861; promoted corporal, date not stated; awarded a Medal of Honor for bravery, at battle of Fredericksburg, Va., December 13, 1862; mustered out with company, May 28, 1863, at Utica, N.Y.; subsequent service in Third Artillery.

559. KELIN, WILLIAM—Age, 22 years. Enlisted, August 22, 1862, at Utica, to serve three years; mustered in as private, unassigned, August 28, 1862; no further record.

560. KELLER, GEORGE B.—Age, 40 years. Enlisted, November 29, 1861, at Rome, to serve unexpired term of two years; mustered in as private, Company E, December 11, 1861, wounded at battle at Groveton, Va., August 30, 1862; died, October 25,

1862, at Trinity Church Hospital, Georgetown, D.C.

561. KELLEY, MARTIN—Age, 36 years. Enlisted, May 8, 1861, at Elmira, to serve three months; mustered in as private, Company E, May 21, 1861; dropped; no further record.

562. KELLOGG, ALPHEUS G.—Age, 23 years. Enlisted, January 8, 1862, at Utica, to serve two years; mustered in as private, Company A, January 9, 1862; mustered out with company, May 28, 1863, at Utica, N.Y.

563. KENEDY, WILLIAM—Age, 24 years. Enlisted, May 1, 1861, at Utica, to serve two years; mustered in as private, Company B, May 21, 1861; captured, December 13, 1862, at Fredericksburg, Va.; paroled, date not stated; mustered out with company, May 28, 1863, at Utica, N.Y; also listed as William Kennedy; subsequent service in Seventeenth Veteran Infantry.

564. KENT, WILLIAM—Age, 27 years. Enlisted, May. 14, 1861, at Elmira, to serve three months; mustered in as private, Company I, May 21, 1861; died, October 8, 1861, at Alexandria, Va.

565. KETCHUM, WILLIAM P.—Age, 24 years. Enlisted, May 14, 1861, at Camden, to serve two years; mustered in as private, Company K, May 21, 1861; mustered out with company, May 28, 1863, at Utica, N.Y.

566. KIDD, WALTER—Age, 36 years. Enlisted, May 3, 1861, at Buffalo, to serve two years; mustered in as private, Company A, May 21, 1861; promoted first sergeant, date not stated; mustered out with company, May 28, 1863, at Utica, N.Y.; subsequent service in Company C, Fourteenth Artillery.

567. KILBURN, HENRY—Age, 18 years. Enlisted, May 7, 1861, at Utica, to serve two years; mustered in as private, Company E, May 21, 1861; mustered out with company, May 28, 1863, at Utica, N.Y.; subsequent service in Third Artillery.

568. KILMER, HENRY C.—Age, 24 years. Enlisted, May 3, 1861, at Utica, to serve two years; mustered in as corporal, Company C, May 21, 1861; reduced, date not stated; mustered out with company, May 28, 1863, at Utica, N.Y.; also listed as Henry C. Kilner.

569. KIMBLE, ANDREW—Age, 22 years. Enlisted, May 3, 1861, at Utica, to serve two years; mustered in as private, Company F, May 21, 1861; mustered out with company, May 28, 1863, at Utica, N.Y.; also listed as Andrew J. Kimball; subsequent service in Company I, Second Artillery.

570. KIMBLE, NORMAN—Age, 33 years. Enlisted, May 3, 1861, at Utica, to serve two years; mustered in as private, Company F, May 21, 1861; mustered out with company, May 28, 1863, at Utica, N.Y.; also listed as Norman Kimball.

571. KIMBLE, WILLIAM—Age, 25 years. Enlisted, May 3, 1861, at Utica, to serve two years; mustered in as private, Company F, May 21, 1861; mustered out with company, May 28, 1863, at Utica, N.Y.; also listed as William Kimball.

572. KING, GEORGE—Age, 30 years. Enlisted, May 2, 1861, at Rochester, to serve two years; mustered in as private, Company H, May 21, 1861; mustered out, May 24, 1863, at Utica, N.Y.; subsequent service in Company H, Sixty-Eighth New York Volunteers.

573. KINGSBURY, GEORGE—Age, 20 years. Enlisted, May 3, 1861, at Utica, to serve two years; mustered in as private, Company C, May 21, 1861; promoted corporal, December 15, 1862; mustered out with company, May 28, 1863, at Utica, N.Y.; also listed as George H. Kingsbury.

574. KINGSBURY, HEZEKIAH—Age, 37 years. Enlisted, November 22, 1861, at Rome, to serve unexpired term of two years; mustered in as private, Company F, December 11, 1861; discharged for disability, December 19, 1862, at Convalescent Camp, Va.

575. KINGSBURY, JOHN T.—Age, 22 years. Enlisted, May 1, 1861, at Utica, as first sergeant, Company B, to serve two years; mustered in as sergeant major, May 21, 1861; as second lieutenant, Company A, August 7, 1861; as first lieutenant, November 5, 1861; as captain, August 30, 1862; mustered out with company, May 28, 1863, at Utica, N.Y.; commissioned second lieutenant; August 14, 1861, with rank from August 7, 1861, original; first lieutenant, November 18, 1861, with rank from November 5, 1861, vice Hay, resigned; captain, November 7, 1862; with rank from August 30. 1862, vice Cossleman, killed in action. Died August 20, 1926.

576. KINGSBURY, LEWIS M.—Age,

18 years. Enlisted, November 19, 1861, at Utica, to serve unexpired term of two years; mustered in as private, Company F, November 22, 1861; wounded, at Antietam, Md.; mustered out with company, May 28, 1863; also listed as Lewis Kingsbury; subsequent service in Third Artillery.

577. KINNEY, JOHN W.—Age, 22 years. Enrolled, May 14, 1861, at Elmira, to serve three months; mustered in as second lieutenant, Company I, May 21, 1861; resigned, August 7, 1861; commissioned second lieutenant, July 4, 1861, with rank from May 13, 1861, original.

578. KIRK, WILLIAM C.—Age, 19 years. Enlisted, May 1, 1861, at Utica, to serve two years; mustered in as private, Company B, May 28, 1861; mustered out with company, May 28, 1863; also listed as William Kirk.

579. KLEINE, WILLIAM—Age, 43 years. Enlisted, May 14, 1861, at Utica, to serve two years; mustered in as private, Company E, May 21, 1861; discharged for disability, March 6, 1862, at Fort Lyon, Va.; also listed as William Klin.

580. KLEINEFIELD, JOSEPH—Age, 22 years. Enlisted, May 7, 1861, at Utica, to serve two years; mustered in as first sergeant, Company E, May 21, 1861; as second lieutenant, December 15, 1862; mustered out with company, May 28, 1863, at Utica, N.Y.; commissioned second lieutenant, February 11, 1863, with rank from December 15, 1862, vice Bacon, died of wounds.

581. KLEINFIELD, LOUIS—Age, 18 years. Enlisted, October 4, 1861, at Utica, to serve three years; mustered in as private, Company E, October 14, 1861; wounded at Groveton, Va.; discharged for disability, November 24, 1862, at Brook's Station, Va.

582. KNEIBEL, FREDERICK—Age, 23 years. Enlisted, October 4, 1861, at Rochester, to serve unexpired term of two years; mustered in as musician, band, same date; discharged, August 16, 1862, at Philadelphia, Pa.

583. KNOX, THOMAS—Age, 22 years. Enlisted, October 22, 1861, at Rochester, to serve three years: mustered in as private, Company G, same date; discharged for disability, July 16. 1862, at Alexandria, Va.

584. KOHLER, CHRISTIAN—Age, 23 years. Enlisted, May 7, 1861, at Utica, to serve two years; mustered in as private, Company E, May 21, 1861; mustered out with company, May 28, 1863, at Utica, N.Y.

585. KOHLER, JOHN—Age, 21 years. Enlisted, May 7, 1861, at Utica, to serve two years; mustered in as sergeant, Company E, May 21, 1861; reduced to private, August 2, 1861; promoted corporal, December—, 1861; sergeant, January 11, 1862; mustered out with company, May 28, 1863, at Utica, N.Y.

586. KONSOHAFZE, WILLIAM—Age, 21 years. Enlisted, May 7, 1861, at Utica, to serve two years; mustered in as private, Company E, May 21, 1861; mustered out with company, May 28, 1863, at Utica, N.Y.; also listed, as William Konshafstky.

587. KREIGER, JOHN—Age, 26 years. Enlisted, May 7, 1861, at Utica, to serve two years; mustered in as private, Company E, May 21, 1861; promoted corporal, date not stated; sergeant, September 14, 1862; mustered out with company, May 28, 1863, at Utica, N.Y.

588. KROTOSHINSKY, ROBERT—Age, 19 years. Enlisted, May 1, 1861, at Utica, to serve two years; mustered in as private, Company A, May 21, 1861; mustered out with company, May 28, 1863, at Utica, N.Y.; also listed as Krottoshinsky.

589. LACKEY, JOHN S.—Age, 21 years. Enlisted, May 7, 1861, at Utica, to serve two years; mustered in as private, Company D, May 21, 1861; discharged for disability, February 11, 1863, at Convalescent Camp, Va.

590. LA CLAER, GEORGE—Age, 22 years. Enlisted, May 13, 1861, at Utica, to serve two years; mustered in as private, Company I, May 21, 1861; deserted, May 1, 1862, at Fort Lyon, Va.

591. LAFORCE, GEORGE—Age, 29 years. Enlisted, December 18, 1861, at Rochester, to serve two years; mustered in as private, Company E, December 19, 1861; wounded at Fredericksburg, Va.; died, January 14, 1863, at Lincoln Hospital, Washington, D C.

592. LANE, ABLE—Age, 19 years. Enlisted, September 12, 1861, at Rochester, to serve three years; mustered in as private, Company G, same date; died of disease, February 20, 1863, at Washington, D.C.

593. LANE, JEREMIAH—Age, 31 years.

Enlisted, May 2, 1861, at Rochester, to serve two years; mustered in as private, Company H, May 21, 1861; wounded, August 30, 1862, at Bull Run, Va.; discharged for disability, November 12, 1862, at Third Division General Hospital, Alexandria, Va.; also listed as Jeramiah Lane.

594. LANG, THOMAS—Age, 30 years. Enlisted, May 2, 1861, at Rochester, to serve two years; mustered in as private, Company G, May 21, 1861; wounded, date and place not stated; discharged on account of wounds, November 5, 1862, at General Hospital, Alexandria, Va.

595. LANGTRY, ROBERT—Age, 44 years. Enlisted, May 2, 1861, at Rochester, to serve two years; mustered in as private, Company H, May 21, 1861; missing, August 30, 1862, at battle of Second Bull Run, Va.; returned to company, November 3, 1862; mustered out, May 24, 1863, at Utica, N.Y.

596. LANPHIER, CHARLES W.—Age, 21 years. Enlisted, May 14, 1861, at Camden, to serve two years; mustered in as private, Company K, May 21, 1861; promoted sergeant, February 1, 1862; mustered out with company, May 28, 1863, at Utica, N.Y.; also listed as Charles W. Lamphier.

597. LAPLANCH, MOSES—Age, 42 years. Enlisted, August 20, 1862, at Utica, to serve three years; mustered in as private, unassigned, same date; no further record.

598. LAQUAY, ORVILLE—Age, 24 years. Enlisted, August 27, 1862, at Utica, to serve three years; mustered in as private, Company K, September 18, 1862; transferred, May 9, 1863, to Eighty-Third Infantry.

599. LARIBE, RICHARD—Age, 25 years. Enlisted, May 3, 1861, at Utica, to serve two years; mustered in as private, Company F, May 21, 1861; promoted sergeant, August 13, 1861; first sergeant, May 1, 1863; mustered out with company, May 28, 1863, at Utica, N.Y.; subsequent service, unassigned; Sixteenth Artillery.

600. LASHER, CHARLES EDWIN—Age, 25 years. Enlisted, May 1, 1861, at Utica, to serve two years; mustered in as private, Company B, May 21, 1861; promoted sergeant, August 7, 1861; mustered as first lieutenant, October 28, 1861; resigned, April 7, 1862; also listed as Charles Edward Lasher; commissioned first lieutenant, November 18, 1861, with rank from October 28, 1861,. vice Barnett resigned.

601. LASHER, WILLIAM—Age, 23 years. Enlisted, May 8, 1861, at Elmira, to serve two years; mustered in as private, Company E, May 21, 1861; discharged for disability, November 21, 1861, at Camp Franklin, Va.; also listed as William Lashier.

602. LAVIN, PATRICK—Age, 28 years. Enlisted, May 2, 1861, at Rochester, to serve three months; mustered in as private, Company H, May 21, 1861; deserted, June 21, 1861, at Adams, Jefferson County, N.Y.

603. LAVIS, ROBERT—Age, 19 years. Enlisted, May 2, 1861, at Rochester, to serve two years; mustered in as private, Company H, May 21, 1861; mustered out, May 24, 1863, at Utica, N.Y.

604. LAWRENCE, JOHN—Age, 23 years. Enlisted, June 19, 1861, at Elmira, to serve two years; mustered in as private, Company K, same date; discharged for disability, February 6, 1863, at Philadelphia, Pa.; also listed as John W. Laurence.

605. LAWRENCE, THOMAS—Age, 24 years. Enlisted, October 30, 1861; at Rochester, to serve three years; mustered in as private, Company H, November 12, 1861; deserted, August 17, 1862, at Rapidan, Va.

606. LAWTON, BENJAMIN F.—Age, 26 years. Enlisted, May 3, 1861, at Utica, to serve two years; mustered in as private, Company C, May 21, 1861; mustered out with company, May 28, 1863, at Utica, N.Y.

607. LAWTON, WILLIAM W.—Age, 23 years. Enlisted, May 7, 1861, at Utica, to serve two years; mustered in as private, Company D, May 21, 1861; mustered out with company, May 28, 1863, at Utica, N.Y.

608. LEACH, CHARLES A.—Age, 18 years. Enlisted, May 3, 1861, at Utica, to serve two years; mustered in as private, Company C, May 21, 1861; discharged for disability, September 14, 1861, at Camp Morx.

609. LEACH, ROMINE W.—Age, 19 years. Enlisted, May 2, 1861, at Rochester, to serve two years; mustered in as drummer, Company G, May 21, 1861; deserted, January 19, 1862, at Alexandria, Va.; also listed as Romeyn W. Leach.

610. LEARY, GEORGE—Age, 29 years. Enlisted, August 28, 1861, at Rochester, to

serve three years; mustered in as private, Company H, September 5, 1861; died; August 13, 1862, in General Hospital at Alexandria, Va.

611. LEAVENS, JOHN—Age, 22 years. Enlisted, May 13, 1861, at Utica, to serve two years; mustered in as private, Company I, May 21, 1861; promoted corporal, January 1, 1863; mustered out with company, May 28, 1863, at Utica, N.Y.

612. LEE, EDWARD—Age, 19 years. Enlisted, May 1, 1861, at Utica, to serve three months; mustered in as private; Company A, May 21, 1861; discharged, June 8, 1861, by order of the court.

613. LEE, FRANK—Age, 18 years. Enrolled, August 7, 1861, at Alexandria, Va., to serve three years; mustered in as second lieutenant, Company G, same date; resigned, October 29, 1862; commissioned second lieutenant, August 14, 1861, with rank from August 7, 1861, original. Died March 20, 1914.

LEFFLER, SAMUEL—see Loeffier, Samuel.

614. LEONARD, GEORGE—Age, 18 years. Enlisted, May 7, 1861, at Utica, to serve two years; mustered in as private, Company D, May 21, 1861; deserted, June 12, 1862, at Front Royal, Va.

615. LEONARD, HUGH—Age, 19 years. Enlisted, May 7, 1861, at Utica, to serve two years; mustered in as sergeant, Company D, May 21, 1861; as second lieutenant, August 7, 1861; killed, August 30, 1862, at the battle of Second Bull Run, Va.; commissioned second lieutenant, August 14, 1861, with rank from August 7, 1861, original.

LEWIN, EDWARD A. ROSS—see Rosslewin, Edward E.

616. LEWIS, JOHN—Age, 32 years. Enlisted, September 20, 1861, at Utica, to serve three years; mustered in as private, Company D, September 28, 1861; deserted, June 26, 1862, at Manassas, Va.

617. LINBECK, HIRAM—Age, 21 years. Enlisted, May 3, 1861, at Utica, to serve two years; mustered in as private, Company F, May 21, 1861; deserted, June 18, 1861, at Elmira, N.Y.

618. LINBECK, MILTON H.—Age, 18 years. Enlisted, May 3, 1861, at Utica, to serve two years; mustered in as private, Company F, May 21, 1861; deserted, September 2, 1861, at Washington, D.C.; also listed as Milton Linbeck.

619. LINCH, MICHAEL—Age, 22 years. Enlisted, May 2, 1861, at Rochester, to serve two years; mustered in as private, Company H, May 21, 1861; mustered out, May 24, 1863, at Utica, N.Y.; also listed as Michael Lynch.

620. LING, JOHN—Age, 18 years. Enlisted, May 2, 1861, at Rochester, to serve two years; mustered in as private, Company H, May 21, 1861; mustered out, May 24, 1863, at Utica, N.Y.; subsequent service, Company C, Twenty-First Cavalry.

621. LINSMAN, CASPER—Age, 21 years. Enlisted, May 1, 1861, at Utica, to serve two years; mustered in as private, Company A, May 21, 1861; promoted corporal, May 1, 1862; reduced, date not stated; wounded, date and place not stated; mustered out with company, May 28, 1863, at Utica, N.Y.

622. LINSMAN, CONRAD—Age, — years. Enlisted, September 3, 1861, at Utica, to serve three years; mustered in as private, Company A, same date; no further record since April 10, 1863.

623. LINSMAN, MARTIN—Age, 23 years. Enlisted, May 1, 1861, at Utica, to serve two years; mustered in as private, Company A, May 21, 1861; promoted corporal, date not stated; sergeant, August 1, 1861; first sergeant, November 5, 1861; died of gunshot wound October 2, 1862, at Judiciary Square Hospital.

624. LIPPEY, PETER—Age, 21 years. Enlisted, May 21, 1861, at Elmira, to serve three months; mustered in as private, Company E, May 21, 1861; no further record.

625. LITTLE, CLARK—Age, 19 years. Enlisted, May 3, 1861, at Utica, to serve two years; mustered in as corporal, Company C, May 21, 1861; reduced, date not stated; captured, August 29 or 30, 1862, at Manassas, Va.; paroled, September 3, 1862, at Groveton Battlefield; reported at Camp Parole, Md., and was sent to Alexandria, Va., November 1862; deserted, February 19, 1863, place not stated.

626. LITTLE, WILLIAM—Age, 19 years. Enlisted, November 12, 1861, at Rochester

to serve three years; mustered in as private, Company A, same date; wounded, April 10, 1863; transferred, April 4, 1864, to Company A, Fortieth New York Volunteers.

627. LOEFFLER, MATHIAS—Age, 25 years. Enlisted, May 7, 1861, at Utica, to serve two years; mustered in as private, Company E, May 21, 1861; mustered out with company, May 28, 1863, at Utica, N.Y.

628. LOEFFLER, SIMON—Age, 25 years. Enlisted, August 4, 1862, at Verona, to serve three years; mustered in as private, Company E,. September 3, 1862; transferred, May 7, 1863, to Company B, Eighty-Third Volunteers; also listed as Samuel Leffier.

629. LOFFLIER, ZEEGIEL—Age, 25 years. Enlisted, August 4, 1862, at Verona, to serve three years; mustered in as private, unassigned, same date; no further record.

630. LONSDALE, JOHN W.—Age, 21 years. Enlisted, August 14, 1861, at Rome, to serve three years; mustered in as private, Company I, August 24, 1861; mustered out with company, May 28, 1863, at Utica, N.Y.

631. LOVE, ANDREW—Age, 20 years. Enlisted, May 2, 1861, at Rochester, to serve two years; mustered in as sergeant, Company G, May 21, 1861; wounded at the battle Fredericksburg, Va., December 13, 1862; died of such wounds, December 14, 1862.

632. LOVELAND, ALBERT—Age, 18 years. Enlisted, May 7, 1861, at Utica, to serve two years; mustered in as private, Company D, May 21, 1861; mustered out with company, May 28, 1863, at Utica, N.Y.

633. LOVELESS, WILLIAM—Age, 19 years. Enlisted, May 10, 1861, at Utica, to serve two years; mustered in as private, Company E, May 21, 1861; mustered out with company, May 28, 1863, at Utica, N.Y.

634. LOVET, THOMAS—Age, 24 years. Enlisted, May 2, 1861, at Rochester, to serve three months; mustered in as private, Company H, May 21, 1861; deserted, June 21, 1861, at Adams, Jefferson County, N.Y.

635. LOWER, HENRY—Age, 23 years. Enlisted, May 2, 1861, at Rochester to serve two years; mustered in as private, Company H, May 21, 1861; mustered out, May 24, 1863, at Utica, N.Y.

636. LUCAS, GEORGE—Age, 18 years. Enlisted, May 1, 1861, at Utica, to serve two years; mustered in as private, Company B, May 21, 1861; transferred to Company E, May 22, 1861; wounded, date and place not stated; mustered out with company, May 28, 1863; at Utica, N.Y.

637. LUDDINGTON, NELSON—Age, 33 years. Enlisted, May 3, 1861, at Utica, to serve two years; mustered in as private, Company C, May 21, 1861; wounded, August 30, 1862; mustered out with company, May 28, 1863, at Utica, N.Y.; subsequent service in Third Artillery.

638. LYNCH, ALBERT D.—Age, 22 years. Enlisted, May 14, 1861, at Camden, to serve two years; mustered in as sergeant, Company K, May 21, 1861; mustered as second lieutenant, August 7, 1861; as first lieutenant, Company D, March 25, 1862; mustered out with company, May 28, 1863, at Utica, N.Y.; commissioned second lieutenant, August 4, 1861, with rank from August 7, 1861, original; first lieutenant, December 20, 1862, with rank from October 19, 1862, vice McLaughlin, promoted.

639. LYNCH, LEANDER—Age, 24 years. Enlisted, May 16, 1861, at Elmira, to serve two years; mustered in as private, Company K, May 21, 1861; wounded at battle of Fredericksburg, Va., December 13, 1862; died, December 15, 1862, at Fredericksburg, Va., of wounds.

LYNCH, MICHAEL—see Linch, Michael.

640. LYNCH, URIAH—Age, 21 years. Enlisted, May 14, 1861, at Camden, to serve two years; mustered in as corporal, Company K, May 21, 1861; mustered out with company, May 28, 1863, at Utica, N.Y.

641. MACKAY, MICHAEL—Age, 29 years. Enlisted, July 26, 1861, at Buffalo, to serve three years; mustered in as private, Company D, August 9, 1861; wounded at Groveton, Va., August 30, 1862; died, September 16, 1862, of such wounds, at Carver Hospital, Washington, D.C.; also listed as Michael Mackey.

642. MADISON, ROBERT—Age, 19 years. Enlisted, August 25, 1862, at Boonville, to serve three years; mustered in as private, Company C, September 18, 1862; wounded at battle of Fredericksburg, Va., December 13, 1862; died, March 5, 1863, at Carver Hospital, Washington, D.C.

643. MAHANEY, GEORGE P.—Age, 22 years. Enlisted, May 8, 1861, at Elmira, to serve two years; mustered in as private, Company E, May 21, 1861; wounded at the battle of Groveton, Va., August 30, 1862; died of such wounds, September 8, 1862, at Armory Square Hospital, Washington, D.C.; also listed as George P. Martus.

644. MAHANY, ANDREW—Age, 22 years. Enlisted, May 7, 1861, at Utica, to serve two years; mustered in as private, Company E, May 21, 1861; mustered out with company, May 28, 1863, at Utica, N.Y.

645. MAHER, JOHN—Age, 31 years. Enlisted, May 2, 1861, at Rochester, to serve two years; mustered in as private, Company H, May 21, 1861; wounded, August 30, 1862, at the battle of Second Bull Run, Va.; mustered out, May 24, 1863, at Utica, N.Y.; subsequent service in First Veteran Cavalry.

646. MAHONEY, MICHAEL—Age, 22.years. Enlisted, May 2, 1861, at Rochester, to serve two years; mustered in as private, Company H, May 21, 1861; promoted corporal, February 20, 1862; deserted, September 16, 1862, at Antietam, Md.

647. MAMPEL, ERNEST—Age, 21 years. Enlisted, May 21, 1861, at Elmira, to serve three months; mustered in as private, Company E, same date; no further record.

648. MANGAN, PATRICK—Age, 19 years. Enlisted, May 2, 1861, at Rochester, to serve three months; mustered in as private, Company H, May 21, 1861; deserted, June 21, 1861, at Elmira, N.Y.; also listed as Patrick Mangin.

649. MANLY, FRANKLIN N.—Age, 21 years. Enlisted, May 14, 1861, at Camden, to serve two years; mustered in as private, Company K, May 21, 1861; wounded, August 30, 1862, at Groveton, Va.; discharged, June 17, 1863, at Albany.

650. MANTAL, HENRY—Age, 41 years. Enlisted, October 3, 1861, at Utica, to serve three years; mustered in as private, Company E, same date; wounded, December 13, 1862, at Fredericksburg, Va.; discharged for disability, February 18, 1863, at Field Hospital, Washington, D.C.

651. MAPES, ALBERT—Age, 27 years. Enlisted, May 7, 1861, at Utica, to serve two years; mustered in as private, Company E, May 21, 1861; promoted corporal, April 15, 1862; mustered out with company, May 28, 1863, at Utica, N.Y.; also listed as Albert Maps.

652. MARKHAM, CHARLES G.—Age, 22 years. Enlisted, August 14, 1862, at Utica, to serve three years; mustered in as private, Company F, August 18, 1862; discharged for disability, March 5, 1863, at Baltimore, Md.; also listed as Charles Markham.

653. MARONEY, PATRICK H.—Age, 22 years. Enlisted, July 30, 1861, at Rochester, to serve three years; mustered in as private, Company H, August 9, 1861; no further record.

654. MARSH, JOHN—Age, 18 years. Enlisted, May 2, 1861, at Rochester, to serve three months; mustered in as private, Company G, May 21, 1861; discharged, September 6, 1861, by order of secretary of war.

655. MARTIN, GEORGE—Age, 21 years. Enlisted, September 16, 1861, at Buffalo, to serve three years; mustered in as private, Company H, same date; transferred to Company D, February 21, 1862; wounded, December 13, 1862, at Fredericksburg, Va.; mustered out with company, May 28, 1863, at Utica, N.Y.; subsequent service in Company B, Twenty-Second Cavalry.

656. MARTIN, LA FOREST J.—Age, 18 years. Enlisted, May 3, 1861, at Utica, to serve two years; mustered in as private, Company C, Ma 21, 1861; killed in action, December 13, 1862, at battle of Fredericksburg, Va.

MARTUS, GEORGE P.—see Mahaney, George P.

657. MARX, JOHN—Age, 30 years. Enlisted, May 21, 1861, at Rochester, to serve three months; mustered in as private, Company F, same date; transferred to field and stuff, date not stated, as musician; mustered out with band, September 10, 1861, at Fort Ellsworth, Va.; reenlisted, October 14, 1861, at Rochester, N.Y., for unexpired term as musician; discharged for disability, June 28, 1862, at Alexandria, Va.; also listed as John Max.

658. MASON, AMASSA—Age, 24 years. Enlisted, August 14, 1861, at Rome, to serve three years; mustered in as private, Company I, August 20, 1861; deserted, September 10, 1861, at Alexandria, Va.

659. MASON, CHARLES—Age, 21

years. Enlisted, May 13, 1861, at Utica, to serve two years; mustered in as private, Company I, May 21, 1861; died of disease, September 15, 1861 at Alexandria Hospital.

660. MASON, GEORGE—Age, 18 years. Enlisted, August 2, 1861, at Rochester, to serve three years; mustered in as private, Company G, August 9, 1861; mustered out with company, May 28, 1863, at Utica, N.Y.; also listed as George W. Mason; subsequent service in Company C, Twenty-First Cavalry.

661. MATCH, LAURENCE—Age, 18 years. Enlisted, May 2, 1861, at Rochester, to serve two years; mustered in as private, Company G, May 21, 1861; mustered out with company, May 28, 1863, at Utica, N.Y.

662. MATHER, CHRIST—Age, 20 years. Enlisted, October 1, 1861, at Utica, to serve three years; mustered in as private, Company A, October 14, 1861; mustered out with company, May 28, 1863, at Utica, N.Y.; also listed as Christopher Mathews.

663. MATHEWS, GEORGE B.—Age, 30 years. Enlisted, August 15, 1862, at Utica, to serve three years; mustered in as private, Company A, same date; transferred, date not stated, to Company B, Eighty-Third New York Volunteers; subsequent service in Ninety-Third Infantry and Tenth Cavalry.

664. MATHEWS, JOHN—Age, 23 years. Enlisted, November 21, 1861, at Utica, to serve unexpired term of two years; mustered in as private, Company A, December 11, 1861; deserted, September 17, 1862, at Sharpsburg, Va.

665. MATHEWS, WILLIAM—Age, 21 years. Enlisted, January 8, 1862, at Utica, to serve three years; mustered in as private, Company A, January 9, 1862; discharged for disability, March 13, 1863; subsequent service in Company C, Sixteenth Artillery.

666. MATTISSON, THOMAS J.—Age, 23 years. Enlisted, May 14, 1861, at Camden, to serve two years; mustered in as private, Company K, May 21, 1861; killed, August 30, 1862, at Groveton, Va.

667. MAY, DAVID—Age, 30 years. Enlisted, May 8, 1861, at Elmira, to serve two years; mustered in as private, Company E, May 21, 1861; mustered out with company, May 28, 1863, at Utica, N.Y.; also listed as David Myers.

668. MAY, WILLIAM—Age, 34 years. Enlisted, September 9, 1861, at Buffalo, to serve three years; mustered in as private, Company G, same date; discharged for disability, May 6, 1862, at Fort Lyon, Va.

669. MAYER, ANTONY—Age, 27 years. Enlisted, October 15, 1862, at Utica, to serve three years; mustered in as private, unassigned, same date; reported as deserted, October 16, 1862, at Utica, N.Y.; no further record.

670. McADAMS, JAMES R.—Age, 18 years. Enlisted, May 13, 1861, at Utica, to serve two years; mustered in as private, Company I, May 21, 1361; discharged for disability, December 30, 1861, at Fort Lyon. Va.; also listed as James McAdams.

671. McCALLISTER, FRANK—Age, 21 years. Enlisted, August 15, 1862, at Utica, to serve three years; mustered in as private, unassigned, September 6, 1862; no further record.

672. McCANN, WILLIAM—Age, 28 years. Enlisted, May 3, 1861, at Utica, to serve two years; mustered in as private, Company C, May 21, 1861; mustered out with company, May 28, 1863, at Utica, N.Y.; subsequent service in Company E, Second Artillery.

673. McCANTY, WILLIAM—Age, 20 years. Enlisted, May 2, 1861, at Rochester, to serve two years; mustered in as private, Company H, May 21, 1861; deserted, June 14, 1862, at Front Royal, Va.

674. McCARRICK, WILLIAM—Age, 24 years. Enlisted, May 1, 1861, at Utica, to serve two years; mustered in as private, Company B, May 21, 1861; mustered out with company, May 28, 1863, at Utica, N.Y.

675. McCARTY, DANIEL—Age, 21 years. Enlisted, September 23, 1861, at Utica, to serve three years; mustered in as private, Company F, September 28, 1861; mustered out with company, May 28, 1863, at Utica, N.Y.

676. McCARTY, JOHN—Age, 20 years. Enlisted, May 1, 1861, at Elmira, to serve two years; mustered in as private, Company B, May 21, 1861; discharged for disability, August 20, 1862, at Fairfax Seminary; also listed as John McCarthy.

677. McCLENTHEN, CHARLES—Age, 34 years. Enlisted, May 2, 1861, at

Rochester, to serve two years; mustered in as private, Company G, May 21, 1861; mustered out with company, May 28, 1863, at Utica, N.Y.; also listed as Charles McClenther; subsequent service in Company G, Fifteenth Cavalry.

678. McCLUSKY, PAUL—Age, 25 years. Enlisted, May 3, 1861, at Utica, to serve two years; mustered in as private, Company F, May 21, 1861; promoted corporal, October 18, 1861; sergeant, September 18, 1862; wounded, December 13, 1862, at battle of Fredericksburg, Va.; died of such wounds, January 11, 1863, at Douglas Hospital, Washington, D.C.

679. McCOMBER, PHILANDER—Age, 34 years. Enlisted, September 13, 1861, at Rochester, to serve three years; mustered in as private, Company D, same date; discharged for disability, March 6, 1862, at Fort Lyon, Va.

680. McCORMACK, SAMUEL—Age, 23 years. Enlisted, May 2, 1861, at Rochester, to serve two years; mustered in as private, Company H, May 21, 1861; mustered out, May 24, 1863, at Utica, N.Y.

681. McCORMICK, JAMES—Age, 34 years. Enlisted, September 3, 1861, at Rochester, to serve three years; mustered in as private, Company H, September 5, 1861; discharged for disability, March 6, 1862, at Fort Lyon, Va.; subsequent service in Thirty-Third Battery.

682. McCRAITH, JOHN—Age, 30 years. Enlisted, May 13, 1861, at Elmira, to serve two years; mustered in as private, Company I, May 21, 1861; discharged for disability, November 12, 1861, at Camp Franklin, Va.; subsequent service in Sixteenth Artillery.

683. McCRAY, ELIGAH—Age, 27 years. Enlisted, May 1, 1861, at Utica, to serve two years; mustered in as private, Company A, May 21, 1861; appointed wagoner, September 16, 1861; mustered out with company, May 28, 1863, at Utica, N.Y.

684. McCULLOUGH, PATRICK—Age, 29 years. Enlisted, May 1, 1861, at Utica, to serve two years; mustered in as private, Company A, May 21, 1861; mustered out with company, May 28, 1863, at Utica, N.Y.; subsequent service in Company F, Third New York Artillery.

685. McDOWELL, WILLIAM—Age, 24 years. Enlisted, September 17, 1861, at Buffalo, to serve three years; mustered in as private, Company H, same date; mustered out, May 24, 1863, at Utica, N.Y.; subsequent service in Company L, Twelfth Cavalry.

686. McFALL, FREDERICK—Age, 34 years. Enlisted, May 3, 1861, at Utica, to serve two years; mustered in as private, Company C, May 21, 1861; mustered out with company, May 28, 1863, at Utica, N.Y.

687. McGARRY, MICHAEL—Age, 40 years. Enlisted, May 2, 1861, at Rochester, to serve two years; mustered in as sergeant, Company H, May 21, 1861; mustered out, May 24, 1863, at Utica, N.Y.; subsequent service in Company I, First Veteran Cavalry.

688. McGENNIS, THOMAS—Age, 19 years. Enlisted, September 16, 1861, at Utica, to serve two years; mustered in as private, Company F, September 17, 1861; deserted, June 22, 1862, at Manassas, Va.

689. McGUIRE, LUKE—Age, 38 years. Enlisted, May 2, 1861, at Rochester, to serve two years; mustered in as sergeant, Company G, May 21, 1861; mustered out with company, May 28, 1863, at Utica, N.Y.

690. McGUIRE, PETER—Age, 22 years. Enlisted, May 7, 1861, at Utica, to serve two years; mustered in as private, Company D, May 21, 1861; promoted corporal, November 19, 1861; sergeant, February 20, 1862; first sergeant, August 30, 1862; reduced to sergeant, date not stated; wounded, December 13, 1862, at battle of Fredericksburg, Va.; mustered out with company, May 28, 1863, at Utica, N.Y.

691. McINTYRE, A. D.—Age, 36 years. Enlisted, October 19, 1861, at Utica, to serve three years; mustered in as private, Company E, October 21, 1861; died of disease, January 4, 1863, at Belle Plain, Va.

692. McLAUGHLIN, JAMES—Age, 19 years. Enlisted, May 14, 1861, at Elmira, to serve two years; mustered in as sergeant, Company I, May 21, 1861; promoted first sergeant, date not stated; mustered in as first lieutenant, January 11, 1862; captain; October 19, 1862; mustered out with company, May 28, 1863, at Utica, N.Y.; subsequent service in Company C, Sixteenth Artillery; commissioned first lieutenant, January 17, 1862, with rank from January 11, 1862, vice Thomson, resigned; captain, December 20,

1862, with rank from October 19, 1862, vice C. B. Coventry, resigned.

693. McLAUGHLIN, ROBERT—Age, 19 years. Enlisted, August 7, 1861, at Utica, to serve two years; mustered in as private, Company C, same date; wounded, August 30, 1862, at Groveton, Va.; discharged by reason of such wounds, December 23, 1862, at Washington, D.C.

694. McMANUS, JOHN—Age, 28 years. Enlisted, May 2, 1861, at Rochester, to serve two years; mustered in as private, Company H, May 21, 1861; discharged for disability, June 17, 1862, at Carver Hospital, Washington, D.C.

695. McMERRICK, ZABINA—Age, 21 years. Enlisted, May 21, 1861, at Elmira, to serve three months; mustered in as private, Company E, same date; no further record.

696. McNACOL, DAVID—Age, 25 years. Enlisted, July 26, 1861, at Buffalo, to serve three years; mustered in as private, Company C, August 9, 1861; transferred to Company G, November 1, 1861; mustered out with company, May 28, 1863, at Utica, N.Y.

697. McNAMARA, MARTIN—Age, 22 years. Enlisted, September 20, 1862, at Utica, to serve three years; mustered in as private, Company E, September 30, 1862; transferred, May 8, 1863, to Company D, Eighty-Third New York Volunteers.

698. McNETT, DAN—Age, date of enlistment, place and term not stated; mustered in as private, Company C; no further record.

699. McNOTT, GEORGE—Age, 40 years. Enlisted, September 4, 1861, at Utica, to serve two years; mustered in as private, Company A, September 5, 1861; mustered out with company, May 28, 1863, at Utica, N.Y.

700. McNOTT, WILLIAM—Age, 20 years. Enlisted, May 1, 1861, at Utica, to serve two years; mustered in as private, Company A, May. 21, 1861; deserted, August 28, 1862.

701. McSLOY, MICHAEL—Age, 20 years. Enlisted, August 12, 1861, at Buffalo, to serve three years; mustered in as private, Company C, September 5, 1861; transferred to Company H, September 9, 1861; deserted, August 8, 1862, at Culpeper, Va.

702. MEDDER, JOHN—Age, 33 years. Enlisted, November 27, 1861, at Rome, to serve unexpired term of two years; mustered in as private, Company E, December 11, 1861; wounded at battle of Groveton, Va., August 30, 1862; discharged for disability, January 22, 1863, at Convalescent Camp, Va.

703. MEEHAN, JOHN—Age, 24 years. Enlisted, May 2, 1861, at Rochester, to serve two years; mustered in as private, Company G, May 21, 1861; captured at Bull Run, Va., August 30, 1862, paroled at Charleston, Va., September 4, 1862; mustered out with company, May 28, 1863, at Utica, N.Y.; subsequent service in Company F, Fourteenth Artillery.

MELLON, JAMES—see Miller, James.

704. MENCH, CHARLES—Age, 18 years. Enlisted, December 28, 1861, at Elmira, to serve unexpired term of two years; mustered in as private, unassigned, January 8, 1862; no further record.

705. MERCER, CHARLES T.—Age, 21 years. Enlisted, May 21, 1861, at Elmira, to serve three months; mustered in as private, Company E, same date; no further record.

706. MERCER, WILLIAM E.—Age, 22 years. Enrolled, May 1, 1861, at Utica, to serve three months; mustered in as first lieutenant, Company A, May 21, 1861; resigned, August 7, 1861; commissioned first lieutenant, July 4, 1861, with rank from May 1, 1861, original.

707. MERINUS, GEORGE—Age, 26 years. Enlisted, December 11, 1861, at Utica, to serve unexpired term of two years; mustered in as private, Company E, same date; wounded at battle of Groveton, Va., August 30, 1862; discharged for disability, February 20, 1863, at Chestnut Hill Hospital, Philadelphia, Pa.; also listed as George W. Morens.

708. MERRILL, DWIGHT W.—Age, 33 years. Enlisted, October 12, 1861, at Rochester, to serve three years; mustered in as private, Company H, October 16, 1861; deserted, June 16, 1862.

709. MEYER, HOWARD C.—Age, 19 years. Enlisted, May 3, 1861, at Utica to serve two years; mustered in as private, Company C, May 21, 1861; promoted sergeant, October 16, 1861; first sergeant, July 24, 1862; killed, December 13, 1862, at battle of Fredericksburg, Va.

710. MILDOLA, THEODORE—Age,

50 years. Enlisted, October 14, 1861, at Rochester, to serve unexpired term of two years; mustered in as musician in band, same date; discharged for disability, April 29, 1862, at Fort Lyon, Va.

711. MILLER, FRANKLIN—Age, 22 years. Enlisted, May 8, 1861, at Utica. to serve two years; mustered in as private, Company D, May 21, 1861; deserted, April 20, 1862, at Fort Lyon, Va.

712. MILLER, GODFREY W.—Age, 20 years. Enlisted, May 1, 1861, at Utica, to serve two years; mustered in as private, Company A, May 21, 1861; promoted corporal, February 20, 1862; sergeant, August 30, 1862; discharged for disability, December 29, 1862, at Mount Pleasant Hospital, Washington, D.C.

713. MILLER, JABEZ L.—Age 20 years. Enlisted, May 1, 1861, at Utica, to serve two years; mustered in as first sergeant, Company A, May 21, 1861; transferred to field and staff, August 7, 1861, and promoted sergeant major; mustered in as second lieutenant, Company H, to date, April 2, 1862; first lieutenant, to date, August 31, 1862; mustered out, May 24, 1863, at Utica, N.Y.; commissioned second lieutenant, April 9, 1862, with rank from April 2, 1862, vice E. E. Rosslewin, promoted; first lieutenant, November 7, 1862, with rank from August 30, 1862, vice E. E. Rosslewin, promoted.

714. MILLER, JAMES—Age, date of enlistment, place and muster-in not stated; private, unassigned; deserted and arrested at Utica, N.Y.; no further record.

715. MILLER, JAMES—Age, 28 years. Enlisted, May 1, 1861, at Utica, to serve two years; mustered in as corporal, Company B, May 21, 1861; reduced, August 24, 1861; mustered out with company, May 28, 1863, at Utica, N.Y.; also listed as James Mellon.

716. MILLER, JOHN—Age, 33 years. Enlisted, May 1, 1861, at Utica, to serve two years; mustered in as private, Company A, May 21, 1861; wounded, December 31, 1862; mustered out with company, May 28, 1863, at Utica, N.Y.

717. MILLER, JOHN—Age, 32 years. Enlisted, October 14, 1861, at Rochester, to serve unexpired term of two years; mustered in as musician in band, same date; mustered out with band, September 4, 1862, at Upton's Hill, Va.

718. MILLER, MATHIAS—Age, 22 years. Enlisted, October 14, 1861, at Rochester, to serve unexpired term of two years; mustered in as musician in band, same date; mustered out with band September 4, 1862, at Upton's Hill, Va.; subsequent service in Company B, Twenty-First Cavalry.

719. MILLER, THOMAS J.—Age, 19 years. Enlisted, August 14, 1861, at Utica, to serve three years; mustered in as private, Company D, August 20, 1861; discharged for disability, February 22, 1863, at Convalescent Camp, Va.

720. MILLS, HENRY—Age, 19 years. Enlisted, September 26, 1861, at Rome, to serve three years; mustered in as private, Company C, same date; discharged for disability, March 6, 1862, at Fort Lyon, Va.

721. MILLS, JAMES—Age, 19 years. Enlisted, May 21, 1861, at Elmira, to serve three months; mustered in as private, Company C, same date; no further record.

722. MILLSPAUGH, OSCAR—Age, 21 years. Enlisted, December 17, 1861, at Elmira, to serve unexpired term of two years; mustered in as private, unassigned, January 3, 1862; no further record.

723. MILSTED, WILLIAM H.—Age, 19 years. Enlisted, August 14, 1861, at Rome, to serve three years; mustered in as private, Company I, August 20, 1861; transferred to Company C, January 14, 1862; mustered in as first lieutenant, October 1, 1862; mustered out with company, May 28, 1863, at Utica; commissioned first lieutenant, December 20, 1862, with rank from October 1, 1862, vice Neill, promoted.

724. MINER, CAREY C.—Age, 25 years Enlisted, May 3, 1861, at Utica, to serve two years; mustered in as private, Company F, May 21, 1861; mustered out with company, May 28, 1863, at Utica, N.Y.; subsequent service in Company E, Fourteenth Artillery.

725. MITCHELL, DANIEL—Age, 21 years. Enlisted, May 1, 1861, at Utica, to serve two years; mustered in as private, Company B, May 21, 1861; mustered out with company, May 28, 1863, at Utica, N.Y.; also listed as Daniel Mitchele.

726. MITCHELL, JOHN O.—Age, 18 years. Enlisted, May 13, 1861, at Utica, to

serve two years; mustered in as private, Company I, May 21, 1861; promoted corporal, date not stated; mustered out with company, May 28, 1863, at Utica, N Y.; also listed as John J. Mitchell.

727. MITCHLER, JACOB—Age, 18 years. Enlisted, May 1, 1861, at Utica, to serve two years; mustered in as private, Company A, May 21, 1861; promoted corporal, April 27, 1862; killed, December 13, 1862, at battle of Fredericksburg, Va.

728. MOLE, FRANCIS—Age, 19 years. Enlisted, May 2, 1861, at Rochester to serve two years; mustered in as private, Company H, May 21, 1861; mustered out with company, May 28, 1863, at Utica, N.Y.; also listed as Francis or "Frank" Moll; subsequent service as sergeant Company C, Fourteenth Artillery. Killed in action July 30, 1864, at Petersburg, Va.

729. MONAGAN, JAMES—Age, 20 years. Enlisted, August 25, 1862, at Boonville, to serve three years; mustered in as private, Company C, September 18, 1862; discharged for disability, August 17, 1863, at Convalescent Camp, Va.; also listed as James Momgan.

730. MONAHAN, PATRICK—Age, 19 years. Enlisted, May 13, 1861, at Elmira, to serve two years; mustered in as private, Company I, May 21, 1861; deserted, May 1, 1862, at Fort Lyon, Va.; also listed as Patrick Monnehan.

731. MONTGOMERY, ELIAS J.—Age, 18 years. Enlisted, May 14, 1861, at Elmira, to serve two years; mustered in as drummer, Company I, May 21, 1861; returned to ranks, date not stated; transferred to Company E, July 1, 1862; mustered out with company, May 28, 1863, at Utica, N.Y.; subsequent service in Company C, Fourteenth Artillery.

732. MOORE, JOHN—Age, 18 years. Enlisted, February 18, 1862, at Utica, to serve three years; mustered in as private, Company F, March 27, 1862; deserted, September 24, 1862, at Sharpsburg, Md.

733. MOORE, WILLIAM C.—Age, 22 years. Enlisted, September 2, 1862, at Utica, to serve two years; mustered in as private, Company G, same date; died of disease, December 1, 1862, at Brook's Station, Va.

734. MORAN, PATRICK—Age, 30 years. Enlisted, August 26, 1862, at Utica, to serve two years; mustered in as private, Company A, September 8, 1862; discharged for disability, October 19, 1862, at Washington, D.C.

735. MOREHEAD, GEORGE—Age, 23 years. Enlisted, May 2, 1861, at Rochester, to serve two years; mustered in as private, Company G, May 21, 1861; mustered out with company, May 28, 1863, at Utica, N.Y.

MORENS, GEORGE W.—see Merinus, George.

736. MORGAN, JOHN—Age, 23 years. Enlisted, August 22, 1861, at Rochester, to serve three years; mustered in as private, Company D, September 16, 1861; deserted, June 13, 1862, at Front Royal, Va.; arrested, August 7, 1862; no further record.

737. MORGAN, LORENZO D.—Age, 21 years. Enlisted, May 13, 1861, at Utica, to serve two years; mustered in as private, Company I, May 21, 1861; wounded, August 30, 1862; captured and paroled, dates not stated; mustered out with company, May 28, 1863, at Utica, N.Y.

738. MORGAN, RAY D.—Age, 21 years. Enlisted, May 13, 1861, at Utica, to serve two years; mustered in as private, Company I, May 21, 1861; captured, August 29, 1862 at Bull Run, Va.; paroled, September 7, 1862, at Gainesville, Va.; mustered out with company, May 28, 1863, at Utica, N.Y.

739. MORGAN, WILLIAM—Age, 24 years. Enlisted, May 7, 1861, at Utica, to serve two years; mustered in as private, Company E, May 21, 1861; killed, August 30, 1862, at Groveton, Va.

740. MORRIS, EDWARD F.—Age, 22 years. Enlisted, May 1, 1861, at Utica, to serve two years; mustered in as private, Company A, May 21, 1861; wounded, December 13, 1862; discharged for disability, March 24, 1863, at Philadelphia, Pa.

741. MOSHIER, DAVISON—Age, 19 years. Enlisted, December 23, 1861, at Elmira, to serve unexpired term of two years; mustered in as private, unassigned, January 3, 1862; no further record.

742. MOSHIER, JOHN—Age, 18 years. Enlisted, December 23, 1861, at Elmira, to serve unexpired term of two years; mustered in as private, unassigned, January 3, 1862; no further record.

743. MOZIER, ALBERT—Age, 21 years.

Enlisted, May 13, 1861, at Utica, to serve two years; mustered in as private, Company I, May 21, 1861; mustered out with company, May 28, 1863, at Utica, N.Y.; also listed as Albert F. Mosher; subsequent service, Company F, Eighth Artillery.

744. MUDDERMAN, EDWIN—Age, 19 years. Enlisted, May 1, 1861, at Utica, to serve two years; mustered in as private, Company B, May 21, 1861; discharged, February 17, 1862, by order of the secretary of war; subsequent service in Twenty-Fourth Cavalry.

745. MULLEN, AMOS—Age, 25 years. Enlisted, May 14, 1861, at Camden, to serve two years; mustered in as private, Company K, May 21, 1861; killed, August 30, 1862, at Groveton, Va.

746. MULLEN, MARTIN—Age, 20 years. Enlisted, May 7, 1861, at Utica, to serve two years; mustered in as private, Company E, May 21, 1861; promoted corporal, November 1, 1862; mustered out with company, May 28, 1863, at Utica, N.Y.; subsequent service in Twenty-Fourth Cavalry.

747. MUNSON, ANSON L.—Age, 19 years. Enlisted, July 29, 1861, at Rochester, to serve three years; mustered in as private, Company C, August 9, 1861; promoted corporal, December 15, 1862; mustered out with company, May 28, 1863, at Utica, N.Y.

748. MUNSON, BUEL—Age, 19 years. Enlisted, July 29, 1861, at Rochester, to serve three years; mustered in as private, Company C, August 9, 1861; wounded, date and place not stated; died, January 2, 1863, at Lincoln Hospital, Washington, D.C.

749. MURETHER, PATRICK—Age, 29 years. Enlisted, May 2, 1861, at Rochester, to serve two years; mustered in as private, Company G, May 21, 1861; mustered out with company, May 28, 1863, at Utica., N.Y.; also listed as Patrick Muretha.

750. MURPHY, DENNIS—Age, 21 years. Enlisted, May 2, 1861, at Rochester, to serve two years; mustered in as private, Company H, May 21, 1861; deserted, May 27, 1862, at Alexandria, Va.

751. MURPHY, MICHAEL—Age, 19 years. Enlisted, May 1, 1861, at Utica, to serve two years; mustered in as private, Company B, May 21, 1861; captured, December 13, 1862; paroled, date not stated; mustered out with company, May 28, 1863, at Utica, N.Y.; subsequent service in Company G, Eighteenth Cavalry.

752. MURPHY, RICHARD—Age, 19 years. Enlisted, May 2, 1861, at Rochester, to serve two years; mustered in as private, Company H, May 21, 1861; deserted, October 1, 1862, at Sharpsburg, Md.

753. MURRAY, ANDREW—Age, 19 years. Enlisted, August 3, 1861, at Rochester, to serve three years; mustered in as private, Company B, August 9, 1861; killed, December 13, 1862, at Fredericksburg, Va.

754. MYERS, CHARLES—Age, 19 years. Enlisted, October 15, 1861, at Rochester, to serve unexpired term of two years; mustered in as musician in band, same date; mustered out with band, September 4, 1862, at Upton's Hill, Va.

MYERS, DAVID—*see* May, David.

755. MYERS, FRED—Age, 19 years. Enlisted, May 1, 1861, at Utica, to serve two years; mustered in as private, Company B, May 21, 1861; promoted corporal, August 24, 1861; sergeant, April 7, 1862; killed, August 30, 1862, at Groveton, Va., also listed as Frederic Meyers.

756. NASH, CHARLES—Age, 19 years. Enlisted, May 3, 1861, at Utica, to serve two years; mustered in as sergeant, Company C, May 21, 1861; reduced, October 1, 1861; discharged for disability, April 25, 1863, at Washington, D.C.

757. NEAR, HENRY—Age, 38 years. Enlisted, December 23, 1861, at Utica, to serve two years; mustered in as private, Company A, December 24, 1861; mustered out with company, May 28, 1863, at Utica, N.Y.; subsequent service in Company C, Sixteenth Artillery.

758. NEAVES, CHAUNCEY—Age, 23 years. Enlisted, June 17, 1861, at Elmira, to serve two years; mustered in as private, Company K, same date; discharged, June 17, 1863, at Albany, N.Y.

759. NEILL, WILLIAM H.—Age, 26 years. Enlisted, May 3, 1861, at Utica, to serve two years; mustered in as sergeant, Company C, May 21, 1861; mustered in as second lieutenant, July 20, 1861; first lieutenant, November 7, 1861; captain, Company D, to date September 10, 1862; wounded, December 13, 1862, at Fredericksburg, Va.; discharged, date not stated;

commissioned second lieutenant, November 18, 1861, with rank from July 20, 1861, vice Herrington, resigned; first lieutenant, November 18, 1861, with rank from November 7, 1861, vice Roberts, resigned; captain, November 7, 1862, with rank from September 9, 1862, vice Arrowsmith, resigned to be appointed lieutenant colonel, One Hundred and Fifty-Seventh Infantry.

760. NELLIS, JAMES—Age, 40 years. Enlisted, December 13, 1861, at Rochester, to serve two years; mustered in as private, Company I, same date; wounded, December 13, 1862, at Fredericksburg, Va.; died, December 27, 1862, at General Hospital, Washington, D.C.

761. NELSON, JOHN—Age, 36 years. Enlisted, May 1, 1861, at Utica, to serve two years; mustered in as private, Company A, May 21, 1861; discharged for disability, November 22, 1861, at Utica, N.Y.

762. NETTLETON, ALBERT—Age, 19 years. Enlisted, May 3, 1861, at Utica, to serve two years; mustered in as private, Company F, May 21, 1861; killed, December 13, 1862, at Fredericksburg, Va.

763. NETTLETON, EUGENE—Age, 20 years. Enlisted, April 1, 1862, at Utica, to serve two years; mustered in as private, Company F, April 25, 1862; transferred, May 8, 1863, to Company D, Eighty-Third Infantry.

764. NEWCOMB, WILLIAM O.—Age, 19 years. Enlisted, May 3, 1861, at Utica, to serve two years; mustered in as private, Company F, May 21, 1861; wounded, August 30, 1862, at Groveton, Va.; died, September 14, 1862, at Washington Hospital, Alexandria, Va.

765. NICHOLAS, JAMES B.—Age, 21 years. Enlisted, May 2, 1861, at Rochester, to serve two years; mustered in as private, Company G, May 21, 1861; deserted, May 18, 1862, at Front Royal, Va.

766. NICHOLSON, JOHN—Age, 19 years. Enlisted, May 2, 1861, at Rochester, to serve two years; mustered in as private, Company H, May 21, 1861; captured, August 30, 1862, at Bull Run, Va.; paroled, date not stated; mustered out, May 24, 1863, at Utica, N.Y.

767. NICHOLSON, THOMAS—Age, 43 years. Enlisted, December 10, 1861, at Rochester, to serve two years; mustered in as private, Company K, same date; wounded, August 30, 1862, at Groveton, Va., at the battle of Second Bull Run, Va.; discharged for disability, February 6, 1863, at Convalescent Camp, Va.; also listed as Thomas J. Nicholson.

768. NIGHTENGALE, RICHARD—Age, 24 years. Enlisted, May 1, 1861, at Utica, to serve two years; mustered in as private Company B, May 21, 1861; mustered out with company, May 28, 1863, at Utica, N.Y.

769. NIVER, GEORGE—Age, 40 years. Enlisted, May 14, 1861, at Camden, to serve two years; mustered in as private, Company K, May 21, 1861; deserted, August 22, 1861, at Alexandria, Va.

770. NORTON, HENRY—Age, 21 years. Enlisted, December 5, 1861, at Utica, to serve unexpired term of two years; mustered in as private, Company K, December 11, 1861; deserted, May 15, 1862, at Brook's Station, Va.

771. NORTON, JOHN H.—Age, 38 years. Enlisted, May 3, 1861, at Utica, to serve two years; mustered in as private, Company C, May 21, 1861; promoted corporal, July 20, 1861; reduced, date not stated; captured, September 5, 1861, at Mount Vernon, Va.; confined, September 19, 1861, at Richmond, Va.; paroled, June 2, 1862, at Washington, D.C.; deserted, December 3, 1862, at Brook's Station, Va.

772. O'BRIEN, JEREMIAH—Age, 25 years. Enlisted, May 7, 1861, at Utica, to serve two years; mustered in as sergeant, Company E, May 21, 1861; mustered out with company, May 28, 1863, at Utica, N.Y.

773. O'BRIEN, ROBERT T.—Age, 19 years. Enlisted, May 2, 1861, at Rochester, to serve two years; mustered in as corporal, Company H, May 21, 1861; promoted sergeant, date not stated; killed, December 13, 1862, at battle of Fredericksburg, Va.

774. O'BRIEN, WILLIAM E.—Age, 19 years. Enlisted, May 4, 1861, at Elmira, to serve two years; mustered in as private, Company H, May 21, 1861; promoted corporal, date not stated; mustered out May 24, 1863, at Utica, N.Y.

775. O'DONNEL, JOHN A.—Age, 28 years. Enlisted, May 1, 1861, at Utica, to serve two years; mustered in as private, Company A, May 21, 1861; mustered out with company, May 28, 1863, at Utica, N.Y.

776. O'FARRELL, MORRIS—Age, 23 years. Enlisted, June 10, 1861, at Elmira, to serve two years; mustered in as private, Company I, same date; mustered out with company, May 28, 1863, at Utica, N.Y.

777. OGSTON, EDWIN—Age, 20 years. Enlisted, June 30, 1861, at Rochester, to serve three years; mustered in as private, Company K, August 9, 1861; drowned, May 22, 1862, at Alexandria, Va.

778. O'HARA, JOHN—Age, 19 years. Enlisted, May 1, 1861, at Utica, to serve two years; mustered in as private Company A, May 21, 1861; went to hospital at Elmira, N.Y., May 13, 1861; dropped in June 1861; no further record.

779. OLDFIELD, JOHN—Age, 40 years. Enlisted, May 7, 1861, at Utica, to serve two years; mustered in as corporal, Company B, May 21, 1861; reduced in September 1861; discharged, June 23, 1863.

780. OLMSTEAD, JAMES M.—Age, 28 years. Enlisted, May 2, 1861, at Rochester, to serve two years; mustered in as private, Company G, May 21, 1861; discharged for disability, March 16, 1862, at Fort Lyon, Va.

781. OMANS, HARVEY S.—Age, 22 years. Enlisted, May 7, 1861, at Utica, to serve two years; mustered in as private, Company D, May 21, 1861; discharged for disability, December 18, 1862, at General Hospital, Fairfax, Va.; subsequent service in Third Artillery.

782. O' NEIL, PATRICK—Age, 28 years. Enlisted, December 5, 1861, at Rochester, to serve two years; mustered in as private, Company H, December 6, 1861; mustered out, May 24, 1863, at Utica, N.Y.

783. ORAN, CHARLES—Age, 21 years. Enlisted, May 2, 1861, at Rochester, to serve two years; mustered in as private, Company G, May 21, 1861; mustered out with company, May 28, 1863, at Utica, N.Y.

784. ORR, JAMES—Age, 22 years. Enlisted, May 8, 1861, at Elmira, to serve two years; mustered in as private, Company E, May 21, 1861; mustered out with company, 28, 1863, at Utica, N.Y.

785. OSBORN, ALLEN W.—Age, 18 years. Enlisted, July 26, 1861, at Utica, to serve three years; mustered in as private; Company D, same date; wounded, August 30, 1862; mustered out with company, May 28, 1863, at Utica, N.Y.; subsequent service in Company C, Fourteenth Artillery.

786. OWENS, THOMAS—Age, 25 years. Enlisted, May 3 1861, at Utica, to serve two years; mustered in as private, Company C, May 21, 1861; wounded, December 13, 1862, at Fredericksburg, Va.; mustered out with company, May 28, 1863, at Utica, N.Y.; also listed as Thomas B. Owens.

787. PALLEN, GEORGE—Age, 30 years. Enlisted, May 7, 1861, at Utica, to serve two years; mustered in as private, Company D, May 21, 1861; mustered out with company, May 28, 1863, at Utica, N.Y.; also listed as George Pullen.

788. PALMER, ADELBERT—Age, 19 years. Enlisted, May 3, 1861 at Utica, to serve two years; mustered in as private, Company F, May 21, 1861; deserted, November 8, 1861, at Alexandria, Va.; arrested at Utica as A. D. Palmer; no further record.

789. PALMER, EUGENE—Age, 19 years. Enlisted, May 13, 1861, at Utica, to serve two years; mustered in as private, Company I, May 21, 1861; deserted, August 23, 1861, at Alexandria, Va.

790. PALMER, JOHN H.—Age, 30 years. Enrolled, May 14, 1861, at Elmira, to serve three months; mustered in as captain, Company I, May 21, 1861; resigned, August 7, 1861; commissioned captain, July 4, 1861, with rank from May 13, 1861, original.

791. PALMER, NORMAN W.—Age, 22 years. Enrolled, May 1, 1861, at Utica, to serve two years; mustered in as first lieutenant, Company B, May 21, 1861; as captain, Company E, to date, August 7, 1861; mustered out with company, May 28, 1863, at Utica, N.Y.; subsequent service, as captain, Company B, Twenty-Fourth Cavalry; commissioned first lieutenant, July 4, 1861, with rank from May 1, 1861, original; captain, August 14, 1861, with rank from August 7, 1861, original.

792. PARDEE, JOHN H.—Age, 21 years. Enlisted, May 7, 1861, at Utica, to serve two years; mustered in as private, Company D, May 21, 1861; discharged for disability, October 10, 1862, at New York City.

793. PARDY, ABBY—Age, 25 years. Enlisted, May 7, 1861, at Utica, to serve two

years; mustered in as private, Company D, May 21, 1861; deserted, June 13, 1862, at Front Royal, Va.

794. PARK, STAUNTON J.—Age, 25 years. Enlisted, May 13, 1861, at Utica, to serve two years; mustered in as private, Company I, May 21, 1861; mustered out with company, May 28, 1863, at Utica, N.Y.

795. PARKHURST, NATHAN—Age, 18 years. Enlisted, December 26, 1861, at Geneseo, to serve two years; mustered in as private, unassigned, January 3, 1862; no further record.

796. PARTRIDGE, WILLIAM H.—Age, 33 years. Enlisted, December 18, 1861, at Geneva, to serve two years; mustered in as private, unassigned, January 3, 1862; no further record.

797. PATTEN, RUFUS D.—Age, 30 years. Enrolled, May 3, 1861, at Utica, to serve two years; mustered in as first lieutenant, Company F, May 21, 1861; resigned, August 7, 1862; commissioned first lieutenant, July 4, 1861, with rank from May 3, 1861, original.

798. PATTERSON, GEORGE—Age, 18 years. Enlisted, July 26, 1861, at Utica, to serve two years; mustered in as private, Company B, August 7, 1861; discharged for disability, November 28, 1862, at Fort McHenry.

799. PATTERSON, HENRY—Age, 19 years. Enlisted, at Utica, to serve two years; mustered in as private, Company B, May 21, 1861; wounded, August 30, 1862, at Bull Run, Va.; mustered out with company, May 28, 1863, at Utica, N.Y.; subsequent service in Third Artillery.

800. PATTERSON, JAMES—Age, 30 years. Enlisted, July 26, 1861, at Utica, to serve two years; mustered in as private, Company B, August 7, 1861; appointed wagoner, date not stated; mustered out with company, May 28, 1863, at Utica, N.Y.; subsequent service in Company L, Fourth Artillery; also in Third Artillery.

801. PATTERSON, JOHN—Age, 18 years. Enlisted, May 3. 1861, at Utica, to serve two years; mustered in as private, Company C, May 21, 1861; wounded, December 13, 1862, at Fredericksburg, Va.; mustered out with company, May 28, 1863, at Utica, N.Y.; subsequent service in Twenty-Fourth Cavalry.

802. PATTERSON, LEWIS—Age, 20 years. Enlisted, May 2, 1861, at Rochester, to serve two years; mustered in as private, Company G, May 21, 1861; promoted corporal, date not stated; mustered out with company. May 28, 1863, at Utica, N.Y.

803. PATTERSON, WILLIAM—Age, 24 years. Enlisted, May 2, 1861, at Rochester, to serve two years; mustered in as private, Company G, May 21, 1861; deserted, May 7, 1862, at Brook's Station, Va.

804. PATTERSON, WILLIAM—Age, 21 years. Enlisted, November 20, 1861, at Buffalo, to serve two years; mustered in as private, Company I, same date; mustered out with company, May 28, 1863, at Utica, N.Y.

805. PAYSON, BURDET—Age, 20 years. Enlisted, May 7, 1861, at Utica, to serve two years; mustered in as private, Company D, May 21, 1861; mustered out with company, May 28, 1863, at Utica, N.Y.; subsequent service in Cos. M and B, Eleventh Cavalry.

806. PEARCE, JOHN W.—Age, 21 years. Enlisted, May 14, 1861, at Camden, to serve two years; mustered in as private, Company K, May 21, 1861; captured, date not stated; paroled, November 8, 1862; mustered out with company, May 28, 1863, at Utica, N.Y.

807. PEASE, HARRISON—Age, 21 years. Enlisted, May 1, 1861, at Utica, to serve two years; mustered in as private, Company A, May 21, 1861; promoted quartermaster sergeant, and transferred to noncommissioned staff; date not stated; reduced and retransferred to Company A, August 22, 1861; discharged, September 4, 1862, by reason of promotion to first lieutenant, Company B, One Hundred and Seventeenth Infantry.

PEIRCE, GARDINER F.—see Pierce, Gardiner F.

808. PELTON, GEORGE B.—Age, 19 years. Enlisted, May 1, 1861, at Utica, to serve two years; mustered in as private, Company B, May 21, 1861; transferred to Company I, February 28, 1862; captured, August 30, 1862, at Bull Run, Va.; paroled, September 1, 1862, at Vienna, Va.; reported absent, sick, in General Hospital, Baltimore, Md., at muster out of company; no further record.

809. PELTON, WILLIAM B.—Age, 21 years. Enlisted, August 1, 1861, at Utica, to serve three years; mustered in as private,

Company C, August 7, 1861; mustered out with company, May 28, 1863, at Utica, N.Y.; subsequent service in Second Infantry.

810. PENFIELD, WARREN—Age, 19 years. Enlisted, October 1, 1861, at Utica, to serve three years; mustered in as private, Company F, October 14, 1861; mustered out with company, May 28, 1863, at Utica, N.Y.

811. PENNER, ALONZO—Age, 31 years. Enlisted, May 3, 1861, at Utica, to serve two years; mustered in as private, Company F, May 21, 1861; mustered out with company, May 28, 1863, at Utica, N.Y.; subsequent service, as sergeant, in Company A, Sixteenth Artillery.

812. PENNER, ANDREW J.—Age, 33 years. Enlisted, May 3, 1861, at Utica, to serve two years; mustered in as private, Company F May 21, 1861; discharged for disability, May 1, 1862, at Fort Lyon, Va.

813. PERKINS, WILLIAM—Age, 22 years. Enlisted, May 1, 1861, at Utica, to serve two years; mustered in as private, Company A, May 21, 1861; mustered out with company, May 28, 1863, at Utica, N.Y.; subsequent service in Third Artillery.

814. PERSONEUS, JOEL W.—Age, 21 years. Enlisted, May 14, 1861, at Camden, to serve two years; mustered in as private, Company K, May 21, 1861; wounded, date and place not stated; mustered out with company, May 28, 1863, at Utica, N.Y.

815. PETUS, VALENTINE—Age, 22 years. Enlisted, May 3, 1861, at Utica, to serve two years; mustered in as sergeant, Company F, May 21, 1861; mustered in as second lieutenant, August 13, 1861; mustered out with company, May 28, 1863, at Utica, N.Y.; also listed as Valentine Peters; commissioned second lieutenant, November 7, 1861, with rank from August 7, 1861, vice Williams, declined.

816. PFISTER, JOSEPH—Age, 30 years. Enlisted, August 30, 1862, at Boonville, to serve three years; mustered in as private, Company C, September 18, 1862; transferred, May 9, 1863, to Company B, Eighty-Third Infantry.

817. PFISTER, PHILLIP—Age, 32 years. Enlisted, August 27, 1862, at Boonville, to serve three years; mustered in as private, Company C, September 18, 1862; killed, December 13, 1862, at battle of Fredericks, Va.

818. PHALEN, ALONZO—Age, 22 years. Enlisted, May 14, 1861, at Camden, to serve two years; mustered in as private, Company K, May 21, 1861; deserted, August 22, 1861, at Alexandria, Va.; mustered in Twenty-Second Regiment North Carolina Confederate Infantry.

819. PHELPS, DANIEL R.—Age, 28 years. Enlisted, May 1, 1861, at Utica, to serve two years; mustered in as sergeant, Company A, May 21, 1861; reduced, July 8, 1861; discharged for disability, November 16, 1861.

820. PHELPS, GEORGE—Age, 20 years. Enlisted, May 1, 1861, at Utica, to serve two years; mustered in as private, Company A, May 21, 1861; transferred to Company D, date not stated; mustered out with company, May 28, 1863, at Utica, N.Y.; subsequent service in Third Artillery.

821. PHILLIPPS, JOHN O.—Age, 20 years. Enlisted, May 7, 1861, at Utica, to serve two years; mustered in as private, Company E, May 21, 1861; killed, August 30, 1862, at Groveton, Va.; also listed as John Phillip.

822. PHILLIPS, WILLIAM D.—Age, 28 years. Enlisted, May 7, 1861, at Utica, to serve two years; mustered in as private, Company D, May 21, 1861; discharged for disability, June 25, 1862, at Alexandria, Va.; also listed as William D. Phelps.

823. PHLER, WILLIAM—Age, 30 years. Enlisted, May 14, 1861, at Utica, to serve two years; mustered in as private, Company E, May 21, 1861; promoted corporal, September 14, 1861; sergeant, January 11, 1862; first sergeant, December 15, 1862; mustered out with company, May 28, 1863, at Utica, N.Y.; also listed as William Pochler.

824. PIERCE, FRANK—Age, 19 years. Enlisted, September 16, 1861, at Buffalo, to serve three years; mustered in as private, Company D, same date; dishonorably discharged, May 15, 1862, by order of general court-martial.

825. PIERCE, GARDINER F.—Age, 33 years. Enlisted, October 7, 1861, at Buffalo, to serve three years; mustered in as corporal, Company A, November 12, 1861; reduced, date not stated; deserted, September 6, 1862, at Washington, D.C.; also listed as Gardiner F. Peirce.

826. PITAM, THOMAS—Age, 24

years. Enlisted, May 1, 1861, at Utica, to serve two years; mustered in as private, Company B, May 21, 1861; mustered out with company, May 28, 1863, at Utica., N.Y.; also listed as Thomas Pittam; subsequent service in Battery C, Third Artillery.

827. PITCHELL, PHILIP—Age, 24 years. Enlisted, date not stated, at Utica, to serve two years; mustered in as private, Company F, August 7, 1861; deserted, July 22, 1862, at Warrenton, Va.; also listed as Philip Pitchinger.

828. PITNEY, BYRON—Age, 31 years. Enlisted, May 14, 1861, at Camden, to serve two years; mustered in as private, Company K, May 21, 1861; wounded, date not stated; mustered out with company, May 28, 1863, at Utica, N.Y.; subsequent service, Company B, Thirteenth Cavalry.

PLATT, JOHN—*see* Blatt, John.

829. PLUNKETT, WILLIAM—Age, 21 years. Enlisted, May 13, 1861, at Utica, to serve two years; mustered in as private, Company I, May 21, 1861; promoted corporal and sergeant, dates not stated; mustered out with company, May 28, 1863, at Utica, N.Y.

POCHLER, WILLIAM—*see* Phler, William.

830. POLLARD, JOHN—Age, 24 years. Enlisted, May 2, 1861, at Rochester, to serve three months; mustered in as private, Company G, May 21, 1861; deserted, June 12, 1861, at Elmira, N.Y.

831. POLLARD, WILLIAM A.—Age, 42 years. Enlisted, May 1, 1861, at Utica, to serve two years; mustered in as private, Company B, May 28, 1861; discharged for disability, July 31, 1862, at De Kalb, Va.; also listed as William H. Pollard.

832. POLLITT, JAMES—Age, 32 years. Enlisted, May 3, 1861, at Utica, to serve two years; mustered in as private, Company F, May 21, 1861; wounded, July 30, 1862, at Groveton, Va.; discharged, June 16, 1863; also listed as James Pollett.

833. POST, WILLIAM—Age, 22 years. Enlisted, May 2, 1861, at Rochester, to serve two years; mustered in as private, Company H, May 21, 1861; discharged for disability, March 6, 1862, at Fort Lyon, Va.

834. POWELL, JEREMIAH—Age, 22 years. Enlisted, May 3, 1861, at Utica, to serve two years; mustered in as corporal, Company F, May 21, 1861; promoted sergeant, February 1, 1862; reduced, September 18, 1862; mustered out with company, May 28, 1863, at Utica, N.Y.

835. POWERS, WILLIAM—Age, 18 years. Enlisted, May 3, 1861, at Utica, to serve two years; mustered in as private, Company C, May 21, 1861; deserted, October 29, 1862, while regiment was on the march.

836. PRATT, LEROY—Age, 18 years. Enlisted, May 7, 1861, at Utica, to serve three months; mustered in as private, Company D, May 21, 1861; deserted, June 5, 1861, at Elmira, N.Y.

PRESTELE, WILLIAM H.—*see* Brestel, William Henry.

837. PRESTON, ORLANDO B.—Age, 22 years. Enlisted, May 14, 1861, at Camden, to serve two years; mustered in as sergeant, Company K, May 21, 1861; reduced, date not stated; promoted corporal, June 10, 1862; mustered out with company, May 28, 1863, at Utica, N.Y.

838. PRIMMER, GEORGE—Age, 19 years. Enlisted, May 7, 1861, at Utica, to serve two years; mustered in as private, Company D, May 21, 1861; mustered out with company, May 28, 1863, at Utica, N.Y.; subsequent service, Company E, Twenty-Second Cavalry.

839. PRINE, JOSIAH—Age, 19 years. Enlisted, May 21, 1861, at Elmira, to serve three months; mustered in as private, Company E, same date; no further record.

840. PRITCHARD, MATHEW—Age, 30 years. Enlisted, May 1, 1861, at Utica, to serve two years; mustered in as private, Company A, May 21, 1861; mustered out with company, May 28, 1863, at Utica, N.Y.

PULLEN, GEORGE—*see* Pallen, George.

841. PYNE, THOMAS—Age, 30 years. Enlisted, August 29, 1861, at Rochester, to serve three years; mustered in as private, unassigned, date not stated; deserted, August 30, 1861.

842. QUANT, LORENZO—Age, 24 years. Enlisted, May 7, 1861, at Utica, to serve two years; mustered in as private, Company D, May 21, 1861; promoted

sergeant, August 9, 1861; killed, August 30, 1862, at battle of Second Bull Run, Va.

843. QUETSHENBACH, VALENTINE—Age, 34 years. Enlisted, December 23, 1861, at Rochester, to serve two years; mustered in as private, Company E, same date; mustered out with company, May 28, 1863, at Utica, N.Y.

844. QUIGLY, HARVY—Age, 19 years. Enlisted, May 2, 1861, at Rochester, to serve two years; mustered in as private, Company H, May 21, 1861; killed at battle of Second Bull Run, Va., August 30, 1862; also listed as Harvey Quigley.

RAGAN, PATRICK—*see* Regan, Patrick.

845. RANDOLPH, GEORGE—Age, 21 years. Enlisted, May 14, 1861, at Camden, to serve two years; mustered in as private, Company K, May 21, 1861; mustered out with company, May 28, 1863, at Utica, N.Y.

846. RAPSON, THOMAS H.—Age, 26 years. Enlisted, May 21, 1861, at Rochester, to serve three months; mustered in as first-class musician, band, same date; mustered out with band at Fort Ellsworth, Va., September 10, 1861; reenlisted, October 14, 1861, for the unexpired term of two years as second-class musician; mustered out with band at Upton's Hill, Va., September 4, 1862.

847. RAPSON, THOMAS H. 2d.—Age, 26 years. Enlisted, May 21, 1861, at Rochester, to serve three months; mustered in as musician, Company H, same date; mustered out, date not stated (expiration of term of service); also listed as Thomas H. Ripson.

848. RAPSON, WILLIAM—Age, 57 years. Enlisted, October 14, 1861, at Rochester, to serve unexpired term of two years; mustered in as third-class musician, band, same date; mustered out with band at Upton's Hill, Va., September 4, 1862.

849. RATCLIFF, WILLIAM—Age, 19 years. Enlisted, May 3, 1861, at Elmira, to serve two years; mustered in as private, Company A, May 21, 1861; appointed drum major, date not stated; discharged as principal musician, November 2, 1862, at Purcellville, Va.; also listed as William Ratcliffe.

850. REDMOND, MARTIN—Age, 18 years. Enlisted, May 2, 1861, at Rochester, to serve two years; mustered in as private, Company H, May 21, 1861; killed, September 17, 1862, at battle of Antietam, Md.

851. REED, ARCHIBALD—Age, 24 years. Enlisted, May 1, 1861, at Utica, to serve two years; mustered in as private, Company A, May 21, 1861; transferred in May 1861, to Company C; captured as Manassas, Va., August 30, 1862; paroled at Manassas, Va., date not stated; mustered out with company, May 28, 1863, at Utica, N.Y.

852. REGAN, PATRICK—Age, 40 years. Enlisted, May 2, 1861, at Rochester, to serve two years; mustered in as private, Company H, May 21, 1861; died, April 28, 1862, at Regimental Hospital, Fort Lyon; also listed as Patrick Ragan.

853. REGERTZ, LEONARD—Age, 32 years. Enlisted, May 3, 1861, at Utica, to serve two years; mustered in as private, Company C, May 21, 1861; mustered out with company, May 28, 1863, at Utica, N.Y.; also listed as Leonard Regetz; subsequent service in Third Artillery.

854. REID, WILLIAM—Age, 18 years. Enlisted, December 17, 1861, at Rochester, to serve two years; mustered in as private, Company K, December 19, 1861; promoted corporal, January 1, 1862; mustered out with company, May 28, 1863, at Utica, N.Y.

855. REIHL, GEORGE—Age, 25 years. Enlisted, May 21, 1861, at Elmira, to serve three months; mustered in as private, Company K, same date; no further record.

856. REMINGTON, JOHN W.—Age, 21 years. Enlisted, May 1, 1861, at Utica, to serve two years; mustered in as private, Company B, May 21, 1861; transferred to Company E, May 22, 1861; discharged for disability, March 10, 1862, at Fort Lyon, Va.; also listed as John Remington.

857. REMORE, DAVID W.—Age, 35 years. Enlisted, May 2, 1861, at Rochester, to serve two years; mustered in as private, Company G, May 21, 1861; promoted corporal, date not stated; mustered out with company, May 28, 1863, at Utica, N.Y.; subsequent service in Company L, First Cavalry.

858. REYNOLDS, GEORGE A.—Age, 41 years. Enlisted, May 13, 1861, at Utica, to serve two years; mustered in as private, Company I, May 21; 1861; transferred to Company A, June 1, 1861; mustered out with company, May 28, 1863, at Utica, N.Y.; also listed as Roger A. Reynolds; subsequent service in Company C, Fourteenth Artillery.

859. REYNOLDS, HIRAM—Age, 25 years. Enlisted, May 3, 1861, at Utica, to serve two years; mustered in as private, Company F, May 21, 1861; deserted, September 1, 1861, at Washington, D.C.

860. REYNOLDS, SIMEON—Age, 25 years. Enlisted, May 2, 1861, at Rochester, to serve two years; mustered in as private, Company H, May 21, 1861; discharged for disability, January 29, 1863, at Washington, D.C.

861. RIBBLE, FREDERICK—Age, 24 years. Enlisted, September 9, 1861, at Buffalo, to serve three years; mustered in as Private, Company G, same date; mustered out with company, May 28, 1863, at Utica, N.Y.; also listed as Frederick H. Riddle.

862. RIBOLIN, WILLIAM—Age, 21 years. Enlisted, May 7, 1861, at Utica, to serve two years; mustered in as private, Company E, May 21, 1861; mustered out with company, May 28, 1863, at Utica, N.Y.

863. RICE, CHANCEY P.—Age, 19 years. Enlisted, May 2, 1861, at Rochester, to serve two years; mustered in as private, Company G, May 21, 1861; discharged for disability, February 20, 1863, at Convalescent Camp, Va.; subsequent service in Company C, Twenty-First Cavalry.

864. RICE, CHARLES M.—Age, 28 years. Enlisted, January 3, 1862, at Rochester, to serve two years; mustered in as private, Company G, same date; discharged for disability, August 25, 1862, at General Hospital, Fairfax Seminary, Va.; also listed as Charles Rice.

865. RICH, GEORGE H.—Age, 32 years. Enlisted, August 28, 1862, at Utica, to serve two years; mustered in as private, Company A, September 2, 1862; discharged for disability, February 11, 1863, at Annapolis, Md.; subsequent service in Company F, Eleventh Cavalry.

RICHARD, ANDREW—see Rickard, Andrew.

866. RICHARD, HENRY—Age, 26 years. Enlisted, May 1, 1861, at Utica, to serve two years; mustered in as private, Company A, May 21, 1861; wounded at Bull Run, Va., August 31, 1862; discharged for disability, December 8, 1862, at Fairfax Seminary.

867. RICHARDS, STEPHEN A.—Age, 40 years. Enlisted, May 4, 1861, at Utica, to serve two years; mustered in as private, Company B, May 21, 1861; transferred to Company C, June 16, 1861; discharged, February 2, 1862, by sentence of general court-martial; also listed as Stephen A. Richard.

868. RICHARDSON, ALVIN—Age, 33 years. Enlisted, May 1, 1861, at Utica, to serve two years; mustered in as private, Company A, May 21, 1861; missing since August 30, 1862; no further record.

869. RICHARDSON, CHARLES B.—Age, 23 years. Enlisted, May 3, 1861, at Utica, to serve two years; mustered in as private, Company F, May 21, 1861; wounded, September 14, 1861, while on picket; discharged for disability, March 4, 1862, at Fort Lyon, Va.

870. RICHARDSON, JAMES P.—Age, 18 years. Enlisted, May 3, 1861, at Utica, to serve two years; mustered in as private, Company F, May 21, 1861; killed, August 30, 1862, at Groveton, Va.

871. RICHARDSON, RICHARD H.—Age, 31 years. Enrolled, May 17, 1861, at Elmira, to serve two years; mustered in as lieutenant colonel, May 21, 1861; as colonel, September 19, 1862; mustered out with regiment, May 28, 1863, at Utica, N.Y.; commissioned lieutenant colonel, June 20, 1861, with rank from May 17, 1861, original; colonel, November 25, 1862, with rank, from September 19, 1862, vice Christian, resigned. Died March 18, 1869.

872. RICHARDSON, SAMUEL W.—Age, 54 years. Enlisted, October 14, 1861, at Rochester, to serve unexpired term of two years; mustered in as first-class musician, band, same date; discharged for disability, June 26, 1862, at Carver Hospital, Washington, D.C.; also listed as Samuel H. Richardson.

873. RICHMOND, HIRAM—Age, 18 years. Enlisted, May 7, 1861, at Utica, to serve two years; mustered in as private, Company D, May 21, 1861; transferred to Company C, June 16, 1861; captured, September 5, 1861; released, May 31, 1862; discharged for disability, February 24, 1863, at Utica, N.Y.; also listed as Hiram H. Richmond.

874. RICHMOND, LEWIS L.—Age, 21. years. Enlisted, May 3, 1861, at Utica, to serve two years; mustered in as private,

Company C, May 21, 1861; wounded and captured at battle of Second Bull Run, Va., August 30, 1862; paroled, date not stated; discharged for disability, November 14, 1862, at Utica, N.Y.

875. RICKARD, ANDREW—Age, 18 years. Enlisted, August 30, 1862, at Utica, to serve three years; mustered in as private Company A, September 1, 1862; wounded at battle of Fredericksburg, December 13, 1862; discharged. for disability, March 12, 1862, at Utica, N.Y.

RIDDLE, FREDERICK H.—*see* Ribble, Frederick.

876. REINHART, ADAM—Age, 19 years. Enlisted, July 26, 1861, at Rochester, to serve three years; mustered in as private, unassigned, August 9, 1861; no further record.

877. RIGHTMIRE, CORNELIUS—Age, 20 years. Enlisted, May 14, 1861, at Camden, to serve two years; mustered in as private, Company K, May 21, 1861; mustered out with company, May 28, 1863, at Utica, N.Y.

878. RIGHTMIRE, SAMUEL—Age, 22 years. Enlisted, May 14, 1861, at Camden, to serve two years; mustered in as private, Company K, May 21, 1861; promoted corporal, February 1, 1862; wounded at Groveton, Va., August 30, 1862; died of wounds, October 4, 1862, in Military Hospital, Washington, D.C.

879. RIMPLE, WILLIAM—Age, 21 years. Enlisted, September 14, 1861, at Buffalo, to serve three years; mustered in as private, Company K, same date; deserted, September 17, 1861.

RIPSON, THOMAS H.—*see* Rapson, Thomas H. 2d.

880. RITTER, GEORGE W.—Age, 27 years. Enlisted, May 13, 1861, at Utica, to serve two years; mustered in as private, Company I, May 21, 1861; mustered out with company, May 28, 1863, at Utica, N.Y.; subsequent service in Twenty-Fourth Cavalry.

881. ROACH, JAMES—Age, 19 years. Enlisted, May 3, 1861, at Utica, to serve two years; mustered in as private, Company C, May 21, 1861; killed, August 30, 1862, at battle of Second Bull Run, Va.

882. ROBATHAN, JAMES—Age, 22 years. Enlisted, May 3, 1861, at Utica, to serve two years; mustered in as private, Company C, May 21, 1861; promoted corporal, November 7, 1861; sergeant, July 24, 1862; first sergeant, December 16, 1862; mustered out with company, May 28, 1863, at Utica, N.Y.

883. ROBERTS, JOHN—Age, 21 years. Enlisted, May 1, 1861, at Utica, to serve two years; mustered in as private, Company B, May 21, 1861; transferred to Company E, May 22, 1861; killed, August 30, 1862, at battle of Second Bull Run, Va.

884. ROBERTS, JOHN C.—Age, 18 years. Enlisted, May 6, 1861, at Utica, to serve two years; mustered in as private, Company C, May 21, 1861; wounded, September 17, 1862, at Antietam, Md.; discharged for disability, December 18, 1862, at Baltimore, Md.

885. ROBERTS, JOSIAH E.—Age, 24 years. Enrolled, May 3, 1861, at Utica, to serve two years; mustered in as first lieutenant, Company C, May 21, 1861; resigned, November 7, 1861; commissioned first lieutenant, July 4, 1861, with rank from May 3, 1861, original.

886. ROBERTS, OWEN—Age, 23 years. Enlisted, May 1, 1861, at Utica, to serve two years; mustered in as private, Company B, May 21, 1861; deserted, August 27, 1862, at Warrenton, Va.

887. ROBERTS, ROBERT C.—Age, 22 years. Enlisted, May 3, 1861, at Utica, to serve two years; mustered in as private, Company F, May 21, 1861; mustered out with company, May 28, 1863, at Utica, N.Y.

888. ROBERTSON, WILLIAM—Age, 33 years. Enlisted, May 2, 1861, at Rochester, to serve two years; mustered in as private, Company H, May 21, 1861; discharged for disability, November 12, 1861, at Camp Franklin, Va.

889. ROBINSON, GEORGE—Age, 37 years. Enlisted, May 2, 1861, at Rochester, to serve two years; mustered in as private, Company H, May 21, 1861; wounded, August 30, 1862, at battle of Second Bull Run, Va.; mustered out, May 24, 1863, at Utica, N.Y.; subsequent service in Company C, Twenty-First Cavalry.

890. ROLFE, LORENZO—Age, 22 years. Enlisted, September 13, 1861, at Buffalo,

to serve three years; mustered in as private, Company G, same date; discharged for disability, October 14, 1862, at Philadelphia, Pa.; also listed as Lorenzo Ross.

891. RONEY, JACOB—Age, 22 years. Enlisted, September 13, 1861, at Buffalo, to serve three years; mustered in as private, Company B, same date; discharged for disability, February 11, 1863, at Convalescent Camp, Va.; also listed as Jacob Rooney.

892. ROONEY, PATRICK—Age, 30 years. Enlisted, September 7, 1861, at Rochester, to serve three years; mustered in as private, Company H, same date; discharged for disability, July 2, 1862, at Manassas Junction, Va.

893. ROSCOE, PETER—Age, 23 years. Enlisted, May 3, 1861, at Utica, to serve two years; mustered in as corporal, Company F, May 21, 1861; reduced, August 19, 1861; mustered out with company, May 28, 1863, at Utica, N.Y.

ROSS, LORENZO—*see* Rolfe, Lorenzo.

894. ROSS, WILLIAM BENJAMIN—Age, 25 years. Enlisted, September 13, 1861, at Buffalo, to serve three years; mustered in as private, Company C, same date; wounded, December 13, 1862, at Fredericksburg, Va.; died, January 9, 1863, at Lincoln Hospital, Washington, D.C.

895. ROSSITER, THOMAS—Age, 21 years. Enlisted, September 25, 1861, at Utica, to serve three years; mustered in as private, Company K, September 28, 1861; transferred to Company F, January 1, 1862; discharged for disability, March 10, 1862, at Fort Lyon, Va.; also listed as Thomas Rossater.

896. ROSSLEWIN, EDWARD E.—Age, 27 years. Enrolled, May 7, 1861, at Elmira, to serve two years; mustered in as second lieutenant, Company H, May 21, 1861; first lieutenant, April 1, 1862; captain, to date August 31, 1862; mustered out, May 24, 1863; also listed as Edward A. Ross Lewin; commissioned second lieutenant, July 4, 1861, with rank from May 2, 1861, original; first lieutenant, April 9, 1862, with rank from April 2, 1862, vice Brown, promoted; captain, November 7, 1862, with rank from August 30, 1862, vice Davis, killed in action.

897. ROTH, JACOB—Age, 19 years. Enlisted, May 1, 1861, at Utica, to serve two years; mustered in as private, Company B, May 28, 1861; deserted, November 7, 1861, at Camp Franklin, Va.

898. ROUNDS, ELBERT—Age, 24 years. Enlisted, May 14, 1861, at Camden, to serve three months; mustered in as private, Company K, May 21, 1861; deserted, June 15, 1861, at Elmira, N.Y.

899. ROWLAND, EDWARD—Age, 26 years. Enlisted, October 24, 1861, at Utica, to serve unexpired term of two years; mustered in as third-class musician, band, same date; mustered out, September 4, 1862, with band, at Upton's Hill, Va.

900. RUDIN, JACOB—Age, 27 years. Enlisted, May 7, 1861, at Utica, to serve two years; mustered in as private, Company E, May 21, 1861; mustered out with company, May 28, 1863, at Utica, N.Y.; subsequent service as sergeant, Company C, Fourteenth Artillery.

901. RYAN, BERNARD—Age, 37 years. Enlisted, September 22, 1862, at Utica, to serve three years; mustered in as private, Company K, same date; transferred to Company D, Eighty-Third Infantry, May 8, 1863.

902. RYAN, WILLIAM—Age, 22 years. Enlisted, August 31, 1861, at Rochester, to serve three years; mustered in as private, Company H, September 5, 1861; mustered out, May 24, 1863, at Utica, N.Y.

903. SABIN, GEORGE A.—Age, 27 years. Enlisted, May 14, 1861, at Camden, to serve two years; mustered in as corporal, Company K, May 21, 1861; mustered out with company, May 28, 1863, at Utica, N.Y.

904. SALMON, WILLIAM R.—Age, 27 years. Enlisted, August 18, 1862, at Utica, to serve three years; mustered in as private, Company B, September 3, 1862; discharged for disability, April 29, 1863, at Convalescent Camp, Va.

905. SAMCO, FREDERICK—Age, 24 years. Enlisted, May 3, 1861, at Elmira, to serve two years; mustered in as private, Company E, May 21, 1861; discharged for disability, October 30, 1862, at Hammond General Hospital.

906. SAMPSON, THOMAS—Age, 43 years. Enlisted, March 14, 1862, at Albany, to serve three years; mustered in as private, Company K, April 23, 1862; deserted, June 5, 1862, at Front Royal, Va.

907. SANDFORD, WALTER—Age, 21 years. Enlisted, May 2, 1861, at Rochester, to serve two years; mustered in as private, Company G, May 21, 1861; died of disease, March 9, 1863, at Fletcher Chapel, Va.

908. SANDS, EDWARD—Age, 19 years. Enlisted, May 12, 1862, at Fredericksburg, to serve three years; mustered in as private, Company F, same date; transferred, date not stated, to Eighty-Third Infantry.

909. SANFORD, WILLIAM H.—Age, 22 years. Enlisted, May 3, 1861, at Utica., to serve two years; mustered in as first sergeant, Company F, May 21, 1861; mustered in as first lieutenant, November 7, 1861; mustered out with company, May 28, 1863, at Utica, N.Y.; commissioned first lieutenant, November 18, 1861, with rank from November 7, 1861, vice Cone, resigned.

910. SANFORD, ZENUS W.—Age, 18 years. Enlisted, May 3, 1861, at Utica, to serve two years; mustered in as private, Company F, May 21, 1861; deserted, May 15, 1862, at Brooks Station, Va.; also listed as Zenus Sanford.

911. SAUER, ADAM.—Age, 52 years. Enlisted, May 21, 1861, at Rochester, to serve two years; mustered in as musician, Company C, same date; transferred to the band, date not stated; mustered out with band, September 10, 1861, at Fort Ellsworth, Va.

912. SAUER, ADAM J.—Age, 25 years. Enlisted, May 21, 1861, at Rochester, to serve two years; mustered in as private, Company F, same date; transferred to band, date not stated; mustered out with band, September 10, 1861, at Fort Ellsworth, Va.; again enlisted and mustered in at Rochester, October 14, 1861, as leader of band; discharged, April 2, 1862.

913. SAUER, ANTHONY—Age, 16 years. Enlisted, May 21, 1861, at Rochester, to serve two years; mustered in as private, Company C, same date; transferred to band, date not stated; mustered out with band, September 10, 1861, at Fort Ellsworth, Va.

914. SAUER, FERDINAND—Age, 38 years. Enlisted, May 21, 1861, at Rochester, to serve three years; mustered in as first-class musician in band, same date; mustered out with band, September 10, 1861, at Fort Ellsworth, Va.; again enlisted as musician, at Rochester, October 14, 1861, and mustered in the same day for unexpired term of two years; discharged for disability, June 23, 1862.

915. SAUER, HENRY—Age, 16 years. Enlisted, May 21, 1861, at Rochester, to serve two years; mustered in as first-class musician in band, same date; mustered out with band, September 10, 1861, at Fort Ellsworth, Va.

916. SAUER, JACOB—Age, 23 years. Enlisted, May 21, 1861, at Rochester, to serve two years; mustered in as musician, Company H, same date; transferred to band, date not stated; mustered out, September 11, 1861, near Alexandria, Va.

917. SAUER, JOHN—Age, 19 years. Enlisted, May 21, 1861, at Rochester, to serve two years; mustered in as first-class musician in band, same date; mustered out with band, September 10, 1861, at Fort Ellsworth, Va.

918. SAUL, FREDERICK—Age, 25 years. Enlisted, May 7, 1861, at Utica, to serve two years; mustered in as sergeant, Company E, May 21, 1861; reduced, September 1, 1861; discharged for disability, May 4, 1862, at General Hospital at Alexandria, Va.

919. SAUNDERS, CHARLES W.—Age, 43 years. Enlisted, date not stated, at Utica, to serve three years; mustered in as private, unassigned, August 7, 1861; died of disease, September 8, 1861.

920. SAUNDERS, JOHN—Age, 24 years. Enlisted, May 21, 1861, at Rochester, to serve two years; mustered in as second-class musician in band, same date; mustered out with band, September 10, 1861, at Fort Ellsworth, Va.; subsequently served in the One Hundred and Eighth Infantry and Eighth Cavalry.

921. SAWYER, ISAIAH—Age, 29 years. Enlisted, September 21, 1861, at Rome, to serve three years; mustered in as private, Company K, same date; mustered out with company, May 28, 1863, at Utica, N.Y.; also listed as Isaiah M. Sawyer.

922. SCALES, JOHN—Age, 19 years. Enlisted, May 2, 1861, at Rochester, to serve two years; mustered in as private, Company G, May 21, 1861; mustered out with company, May 28, 1863, at Utica, N.Y.

923. SCANLON, RICHARD—Age, 22 years. Enlisted, May 2, 1861, at Rochester,

to serve two years; mustered in as private, Company H, May 21, 1861; promoted sergeant, date not stated; mustered out, May 24, 1863, at Utica, N.Y.; also listed as Richard Scanlin.

924. SCHMIDT, CHARLES—Age, 25 years. Enlisted, May 7, 1861, at Utica, to serve two years; mustered in as corporal, Company E, May 21, 1861; mustered in as second lieutenant, August 7, 1861; as first lieutenant, January 11, 1862; mustered out with company, May 28, 1863, at Utica, N.Y.; also listed as Charles T. Smith; commissioned second lieutenant, August 14, 1861, with rank from August 7, 1861, original; first lieutenant, January 17, 1862, with rank from January 11, 1862, vice C. B. Coventry, promoted.

925. SCHMIDT, WILLIAM—Age, 26 years. Enlisted, October 14, 1862, at York Mills, to serve three years; mustered in as private, unassigned, October 15, 1862; deserted, October 18, 1862, at Utica, N.Y.

926. SCHREMPS, WENDLE—Age, 18 years. Enlisted, May 3, 1861, at Elmira, to serve two years; mustered in as private, Company A, May 21, 1861; transferred to Company E, date not stated; mustered out with company, May 28, 1863, at Utica, N.Y.; also listed as Wendelin Schremp.

927. SCHUBERT, JOHN—Age, 35 years. Enlisted, July 26, 1861, at Rochester, to serve three years; mustered in as private, Company E, August 9, 1861; mustered out with company, May 28, 1863, at Utica, N.Y.; also listed as John Shurbert.

SCHWAB—*see* Suob.

928. SCHWAB, VALENTINE—Age, 21 years. Enlisted, January 8, 1862, at Rochester, to serve two years; mustered in as private, Company E, same date; mustered out with company, May 28, 1863, at Utica, N.Y.

929. SCOTT, AARON—Age, 26 years. Enlisted, May 3, 1861, at Utica, to serve two years; mustered in as private, Company C, May 21, 1861; discharged for disability, June 8, 1862, at hospital, Alexandria, Va.

930. SCOTT, HENRY—Age, 18 years. Enlisted, June 1, 1861, at Elmira, to serve two years; mustered in as private, Company C, same date; discharged for disability, September 4, 1861, near Alexandria, Va.; also listed as Henry F. Scott.

931. SCOTT, JAMES—Age, 32 years. Enlisted, May 2, 1861, at Rochester, to serve two years; mustered in as corporal, Company G, May 21, 1861; deserted, October 7, 1862, at Utica, N.Y.

932. SCOVELL, CHARLES—Age, 20 years. Enlisted, May 3, 1861, at Utica, to serve three years; mustered in as private, Company F, May 21, 1861; mustered out with company, May 28, 1863, at Utica, N Y.; also listed as Charles Scoville.

933. SCRIME, SAMUEL—Age, 21 years. Enlisted, May 3, 1861, at Utica, to serve two years; mustered in as private, Company C, May 21, 1861; killed, August 30, 1862, at battle of Second Bull Run, Va.

934. SEARLE, ICHABOD H.—Age, 30 years. Enrolled, September 2, 1862, at Washington, D.C., to serve two years; mustered in as assistant surgeon, same date; mustered out with regiment, May 28, 1863, at Utica, N.Y.; commissioned assistant surgeon, August 27, 1862, with rank from August 18, 1862, original.

935. SEEDS, JAMES—Age, 21 years. Enlisted, May 8, 1861, at Utica, to serve two years; mustered in as private, Company D, June 1, 1861; transferred to Company H, January 22, 1862; deserted, June 14, 1862, at Front Royal, Va.

936. SEELY, CHARLES H.—Age, 24 years. Enlisted, May 14, 1861, at Camden, to serve two years; mustered in as private, Company K, May 21, 1861; mustered out with company, May 28, 1863, at Utica, N.Y.

937. SEELY, JOHN T.—Age, 28 years. Enlisted, September 3, 1861, at Utica, to serve two years; mustered in as private, Company B, September 5, 1861; wounded, December 13, 1862, at battle of Fredericksburg, Va.; mustered out with company, May 28, 1863, at Utica, N.Y.

938. SEELYE, DUANE—Age, 18 years. Enlisted, May 1, 1861, at Utica, to serve two years; mustered in as private, Company A, May 21, 1861; promoted corporal, date not stated; sergeant, February 20, 1862; first sergeant, October 2, 1862; wounded at battle of Fredericksburg, Va., December 13, 1862; died of such wounds, December 15, 1862, at Falmouth, Va.

939. SEIFERT, FRANK—Age, 22 years. Enlisted, May 2, 1861, at Rochester, to serve

two years; mustered in as private, Company G, May 21, 1861; mustered out with company, May 28, 1863, at Utica, N.Y.

940. SENATE, ROBERT—Age, 21 years. Enlisted, September 13, 1861, at Buffalo, to serve three years; mustered in as private, Company G, same date; mustered out with company, May 28, 1863, at Utica, N.Y.; also listed as Robert Sennett; subsequent service in Company L, Fourth Artillery.

941. SEYMOUR, EDGAR—Age, 20 years. Enlisted, May 7, 1861, at Utica, to serve two years; mustered in as private, Company D, May 21, 1861; mustered out with company, May 28, 1863, at Utica, N.Y., as Edger W. Seymour; subsequent service in Third Artillery.

942. SHAPLEY, HIRAM H.—Age, 23 years. Enlisted, May 7, 1861, at Utica, to serve three years; mustered in as private, Company D, May 21, 1861; mustered out with company, May 28, 1863, at Utica, N.Y.; subsequent service in Company G, Thirteenth Artillery.

943. SHAROR, EDWARD—Age, 23 years. Enlisted, June 9, 1861, at Elmira, to serve two years; mustered in as private, Company D, same date; discharged for disability, December 3, 1861; also listed as Edward P. Shaver.

944. SHEAR, CHARLES—Age, 18 years. Enlisted, May 1, 1861, at Utica, to serve three months; mustered in as private, Company B, May 21, 1861; discharged for disability, July 20, 1861, at Washington, D.C., as Charles Spier.

945. SHELDON, OLIVER W.—Age, 26 years. Enrolled, May 7, 1861, at Utica, to serve three months; mustered in as first lieutenant, Company E, May 21, 1861; resigned, August 7, 1861; commissioned first lieutenant, July 4, 1861, with rank from May 7, 1861, original.

946. SHEPARD, ALBERT B.—Age, 33 years. Enlisted, May 13, 1861, at Utica, to serve two years; mustered in as private, Company I, May 21, 1861; mustered out with company, May 28, 1863, at Utica, N.Y.; subsequent service in Company C, Fourteenth Artillery.

947. SHEPHERD, ANDREW J.—Age, 19 years. Enlisted, July 20, 1861, at Washington, D.C., to serve two years; mustered in as private, Company C, same date; deserted, August 20, 1862, while on the march from Rapidan Station.

948. SHERMAN, CHARLES—Age, 18 years. Enlisted, May 7, 1861,. at Utica, to serve two years; mustered in as private, Company D, May 21, 1861; wounded, August 30, 1862, at Groveton, Va.; discharged for disability, March 14, 1863, at United States General Hospital, Philadelphia, Pa.

949. SHERMAN, ELMER—Age, 19 years. Enlisted, May 2, 1861, at Rochester, to serve two years; mustered in as private, Company G,. May 21, 1861; mustered out with company, May 28, 1863, at Utica, N.Y.

950. SHERPE, THOMAS—Age, 22 years. Enlisted, September 16, 1861, at Utica, to serve two years; mustered in as private, Company F, September 17, 1861; deserted, March 19, 1862, at Fort Lyon, Va.

951. SHERRY, WILLIAM—Age, 32 years. Enlisted, September 16, 1861, at Buffalo, to serve three years; mustered in as private, Company H, same date; captured, date not stated, while on picket duty; escaped, June 1862; deserted, November 7, 1862.

SHIER, CHARLES—see Shear, Charles.

952. SHOEMAKER, CHRISTOPHER—Age, 23 years. Enlisted, May 2, 1861, at Rochester, to serve two years; mustered in as private, Company G, May 21, 1861; mustered out with company, May 28, 1863, at Utica, N.Y.; also listed as Christopher Shoenmaker.

953. SHOLES, HIRAM—Age, 18 years. Enlisted, May 7, 1861, at Utica, to serve two years; mustered in as private, Company D, May 21, 1861; wounded, December 13, 1862, at battle of Fredericksburg, Va.; discharged, June 4, 1863, at Utica, N.Y.

954. SHUBERT, MARTIN—Age, 22 years. Enlisted, May 7, 1861, at Utica, to serve two years; mustered in as private, Company E, May 21, 1861; promoted corporal, December 22, 1862; mustered out with company, May 28, 1863, at Utica, N.Y.; subsequent service, unassigned, Fourteenth Artillery; awarded a Medal of Honor, by act of Congress, for most distinguished gallantry at the battle of Fredericksburg, Va.

955. SHURLEY, EDWARD R. P.—Age, 32 years. Enrolled, May 2, 1861, at Rochester, as second lieutenant, to serve three months;

mustered in as first lieutenant, Company G, May 21, 1861; as captain, Company C, August 7, 1861; wounded, December 13, 1862, at battle of Fredericksburg, Va.; honorably discharged, April 25, 1863, on account of wounds; commissioned second lieutenant, date not stated, with rank from May 2, 1861, original; not mustered first lieutenant, July 4, 1861, with rank from May 18, 1861, original; captain, August 14, 1861, with rank from August 7, 1861, original.

956. SIDNEY, SHERMAN—Age, 35 years. Enlisted, May 3, 1861, at Utica, to serve two years; mustered in as private, Company F, May 21, 1861; mustered out with company, May 28, 1863, at Utica, N.Y.; subsequent service in Third Artillery.

957. SIMMONS, SAMUEL—Age, 23 years. Enlisted, May 2, 1861, at Elmira, to serve two years; mustered in as private, Company G, May 21, 1861; discharged for disability, June 19, 1862, at General Hospital, Alexandria, Va.

958. SIMON, BASSET—Age, 38 years. Enlisted, August 4, 1862, at Verona, to serve three years; mustered in as private, unassigned, same date; no further record.

959. SKINNER, CHARLES—Age, 22 years. Enlisted, May 7, 1861, at Utica, to serve two years; mustered in as private, Company D, May 21, 1861; killed, December 13, 1862, at battle of Fredericksburg, Va.

960. SLATER, GEORGE—Age, 19 years. Enlisted, May 2, 1861, at Rochester, to serve three years; mustered in as private, Company H, May 21, 1861; deserted, June 21, 1861, at Ontario County, N.Y.

961. SLAVIN, MICHAEL—Age, 20 years. Enlisted, May 2, 1861, at Rochester, to serve two years; mustered in as private, Company H, May 21, 1861; mustered out, May 24, 1863, at Utica, N.Y.; also listed as Michael Slaven.

962. SLOAN, CHARLES A.—Age, 19 years. Enlisted, May 8, 1861, at Utica, to serve two years; mustered in as private, Company C, May 21, 1861; mustered out with company, May 28, 1863, at Utica, N.Y.; subsequent service in Company L, Fourth Artillery.

963. SMEARS, BARNEY—Age, 30 years. Enlisted, February 27, 1862, at Rochester, to serve two years; mustered in as private Company G, March 27, 1862; deserted, June 12, 1862, at Front Royal, Va.

964. SMITH, BENJAMIN—Age, 19 years. Enlisted, May 3, 1861, at Utica, to serve two years; mustered in as private, Company C, May 21, 1861; discharged for disability, March 4, 1863, at Convalescent Camp, Va.; subsequent service in Twenty-Fourth Cavalry.

965. SMITH, CHARLES A.—Age. 23 years. Enlisted, May 7, 1861, at Utica, to serve two years; mustered in as private, Company E, May 21, 1861; mustered out with company, May 28, 1863, Utica, N.Y.

966. SMITH, CHARLES A.—Age, 30 years. Enlisted, July 29, 1861, at Rochester, to serve three years; mustered in as private, Company D, August 9, 1861; mustered out with company, May 28, 1863, at Utica, N.Y.; subsequent service in Third Artillery.

967. SMITH, CHARLES F.—Age, 30 years. Enlisted, May 10, 1861, at Utica, to serve three months; mustered in as private, Company E, May 21, 1861; dropped; name only appears on company muster-in roll.

SMITH, CHARLES T.—see Schmidt, Charles.

968. SMITH, DANIEL H.—Age, 25 years. Enlisted, May 1, 1861, at Utica, to serve two years; mustered in as private, Company A, May 21, 1861; promoted corporal, date not stated; reduced, September 16, 1861; discharged for disability, February 8, 1862, at Fort Lyon, Va.

969. SMITH, DAVID Jr.—Age, 23 years. Enrolled, May 3, 1861, at Utica, as captain, Company C, to serve two years; appointed first lieutenant and adjutant and mustered in as such, May 21, 1861; resigned, August 7, 1861; not commissioned adjutant; commissioned not mustered captain, July 4, 1861, with rank from May 3, 1861, original.

970. SMITH, ELIJAH—Age, 19 years. Enlisted, May 16, 1861, at Elmira, to serve two years; mustered in as private, Company K, May 21, 1861; discharged for disability, August 7, 1862, at Fairfax Seminary, Va.

971. SMITH, EMERY F.—Age, 29 years. Enlisted, February 18, 1862, at Rochester, to serve three years; mustered in as private, Company H, March 27, 1862; wounded, August 30, 1862, at battle of Second Bull Run, Va.; discharged for disability, November 28, 1862.

972. SMITH, HENRY—Age, 25 years.

Enlisted, July 30, 1861, at Elmira, to serve three years; mustered in as private, Company E, August 9, 1861; discharged, October 16, 1861, at Camp Franklin, near Alexandria, Va.

973. SMITH, HOLLISTER T.—Age, 21 years. Enlisted, May 2, 1861, at Rochester, to serve three months; mustered in as private, Company H, May 21, 1861; deserted, May 24, 1861, at Ontario County, N.Y.

974. SMITH, IRA—Age, — years. Enrolled, May 15, 1861, at Candor, to serve two years; mustered in as chaplain, May 21, 1861; resigned, September 13, 1861; commissioned chaplain, August 14, 1861; with rank from May 21, 1861, original.

975. SMITH, JACOB—Age, 33 years. Enlisted, May 7, 1861, at Utica, to serve two years; mustered in as private, Company D, May 21, 1861; transferred to Company K, June 2, 1861; deserted, June 5, 1862 at Front Royal, Va.

976. SMITH, JAMES—Age, 18 years. Enlisted, May 1, 1861, at Utica, to serve three months; mustered in as private, Company A, May 21, 1861; deserted, June 21, 1861.

977. SMITH, JAMES—Age, 19 years. Enlisted, May 2, 1861, at Rochester, to serve two years; mustered in as private, Company H, May 21, 1861; deserted, August 8, 1862, at Culpeper, Va.

978. SMITH, JOHN—Age, 35 years. Enlisted, May 3, 1861, at Utica, to serve two years; mustered in as private, Company C, May 21, 1861; promoted corporal, January 1, 1862; sergeant, December 13, 1862; mustered out with company, May 28, 1863, at Utica, N.Y.

979. SMITH, JOHN T.—Age, — years. Enlisted, June 1, 1861, at Elmira, to serve— years; mustered in as private, Company G, date not stated; dropped; no further record.

980. SMITH, LEROY—Age, 20 years. Enlisted, May 7, 1861, at Utica, to serve two years; mustered in as private, Company D, May 21, 1861; mustered out with company, May 28, 1863, at Utica, N.Y.; subsequent service in Third Artillery. Died March 2, 1866.

981. SMITH, NOAH P.—Age, 22 years. Enlisted, October 9, 1861, at Utica, to serve three years; mustered in as private, Company I, same date; deserted, November 12, 1861, at Alexandria, Va.

982. SMITH, ROBERT—Age, 28 years. Enlisted, May 4, 1861, at Rochester, to serve three months; mustered in as private, Company H, May 21, 1861; deserted, August 30, 1861, at Alexandria, Va.

983. SMITH, THOMAS E.—Age, 42 years. Enlisted, August 12, 1862, at Utica, to serve three years; mustered in as private, Company G, August 15, 1862; transferred, May 8, 1863, to Eighty-Third Infantry.

984. SMITH, WILLIAM—Age, 21 years. Enlisted, September 13, 1861, at Buffalo, to serve three years; mustered in as private, unassigned, same date; no further record.

985. SMITH, WILLIAM—Age, 25 years. Enlisted, November 15, 1861, at Utica, to serve unexpired term of two years; mustered in as private, Company B, November 16, 1861; mustered out with company, May 28, 1863, at Utica, N.Y.; subsequent service in Third Artillery.

986. SMITH, WILLIAM H.—Age, 19 years. Enlisted, May 1, 1861, at Utica, to serve two years; mustered in as private, Company A, May 21, 1861; wounded, date not stated; discharged, May 1, 1863, at Providence, R.I.

987. SMITH, WILLIAM H.—Age, 21 years. Enlisted, May 7, 1861, at Utica, to serve two years; mustered in as private, Company E, May 21, 1861; mustered out with company, May 28, 1863; at Utica, N.Y.

988. SNOW, FEILDER—Age, 19 years. Enlisted, May 7, 1861, at Utica, to serve two years; mustered in as private, Company D, May 21, 1861; mustered out with company, May 28, 1863, at Utica, N.Y., as Feilder H. Snow.

989. SNOW, NATHAN—Age, 23 years. Enlisted, May 7, 1861, at Utica, to serve two years; mustered in as private, Company D, May 21, 1861; mustered out with company, May 28, 1863, at Utica, N.Y.

990. SNYDER, READ—Age, 23 years. Enlisted, September 4, 1861, at Utica, to serve two years; mustered in as private, Company A, September 5, 1861; discharged, December 27, 1862, at Mount Pleasant Hospital; subsequent service in Twenty-Fourth Cavalry.

991. SOHRERBER, JACOB—Age, 23 years. Enlisted, May 7, 1861, at Utica, to serve two years; mustered in as private,

Company E, May 21, 1861; mustered out with company, May 28, 1863, at Utica, N.Y.; also listed as Jacob Schrieber.

992. SOLAN, PATRICK—Age, 29 years. Enlisted, May 3, 1861, at Utica, to serve two years; mustered in as private, Company C, May 24 1861; wounded, August 30, 1862, at battle of Second Bull Run, Va., and December 13, 1862, at battle of Fredericksburg, Va.; mustered out with company, May 28, 1863, at Utica, N.Y.; subsequent service in Third Artillery.

993. SOLES, ORINTON—Age, 28 years. Enlisted, December 6, 1861, at Utica, to serve unexpired term of two years; mustered in as private, Company K, December 11, 1861; wounded, August 30, 1862, at Groveton, Va.; discharged for disability, February 16, 1863, at Camp Banks, Va.; also listed as Orinton L. Soles.

994. SOLOMON, JAMES T.—Age, 22 years. Enlisted, May 1, 1861, at Utica, to serve two years; mustered in as private, Company B, May 21, 1861; mustered out with company, May 28, 1863, at Utica, N.Y.

995. SORGE, AUGUSTUS—Age, 20 years. Enlisted, May 1, 1861; at Utica, to serve two years; mustered in as private, Company B, May 28, 1861; wounded, September 1862; mustered out with company, May 28, 1863, at Utica, N.Y.

996. SPENCER, REUBEN D.—Age, 24 years. Enlisted, May 13, 1861, at Utica, to serve two years; mustered in as private, Company I, May 21, 1861; promoted corporal, November 4, 1862; mustered out with company, May 28, 1863, at Utica, N.Y.

997. SPIES, MIERON—Age, 24 years. Enlisted, May 14, 1861, at Camden, to serve two years; mustered in as private, Company K, May 21, 1861; promoted corporal, December 30, 1861; sergeant, January 1, 1862; wounded, September 17, 1862, at the battle of Antietam, Md.; died of such wounds, October 13, 1862, at Fredericksburg, Va.; also listed as Myron Spies.

998. SPOOR, JOSEPH—Age, 26 years. Enlisted, May 2, 1861, at Rochester, to serve two years; mustered in as private, Company G, May 21, 1861; mustered out with company, May 28, 1863, at Utica, N.Y.

999. STAFFORD, BENJAMIN—Age, 23 years. Enlisted, May 13, 1861, at Utica, to serve two years; mustered in as private, Company I, May 21, 1861; wounded at Antietam, Md.; mustered out with company, May 28, 1863, at Utica, N.Y.

1000. STAFFORD, JAMES—Age, 23 years. Enlisted, May 1, 1861, at Utica, to serve two years; mustered in as private, Company A, May 21, 1861; killed, August 31, 1862.

1001. STAFFORD, JOHN—Age, 19 years. Enlisted, May 13, 1861, at Utica, to serve two years; mustered in as private, Company I, May 21, 1861; mustered out with company, May 28, 1863, at Utica, N.Y.

1002. STAFFORD, THOMAS—Age, 23 years. Enlisted, May 1, 1861, at Elmira, to serve two years; mustered in as private, Company B, May 21, 1861; captured, August 28 or 30, 1862, at Warrenton Junction, Va.; paroled, date not stated; mustered out with company, May 28, 1863, at Utica N.Y.

1003. STAMCLIFF, GEORGE—Age, 22 years. Enlisted, May 1, 1861, at Utica, to serve two years; mustered in as private, Company A, May 21, 1861; wounded, December 13, 1862, at the battle of Fredericksburg, Va.; died of such wounds, December 14, 1862; also listed as George Stancliffe.

1004. STANLEY, EDWARD—Age, 21 years. Enlisted, May 1, 1861, at Rochester, to serve two years; mustered in as private, Company A, same date; promoted corporal, February 20, 1862; sergeant, December 15, 1862; mustered out with company, May 28, 1863, at Utica, N.Y.; subsequent service in Third Artillery.

1005. STARING, DE WITT C.—Age, 22 years. Enlisted, May 1, 1861, at Utica, to serve two years; mustered in as private, Company A, May 21, 1861; promoted quartermaster sergeant, August 22, 1861; promoted regimental quartermaster, November 1, 1862; mustered in, February 1, 1863; mustered out with regiment, May 28, 1863, at Utica, N.Y.; commissioned quartermaster, February 11, 1863, with rank from November 1, 1862, vice W. B. Blackwell, resigned.

1006. STARK, FREDERICK—Age, 21 years. Enlisted, October 1, 1861, at Utica, to serve three years; mustered in as private, Company E, October 14, 1861; mustered out with company, May 28, 1863, at Utica, N.Y.; subsequent service as wagoner in Company A, Sixteenth Artillery.

1007. STARKWEATHER, EDWIN A.—Age, 18 years. Enlisted, May 22, 1861, at Elmira, to serve two years; mustered in as private, Company K, same date; died, November 3, 1861, at Alexandria, Va.

1008. STEEL, HENRY—Age, 18 years. Enlisted, May 2, 1861, at Rochester, to serve two years; mustered in as private, Company G, May 21, 1861; mustered out with company, May 28, 1863, at Utica, N.Y.

1009. STEEL, HENRY—Age, 18 years. Enlisted, October 7, 1862, at York Mill, to serve three years; mustered in as drummer, Company A, same date; transferred, date not stated, to Company A, Eighty-Third Infantry.

1010. STEEL, JAMES—Age, 18 years. Enlisted, May 1, 1861, at Utica, to serve two years; mustered in as private, Company A, May 2, 1861; mustered out with company, May 28, 1863, at Utica, N.Y.

1011. STEEL, JOSEPH—Age, 25 years. Enlisted, May 1, 1861, at Utica, to serve two years; mustered in as private, Company A, May 21, 1861; promoted corporal, February 20, 1862; discharged for disability, February 16, 1863; also listed as Joseph Steele.

1012. STEELE, AARON J.—Age, 23 years. Enrolled, May 17, 1861, at Utica, to serve two years; mustered in as assistant surgeon, May 21, 1861; discharged, November 9, 1862, to accept commission as surgeon, Thirty-Eighth Infantry; commissioned assistant surgeon, July 4, 1861, with rank from May 17, 1861, original.

1013. STEELE, CHARLES H.—Age, 21 years. Enlisted, April 1, 1862, at Utica, to serve three years; mustered in as private, Company F, April 25, 1862; deserted, August 31, 1862, at Centreville, Va.

1014. STEELE, WALSTEIN L.—Age, 25 years. Enlisted, April 1, 1S62, at Utica, to serve three years; mustered in as private, Company F, April 25, 1862; discharged for disability, April 7, 1863, from hospital at Alexandria, Va.

1015. STEMP, JOHN W.—Age, 36 years. Enlisted, December 12, 1861, at Utica, to serve two years; mustered in as private, Company A, December 20, 1861; mustered out with company, May 28, 1863, at Utica, N.Y.; subsequent service in Third Artillery.

1016. STEPHENS, FRANCIS M.—Age, 21 years. Enlisted, September 9, 1861, at Utica, to serve two years; mustered in as private, Company B, September 17, 1861; transferred to Company D, November 1, 1861; mustered out with company, May 28, 1863, at Utica, N.Y.

1017. STIEN, CHRISTOFF—Age, 24 years. Enlisted, September 30, 1862, at Utica, to serve three years; mustered in as private, Company K, October 2, 1862; transferred, May 8, 1863, to the Eighty-Third New York Volunteers.

1018. STOORES, MERRITT B.—Age, 22 years. Enlisted, May 1, 1861, at Utica, to serve two years; mustered in as private, Company A, May 21, 1861; mustered out with company, May 28, 1863, at Utica, N.Y.; also listed as Merritt B. Stoors.

1019. STORY, EDWARD F.—Age, 22 years. Enlisted, May 4, 1861, at Elmira, to serve two years; mustered in as private, Company H, May 21, 1861; wounded, December 13, 1862, at battle of Fredericksburg, Va.; mustered out, May 24, 1863, at Utica, N.Y.

1020. STRAUB, ALEXANDER—Age, 26 years. Enlisted, November 26, 1861, at Rome, to serve unexpired term of two years; mustered in as private, Company E, December 11, 1861; killed, August 30, 1862, at Groveton, Va.

1021. STREBLER, MICHAEL—Age, 22 years., Enlisted, May 2, 1861, at Rochester, to serve two years; mustered in as private, Company G, May 21, 1861; mustered out with company, May 28, 1863, at Utica, N.Y.; also listed as Michael Streblen; subsequent service in Company C, Twenty-First Cavalry.

1022. STUBBS, JAMES—Age, 34 years. Enlisted, July 10, 1862, at Utica, to serve three years; mustered in as private, unassigned, same date; died, August 13, 1862.

1023. SULLIVAN, JAMES—Age, 21 years. Enlisted, December 10, 1861, at Rochester, to serve two years; mustered in as private, Company F, same date; mustered out with company, May 28, 1863, at Utica, N.Y.

1024. SULLIVAN, JOHN—Age, 21 years. Enlisted, May 2, 1861, at Rochester, to serve two years; mustered in as private, Company G, May 21, 1861; discharged for disability, July 2, 1862, at Manassas, Va.

1025. SULLIVAN, PATRICK—Age, 20 years. Enlisted, November 18, 1862, at Utica, to serve three years; mustered in as private, Company B, November 21, 1862; transferred, May 7, 1863, to Eighty-Third Infantry.

1026. SULLIVAN, TIMOTHY—Age, 19 years. Enlisted, May 1, 1861, at Utica, to serve two years; mustered in as private, Company B, May 21, 1861; wounded, August 31, 1862; mustered out with company, May 28, 1863, at Utica, N.Y.

1027. SUOB, FREDERICK—Age, 22 years. Enlisted, May 11, 1861, at Utica, to serve two years; mustered in as a private, Company E, May 21, 1861; wounded, date not stated; mustered out with company, May 28, 1863, at Utica, N.Y.; also listed as Frederick Schwab.

1028. SUOB, JACOB—Age, 21 years. Enlisted, May 14, 1861, at Utica, to serve two years; mustered in as private, Company E, May 21, 1861; mustered out with company, May 28, 1863, at Utica, N.Y.; also listed as Jacob Schwab.

1029. SWAN, ALFRED—Transferred as corporal from Company G, One Hundred and Fortieth Infantry, to Company G, this regiment; mustered in as second lieutenant, November 1, 1862; mustered out with company, May 28, 1863, at Utica, N.Y.; commissioned second lieutenant, December 20, 1862, with rank from November 1, 1862, vice Lee, resigned.

1030. SWAN, JAMES—Age, 19 years. Enlisted, May 1, 1861, at Utica, to serve two years; mustered in as private, Company A, May 21, 1861; wounded, August 31, 1862, at Bull Run, Va.; mustered out with company, May 28, 1863, at Utica, N.Y.; subsequent service in Company H, Second Infantry.

1031. SWEENEY, WILLIAM—Age, 26 years. Enlisted, December 26, 1861, at Elmira, to serve unexpired term of two years; mustered in as private, unassigned, January 3, 1861; no further record.

1032. SYME, CHARLES M.—Age, 24 years. Enlisted, May 2, 1861, at Rochester, to serve two years; mustered in as first sergeant, Company G, May 21, 1861; mustered out with company, May 28, 1863, at Utica, N.Y.

1033. TAFT, JOHN—Age, 23 years. Enlisted, September 13, 1861, at Buffalo, to serve three years; mustered in as private, Company D, same date; mustered out with company, May 28, 1863, at Utica, N.Y.

1034. TATE, WILLIAM C.—Age, 24 years. Enlisted, May 1, 1861, at Elmira, to serve unexpired term of two years; mustered in as private, Company B, May 28, 1861; deserted, November 7, 1861, at Alexandria, Va.

1035. TAYLOR, WILLIAM H.—Age, 25 years. Enlisted, May 2, 1861, at Rochester, to serve three years; mustered in as private, Company G, May 21, 1861; mustered out with company, May 28, 1863, at Utica, N.Y.; subsequent service in First Veteran Cavalry and Fourteenth Artillery.

1036. TESSEY, JOSEPH—Age, 18 years. Enlisted, May 6, 1861, at Utica, to serve two years; mustered in as private, Company C, May 21, 1861; mustered out with company, May 28, 1863, at Utica, N.Y.

1037. THERIDGE, W. I.—Age, 20 years. Enlisted, September 23, 1861, at Utica, to serve three years; mustered in as private, unassigned, September 28, 1861; no further record.

1038. THOMA, JAMES K.—Age, — years. Enlisted, October 8, 1861, at Buffalo, to serve three years; mustered in as private, Company I, same date; wounded, December 13, 1862, at Fredericksburg, Va.; discharged for disability, March 4, 1863, at Washington, D.C.

1039. THOMAS, FRANCIS—Age, 25 years. Enlisted, November 12, 1861, at Utica, to serve two years; mustered in as private, unassigned, November 22, 1861; no further record.

1040. THOMAS, GEORGE—Age, 25 years. Enlisted, May 3, 1861, at Utica, to serve three years; mustered in as private Company F, May 21, 1861; mustered out with company, May 28, 1863, at Utica, N.Y.; also listed as George P. Thomas; subsequent service in Company C, Eleventh Cavalry.

1041. THOMAS, HUGH—Age, 24 years. Enlisted, May 3, 1861, at Utica, to serve two years; mustered in as private, Company F, May 21, 1861; deserted, July 17, 1862, at Culpepper, Va.; arrested August 8, 1862; no further record.

1042. THOMAS, LEWIS—Age, 18 years. Enlisted, August 21, 1862, at Utica, to serve three years; mustered in as private, Company B, same date; discharged for disability, November 26, 1862, at Washington, D.C.; also listed as Louis Thomas.

1043. THOMPKINS, WILLIAM—Age, 18 years. Enlisted, May 3, 1861, at Utica, to serve two years; mustered in as private, Company C, May 21, 1861; transferred to Company I, in July or August 1861; wounded and captured, August 30, 1862; paroled in September 1862; no further record; also listed as William Tompkins.

1044. THOMPSON, ALONZO A.—Age, 26 years. Enlisted, May 1861, at Elmira, to serve two years; mustered in as corporal, Company I, May 21, 1861; as first lieutenant, to date, August 7, 1861; resigned, January 11, 1862; commissioned first lieutenant August 14, 1861, with rank from August 7, 1861, original.

1045. THOMPSON, CHARLES—Age, 18 years. Enlisted, date not stated, at Utica, to serve three years; mustered in as private, Company F, August 7, 1861; deserted, June 22, 1862, at Manassas, Va.; also listed as Charles H. Thompson.

1046. THOMPSON, DAVID A.—Age, 44 years. Enlisted, July 27, 1861, at Rochester, to serve three years; mustered in as private, Company I, August 9, 1861; deserted, June 16, 1862, at Front Royal, Va.

1047. THOMPSON, EVERETT—Age, 20 years. Enlisted, May 1861, at Utica, to serve two years; mustered in as private, I, May 21, 1861; wounded, August 30, 1862, at battle of Second Bull Run, Va.; discharged for disability, January 6, 1863, at Hammond General Hospital, Point Lookout, Md.; subsequent service in Twenty-Fourth Cavalry.

1048. THORN, JOSEPH—Age, 21 years. Enlisted, May 1, 1861, Utica, to serve two years; mustered in as private, Company A, 21, 1861; mustered out with company, May 28, 1863, at Utica, N.Y.

1049. THORNTON, JOHN—Age, 19 years. Enlisted December 28, 1861, at Geneva, to serve two years; mustered in as private, unassigned, January 3, 1861; no further record.

1050. THORNTON, JOHN—Age, 35 years. Enlisted, August 12, 1862, at Utica, to serve three years; mustered in as private, Company E, September 3, 1862; deserted, September 14, 1862, at battle of South Mountain, Md.

1051. THORNTON, RILEY—Age, 18 years. Enlisted, May 1, 1861, at Utica, to serve two years; mustered in as private, Company A, May 21, 1861; died, January 27, 1862, at Fort Lyon, Va.

1052. TIFFANY, BYRON L.—Age, 23 years. Enlisted, May 21, 1861, at Elmira, to serve three months; mustered in as private, Company E, same date; no further record.

1053. TILLEPAUGH, GEORGE—Age, 19 years. Enlisted, July 10, 1861, at Washington, D.C., to serve three years; mustered in as private, Company H, same date; deserted, August 8, 1862, at Culpeper, Va.

TINIEN, EDWARD—*see* Finien, Edward.

1054. TINSMAN, CONRAD—Age, 19 years. Enlisted, October 9, 1861, at Utica, to serve three years; mustered in as private, Company A, October 14, 1861; mustered out with company, May 28, 1863, at Utica, N.Y.; also listed as Conrad Dinsman.

1055. TOBEY, LEROY—Age, 19 years. Enlisted, July 27, 1861, at Buffalo, to serve three years; mustered in as private, Company G, August 9, 1861; wounded, December 13, 1862, at battle of Fredericksburg, Va.; mustered out, August 10, 1864, at Rochester, N.Y.

1056. TOBIN, JOHN—Age, 23 years. Enlisted, May 2, 1861, at Rochester, to serve two years; mustered in as private, Company G, May 21, 1861; mustered out with company, May 28, 1863, at Utica, N.Y.

TOMPKINS, WILLIAM—*see* Thompkins, William.

1057. TOOLE, GERRITT—Age, 21 years. Enlisted, May 7, 1861, at Utica, to serve two years; mustered in as private, Company D, May 21, 1861; wounded, August 30, 1862, at Groveton, Va.; discharged for disability, November 19, 1862, at New York City.

1058. TOWLE, WILLIAM—Age, 18 years. Enlisted, May 1, 1861, at Utica, to serve two years; mustered in as private, Company B, May 28, 1861; mustered out with company, May 28, 1863, at Utica, N.Y.; subsequent service in Company G, Fourteenth Artillery.

1059. TOWNSEND, ORRIN A.—Age, 22 years. Enlisted; May 7, 1861, at Utica, to serve two years; mustered in as private, Company D, May 21, 1861; promoted corporal,

February 20, 1861; sergeant, August 30, 1862; mustered out with company, May 28, 1863, at N.Y.; subsequent service in Third Artillery.

1060. TRAIR, BENJAMIN—Age, 33 years. Enlisted, May 2, 1861, at Rochester, to serve two years; mustered in as private, Company H, May 21, 1861; mustered out, May 24, 1863, at Utica, N.Y.; also listed as Benjamin Trayer.

1061. TRASK, HERBERT S.—Age, 18 years. Enlisted, May 1, 1861, at Utica, to serve two years; mustered in as private, Company B, May 21, 1861; captured, August 30, 1862, at battle of Second Bull Run, Va.; no further record.

1062. TRASK, NATHANIEL—Age, 21 years. Enlisted, May 3, 1861, at Utica, to serve two years; mustered in as private, Company F, May 21, 1861; wounded, December 13, 1862, at Fredericksburg, Va.; discharged, February 13, 1863, at St. Elizabeth Hospital, Washington, D.C., on account of wounds.

TRAYER, BENJAMIN—*see* Trair, Benjamin.

1063. TREAT, SAMUEL—Age, 27 years. Enlisted, May 1, 1861, at Utica, to serve two years; mustered in as private, Company B, May 21. 1861; captured and paroled, dates not stated; mustered out with company, May 28, 1863, at Utica, N.Y.; subsequent service, unassigned, Fourteenth Artillery.

1064. TREGILGUS, JOHN—Age, 27 years. Enlisted, December 2, 1861, at Rochester, to serve unexpired term of two years; mustered in as private, Company H, December 11, 1861; captured, August 30, 1862, at Bull Run, Va.; paroled, date not stated; discharged for disability, September 29, 1862, at General Hospital, Philadelphia, Pa.

1065. TRIPP, EUGENE W.—Age, 24 years. Enlisted, May 17, 1861, at Utica, to serve two years; mustered in as corporal, Company D, May 21, 1861; promoted sergeant, August 30, 1862; wounded, September 17, 1862, at battle of Antietam, Md.; mustered out with company, May 28, 1863, at Utica, N.Y.

1066. TULLER, HENRY—Age, 28 years. Enlisted, July 31, 1862, at Utica, to serve three years; mustered in as private, unassigned, September 22, 1862; reported as being rejected.

1067. TULLER, WILLIAM H.—Age, 25 years. Enlisted, May 1, 1861, at Utica, to serve two years; mustered in as private, Company B, May 21, 1861; discharged for disability, May 28, 1862, at Carver Hospital, Washington, D.C.

1068. TUTTLE, WILLIAM E.—Age, 23 years. Enlisted, May 3, 1861, at Utica, to serve two years; mustered in as private, Company F, May 21, 1861; promoted corporal, January 1, 1862; died of disease, September 8, 1862, at Washington Street Hospital, Alexandria, Va.

1069. TWILIGAR, IRA—Age, 19 years. Enlisted, July 30, 1861, at Buffalo, to serve three years; mustered in as private, unassigned, August 9, 1861; deserted in August 1861, place not stated.

1070. ULLMANN, JULIUS—Age, — years. Enlisted, May 7, 1861, at Utica, to serve two years; mustered in as private, Company E, date not stated; appointed commissary sergeant, date not stated; mustered as second lieutenant, Company B, September 28, 1862; mustered out with company, May 28, 1863, at Utica, N.Y.; commissioned second lieutenant, February 11, 1863, with rank from August 30, 1862, vice Leonard, killed in action.

1071. URICH, JACOB—Age, 26 years. Enlisted, November 29, 1861, at Rome, to serve unexpired term of two years; mustered in as private, Company E, December 11, 1861; mustered out with company, May 28, 1863, at Utica, N.Y.; also listed as Jacob Ulrich; subsequent service in Third Artillery.

1072. VALENTINE, ELEAZER—Age, 22 years. Enlisted, May 14, 1861, at Camden, to serve two years; mustered in as private, Company K, May 21, 1861; deserted, August 13, 1862, at Culpepper, Va.

1073. VANAKEN, FRANKLIN—Age, 21 years. Enlisted, December 13, 1861, at Rochester, to serve two years; mustered in as private, Company K, same date; transferred to Company C, March 21, 1862; discharged for disability, February 25, 1863, at Carver Hospital, Washington, D.C.; also listed as Franklin Van Aken and Franklin L. Vanunken.

1074. VAN AUKEN, JOHN—Age, date

of enlistment, muster-in and term not stated; mustered in as private, Company G; no further record.

1075. VANDERHAVEN, JOHN—Age, 42 years. Enlisted, May 21, 1861, at Rochester, to serve two years; mustered in as second class musician, Company B, same date; transferred to the band, date not stated; mustered out with band, September 10, 1861, at Fort Ellsworth, Va.

1076. VANDERMARK, JOHN—Age, 23 years. Enlisted, May 14, 1861, at Camden, to serve two years; mustered in as private, Company. K, May 21, 1861; wounded, August 30, 1862, at Groveton, Va.; mustered out with company, May 28, 1863. at Utica, N.Y.

1077. VANDERMARK, JONATHAN—Age, 21 years. Enlisted, May 1, 1861, at Elmira, to serve two years; mustered in as private, Company B, June 17, 1861; discharged for disability, July 15, 1862, at Warrenton.

1078. VAN EPPS, JAMES—Age, 22 years. Enlisted, May 2, 1861, at Rochester, to serve two years; mustered in as private, Company G, May 21, 1861; mustered out with company, May 28, 1863, at Utica, N.Y.; subsequent service in Company C, Twenty-First Cavalry.

1079. VANHUSEN, ISAAC—Age, 28 years. Enlisted, December 5, 1861, at Rochester, to serve two years; mustered in as private, Company K, same date; wounded, at Groveton, Va.; discharged, December 30, 1862, at Detroit, Mich., on account of wounds; also listed as Isaac Van Husen.

1080. VANLOAN, JACOB V.—Age, 26 years. Enlisted, June 10, 1861, at Elmira, to serve two years; mustered in as private, Company K, same date; promoted sergeant, October 16, 1862; mustered out with company, May 28, 1863, at Utica, N.Y.

1081. VANOCKEN, ELIJAH—Age, 21 years. Enlisted, June 1, 1861, at Elmira, to serve two years; mustered in as private, Company K, same date; deserted, July 28, 1862, at Waterloo, Va.; also listed as Elijah Van Ocken.

1082. VAN ORDEN, MORIMUS—Age, 24 years. Enlisted, May 2, 1861, at Rochester, to serve two years; mustered in as private, Company G, May 21, 1861; promoted corporal, October 7, 1862; sergeant, November 1, 1862; mustered out with company, May 28, 1863, at Utica, N.Y.; also listed as Marinus Van Orden.

1083. VAN SCHOTEN, HIRAM—Age, 21 years. Enlisted, September 23, 1861, at Utica, to serve three years; mustered in as private, Company D, September 26, 1861; died of disease, February 24, 1862, at Fort Lyon, Va.

1084. VAN VLECK, JAMES—Age, 20 years. Enrolled, May 7, 1861, at Utica, to serve three months; mustered in as second lieutenant, Company E, May 21, 1862; resigned, August 7, 1861; commissioned second lieutenant, July 4, 1861, with rank from May 7, 1861, original.

1085. VAN VOLKENBURGH, HENRY—Age, 25 years. Enlisted, May 1, 1861, at Utica, to serve two years; mustered in as corporal, Company B, May 21, 1861; promoted sergeant, September 1, 1862; wounded, December 13, 1862, at battle of Fredericksburg, Va.; mustered out with company, May 28, 1863, at Utica, N.Y.; subsequent service in Company C, Fourteenth Artillery.

1086. VAUGHN, WILLIAM D.—Age, 22 years. Enlisted, September 2, 1861, at Rochester, to serve three years; mustered in as private, Company H, September 5, 1861; transferred to Company D, January 22, 1862; captured, August 31, 1862, at battle of Second Bull Run, Va.; sent to regiment, November 19, 1862; mustered out with company, May 28, 1863, at Utica, N.Y.; subsequent service, Company C, Fourteenth Artillery; also listed as William D. Vaughan.

1087. VENN, WILLIAM T.—Age, 22 years. Enlisted, May 21, 1861, at Elmira, to serve three months; mustered in as private, Company C, same date, no further record.

1088. VERHAGE, JACOB—Age, 22 years. Enlisted, May 2, 1861, at Rochester, to serve two years; mustered in as corporal, Company G, May 21, 1861; discharged for disability, October 14, 1861, near Fairfax Seminary, Va.

1089. VERNON, PETER D.—Age, 23 years. Enlisted, May 2, 1861, at Rochester, to serve two years; mustered in as private, Company H, May 21, 1861; wounded, December 13, 1862, at battle of Fredericksburg, Va.; mustered out, May 24, 1863, at Utica, N.Y.

1090. VIBBARD, LORENZO—Age, 27 years. Enlisted, May 7, 1861, at Utica, to serve two years; mustered in as private, Company D, May 21, 1861; promoted corporal, August 10, 1861; sergeant, February 20, 1862; reduced, date not stated; died of gunshot wound, September 9, 1862, near Washington, D.C.

1091. VICTOR, NELSON—Age, 26 years. Enlisted, May 7, 1861, at Utica, to serve two years; mustered in as private, Company E, May 21, 1861; died of disease, November 11, 1862, at Camp Parole, Md.; also listed as Allen Victor.

1092. VOSBURG, DANIEL—Age, 23 years. Enlisted, May 7, 1861, at Utica, to serve three months; mustered in as private, Company E, May 21, 1861; deserted, August 1, 1861, at Elmira, N.Y.

1093. WADE, WILLIAM H.—Age, 21 years. Enlisted, August 21, 1862, at Utica, to serve three years; mustered in as private, Company A, same date; transferred, date not stated, to Eighty-Third Infantry.

1094. WAGHORN, JOHN—Age, 23 years. Enlisted, May 3, 1861, at Utica, to serve two years; mustered in as private, Company F, May 21, 1861; deserted, July 7, 1862, at Warrenton, Va.

1095. WAGNER, CONRAD—Age, 24 years. Enlisted, October 14, 1861, at Buffalo, to serve three years; mustered in as private, Company E, same date; mustered out with company, May 28, 1863, at Utica, N.Y.; subsequent service, Company M, Twelfth Cavalry.

1096. WAIT, HENRY O.—Age, 21 years. Enlisted, May 14, 1861, at Camden, to serve two years; mustered in as corporal, Company K, May 21, 1861; reduced, August 1, 1861; mustered out with company, May 28, 1863, at Utica, N.Y.

1097. WAITE, EUPHRATUS—Age, 25 years. Enlisted, July 30, 1861, at Buffalo, to serve three years; mustered in as private, Company D, August 9, 1861; promoted corporal, date not stated; reduced July 20, 1862; deserted, August 30, 1862, at Manassas, Va.; also listed as Epophraditos Waite.

1098. WALKER, ANDREW G.—Age, 18 years. Enlisted, May 14, 1861, at Camden, to serve two years; mustered in as private, Company K, May 21, 1861; wounded, August 31, 1862, at battle of Second Bull Run, Va.; mustered out with company, May 28, 1863, at Utica, N.Y.

1099. WALKER, ISAAC M.—Age, 44 years. Enlisted, May 14, 1861, at Camden, to serve two years; mustered in as private, Company K, May 21, 1861; discharged for disability, November 11, 1861, at Camp Franklin, Va.; also listed as Isaac W. Walker.

1100. WALKER, JAMES—Age, 25 years. Enlisted, September 10, 1861, at Utica, to serve two years; mustered in as private, Company F, September 17, 1861; deserted, May 15, 1862, at Brook's Station, Va.

WALKER, JOHN—see Walter, John.

1101. WALKER, JOHN—Age, 25 years. Enlisted, July 30, 1861, at Rochester, to serve three years; mustered in as private, Company I, August 9, 1861; wounded, August 30, 1862, at battle of Second Bull Run, Va.; discharged for disability, in March 1863; also listed as John W. Walker; subsequent service in Company H, Twelfth Cavalry.

1102. WALKER, THOMAS J.—Age, 21 years. Enlisted, May 7, 1861, at Utica, to serve two years; mustered in as private, Company E, May 21, 1861; mustered out with company, May 28, 1863, at Utica, N.Y.

1103. WALLACE, FRANKLIN—Age, 24 years. Enlisted, May 1, 1861, at Utica, to serve two years; mustered in as private, Company B, May 21, 1861; transferred to Company E, May 22, 1861; wounded, date and place not stated; mustered out with company, May 28, 1863, at Utica, N.Y.

1104. WALSH, JOHN—Age, 43 years. Enlisted, July 29, 1862, at Utica, to serve three years; mustered in as private, Company B, August 19, 1862; wounded, December 13, 1862, at battle of Fredericksburg, Va.; discharged, date and place not stated.

1105. WALTER, JOHN—Age, 23 years. Enlisted, May 1, 1861, at Utica, to serve two years; mustered in as private, Company B, May 21, 1861; mustered out with company, May 28, 1863, at Utica, N.Y.; also listed as John Walker; subsequent service in Third Artillery.

1106. WALTER, JOSEPH—Age, 40 years. Enlisted, July 30, 1861, at Buffalo, to serve three years; mustered in as private, Company E, August 9, 1861; killed, August 30, 1862, at battle of Second Bull Run, Va.; also listed as Joseph Walters.

1107. WAMPLE, CHARLES H.—Age, 28 years. Enlisted, May 1, 1861, at Utica, to serve two years; mustered in as corporal, Company B, May 21, 1861; promoted sergeant, same date; mustered in as second lieutenant, April 7, 1862; resigned, February 24, 1863; also listed as Charles H. Wampel; commissioned second lieutenant, April 14, 1862, with rank from April 7, 1862, vice Harlow, promoted.

1108. WARD, JOHN—Age, 27 years. Enlisted, August 18, 1862, at Utica, to serve three years; mustered in as private, unassigned, same date; no further record.

1109. WARD, JOHN G.—Age, 18 years. Enlisted, May 13, 1861, at Utica, to serve two years; mustered in as private, Company I, May 21,. 1861; promoted corporal, November 4, 1862; mustered out with company, May 28, 1863, at Utica, N.Y.

1110. WARNER, BARNEY—Age, 22 years. Enlisted, May 2, 1861, at Rochester, to serve two years; mustered in as private, Company G, May 21, 1861; mustered out with company, May 28, 1863, at Utica, N.Y.

1111. WARNER, JAMES—Age, 22 years. Enlisted, May 14, 1861, at Camden, to serve two years; mustered in as private, Company K, May 21, 1861; mustered out with company, May 28, 1863, at Utica, N.Y.; subsequent service in Company B, Twenty-First Cavalry.

1112. WARNER, LORENZO—Age, 20 years. Enlisted, May 14, 1861, at Camden, to serve two years; mustered in as private, Company K, May 21, 1861; killed, August 30, 1862, at battle of Second Bull Run, Va.

1113. WARREN, DANIEL—Age, 19 years. Enlisted, May 1, 1861, at Utica, to serve two years; mustered in as private, Company A, May 21, 1861; mustered out with company, May 28, 1863, at Utica, N.Y.

1114. WATERMAN, JOHN G.—Age, 21 years. Enlisted, May 7, 1861, at Utica, to serve two years; mustered in as private, Company E, May 21, 1861; died of disease, February 12, 1863, at Union Hotel Hospital, Georgetown, D.C.

1115. WATSON, ALVIN—Age, 16 years. Enlisted, April 1, 1862, at Rochester, to serve years; mustered in as private, Company F, date not stated; no record subsequent to August 1862.

1116. WATSON, JAMES—Age, 19 years. Enlisted, May 1, 1861, at Utica, to serve two years; mustered in as private, Company A, May 21, 1861; promoted corporal, December 12, 1862; mustered out with company, May 28, 1863, at Utica, N.Y.

1117. WEAVER, NICHOLAS W.—Age, 27 years. Enlisted August 29, 1862, at Deerfield, to serve three years; mustered in as private, Company F, September 18, 1862; transferred, May 8, 1863, to Company D, Eighty-Third Infantry; also listed as Nicholas Weaver.

1118. WEBSTER, HENRY N.—Age, 19 years. Enlisted, May 13, 1861, at Utica, to serve two years; mustered in as private, Company I, May 21 1861; wounded, December 13, 1862, at battle of Fredericksburg, Va.; mustered out with company, May 28, 1863, at Utica, N.Y.

1119. WEECKMAN, SEBASTIAN—Age, 44 years. Enlisted, September 27, 1861, at Rome, to serve three years; mustered in as private, Company E, same date; discharged for disability, March 8, 1862, at Fort Lyon, Va.; also listed as Sebastian Wickman.

1120. WEISENBORN, JOHN—Age, 18 years. Enlisted, April 1, 1862, at Springfield, Va., to serve two years; mustered in as private, Company G, same date; deserted, August 9, 1862, at Warrenton, Va.

1121. WELCH, GILBERT—Age, 29 years. Enlisted, May 3, 1861, at Utica, to serve two years; mustered in as private, Company F, May 21, 1861; mustered out with company, May 28, 1863, at Utica, N.Y.; subsequent service in Third Artillery.

1122. WELCH, MICHAEL—Age, 28 years. Enlisted, May 3, 1861, at Utica, to serve two years; mustered in as private, Company C, May 21, 1861; wounded, August 30, 1862, at battle of Second Bull Run, Va.; mustered out with company, May 28, 1863, at Utica, N.Y.

1123. WELCH, THOMAS—Age, 18 years. Enlisted, May 3, 1861, at Utica, to serve two years; mustered in as private, Company F, May 21, 1861; mustered out with company, May 28, 1863, at Utica, N.Y.; subsequent service in Third Artillery.

1124. WELLMAN, JACOB H.—Age, 21 years. Enlisted, October 28, 1861, at Rochester, to serve two years; mustered in as private, Company H, November 20, 1861; died, March 25, 1862, in Regimental Hospital, Alexandria; Va.; also listed as Jacob Wellinan.

1125. WERNET, GEORGE—Age, 18 years. Enlisted, May 2, 1861, at Rochester, to serve two years; mustered in as private, Company H, May 21, 1861; deserted, May 26, 1862, at Alexandria, Va.

1126. WEST, WILLIAM P.—Age, 20 years. Enrolled, May 7, 1861, at Utica, to serve two years; mustered in as first lieutenant, Company D, May 21, 1861; as captain, Company I, August 7, 1861; resigned, January 11, 1862; commissioned first lieutenant, July 4, 1861, with rank from May 7, 1861, original; captain, August 14, 1861, with rank from August 7, 1861, original.

1127. WESTBROOK, AMASA—Age, 19 years. Enlisted, May 14, 1861, at Camden, to serve two years; mustered in as private, Company K, May 21, 1861; mustered out with company, May 28, 1863, at Utica, N.Y.

1128. WESTFALL, ELI F—Age, 20 years. Enlisted, May 14, 1861, at Camden, to serve two years; mustered in as private, Company K, May 21, 1861; deserted August 15, 1861; discharged by sentence of general court-martial, February 2, 1862; subsequent service in Company B, Twenty-First Cavalry.

1129. WETMORE, EZRA F.—Age, 40 years. Enrolled, May 3, 1861, at Utica, to serve two years; mustered in as captain, Company F, May 21, 1861; as major, September 19, 1862; mustered out with regiment, May 28, 1863, at Utica, N.Y.; commissioned captain, July 4, 1861, with rank from May 3, 1861, original; major, November 25, 1862, with rank from September 19, 1862, vice Gilbert S. Jennings, promoted.

1130. WHALEY, ELEAZER H.—Age, 24 years. Enlisted, May 7, 1861, at Utica, to serve two years; mustered in as private, Company D, same date; discharged for disability, December 15, 1861, at Fort Lyon, Va.; also listed as Edgar H. Whaley.

1131. WHEAT, CHARLES—Age, 18 years. Enlisted, May 25, 1861, at Elmira, to serve two years; mustered in as private, Company K, same date; discharged for disability, August 14, 1862, at General Hospital, Fairfax Seminary, Va.

1132. WHEELER, CHARLES—Age, 21 years. Enlisted, July 28, 1861, at Rochester, to serve three years; mustered in as private, unassigned, August 9, 1861; no further record.

1133. WHEELER, JOHN H.—Age, 20 years. Enlisted, May 14, 1861, at Camden, to serve two years; mustered in as private, Company K, May 21, 1861; mustered out with company, May 28, 1863, at Utica, N.Y.; also listed as John W. Wheeler.

1134. WHITE, CHARLES. S.—Age, 19 years. Enlisted, May 7, 1861, at Utica, to serve two years; mustered in as private, Company D, May 21, 1861; promoted corporal, February 28, 1862; wounded at battle of Fredericksburg, Va., December 13, 1862; discharged for disability, April 6, 1863, at Armory Square hospital.

1135. WHITE, GEORGE—Age, 28 years. Enlisted, May 1, 1861, at Utica, to serve two years; mustered in as sergeant, Company A, May 21, 1861; reduced, August 21, 1861; mustered out with company, May 28, 1863, at Utica, N.Y.

1136. WHITE, JOHN J.—Age, 32 years. Enlisted, May 1, 1861, at Elmira, to serve two years; mustered in as private, Company B, May 28, 1861; wounded, August 30, 1862; mustered out with company, May 28, 1863, at Utica, N.Y.

1137. WHITE, JOSEPH—Age, 23 years. Enlisted, May 1, 1861, at Utica, to serve two years; mustered in. as private, Company B, May 21, 1861; wounded at battle of Second Bull Run, Va., August 30, 1862; mustered out with company, May 28, 1863, at Utica, N.Y.

1138. WHITEMAN, WILLIAM U.—Age, 19 years. Enlisted, June 5, 1861, at Elmira, to serve two years; mustered in as private, Company K, same date; captured and paroled, dates and place not, stated; transferred, October 9, 1862, to regular cavalry.

1139. WHITMORE, SETH—Age, 26 years. Enlisted, December 20, 1861, at Geneva, to serve two years; mustered in as private, unassigned, January 3, 1862; no further record.

1140. WHITTON, STEPHEN—Age, 18 years. Enlisted, May 8, 1861, at Elmira, to serve two years; mustered in as private,

Company D, May 21, 1861; transferred to Company B in June 1861; mustered out with company, May 28, 1863, at Utica, N.Y.; also listed as Stephen A. Whitten; subsequent service in Third Artillery.

1141. WIGGINS, ROBERT—Age, 41 years. Enlisted, May 1, 1861, at Elmira, to serve two years; mustered in as private, Company B, May 21, 1861; mustered out with company, May 28, 1863, at Utica, N.Y.

1142. WIGHT, CHAS. M.—Age, 28 years. Enrolled, November 20, 1862, at Washington, D.C., to serve two years; mustered in as assistant surgeon, same date; no record of service; commissioned assistant surgeon, November 5, 1862, with rank from October 28, 1862, vice Steele, resigned.

1143. WILBUR, NATHAN C.—Age, 20 years. Enlisted, May 7, 1861, at Elmira, to serve two years; mustered in as sergeant, Company D, May 21, 1861; promoted first sergeant, August 7, 1861; captured at Manassas, Va., August 29, 1862; paroled, December 8, 1862; mustered out with company, May 28, 1863, at Utica. N.Y.

1144. WILCOX, CHARLES—Age, 22 years. Enlisted, May 7, 1861, at Utica, to serve two years; mustered in as private, Company D, May 21, 1861; promoted corporal, February 28, 1862; wounded at battle of Antietam, Md., September 17, 1862; mustered out with company, May 28, 1863, at Utica, N.Y.; subsequent service as corporal in Company C, Fourteenth Artillery.

1145. WILCOX, CHARLES D.—Age, 18 years. Enlisted, May 7, 1861, at Utica, to serve two years; mustered in as private, Company D, May 21, 1861; discharged for disability, September 15, 1862, at Alexandria, Va.

1146. WILCOX, DELOS—Age, 24 years. Enlisted, May 7, 1861, at Utica., to serve two years; mustered in as private, Company D, May 21, 1861; mustered out with company, May 28, 1863, at Utica, N.Y.; also listed as Devolson Wilcox; subsequent service in Eighth Independent Battery as Derolson Wilcox.

1147. WILL, FREDERICK—Age, 43 years. Enlisted, May 18, 1861, at Utica, to serve two years; mustered in as private, Company E, May 21, 1861; died of disease, January 14, 1862, at Military Hospital at Alexandria, Va.

1148. WILLARD, EPHRAIM JAY—Age, 21 years. Enlisted, May 13, 1861, at Utica, to serve two years; mustered in a. private, Company I, May 21, 1861; discharged for disability, February 6, 1863, at Frederick, Md.

1149. WILLIAMS, CHARLES P.—Age, 18 years. Enlisted, May 13, 1861, at Utica, to serve two years; mustered in as private, Company I, May 21, 1861; wounded at battle of Second Bull Run, Va., August 30, 1862; mustered out with company, May 28, 1863, at Utica, N.Y.; subsequent service in Twenty-Fourth Cavalry.

1150. WILLIAMS, FRANCIS—Age, 38 years. Enlisted, May 1, 1861, at Utica, to serve two years; mustered in as private, Company B, May 21, 1861; mustered out with company, May 28, 1863, at Utica, N.Y.

1151. WILLIAMS, JACOB—Age, 21 years. Enlisted, September 16, 1861, at Buffalo, to serve two years; mustered in as private, Company H, same date; promoted corporal, date not stated; mustered out, May 24, 1863, at Utica, N.Y.

1152. WILLIAMS, JOHN—Age, 23 years. Enlisted, May 3, 1861, at Utica, to serve two years; mustered in as private, Company F, May 21, 1861; promoted corporal, date not stated; wounded, date and place not stated; mustered out with company, May 28, 1863, at Utica, N.Y.; commissioned, not mustered, second lieutenant, August 14, 1861, with rank from August 7, 1861; original; declined.

1153. WILLIAMS, OLIVER—Age, 23 years. Enlisted, May 14, 1861, at Camden, to serve two years; mustered in as private, Company K, May 21, 1861; deserted, September 15, 1861, at Alexandria, Va.

1154. WILSEY, HIRAM—Age, 22 years. Enlisted, May 3, 1861, at Utica, to serve two years; mustered in as private, Company C, May 21, 1861; mustered out with company, May 28, 1863, at Utica N.Y.; subsequent service in Twenty-Fourth Cavalry.

1155. WILSON, CLARK—Age, 22 years. Enlisted, May 2, 1861, at Rochester, to serve two years; mustered in as private, Company H, May 21, 1861; mustered out, May 24, 1863, at Utica, N.Y.

1156. WILSON, JAMES—Age, 22 years. Enlisted, August 13, 1861, at Rochester, to serve three years; mustered in as private, Company C, September 5, 1861; promoted corporal, January 1, 1862; wounded at battle of Antietam, Md., September 17, 1862; reduced to the ranks, February 28, 1863; mustered out with company, May 28, 1863, at Utica, N.Y.

1157. WINCHELL, JAMES N.—Age, 19 years. Enlisted, May 14, 1861, at Camden, to serve two years; mustered in as private, Company K, May 21, 1861; wounded, August 30, 1862, at Groveton, Va.; discharged for disability, October 21, 1862, at Carver Hospital, Washington, D.C.

1158. WINCHELL, PHILIP D.—Age, 25 years. Enlisted, May 3, 1861, at Utica, to serve two years; mustered in as private, Company C, May 21, 1861; wounded, August 30, 1862, at battle of Second Bull Run, Va.; mustered out with company, May 28, 1863, at Utica, N.Y.

1159. WING, CYRENUS—Age, 21 years. Enlisted, May 1, 1861, at Utica, to serve three months; mustered in as private, Company B, May 21, 1861; deserted, September 3, 1861, at Alexandria, Va.

1160. WINSLER, PAUL—Age, 21 years. Enlisted, May 1, 1861, at Elmira, to serve two years; mustered in as private, Company B, May 21, 1861; captured, August 24, 1861, place not stated; paroled, May 28, 1862; wounded, December 13, 1862, at battle of Fredericksburg, Va.; mustered out with company, May 28, 1863, at Utica, N.Y.

1161. WINSTON, THOMAS—Age, 25 years. Enlisted, September 9, 1861, at Utica, to serve two years; mustered in as private, Company C, September 17, 1861; mustered out with company, May 28, 1863, at Utica, N.Y.

1162. WITHERELL, JAMES—Age, 19 years. Enlisted, May 14, 1861, at Camden, to serve two years; mustered in as private, Company K, May 21, 1861; deserted, August 13, 1862, at Culpeper, Va.

1163. WOOD, EUGENE K.—Age, 20 years. Enlisted, May 14, 1861, at Elmira, to serve two years; mustered in as private, Company I, May 21, 1861; transferred to Company C, June 1, 1861; to Company K, October 1, 1861; mustered out with company, May 28, 1863, at Utica, N.Y.; subsequent service in Company C, Sixteenth Artillery.

1164. WOODALL, JOHN—Age, 19 years. Enlisted, May 13, 1861, at Utica, to serve two years; mustered in as private, Company I, May 21, 1861; captured, August 29, 1862, at Manassas, Va.; paroled at Manassas, Va., date not stated; mustered out with company, May 28, 1863, at Utica, N.Y.

1165. WOODHULL, ROSELL—Age, 18 years. Enlisted, September 3, 1861, at Utica, to serve two years; mustered in as private, Company B, September 5, 1861; mustered out with company, May 28, 1863, at Utica, N.Y.

1166. WOOLE, GOTTLEIB—Age, 19 years. Enlisted, May 2, 1861; at Rochester, to serve two years; mustered in as drummer, Company H, May 21, 1861; wounded, December 13, 1862, at battle of Fredericksburg, Va.; died of such wounds, January 23, 1863, in hospital at Washington, D.C.

1167. WOOLEY, MICHAEL—Age, 18 years. Enlisted, June 1, 1861, at Elmira, to serve two years; mustered in as private, Company C, same date; discharged for disability, January 16, 1863, at Annapolis, Md.

1168. WORDEN, WILLIAM W.—Age, 19 years. Enlisted, May 3, 1861, at Utica, to serve two years; mustered in as private, Company C, May 21, 1861; deserted, October 24, 1861, from Camp Franklin, Va.

1169. WORTH, JOHN A.—Age, 20 years. Enlisted, May 2, 1861, at Rochester, to serve two years; mustered in as corporal, Company G, May 21, 1861; discharged for disability, February 7, 1863, at Convalescent Camp, Va.

1170. WRENN, BARNY—Age, 19 years. Enlisted, May 2, 1861, at Rochester, to serve two years; mustered in as private, Company H, May 21, 1861; mustered out, May 24, 1863, at Utica, N.Y.; also listed as Bernard Wren.

1171. WRIGHT, AMZI W.—Age, 22 years. Enlisted, May 14, 1861, at Camden, to serve two years; mustered in as private, Company K, May 21, 1861; mustered out, May 24, 1863, at Utica, N.Y.

1172. WRIGHT, MARTIN R.—Age, 43 years. Enlisted, July 27, 1861, at Rochester, to serve three months; mustered in as private, Company E, August 9, 1861; reported deserted, to date, August 2, 1861.

1173. WRIGHT, PHILIP—Age, 31 years. Enlisted, May 1, 1861, at Utica, to serve two years; mustered in as private, Company A, May 21, 1861; deserted, September 6, 1862, at Washington, D.C.

1174. WRIGHT, SILAS—Age, 29 years. Enlisted, May 1, 1861, at Utica, to serve two years; mustered in as private, Company A May 21, 1861; mustered out with company, May 28, 1863, at Utica, N.Y.

1175. WYATT, ROMANCE—Age, 36 years. Enlisted, August 22, 1862, at Utica, to serve two years; mustered in as private, Company K, September 16, 1862; transferred, May 8, 1863, to Company A, Eighty-Third New York Volunteers.

1176. WYCH, THOMAS P.—Age, 34 years. Enlisted, May 2, 1861, at Rochester, to serve two years; mustered in as sergeant, Company G, May 21, 1861; mustered out with company, May 28, 1863, at Utica, N.Y.; subsequent service in Company C, Twenty-First Cavalry.

1177. YALE, DANIEL N.—Age, 38 years. Enlisted, May 14, 1861, at Elmira, to serve two years; mustered in as first sergeant, Company I, May 21, 1861; discharged for disability, December 8, 1861, at Fort Lyon, Va.; subsequent service in Company C, Sixteenth Artillery.

1178. YOURDON, JOHN—Age, 31 years. Enlisted, May 3, 1861, at Utica, to serve two years; mustered in as private, Company C, May 21, 1861; wounded, December 13, 1862, at battle of Fredericksburg, Va.; discharged for disability, March 28, 1863, at Mount Pleasant.

1179. ZIMMERMAN, SIMON—Age, 22 years. Enlisted, May 7, 1861, at Utica, to serve two years; mustered in as private, Company E, May 21, 1861; mustered out with company, May 28, 1863, at Utica, N.Y.

1180. ZORN, FREDERICK—Age, 19 years. Enlisted, October 15, 1861, at Rochester, to serve unexpired term of two years; mustered in as third-class musician, band, same date; mustered out, September 4, 1862, with band, at Upton's Hill, Va.

1181. ZORN, JOSEPH—Age, 27 years. Enlisted, October 14, 1861, at Rochester, to serve unexpired term of two year; mustered in as first-class musician, band, same date; mustered out September 4, 1862, with band, at Upton's Hill, Va.

1182. ZORN, WILLIAM—Age, 23 years. Enlisted, October 14, 1861, at Rochester, to serve unexpired term of two years; mustered in as first-class musician, band, same date; mustered out, September 4, 1862, with band, at Upton's Hill, Va.

Chapter Notes

Preface

1. New York Historical Resources Center, *Guide to Historical Resources in Oneida County, New York, Repositories* (Ithaca, N.Y.: New York Historical Resources Center, Olin Library, Cornell University), 1983.

Chapter 1

1. J. H. French, *Gazetteer of the State of New York* (Syracuse, N.Y.: R. Pearsall Smith, 1860), pp. 458, 472.
2. Millard Family letter dated January 24, 1860, collection of the author; Daniel E. Wager, ed., *Our County and its People: A Descriptive Work on Oneida County, New York* (Boston: Boston History Co., 1896), pp. 195–196.
3. Theophilus F. Rodenbough, ed., *The Army of the United States: Historical Sketches of Staff and Line* (New York: Maynard Merrill and Co., 1896).
4. New York (State) Adjutant General's Office, *A Record of the Commissioned Officers, Non-commissioned Officers, Privates, of the Regiments Which Were Organized in the State of New York and Called Into the Service of the United States to Assist in Suppressing the Rebellion, Caused by the Secession of Some of the Southern States From the Union, A.D. 1861, As Taken From the Muster-in Rolls on File in the Adjutant-General's Office, S. N. Y., Vol. 1* (Albany: Comstock & Cassidy Printers, 1864), pp. 5–7, 10, 14; William Holstead, letter to his parents dated April 14, 1861, Charles Rodgers Collection, Northridge, CA; Charles McClenthen letter to his sister dated May 19, 1861, Charles McClenthen papers, #1304m, Rare and Manuscript Collections, Cornell University Library.
5. *Utica Daily Herald and Morning Gazette*, April 28, 1861; James McQuade, "Military History of Utica" in *Semi-Centennial of the City of Utica* (Utica, N.Y.: Oneida Historical Society, 1882), p. 50; Mary P. Ryan, *Cradle of the Middle Class: The Family in Oneida County, New York, 1790–1865* (New York: Cambridge University Press, 1983), p. 213.
6. A company usually consisted of 50 to 100 soldiers. A regiment usually had ten companies.
7. New York (State) Bureau of Military Statistics, *Third Annual Report of the Bureau of Military Record of the State of New York* (Albany, N.Y.: C. Wendell Printer, 1866), pp. 194–195; *Hornellsville (N.Y.) Tribune*, June 27, 1861.
8. Guy James Giffen, *California Expedition: Stevenson's First New York Regiment of Volunteers* (Oakland, Calif.; Bio-books, 1951), p. 35; Roger Hunt and Jack Brown, *Brevet Brigadier Generals in Blue* (Gaithersburg, MD: Olde Soldier Books, 1990), p. 110; Stewart Sifakis, *Who Was Who in the Union* (New York: Facts on File, 1998), p. 76; Francis B. Heitman, *Historical Register and Dictionary of the United States Army From Its Organization, September 29, 1789, to March 2, 1903*, 2 vols. (Washington, D.C.: Government Printing Office, 1903), p. 300; Christian obituary, *Utica Daily Press*, May 9, 1887.
9. Company C Descriptive Roll, Twenty-Sixth New York bound volume, New-York Historical Society, New York, N.Y.; Company E Descriptive Roll, Charles Ackerman papers, #3966, Division of Rare and Manuscript Collections, Cornell University Library; New York (State) Adjutant General's Office, *A Record of the Commissioned Officers, Non-commissioned Officers*, p. 596; James S. Page, ed., *Ethnic Utica* (Utica, N.Y.: Utica College, 2002), p. 53; Howard Thomas, *Boys in Blue from the Adirondack Foothills* (Prospect, N.Y.: Prospect Books, 1960), p. 16.
10. Washington Eliot to William Christian, photocopy of letter dated May 20, 1861, collection of the author; Edward K. Eckert and Nicholas J. Amato, ed., *Ten Years in the Saddle: The Memoir of William Woods Averell 1851–1862* (San Rafael, CA: Presidio Press, 1978), p. 281.
11. Timothy Gaffney, letter dated May 16, 1861, Don Wisnoski collection, Chadwicks, N.Y.; Michael Horigan, *Elmira: Death Camp of the North* (Mechanicsburg, PA: Stackpole, 2002), pp. 8–9.
12. New York (State) Adjutant General's Office, *Annual Report of the Adjutant-General of the State of New York for the Year 1899, Serial No. 21* (Albany: James B. Lyon, 1900), p. 31.
13. John S. Applegate, *Reminiscences and Letters of George Arrowsmith, Late Lieutenant-Colonel of the One Hundred and Fifty-Seventh Regiment, New York State Volunteers* (Red Bank, N.J.: John H. Cook, 1893), pp. 36–41. Arrowsmith served in the Twenty-Sixth New York from May 1861, through early September 1862, at which time he joined the 157th New York Regiment; *Utica Morning Herald and Daily Gazette*, May 1, 1861.

14. *O. R.*, ser. 3, vol. 1, p. 268; Applegate, pp. 36–41.
15. *Rochester Evening Express*, May 27, 1861.
16. Edmund R. P. Shurly, "Reminiscences of the War in 1861," Bentley Historical Library, University of Michigan; Thomas R. Proctor, compiler, *Presentation of the Battle Flags of the Oneida County Regiments to the Oneida Historical Society* (Utica, N.Y.: Oneida Historical Society, 1898), pp. 8–9,25; *Washington Evening Star*, June 22, 1861; Record Series A4134: "Historical Notes on the 26th New York Volunteer Regiment," New York State Archives, Albany, N.Y.; Ruth Marsh, "A History of Rochester's Part in the Civil War." *Rochester in the Civil War* (Rochester, N.Y.: Rochester Historical Society, 1944), p. 26.
17. *Rochester Evening Express*, June 20, 1861; *Utica Daily Observer*, June 21 and 28, 1861; Cornelius Rightmire, Letter and brief memoir written to his son, dated June 4, 1912, United States Army Military History Institute (hereafter referred to as USAMHI), Carlisle, Pa.
18. Col. Edward F. Jones report, *O. R.*, ser. 1, vol. 2, pp. 7–8; George William Brown, *Baltimore and the Nineteenth of April, 1861* (Baltimore, MD: N. Murray, 1887), pp. 49–53; Applegate, p. 41.
19. *Baltimore Sun*, June 24, 1861; Fred Smith, journal entry dated June 22, 1861, http://www.letterscivilwar.com/journal_fred_smith_8th_mass.html. Smith served with the Eighth Massachusetts; Applegate, pp. 44–45; C. Rightmire letter; *Washington Evening Star*, June 22, 1861.
20. C. DeWitt Staring letter to his brother dated June 26, 1861, collection of the author.
21. Oliver Otis Howard, *Autobiography of Oliver Otis Howard*, 2 vols. (New York: Baker and Taylor, 1907), pp. 137–138.
22. Michael Shiner diary, June 1, 1861, Library of Congress, Washington, D.C.

Chapter 2

1. Bacon, pp. 20–21; *Washington Evening Star*, July 14, 1861; Timothy Gaffney, letter dated July 7, 1861, Don Wisnoski collection, Chadwicks, N.Y.
2. Albert Collier, letter dated June 30, 1861, USAMHI, Carlisle, Pa.; Cornelius Rightmire letter and memoir.
3. Erna Risch, *Quartermaster Support of the Army: A History of the Corps, 1775–1939* (Washington D.C.: Center of Military History-United States Army, 1989), pp. 334–335.
4. *Utica Daily Observer*, July 19, 1861; Risch, pp. 354–355; William T. Sherman, *Memoirs of General W. T. Sherman*, 2 vols. (New York: D. Appleton, 1875), vol. 1, p. 178.
5. *Utica Daily Observer*, July 19, 1861; Risch, pp. 354–355; vol. 1, p. 178.
6. Applegate, pp. 46–47.
7. William Harrar, *With Drum and Gun in '61* (Greenville, PA: Beaver Printing Co., 1906), pp. 12–13.
8. Lucius E. Chittenden, *Invisible Siege: The Journal of Lucius E. Chittenden* (San Diego, CA: Americana Exchange Press, 1969), pp. 121–122; *Utica Daily Observer*, July 9, 1861; Margaret Leech, *Reveille in Washington 1860–1865* (New York: Harper and Row, 1941), p. 101.
9. *Washington Evening Star*, July 10, 1861; *Utica Daily Observer*, July 16, 1861.
10. *Utica Daily Observer*, July 16, 1861.
11. *O. R.*, ser. 1, vol. 2, p. 751; Cornelius Rightmire letter and memoir; Thomas, p. 27; *Utica Daily Observer*, July 25, 1861.
12. James Barber, *Alexandria in the Civil War* (Lynchburg, VA: H. E. Howard, 1988), p. 14.
113. Howard, p. 142; T. Michael Miller, ed., *Pen Portraits of Alexandria, Virginia, 1739–1900* (Bowie, MD: Heritage Books, 1987), p. 201.
14. *O. R.*, ser. 1, vol. 2, p. 751; Applegate, pp. 52–55; *Utica Daily Herald and Morning Gazette*, July 25, 1861; *Utica Daily Observer*, July 25, 1861; H. F. Pitcher journal, July 21, 1861, Booth Library, Chemung County Historical Society, Elmira, N.Y.; Thomas, p. 27.
15. Ezra J. Warner, *Generals in Blue* (Baton Rouge: University of Louisiana Press, 1989), pp. 290–292.
16. *Washington Evening Star*, July 27, 1861.
17. *Washington Evening Star*, July 30, 1861; Cornelius Rightmire letter and memoir; Charles A. Smith letter dated July 30, 1861, Ohio Historical Society, Columbus, Ohio.
18. Newton Martin Curtis, *From Bull Run to Chancellorsville: The Story of the Sixteenth New York* (New York: G. P. Putnams, 1906), p. 59; *Roman Citizen*, August 16, 1861; New York Adjutant General's Office, pp. 587–607; *O. R.*, ser. 3, vol. 1, p. 267; Photocopy of Special Order No. 325, Donald Wisnoski Collection, Chadwicks, N.Y.
19. William Johnson Bacon, *Memorial of William Kirkland Bacon, Late Adjutant of the Twenty-Sixth Regiment of New York State Volunteers* (Utica, N.Y.: Roberts Printing, 1863), pp. 18–19; Gaffney letter, August 12, 1861; Thomas, p. 32.
20. Norman L. Ritchie, ed., *Four Years in the First New York Light Artillery: The Papers of David F. Ritchie* (Hamilton, N.Y.: Edmonston, 1997), p. 11. Ritchie served in the Fourteenth New York Infantry prior to his transfer to the artillery branch of the service. Fritz Updike, "Rome in the Civil War," Rome Historical Society, Rome, N.Y.
21. Brooks D. Simpson and Jean D. Berlin, eds., *Sherman's Civil War: Selected Correspondence of William T. Sherman, 1860–1865* (Chapel Hill, N.C.: University of North Carolina Press, 1999), pp. 130–132; Horatio N. Taft diary, August 14, 1861, Library of Congress; George B. McClellan, *McClellan's Own Story* (New York: Charles L. Webster and Co., 1887), p. 86; Photocopy of John Babcock letter to his sister dated August 11, 1861, collection of the author; Applegate, p. 77.
22. *Washington Evening Star*, August 15, 1861.
23. Applegate, p. 75; George W. Bicknell, *History of the Fifth Regiment Maine Volunteers* (Portland, ME: Hall L. Davis, 1871), p. 44.
24. Applegate, pp. 79–83.
25. Col. Thomas Davis order, dated August 20, 1861, Guard Report and Order Book of the Twenty-Sixth New York Volunteer Infantry, Record Group 94: Records of the Adjutant General's Office, National Archives, Washington, D.C.

26. Emily Bancroft, ed., *Memorial and Letters of Reverend John R. Adams, D. D., Chaplain, 5th Maine* (Cambridge: privately printed, 1890), pp. 34–35; Howard, pp. 168–169.
27. United States Sanitary Commission Records, Series 7, Camp Inspection Report of the Twenty-Sixth New York Infantry dated August 26, 1861, Manuscripts and Archives Division, New York Public Library, New York, N.Y.
28. Christian order, dated September 2, 1861, Guard Report and Order Book of the Twenty-Sixth New York Volunteer Infantry, Record Group 94: Records of the Adjutant General's Office, National Archives, Washington, D.C.; Stephen Sears, ed., *The Civil War Papers of George B. McClellan: Selected Correspondence 1860–1865* (New York: Ticknor & Fields, 1989), p. 93.
29. *Utica Daily Observer,* October 10, 1861.
30. John W. Brinsfield, William C. Davis, Benedict Maryniak, and James I. Robertson Jr., eds., *Faith in the Fight: Civil War Chaplains* (Mechanicsburg, PA: Stackpole, 2003), p. 137.
31. Bacon, pp. 21–22, 25; Applegate, pp. 114–115; *Utica Morning Herald and Daily Gazette,* December 10, 1861; *Utica Daily Observer,* December 16, 1861.
32. Timothy Gaffney, letter of September 25, 1861, Don Wisnoski collection, Chadwicks, N.Y.
33. *Utica Daily Observer,* February 15, 1862; Thomas, pp. 35–36.
34. *O. R.,* ser. 1, vol. 5, pp. 236–237; William B. Westervelt, *Lights and Shadows of Army Life As Seen by a Private Soldier* (Marlboro, N.Y.: C. H. Cochrane, 1886), pp. 6–7. Westervelt was in the Twenty-Seventh New York during this affair; Charles B. Fairchild, *History of the 27th Regiment New York Volunteers* (Binghamton, N.Y.: Carl & Matthews, 1888), p. 23; *Utica Morning Herald and Daily Gazette,* October 10, 1861; New York Monuments Commission, *In Memoriam: Henry Warner Slocum 1826–1894* (Albany, N.Y.: J. B. Lyons Printers, 1904), p. 71; Curtis, p. 72.
35. William H. Christian, Civil War Military Service File, order dated October 10, 1861, to William Franklin directing charges be preferred against Christian, National Archives, Washington.
36. *Utica Daily Observer,* October 10, 1861.
37. William H. Christian, Civil War Military Service File, letter dated November 5, 1861, requesting leave of absence, National Archives, Washington, D.C.; Richard Richardson, Civil War Military Service File, National Archives, Washington, D.C.; *Utica Morning Herald and Daily Gazette,* November 15, 1861; *Utica Daily Observer,* November 30, 1861.

Chapter 3

1. Timothy Gaffney, letter to his father dated October 11, 1861, Donald Wisnoski collection, Chadwicks, N.Y.
2. Miller, p. 214.
3. Barnard Report, *O. R.,* ser. 1, vol. 5, p. 680; Benjamin Franklin Cooling and Walton H. Owen, *Mr. Lincoln's Forts: A Guide to the Civil War Defenses of Washington* (Shippensburg, PA: White Mane, 1988) p. 60.
4. *Utica Morning Herald and Daily Gazette,* November 15, 1861.
5. *Waterville (N.Y.) Times,* September 20 and October 10, 1861; McClellan, p. 155.
6. *Utica Morning Herald and Daily Gazette,* November 15, 1861; Crigier Family Papers, James Fuller, Boyne City, Mich.
7. Gilbert S. Jennings, Civil War Military Service File, National Archives, Washington, D.C.
8. *Utica Daily Observer,* November 20, 1861.
9. Applegate, pp. 116–117; *Utica Daily Observer,* November 30, 1861.
10. *Utica Daily Observer,* November 30, 1861.
11. *O. R.,* ser. 1, vol. 5, p. 671; *Allegan Journal,* November 25, 1861; Stephen Sears, ed., *For Country, Cause, and Leader: The Civil War Journal of Charles B. Haydon* (New York: Ticknor and Fields, 1993).
12. U.S. Sanitary Commission Papers, Camp Inspection Report dated December 14, 1861.
13. *Utica Daily Observer,* January 9, 1862.
14. Court-martial transcripts and records, Record Group 153, II562, Private Stephen A. Richards, Company C, Private George F. Childs, Company H, and Private Eli F. Westfall, Company K, 26th New York Regiment, National Archives, Washington D.C.
15. Robert Knox Sneden, *Eye of the Storm: A Civil War Odyssey* (New York: The Free Press, 2000), pp. 19–20; Robert Knox Sneden, *Images from the Storm* (New York: The Free Press, 2001), p. 18; Ritchie, pp. 23–24.
16. Sears, *For Country,* p. 210.
17. *Utica Daily Observer,* February 15, 1862.
18. Shurly, reminiscences.
19. Thomas Huntly letter dated April 7, 1862, *The Civil War Letters of Fannie Austin;* http://freepages.genealogy.rootsweb.com/~snugaza/austin/index.html.
20. U.S. Sanitary Commission Papers, Camp Inspection Report dated April 22, 1862.
21. DeWitt Staring letter dated February 20, 1862, collection of author. Warner, pp. 403–404.

Chapter 4

1. Court-martial transcripts and records, Record Group 153, II873, Private Frank R. Pierce, Company D, 26th New York Regiment, National Archives, Washington, D.C.
2. Janet B. Hewet, ed., *Supplement to the Official Records of the Union and Confederate Armies,* vol. 43 (Wilmington, N.C.: Broadfoot, 1994–1996), pp. 373, 383–384. Hereafter referred to as *S. O. R.;* Warren S. Firman, diary, May 3, 1862, Rochester Museum and Science Center, Rochester, N.Y.; *Utica Daily Observer,* May 27, 1862.
3. *Utica Daily Observer,* May 27, 1862.
4. *O. R.,* ser. 1, vol. 101, pt. 1, p. 607; Firman diary, May 9, 1862.
5. *Utica Daily Observer,* May 20, 27, 1862.
6. Applegate, pp. 129–130.
7. *O. R.,* ser. 1, vol. 12. pt. 3, p. 232; *S. O. R.,* vol. 43, p. 384.

8. McDowell, *O. R.*, ser. 1, vol. 12, pt. 3, p. 326.
9. Shurly reminiscence; John Vautier, *History of the 88th Pennsylvania Volunteers* (Philadelphia: J. B. Lippincott, 1894), pp. 34–35; Applegate, pp. 188–189; *O. R.*, ser. 1, vol. 12. pt. 3, p. 390.
10. *O. R.*, ser. 1, vol. 101, pt. 1, p. 77; Samuel P. Bates, *History of Pennsylvania Volunteers, 1861– 65*, vol. 3 (Harrisburg, PA: Pennsylvania State Printer, 1870) p. 151.
11. Richard H. Richardson, Civil War Military Service and Pension Files, National Archives, Washington, D.C.
12. *O. R.*, ser. 1, vol. 12, pt. 3, p. 328.
13. *Utica Morning Herald and Daily Gazette*, July 7, 1862.
14. Nelson L. Wandell journal, August 13, 1862, Brooks Memorial Library, Brattleboro, VT.
15. William H. Christian, Civil War Pension File, National Archives, Washington, D.C.
16. *Oneida Weekly Herald*, August 5, 1862; Wager, p. 196.
17. Firman diary, July 12, 1862; D. T. Arnold, letter dated July 13, 1862, George A. Forman Collection, Historical Society of Pennsylvania, Philadelphia; Adrian Root letter dated July 28, 1862, Mss. W-35, Buffalo and Erie County Historical Society Archives, Buffalo, N.Y.
18. Applegate, pp. 146–149; Adrian Root letter dated August 3, 1862, Robert C. Ogden Papers, Library of Congress. Root was the colonel of the Ninety-Fourth New York within Tower's brigade; Vautier, p. 40; Firman diary, August 8, 1862.
19. Ricketts Report, *O. R.*, ser. 1, vol. 12, pt. 2, p. 170.
20. James Durkin, ed., *"This War is an Awful Thing": Civil War Letters of the National Guards, The 19th and 90th Pennsylvania Volunteers* (Glenside, PA: Santarelli, 1994), p. 222; Peter Cozzens and Robert I. Girardi, eds., *The Military Memoirs of General John Pope*, Chapel Hill, N.C.: University of North Carolina Press, 1998), p. 137.
21. McDowell Report, *O. R.*, ser. 1, vol. 12, pt. 2, pp. 327–328; *Utica Morning Herald and Daily Gazette*, August 15, 1862; Ephraim A. Wood Civil War Journal, August 10, 1862, Accession #12021, Albert and Shirley Small Special Collections Library, University of Virginia Library, Charlottesville, Va.; Tower Report, *O. R.*, ser. 1, vol. 12, pt. 2, p. 173.
22. Ricketts Report, *O. R.* ser. 1, vol. 12, pt. 2, p. 170; Tower Report, *O. R.*, ser. 1, vol. 12, pt. 2, pp. 173–174; Tillson Report, *O. R.*, ser. 1, vol. 12, pt. 2, p. 171; Charles S. McClenthen, *A Sketch of the Campaign in Virginia and Maryland from Cedar Mountain to Antietam*, (Syracuse, N.Y.: Masters and Lee, 1862), pp. 3–4; Adrian Root letter dated August 12, 1862, Mss. W-35, Buffalo and Erie County Historical Society Archives, Buffalo, N.Y.
23. Firman diary, August 11, 1862.
24. *Utica Daily Observer*, August 24, 1862; McClenthen, *Sketch*, pp. 4–5; Vautier, p. 43; Jackson Report, *O. R.* ser. 1, vol. 12, pt. 2, pp. 183–184; Charles McClenthen letter to his father, August 17, 1862, Charles McClenthen papers, #1304m, Division of Rare and Manuscript Collections, Cornell University Library; Ephraim A. Wood journal, August 11, 1862.
25. Jackson Report, *O. R.* ser. 1, vol. 12, pt. 2, pp. 183–184; McClenthen, *Sketch*, pp. 4–5.
26. Vautier, p.46; McClenthen, pp. 5–6; Sparks, p. 125; Ricketts Report, *O. R.*, ser. 1, vol. 12, pt. 2, p. 383; McDowell Report, *O. R.*, ser. 1, vol. 12, pt. 2, p. 330; Firman diary, August 20, 1862.
27. *Utica Daily Observer*, August 26, 1862; McClenthen, p. 7.
28. Shurly reminiscence, *National Tribune*, March 31, 1892.

Chapter 5

1. McDowell Report, *O. R.*, ser. 1, vol. 12, pt. 2, p. 331; Pope Report, *O. R.*, ser. 1, vol. 12, pt. 2, p. 13; Ricketts Report, *O. R.*, ser. 1, vol. 12, pt. 2, p. 383; Firman diary, August 23, 1862; McClenthen, p. 8.
2. Shurly reminiscence, *National Tribune*, December 16, 1897.
3. McClenthen, pp. 9–11.
4. Ibid, pp. 10–11, 15; William Christian letter to James McQuade dated July 15, 1878, Fitz-John Porter Papers, Library of Congress, Washington, D.C.; Charles McClenthen letter to his father, September 4, 1862, Charles McClenthen Papers, #1304m, Division of Rare and Manuscript Collections, Cornell University Library.
5. Ricketts Report, *O. R.*, ser. 1, vol. 12, pt. 2, p. 384; McDowell Report, *O. R.*, ser. 1, vol. 12, pt. 2, p. 337; John J. Hennessy, *Return to Bull Run: The Campaign and Battle of Second Manassas* (New York: Simon and Schuster, 1993), pp. 154–156.
6. Uncredited 94th New York Report on Manassas Campaign, T. C. H. Smith Papers, Ohio Historical Society, Columbus, Ohio.
7. McClenthen, pp. 12–14; Zealous Tower letter to Fitz-John Porter dated July 16, 1878, Fitz-John Porter Papers, Library of Congress, Washington, D.C.
8. John Hennessy, *Second Manassas Battlefield Map Study* (Lynchburg, VA: H. E. Howard, 1985), p. 175; Frank Jennings letter dated January 7, 1867 (90th Pa.), Civil War Times Illustrated Collection, USAMHI; John Vautier memoir (88th Pa.), USAMHI.
9. Ricketts Report, *O. R.*, ser. 1, vol. 12, pt. 2, p. 384; John Hennessy, *Battlefield Map Study*, p. 267; Zealous Tower letter dated June 6, 1865, Manassas National Battlefield Park Library; Warner, p. 628.
10. William H. Christian, Civil War Pension File, National Archives, Washington, D.C. *New York Daily Tribune*, September 6, 1862; *Utica Morning Herald and Daily Gazette*, September 15, 1862; William Christian letter to James McQuade dated July 15, 1878, Fitz-John Porter Papers, Library of Congress, Washington, D.C.
11. Richardson Report, *O. R.* ser. 1, vol. 12, pt. 2, pp. 389–390; Firman diary, August 30, 1862; Vautier, p. 55; Tower letter, June 6, 1865; McClenthen, p. 18; Bacon, p. 27.
12. Alexander Hunter, *Johnny Reb and Billy Yank* (New York: Neale, 1905), p. 253.
13. Bacon, pp. 32–33; McClenthen letter, September 4, 1862.

14. Charles E. Davis, *Three Years in the Army: The Story of the Thirteenth Massachusetts Volunteers from July 16, 1861 to August 1, 1864* (Boston: Estes and Lauriat, 1894), p. 109; Zealous Tower to Gen. Samuel Beck, adjutant general, undated, entry 713-box 7, file: WRO1450 (1897), Records of the Adjutant General's Office, Record Group 94, National Archives, Washington, D.C.; U. S. Congress, *Report of the Joint Committee on the Conduct of the War*, vol. 8 (Wilmington, N.C.: Broadfoot, 1998), p. 173; McDowell Report.
15. McClenthen, p. 17–20; Ezra Wetmore deposition, William H. Christian Pension File, National Archives, Washington, D.C.; Hunter, p. 253.
16. Willard L. Cook journal, Manassas National Battlefield Park Library, p. 54. Cook was with the Ninety-Fourth New York; Littlefield Report, *O. R.* ser. 1, vol. 12, pt. 2, pp. 390–391; Richardson Report, *O. R.* ser. 1, vol. 12, pt. 2, pp. 389–390; McClenthen, p. 17–20; Gilbert Jennings account, *Rochester Evening Express*, September 9, 1862.
17. Vautier, p. 58; Sigel Report, *O. R.*, ser. 1, vol. 12, pt. 2, pp. 268–269; Pope Report, *O. R.*, ser. 1, vol. 12, pt. 2, p. 43.
18. Montgomery Cossleman, Civil War Pension File, National Archives, Washington, D.C.; Samuel Rightmire letter dated September 16, 1862, USAMHI.
19. McClenthen, *Sketch*, p. 20; Vautier, p. 67; McClenthen letter, September 4, 1862; Jabez Miller deposition, William Christian Civil War Pension File, National Archives Washington D.C.; Norman W. Palmer deposition, William Christian Civil War Pension File, National Archives, Washington, D.C.; *New York Daily Tribune*, September 6, 1862.
20. Charles Jennings letter, *Rochester Union and American*, September 10, 1862; Charles Jennings, Civil War Pension File, National Archives, Washington, D.C.
21. Francis Crigier, Civil War Pension File, National Archives, Washington, D.C.
22. *Utica Daily Observer*, September 9, 1862.
23. William F. Fox, *Regimental Losses in the American Civil War* (Albany, N.Y.: Albany Publishing Co., 1899), p. 431; *O. R.*, ser. 1, vol. 12, pt. 3, pp. 581–588.
24. Vautier, p. 67; McClenthen, p. 24; McDowell Report, p. 344.
25. McClenthen letter, September 4, 1862.
26. Ezra M. Wetmore, Civil War Pension File, National Archives, Washington, D.C.
27. The Hall's Hill area today is located in Arlington's Highview Park neighborhood, just north of Lee Highway.
28. McClenthen letter, September 4, 1862; 26th New York Regimental Survey File, Grand Army of the Republic Papers, New York State Archives, Albany, N.Y.; Durkin, p. 81.
29. McClenthen, pp. 28–29; Firman diary, September 5–8, 1862.

Chapter 6

1. Lee Report, *O. R.*, ser. 1, vol. 19, pt. 1, pp. 144–145.
2. *O. R.*, ser. 1, vol. 19, pt. 1, p. 25.
3. Ephraim A. Wood journal, September 6–7, 1862.
4. Samuel W. Moore, diary, September 7, 1862, Antietam National Battlefield Park Library. Moore served with the Ninetieth Pennsylvania; Firman diary, September 7–8, 1862.
5. Moore diary, September 13, 1862; McClenthen, p. 29; Vautier, pp. 69–70; *S. O. R.*, vol. 43, pp. 373, 376, 381.
6. Ricketts Report, *O. R.* ser. 1, vol. 19, pt. 1, p. 258.
7. *O. R.*, ser. 1, vol. 19, pt. 1, pp. 246, 263; John Michael Priest, *Before Antietam: The Battle for South Mountain* (Shippensburg, PA: White Mane, 1992), p. 261.
8. Richardson Report, *O. R.*, ser. 1, vol. 19, pt. 1, p. 263; McClenthen, pp. 32–33; Priest, p. 263.
9. Moore diary, September 15, 1862; McClenthen, p. 33–34.
10. Ibid.; Vautier, p. 72.
11. McClenthen, p. 35.
12. The Union garrison at Harper's Ferry, numbering about 12,000 men, had in fact surrendered on September 15, 1862, after being surrounded and outnumbered by Confederate forces under Stonewall Jackson.
13. William Henry Locke, *The Story of the Regiment* (New York: J. Miller, 1872), p. 125. The title references the Eleventh Pennsylvania Infantry which fought within Ricketts' division; McClenthen, pp. 37–38.
14. Vautier, p. 73.
15. W. H. Holstead, letter dated March 9, 1893, Antietam National Battlefield Park Library; 26th New York File, pp. 9–10; Palmer deposition, William Christian Civil War Pension File, National Archives, Washington D.C.; Vautier, p. 74; David V. Finnell, "The Sad Case of Colonel William Henry Christian, 26th New York Volunteer Infantry," *Civil War*, 12 (March 1988): p. 64.
16. Durkin, *Last Man*, p. 87.
17. Richardson Report, *O. R.*, ser. 1, vol. 19, pt. 1, p. 263; Myers Report, *O. R.*, ser. 1, vol. 19, pt. 1, p. 265; Palmer deposition, William Christian Civil War Pension File, National Archives, Washington, D.C.
18. Richardson Report, *O. R.*, ser. 1, vol. 19, pt. 1, p. 263; McClenthen, p. 39; Holstead letter; Ripley Report, *O. R.*, ser. 1, vol. 19, pt. 1, p. 1,033.
19. Charles F. Cleveland, Civil War Pension File, National Archives, Washington, D.C.; Wager, pt. 3, p. 222; Richardson Report, *O. R.*, ser. 1, vol. 19, pt. 1, p. 263.
20. Richardson Report, *O. R.*, ser. 1, vol. 19, pt. 1, p. 263; Firman diary, September 17, 1862; McClenthen, pp. 40–41; Sears, *Landscape Turned Red*, pp. 198–199.
21. Ricketts Report, *O. R.*, ser. 1, vol. 19, pt. 1, p. 260; McClenthen, p. 42.
22. Richardson Report, *O. R.*, ser. 1, vol. 19, pt. 1, p. 263.
23. U.S. Congress, *Report of the Joint Committee on the Conduct of the War*, vol. 1 (Wilmington, N.C.: Broadfoot Publishing Co., 1998), p. 368.
24. Warner, p. 404.
25. William H. Christian, Civil War Military Service File, National Archives, Washington, D.C.; Moore diary, September 19, 1862.

26. *Utica Morning Herald and Daily Gazette*, September 23, 1862; *O. R.* ser. 1, vol. 19, pt. 2, p. 315.
27. Moore diary, September 19, 1862; Joseph G. Patterson, letter dated October 1862, Joseph G. Patterson Papers, Musselman Library, Gettysburg College, Gettysburg, Pa.; Ezra Carman, "History of the Maryland Campaign," Ezra Carman Papers, Library of Congress, Washington D.C. Carman was also on the field at Antietam serving in the Thirteenth New Jersey Infantry; Charles McClenthen, *Narrative of the Fall and Winter Campaign* (Syracuse, N.Y.: Masters and Lee, 1863), p. 29.
28. Daniel Jones, letter dated September 19, 1862, Daniel Jones Papers, Historical Society of Pennsylvania, Philadelphia, Pa.; Allen Nevins, ed., *A Diary of Battle: The Personal Journals of Colonel Charles S. Wainwright 1861–1865* (New York: Harcourt Brace and World, 1962), p. 108; George Meade, *The Life and Letters of George Gordon Meade*, Vol. 1 (New York: Charles Scribners Sons, 1913), p. 318.
29. *O. R.* ser. 1, vol. 19, pt. 2, p. 322; Ephraim C. Brown Diary, p. 25, Patricia Murphy collection, Lakeland, Fla.
30. McClenthen, p. 43.
31. Letter dated October 9, 1862, from Frank Ingersoll to Charles Ackerman, Charles Ackerman Papers, #3966. Division of Rare and Manuscript Collections, Cornell University Library; New York (State) Adjutant General's Office, *Annual Report of the Adjutant-General of the State of New York for the Year 1899*, ser. no. 21 (Albany, N.Y.: James B. Lyon, 1900), p. 39; United States Army, Surgeon-General's Office, *The Medical and Surgical History of the War of the Rebellion*, vol. 7 (Wilmington, N.C.: Broadfoot, 1991), p. 114.
32. United States Army, Surgeon-General's Office, *The Medical and Surgical History of the War of the Rebellion*, vol. 7 (Wilmington, N.C.: Broadfoot, 1991), p. 208.
33. Charles McClenthen, *Narrative of the Fall and Winter Campaign*, p. 5; Adrian Root letter dated October 10, 1862, Mss. W-35, Buffalo and Erie County Historical Society Archives, Buffalo, N.Y.
34. Charles McClenthen, *Narrative of the Fall*, p. 5.
35. Abner R. Small, *The Road to Richmond: The Civil War Memoirs of Major Abner R. Small of the Sixteenth Maine Volunteers* (Berkeley, CA: University of California Press, 1939), p. 53.
36. McClellan report, *O. R.*, ser. 1, vol. 19, pt. 1, p. 87.

Chapter 7

1. Richard H. Richardson, Civil War Military Service and Pension Files, National Archives, Washington, D.C.; Court-martial records, Record Group 153, KK739, Captain James B. Caryl, Company K, 26th New York Regiment (Deposition of Dr. Walter Coventry), National Archives, Washington, D.C., p. 24
2. McClenthen, *Narrative of the Fall*, p. 13, 18–19; *Utica Morning Herald and Daily Gazette*, November 15, 1862; McClellan, *O. R.*, ser. 1, vol. 19, pt. 1, p. 88; Small, p. 54. The Sixteenth Maine was now in the same division (Gibbons') as the Twenty-Sixth New York.
3. David S. Sparks, ed., *Inside Lincoln's Army: The Diary of Marsena Rudolph Patrick, Provost Marshal General, Army of the Potomac* (New York: Thomas Yoseloff, 1964), p. 153; *O. R.*, ser. 1, vol. 19, pt. 2, p. 533; Warner, p. 171, 404.
4. James Durkin, *The Last Man and the Last Life: The Bloody Journey of the Philadelphia National Guards Regiment May 1861 to May 1864; 19th P. V., Three Months Service, 90th P. V. Three Years Service* (Glenside, PA: Santarelli, 2000), pp. 101–102.
5. *Utica Morning Herald and Daily Gazette*, November 15, 1862.
6. Richard H. Richardson, Civil War Military Service File, National Archives, Washington, D.C.; Deposition of Milton H. Thomson, New York Life Insurance Co. agent, re Richard Richardson, Civil War Pension File, National Archives, Washington, D.C.
7. John Gibbon, *Personal Recollections of the Civil War* (G. P. Putnam's Sons, 1928), p. 102; *Oneida Weekly Herald & Gazette & Courier*, December 16, 1862.
8. Gibbon, p. 102.
9. Reynolds Report, *O. R.*, ser. 1, vol. 21, p. 453.
10. Franklin Report, *O. R.*, ser. 1, vol. 21, p. 450; Reynolds Report.
11. Wetmore Report, *O. R.*, ser. 1, vol. 21, p. 499; Bacon, p. 57; Francis Augustin O'Reilly, *The Fredericksburg Campaign: Winter War on the Rappahannock* (Baton Rouge, LA: Louisiana State University Press, 2003), p. 187; Benjamin F. Cook, *The Twelfth Massachusetts Volunteers (Webster Regiment)* (Boston: Twelfth Regiment Association, 1883), p. 80.
12. Wetmore Report; Bacon, p. 37; Small, p. 63.
13. Meade, p. 337; Reynolds Report, *O. R.*, ser. 1, vol. 21, p. 454; U. S. Congress, *Report of the Joint Committee on the Conduct of the War*, vol. 1 (Wilmington, N.C.: Broadfoot, 1998), p. 691.
14. Charles W. Turner, ed., *Captain Greenlee Davidson, C.S.A., Diary and Letters, 1861–1865* (Verona, VA: McClure Press, 1975), p. 64.
15. McClenthen, *Narrative*, p. 37; Wetmore Report, p. 499; Ezra Wetmore, "Story of a New York Boy at Fredericksburg," *National Tribune*, May 9, 1895.
16. Wetmore Report; Lyle Report, *O. R.*, ser. 1, vol. 21, p. 496; Root Report, *O. R.* ser. 1, vol. 21, pp. 486–487; Gibbon, p. 104; O' Reilly, p. 192.
17. Leech Report, *O. R.* ser. 1, vol. 21, p. 501.
18. Wetmore Report; Lyle Report, p. 496.
19. United States Army, Surgeon-General's Office, *The Medical and Surgical History of the War of the Rebellion*, vol. 7 (Wilmington, N.C.: Broadfoot, 1991), p. 116; Joseph Keene, Civil War Military Service and Pension Files, National Archives, Washington, D.C.
20. W. F. Beyer and O. F. Keydel, *Deeds of Valor: How America's Civil War Heroes Won the Congressional Medal of Honor* (Detroit: Perrien-Keydel Co, 1903), pp. 116–117.
21. Wetmore, "Story of a New York Boy"; Lyle Report, *O. R.*, ser. 1, vol. 21, pp. 496–497; McCoy Report, ser. 1, vol. 21, p. 495; McClenthen, *Narrative of the Fall*, p. 40; Mary Warner Thomas and

Richard Sauers, eds., *The Civil War Letters of First Lieutenant James B. Thomas* (Baltimore: Butternut and Blue, 1995), p. 127, 130. Thomas served in the One Hundred and Seventh Pennsylvania.
22. Wetmore Report; Bacon, p. 38–39.
23. Locke, p. 166. Locke writes of the Eleventh Pennsylvania Infantry, which also served in Gibbon's division; Alex Montgomery, diary, December 13, 1862, Dawson-Montgomery Family Papers, Senator John Heinz Pittsburgh Regional History Center, Pittsburgh, Pa.; Jerome Frazier, Civil War Pension File, National Archives, Washington, D.C.
24. Wetmore Report; Thomas and Sauers, pp. 127, 130.
25. *Oneida Weekly Herald and Gazette and Courier*, January 27, 1863; McClenthen, *Narrative of the Fall*, p. 44.
26. *O. R.* ser. 1, vol. 21, p. 138; Ezra Wetmore, "Story of a New York Boy"; Fox, *Regimental Losses*, p. 31, 434.
27. Norman Palmer, Civil War Pension File, National Archives, Washington, D.C.; *Utica Morning Herald and Daily Gazette*, December 20, 1862.
28. Reynolds Report; Wetmore Report.
29. McClenthen, *Narrative of the Fall*, p. 48.

Chapter 8

1. Transcript of court-martial proceedings dated January 8, 1863, Charles Ackerman papers, #3966. Division of Rare and Manuscript Collections, Cornell University Library; William H. Holstead, diary, February 3 and 9, 1863, Charles Rogers Collection, Northridge, Calif.; U. S. Adjutant General's Office, *Official Army Register of the Volunteer Force of the United States Army, 1861–1865, pt. 2* (Washington D.C.: 1865), p. 461.
2. Statistical analysis of Appendix B.
3. Nevins, p. 162.
4. McClenthen, *Narrative of the Fall*, pp. 50–51.
5. Richard H. Richardson, Civil War Pension File, National Archives, Washington, D.C.
6. McClenthen, *Narrative of the Fall*, pp. 50–51; Cook, p. 86.
7. Raymond G. Barber and Gary E. Swinson, eds., *The Civil War Letters of Charles Barber, Private, 104th New York Volunteer Infantry* (Torrance, CA: self-published, 1991), p. 112.
8. George A. Turner, ed., *Civil War Letters from Soldiers and Sailors of Columbia County, Pennsylvania* (New York: American Heritage Publishing, 1996), p. 302; McClenthen, *Narrative of the Fall*, pp. 52–53.
9. Chris Bishop and Ian Drury, *1400 Days: The Civil War Day by Day* (New York: Gallery Books, 1990), p. 118.
10. *O. R.* ser. 1, vol. 25, pt. 2, p. 855; Roy P. Basler, ed., *The Collected Works of Abraham Lincoln*, vol. 6 (New Brunswick, N.J.: Rutgers University Press, 1953), pp. 78–79.
11. Court-martial transcripts and records, Record Group 153, KK739, Captain James B. Caryl, Company K, 26th New York Regiment, National Archives, Washington, D.C.; Thomas, p. 123.
12. Holstead diary, February 13 and 23, 1863; Firman diary, February 13, 1863.
13. *O. R.*, ser. 1, vol. 25, pt. 2, p. 57.
14. *O. R.*, ser. 1, vol. 25, pt. 2, p. 38; Davis Jr., pp. 194–195.
15. Transcript of Court-Martial Proceedings, Charles Ackerman Papers, Carl A. Kroch Library, Cornell University, Ithaca, N.Y.
16. Durkin, *The Last Man*, p. 135.
17. Small, p. 80; Warner, pp. 25, 496; *O. R.*, ser. 1, vol. 25, pt. 2, p. 229.
18. Francis Thomas letter, undated (1863), Charles Ackerman papers, #3966. Division of Rare and Manuscript Collections, Cornell University Library.

Chapter 9

1. *Utica Daily Herald and Morning Gazette*, March 6, 1863; Turner, *Columbia County*, p. 313.
2. *Utica Daily Herald and Morning Gazette*, March 6, 1863.
3. Charles McClenthen letter to his father dated April 19, 1863, Charles McClenthen papers, #1304m, Division of Rare and Manuscript Collections, Cornell University Library.
4. *O. R.* ser. 1, vol. 25, pt. 2, pp. 233–234; Walter H. Hebert, *Fighting Joe Hooker* (Lincoln, NE: University of Nebraska Press, 1999), p. 183; John Bigelow Jr., *The Campaign of Chancellorsville* (New Haven, CT: Yale University Press, 1910), pp. 168–169; United States Congress, *Report of the Joint Committee on the Conduct of the War*, vol. 4, p. 219.
5. Gilbert Jennings order dated April 26, 1863, Charles Ackerman papers, #3966. Division of Rare and Manuscript Collections, Cornell University Library; Holstead diary, April 28, 1863; Firman diary, April 28 & 29, 1863; Sparks, ed., p. 238; Chester Sternberg diary, April 28, 1863, Buffalo and Erie County Historical Society Archives, Buffalo, N.Y.
6. *Ramapo to Chancellorsville and Beyond*, p. 127, http://www.talkeetna.com/Pierson/Ramapo-ToChancellorsville.pdf; J. Gregory Acken, ed., *Inside the Army of the Potomac: The Civil War Experience of Captain Francis Adams Donaldson* (Mechanicsburg, PA: Stackpole Books, 1998), p. 266; *O. R.*, ser. 1, vol. 25, pt. 2, p. 302.
7. Richard H. Richardson, Civil War Military Service and Pension Files, National Archives, Washington, D.C.
8. McClenthen letter, April 19, 1863; Locke, p. 195.
9. Robinson report, *O. R.*, ser. 1, vol. 25, pt. 1, p. 276; Reynolds report, *O. R.*, ser. 1, vol. 25, pt. 1, pp. 253–257; Davis, p. 203; Holstead diary.
10. Root report, *O. R.*, ser. 1, vol. 25, pt. 1, p. 279.
11. Nevins, p. 190.
12. Frank O' Reilly and Erik J. Mink, Battle of Chancellorsville Maps, map 5 of 12, illustrated and produced by John Dove, 1998.
13. Abner Doubleday, *Chancellorsville and Gettysburg: Campaigns of the Civil War*, vol. 6 (New York: Charles Scribners Sons, 1882), pp. 42–43;

George A. Hussey and William Todd, *History of the Ninth Regiment N.Y.S.M. (Eighty-Third New York Volunteers)* (New York: Veterans of the Regiment, 1889), p. 246; Small, p. 86.

14. Nichols, p. 174; Robinson *O. R.* report; Durkin, *Last Man*, pp. 145–146; Firman diary, May 3, 1863.

15. Benjamin F. Cook Diary, Special Collections Library, Duke University, Durham, N.C. Cook served in the Twelfth Massachusetts; Sears, *Chancellorsville*, p. 406.

16. Robinson *O. R.* report; Wager, pt. 3, pp. 119–120; Firman diary, May 4, 1863.

17. Meade report, *O. R.* ser. 1, vol. 25, pt. 1, p. 510; Reynolds report, *O. R.*, ser. 1, vol. 25, pt. 1, pp. 253–257; *Battles and Leaders*, vol. 3, p. 222; Sears, *Chancellorsville*, p. 405.

18. Durkin, *Last Man*, p. 101; Nevins, p. 201.

19. Reynolds report; Firman diary, May 5 and 6, 1863; Stephen W. Sears, *Chancellorsville* (Boston: Houghton Mifflin, 1996), pp. 420–421; *13th Independent Battery—NY Light Artillery*—"Letter of Lieut. William Wheeler dated May 14, 1863." http://www.13nybattery.com/battles/ww630514-chanc.htm. Wheeler served in the Thirteenth Independent Battery—NY Light Artillery assigned to Reynold's corps during the final days of the Chancellorsville battle.

20. Frederick Phisterer, *New York in the War of the Rebellion: 1861 to 1865*, 5 volumes (Albany, N.Y.: J. B. Lyon and Co., 1912), vol. 3, p. 2,027.

21. Charles Augustus Wheeler, letter dated May 10, 1863, Pearce Collection, Navarro College, Corsicana, Texas; John Reynolds, letter to his sisters dated May 9, 1863, Franklin and Marshall College, Special Collections Department, Lancaster, Pa.

22. Holstead diary; Firman diary, May 7–8, 1863; New York (State) Bureau of Military Statistics, *Third Annual Report of the Bureau of Military Record of the State of New York* (Albany, N.Y.: C. Wendell Printer, 1866), p. 198; Gilbert Jennings order dated May 12, 1863, Charles Ackerman papers, #3966. Division of Rare and Manuscript Collections, Cornell University Library.

23. Harrer, pp. 116–118; Holstead diary, May 20, 1863; *Utica Morning Herald and Daily Gazette*, May 21, 1863; Thomas, pp. 141–142.

Chapter 10

1. Richard H. Richardson, Civil War Military Service and Pension Files, National Archives, Washington, D.C.

2. *O. R.*, ser. 1, vol. 37, pt. 1, pp. 474, 699; *O. R.*, ser. 3, vol. 5, p. 562; Guy V. Henry, *Military Record of Civilian Appointments in the United States Army* (New York: D. Van Nostrand, 1873), p. 350.

3. Thomas, p. 143; Twenty-Sixth New York newspaper clippings file, New York State Military Museum and Veterans Research Center, Saratoga Springs, New York.

4. Wetmore obituary, *Utica Saturday Globe*, July 29, 1905.

5. New York (State) Adjutant General's Office, *Proceedings Attending the Presentation of Regimental Colors to the Legislature, April 20, 1864* (Albany, N.Y.: Van Benthuysen's Steam Printing House, 1864), pp. 43–44.

6. Invitation to William Christian to attend One Hundred and Seventeenth New York Infantry reunion, dated June 6, 1877, Donald Wisnoski Collection, Chadwicks, N.Y; *Roman Citizen (Rome, N.Y.)*, May 13, 1887; *Utica Daily Press*, May 9, 1887; Christian Pension File.

7. Gilbert Jennings, letter dated July 30, 1866, Rush Rhees Library, University of Rochester, Rochester, New York; Heitman, p. 572; *Detroit Evening News*, November 2, 1893.

8. Richard H. Richardson, Civil War Pension File, National Archives, Washington, D.C.

9. Proctor, pp. 8–9, 25.

Chapter 11

1. Those New York infantry regiments were the Fourteenth, Ninety-Seventh, One Hundred and Seventeenth, and One Hundred and Forty-Sixth.

2. Ella Lonn, *Desertion During the Civil War* (Gloucester, MA: Peter Smith, 1966), p. 138; The U.S. Sanitary Commission "Camp Inspection Reports" placed the number of Germans at roughly 20 percent with the number of Irish also at roughly 20 percent.

Appendix B

1. New York (State) Adjutant General's Office, *Annual Report of the Adjutant-General of the State of New York for the Year 1899, Serial No. 21* (Albany: James B. Lyon, 1900), pp. 1–142. The vast majority of the information in this roster is taken from this publication. The author has corrected information and added to it as research warranted. Dashes within entries indicate information not known or unavailable to the original compilers and the author.

Bibliography

Unpublished Manuscript Collections

Antietam National Battlefield Park Library, Sharpsburg, Va.
    Twenty-Sixth New York Infantry File: William H. Holstead. Letters.
    Samuel W. Moore. Diary [90th Pennsylvania].
Brooks Memorial Library, Brattleboro, Vermont
    Nelson L. Wandell. Journal [9th Vermont].
Buffalo and Erie County Historical Society, Buffalo, N.Y.
    Adrian Root. Letters. [94th New York]
    Chester W. Sternberg. Diary. [21st New York]
Central Michigan University, Clarke Historical Library, Mt. Pleasant, Mich.
    William E. Limbocker. Diary [4th Michigan].
Charles Rogers Collection, Northridge, Calif.
    William Holstead. Letters and Diary.
Chemung Valley Historical Society, Booth Library, Elmira, N.Y.
    H. F. Pitcher. Journal.
Cornell University, Carl A. Kroch Library, Ithaca, N.Y.
    Charles Ackerman. Papers.
    Charles McClenthen. Civil War Letters.
Donald Wisnoski Collection, Chadwicks, N.Y.
    Timothy Gaffney. Letters.
    William Christian. Letters.
Duke University, Special Collections Library, Durham, N.C.
    Benjamin F. Cook. Diary.
Franklin and Marshall College, Special Collections, Lancaster, Pa.
    John Reynolds. Family Papers.
Historical Society of Pennsylvania, Philadelphia, Pa.
George Albright Foreman Collection:
    D. T. Arnold. Letters [90th Pennsylvania].
    Daniel Jones Papers [88th Pennsylvania]
Heinz Regional Pittsburgh History Center, Pittsburgh, Pa.
    Alex Montgomery. Diary [136th Pennsylvania].
James Fuller Collection, Boyne City, Mich.
    Crigier/Fuller Family Papers.
Library of Congress, Manuscripts Division, Washington, D.C.
    Ezra Carman. Papers.
    Samuel Heintzelman. Papers.
    Robert C. Ogden. Papers:
        Adrian Root. Letter [94th New York].
    Fitz-John Porter. Papers:
        William H. Christian. Letter.
        Zealous Tower. Letter.
    Michael Shiner. Diary.
    N. A. Strait Regimental Papers
    Horatio Nelson Taft. Diary.
Manassas National Battlefield Park Library, Manassas, Va.
    Fanny Ricketts. Diary.
    Ninety-Fourth New York Infantry File: Willard L. Cook. Journal.
    Twenty-Sixth New York Infantry File: Cornelius Rightmire. Letter and Memoir.
    Charles McClenthen. Diary.
    Zealous Tower. Letter.
Musselman Library, Gettysburg College, Gettysburg, Pa.
    Joseph G. Patterson. Papers. [90th Pennsylvania[
National Archives, Washington, D.C.
    Record Group M551: Civil War Military / Pension Records
    Record Group 94: Records of the Adjutant General's Office
    Record Group 153: Registers of the Bureau of Military Justice

Navarro College, Corsicana, Tx.
   Pearce Civil War Collection:
      Charles Augustus Wheeler. Letters [12th Massachusetts].
New York Historical Society, New York, N.Y.
   Descriptive and Clothing Books, 2 vols., Twenty-Sixth New York, Company C
New York Public Library, New York, N.Y.
   United States Sanitary Commission. Papers.
New York State Archives, Albany, N.Y.
   Grand Army of the Republic Papers: Twenty-Sixth New York Infantry Regimental Survey File
   Record Series A4134: Historical Notes on the New York State Volunteer Regiments, 1861–1865.
   Record Series A4104: Incoming Correspondence From Medical Officers of New York State Volunteer Units.
   Record Series B0311: Rosters of Medical Staff of New York State Volunteer Units.
Ohio Historical Society, Columbus, Oh.
   Thomas C. H. Smith Papers:
      94th New York Report on Second Manassas
      Charles A. Smith. Letter.
Patricia A. Murphy Collection, Lakeland, Fla.
   Ephram C. Brown. Diary.
Paul Taylor Collection, Clinton Township, Mich.
   Twenty-Sixth New York Collection.
   Millard Family. Letters.
Rochester Museum and Science Center, Schuyler C. Townson Library, Rochester, N.Y.
   Warren S. Firman. Diaries.
Rome Historical Society, Rome, N.Y.
   Fritz Updike. "Rome in the Civil War."
University of Michigan, Bentley Historical Library, Ann Arbor, Mich.
   Edmund R. P. Shurly. Memoir.
University of Rochester, Rush Rhees Library, Rochester, N.Y.
   Gilbert S. Jennings. Letters.
University of Virginia, Albert and Shirley Smalls Library, Charlottesville, Va.
   Ephraim A. Wood. Journal.
United States Army Military History Institute, Carlisle, Pa.
   Albert A. Collier. Letter.
   Frank Jennings. Letter [90th Pennsylvania].
   Samuel Rightmire. Letter.
   John Vautier. Diary and Memoir [88th Pennsylvania].
Warsaw Community Library, Warsaw, Ind.
   William Hemphill. Journal [12th Indiana].

Published State and Federal Government Documents

Hewet, Janet B., ed. *Supplement to the Official Records of the Union and Confederate Armies.* 100 vols. Wilmington, N.C.: Broadfoot, 1994–1996.

New York (State) Adjutant General's Office. *A Record of the Commissioned Officers, Non-commissioned Officers, Privates, of the Regiments Which Were Organized in the State of New York and Called Into the Service of the United States to Assist in Suppressing the Rebellion, Caused by the Secession of Some of the Southern States From the Union, A.D. 1861, As Taken From the Muster-in Rolls on File in the Adjutant-General's Office, S. N. Y.* Albany: Comstock & Cassidy Printers, 1864–68.

New York (State) Adjutant General's Office. *Annual Report of the Adjutant-General of the State of New York for the Year 1899, Serial No. 21.* Albany: James B. Lyon, 1900.

New York (State) Adjutant General's Office. *Proceedings Attending the Presentation of Regimental Colors to the Legislature, April 20, 1864.* Albany, N.Y.: Van Benthuysen's Steam Printing House, 1864.

New York (State) Bureau of Military Statistics. *Third Annual Report of the Bureau of Military Record of the State of New York.* Albany, N.Y.: C. Wendell Printer, 1866.

United States Army, Surgeon-General's Office. *The Medical and Surgical History of the War of the Rebellion.* 1870–1888. Reprint, Wilmington, N.C.: Broadfoot, 1991.

United States Army, Adjutant General's Office. *Official Army Register of the Volunteer Force of the United States Army, 1861–1865.* Washington, D.C.: 1865.

United States Congress. *Report of the Joint Committee on the Conduct of the War.* 8 Volumes. 1863–1866. Reprint, Wilmington, N.C.: Broadfoot, 1998.

United States War Department. *The War of*

the Rebellion: A Compilation of the Official Records of the Union and Confederate Armies. 128 Volumes. Washington, D.C., 1881–1902.

United States War Department. *Atlas to Accompany the Official Records of the Union and Confederate Armies.* 2 Vols. Washington, D.C., 1891–1895.

Newspapers

Alexandria (Virginia) Gazette
Allegan (Michigan) Journal
Baltimore Sun
Detroit Evening News
Grand Army Scout and Soldiers Mail (Philadelphia)
Harper's Weekly
Hornellsville (New York) Tribune
National Tribune (Washington, D. C.)
New York Daily Tribune
New York Illustrated News
New York Times
Oneida (New York) Weekly Herald and Gazette and Courier
Rochester (New York) Union and American
Rochester (New York) Evening Express
Roman Citizen (Rome, New York)
Utica (New York) Daily Observer
Utica (New York) Daily Press
Utica (New York) Morning Herald and Daily Gazette
Utica (New York) Saturday Globe
Washington (D. C.) Evening Star
Waterville (New York) Times

Books and Articles: Primary Sources

Acken, J. Gregory, ed. *Inside the Army of the Potomac: The Civil War Experience of Captain Francis Adams Donaldson.* Mechanicsburg, Pa.: Stackpole Books, 1998.

Applegate, John S. *Reminiscences and Letters of George Arrowsmith of New Jersey, Late Lieutenant-Colonel of the One hundred and Fifty-Seventh Regiment, New York State Volunteers.* Red Banks, N.J.: John H. Cook, 1893.

Bacon, William Johnson. *Memorial of William Kirkland Bacon, Late Adjutant of the Twenty-Sixth Regiment of New York State Volunteers.* Utica, N.Y.: Roberts Printing, 1863.

Bancroft, Emily, ed. *Memorial and Letters of Reverend John R. Adams, D. D., Chaplain, 5th Maine.* Cambridge: Privately Printed, 1890.

Barber, Raymond G., and Gary E. Swinson, eds. *The Civil War Letters of Charles Barber, Private, 104th New York Volunteer Infantry.* Torrence, CA:, self-published, 1991.

Basler, Roy P., ed. *The Collected Works of Abraham Lincoln.* New Brunswick, N.J.: Rutgers University Press, 1953.

Beyer, W. F., and O. F. Keydel. *Deeds of Valor: How America's Civil War Heroes Won the Congressional Medal of Honor.* Detroit: Perrien-Keydel, 1903.

Bicknell, George W. *History of the Fifth Regiment Maine Volunteers.* Portland, ME: Hall L. Davis, 1871.

Brown, George William. *Baltimore and the Nineteenth of April, 1861.* Baltimore: N. Murray, 1887.

Chittenden, Lucius E. *Invisible Siege: The Journal of Lucius E. Chittenden.* San Diego: Americana Exchange Press, 1969.

Cook, Benjamin F. *The Twelfth Massachusetts Volunteers (Webster Regiment).* Boston: Twelfth Regiment Association, 1883.

Cozzens, Peter, and Robert I. Girardi, eds. *The Military Memoirs of General John Pope.* Chapel Hill, N.C.: University of North Carolina Press, 1998.

Curtis, Newton Martin. *From Bull Run to Chancellorsville: The Story of the Sixteenth New York.* New York: G. P. Putnam's, 1906.

Davis, Charles E., Jr. *Three Years in the Army: The Story of the Thirteenth Massachusetts Volunteers.* Boston: Estes and Lauriat, 1894.

Doubleday, Abner. *Chancellorsville and Gettysburg: Campaigns of the Civil War, Volume 6.* New York: Charles Scribners Sons, 1882.

Durkin, James, ed. *"This War Is an Awful Thing": Civil War Letters of the National Guards, The 19th and 90th Pennsylvania Volunteers.* Glenside, PA: Santarelli, 1994.

Eckert, Edward K., and Nicholas J. Amato, eds. *Ten Years in the Saddle: The Memoir of William Woods Averell 1851–1862.* San Rafael, CA.: Presidio Press, 1978.

Fairchild, Charles B. *History of the 27th Regiment New York Volunteers.* Binghamton, N.Y.: Carl & Matthews, 1888.

Gardner, Alexander. *Gardner's Photographic Sketchbook of the American Civil War.*

1866. Reprint, New York: Delano Greenidge Editions, 2001.

Gibbon, John. *Personal Recollections of the Civil War.* New York: G. P. Putnam's Sons, 1928.

Haddock, John A., comp. "The 94th New York Infantry" in *The Growth of a Century: As Illustrated in the History of Jefferson County, New York from 1793 to 1894.* Albany: Weed-Parsons Printing Co., 1895.

Hall, H. Seymour. "Experience in the Peninsular and Antietam Campaigns" in *Military Order of the Loyal Legion of the United States—Kansas.* vol. 1. Wilmington, N.C.: Broadfoot, 1992.

Harrar, William. *With Drum and Gun in '61.* Greenville, PA: Beaver Printing Co., 1906.

Howard, Oliver Otis. *Autobiography of Oliver Otis Howard.* 2 vols. New York: Baker and Taylor, 1907.

Hunter, Alexander. *Johnny Reb and Billy Yank.* New York: Neale, 1905.

Hussey, George A., and William Todd. *History of the Ninth Regiment N.Y.S.M. (Eighty-third New York Volunteers).* New York: Veterans of the Regiment, 1889.

Johnson, Robert U., and Clarence Buel, eds. *Battles and Leaders of the Civil War.* 4 vols. 1887–1888. Reprint, New York: Thomas Yoseloff, 1956.

Locke, William Henry. *The Story of the Regiment.* New York: J. Miller, 1872.

Longstreet, James. "Our March Against Pope." *The Century Magazine* 31:4 (February 1886).

McClellan, George B. *McClellan's Own Story.* New York: Charles L. Webster, 1887.

McClenthen, Charles S. *Narrative of the Fall and Winter Campaign by a Private Soldier.* Syracuse, N.Y.: Masters and Lee, 1863.

_____. *A Sketch of the Campaign in Virginia and Maryland from Cedar Mountain to Antietam.* Syracuse, N.Y.: Masters and Lee, 1862.

McQuade, James. "Military History of Utica" in *Semi-Centennial of the City of Utica.* Utica, N.Y.: Oneida Historical Society, 1882.

Meade, George. *The Life and Letters of George Gordon Meade.* 2 vols. New York: Charles Scribners Sons, 1913.

Nevins, Allen, ed. *A Diary of Battle: The Personal Journals of Colonel Charles S. Wainwright 1861–1865.* New York: Harcourt Brace and World, 1962.

Proctor, Thomas R., comp. *Presentation of the Battle Flags of the Oneida County Regiments to the Oneida Historical Society.* Utica, N.Y.: Oneida Historical Society, 1898.

Ritchie, Norman L., ed. *Four Years in the First New York Light Artillery: The Papers of David F. Ritchie.* Hamilton, N.Y.: Edmonston, 1997.

Sears, Stephen, ed. *The Civil War Papers of George B. McClellan: Selected Correspondence 1860–1865.* New York: Ticknor & Fields, 1989.

_____. *For Country, Cause, and Leader: The Civil War Journal of Charles B. Haydon.* New York: Ticknor and Fields, 1993.

Sherman, William T. *Memoirs of General W. T. Sherman.* 2 vols. New York: D. Appleton, 1875.

Simpson, Brooks D., and Jean D. Berlin, eds. *Sherman's Civil War: Selected Correspondence of William T. Sherman, 1860–1865,* Chapel Hill, N.C.: University of North Carolina Press, 1999.

Small, Abner R. *The Road to Richmond: The Civil War Memoirs of Major Abner R. Small of the Sixteenth Maine Volunteers.* Berkeley, CA: University of California Press, 1939.

Sneden, Robert Knox. *Eye of the Storm: A Civil War Odyssey.* New York: The Free Press, 2000.

_____. *Images from the Storm.* New York: The Free Press, 2001.

Sparks, David S., ed. *Inside Lincoln's Army: The Diary of Marsena Rudolph Patrick, Provost Marshal General, Army of the Potomac.* New York: Thomas Yoseloff, 1964.

Thomas, Mary Warner, and Richard Sauers, ed. *The Civil War Letters of First Lieutenant James B. Thomas, Adjutant, 107th Pennsylvania Volunteers.* Baltimore: Butternut and Blue, 1995.

Turner, Charles W., ed. *Captain Greenlee Davidson, C. S. A., Diary and Letters, 1861–1865,* Verona, VA: McClure Press, 1975.

Turner, George A., ed. *Civil War Letters from Soldiers and Sailors of Columbia County, Pennsylvania.* New York: American Heritage Publishing, 1996.

Vautier, John. *History of the 88th Pennsylvania Volunteers.* Philadelphia: J. B. Lippincott, 1894.

Westervelt, William B. *Lights and Shadows of Army Life As Seen by a Private Soldier.* Marlboro, N.Y.: C. H. Cochrane, 1886.

Books and Articles: Secondary Sources

Barber, James. *Alexandria in the Civil War.* Lynchburg, VA: H. E. Howard, 1988.

Bates, Samuel P. *History of Pennsylvania Volunteers, 1861–65.* 5 vols. Harrisburg, PA: Pennsylvania State Printer, 1869–71.

Bigelow, John, Jr. *The Campaign of Chancellorsville.* New Haven, CT: Yale University Press, 1910.

Bishop, Chris, and Ian Drury. *1400 Days: The Civil War Day by Day.* New York: Gallery Books, 1990.

Brinsfield, John W., William C. Davis, Benedict Maryniak, and James I. Robertson Jr., eds. *Faith in the Fight: Civil War Chaplains.* Mechanicsburg, PA: Stackpole, 2003.

Cooling, Benjamin Franklin, and Walton H. Owen. *Mr. Lincoln's Forts: A Guide to the Civil War Defenses of Washington.* Shippensburg, PA.: White Mane Publishing, 1988.

Durkin, James. *The Last Man and the Last Life: The Bloody Journey of the Philadelphia National Guards Regiment May 1861 to May 1864; 19th P. V., Three Months Service, 90th P. V. Three Years Service.* Glenside, PA: Santarelli, 2000.

Finnell, David V. "The Man Who Walked Spanish: The Sad Case of Colonel William Henry Christian, 26th New York Volunteer Infantry." *Civil War* 12 (March 1988): 60–65.

Foote, Robert. *Bridgewater's Boys in Blue, 1861–1865.* Bridgewater, N.Y.: self-published, n.d.

Fox, William F. *Regimental Losses in the American Civil War.* Albany, N.Y.: Albany Publishing Co., 1899.

French, J. H. *Gazetteer of the State of New York.* Syracuse, N.Y.: R. Pearsall Smith, 1860.

Giffen, Guy James. *California Expedition: Stevenson's First New York Regiment of Volunteers.* Oakland: Bio-Books, 1951.

Hebert, Walter H. *Fighting Joe Hooker.* Lincoln, NE: University of Nebraska Press, 1999.

Heitman, Francis B. *Historical Register and Dictionary of the United States Army From Its Organization, September 29, 1789, to March 2, 1903.* 2 vols. Washington D.C.: Government Printing Office, 1903.

Hennessy, John J. *Return to Bull Run: The Campaign and Battle of Second Manassas.* New York: Simon and Schuster, 1993.

———. *Second Manassas Battlefield Map Study.* Lynchburg, VA: H. E. Howard, 1985.

Henry, Guy V. *Military Record of Civilian Appointments in the United States Army.* New York: D. Van Nostrand, 1873.

Horigan, Michael. *Elmira: Death Camp of the North.* Mechanicsburg, PA: Stackpole, 2002.

Hunt, Roger, and Jack Brown. *Brevet Brigadier Generals in Blue.* Gaithersburg, MD: Olde Soldier Books, 1990.

Kimmel, Stanley. *Mr. Lincoln's Washington.* New York: Coward-McCann, 1957.

Krick, Robert K. *Stonewall Jackson at Cedar Mountain.* Chapel Hill, N.C.: University of North Carolina Press, 1990.

Leech, Margaret. *Reveille in Washington 1860–1865.* New York: Harper and Row, 1941.

Lonn, Ella. *Desertion During the Civil War.* 1928. Reprint, Gloucester, MA: Peter Smith, 1966.

McKelvey, Blake, ed. *Rochester in the Civil War.* Rochester, N.Y.: Rochester Historical Society, 1944.

Miller, T. Michael, ed. *Pen Portraits of Alexandria, Virginia, 1739–1900.* Bowie, MD: Heritage Books, 1987.

Murfin, James W. *The Gleam of Bayonets.* 1965. Reprint, Baton Rouge: Louisiana State University Press, 1982.

New York Historical Resources Center. *Guide to Historical Resources in Oneida County, New York, Repositories.* Ithaca, N.Y.: New York Historical Resources Center, Olin Library, Cornell University, 1983.

New York Monuments Commission. *In Memoriam: Henry Warner Slocum 1826–1894.* Albany, N.Y.: J. B. Lyons Printers, 1904.

Nichols, Edward J. *Toward Gettysburg: A Biography of General John Reynolds.* University Park, PA: Pennsylvania State University Press, 1958.

O'Reilly, Francis Augustin. *The Fredericksburg Campaign: Winter War on the Rappahannock.* Baton Rouge: Louisiana State University Press, 2003.

Phisterer, Frederick. *New York in the War of the Rebellion: 1861 to 1865.* 5 vols. Albany, N.Y.: J. B. Lyon, 1912.

Priest, John Michael. *Before Antietam: The Battle for South Mountain.* Shippensburg, PA: White Mane, 1992.

Rable, George C. *Fredericksburg! Fredericks-*

burg!. Chapel Hill, N.C.: University of North Carolina Press, 2002.
Risch, Erna. *Quartermaster Support of the Army: A History of the Corps, 1775–1939.* 1962. Reprint, Washington, D.C.: Center of Military History-United States Army, 1989.
Rodenbough, Theophilus F., ed. *The Army of the United States: Historical Sketches of the Staff and Line.* New York: Maynard Merrill and Co., 1896.
Ryan, Mary P. *Cradle of the Middle Class: The Family in Oneida County, New York, 1790–1865,* Cambridge, N.Y.: Cambridge University Press, 1983.
Sears, Stephen W. *Chancellorsville.* Boston: Houghton Mifflin, 1996.
———. *Landscape Turned Red: The Battle of Antietam.* New York: Ticknor & Fields, 1983.
Sifakis, Stewart. *Who Was Who in the Union.* New York: Facts on File, 1998.
Stackpole, Edward J. *From Cedar Mountain to Antietam.* Harrisburg, PA: Stackpole, 1959.
Tanner, Robert G. *Stonewall in the Valley: Thomas J. "Stonewall" Jackson's Shenandoah Valley Campaign Spring 1862.* New York: Doubleday, 1976.
Thomas, Howard. *Boys in Blue from the Adirondack Foothills.* Prospect, N.Y.: Prospect Books, 1960.
Wager, Daniel E., ed. *Our County and Its People: A Descriptive Work on Oneida County, New York.* Boston: Boston History Co., 1896.
Warner, Ezra J. *Generals in Blue.* Baton Rouge: Louisiana State University Press, 1964.
Yandoh, Judy. "Brief Breach at Fredericksburg." *America's Civil War* 14:5 (November 2001).

Maps

O' Reilly, Frank A., and Eric J. Mink. "The Battle of Chancellorsville." 12 maps. Illustrated and produced by John Dove, 1998.

Internet Sources

The Civil War Letters of Fannie Austin, http://freepages.genealogy.rootsweb.com/~snugaza/austin/index.html.
Letters of the Civil War: A Compilation of Letters, Stories, Diaries From the Soldiers, Sailors, Nurses, Politicians, Ministers, Journalists and Citizens During the War of the Rebellion From the Newspapers of Massachusetts, http://www.letterscivilwar.com.
Ramapo to Chancellorsville and Beyond, http://www.talkeetna.com/Pierson/RamapoToChancellorsville.pdf.
13th Independent Battery—NY Light Artillery, http://www.13nybattery.com/index2.htm.

Index

Numbers in *italic* indicate illustrations.

Alexandria Local News 33
Alexandria, Va. 19–20, 26, 43, 47; slave pen at 19, 22
Antietam, Battle of 79–84; casualties at 83–84, 85–86
Army of Virginia 48, 54, 55
Arrowsmith, George 5, 9, *15*, 16, 20, 24, 25, 26, 34, 35, 45, 49–50
Ashley, Theodore 63
Averell, William 7, 10

Babcock, John 24
Bacon, William 14, 23, 28, 65, *95*, 100, 102, 123
Bailey's Crossroads, Va. 25, 35
Baker, Thomas: execution of 47–48
Baltimore, Md. 11
Banks, Nathan 51–52
Baxter, Henry 111, 114, 118, 121
Beauregard, Pierre G. T. 18
Belle Plain, Va. 103, 108, 115
Benedick, Samuel *53*
Berlin, Md. *88*, 89
Blackwell, George 25
Blake, George 36–37
Boonesboro, Md. 78
Bowen, William 54
Brindle, Anton 5, 7
Bristoe Station, Va. 61
Bristol, Daniel 28, 37, 87, *102*; resignation of 104
Brook's Station, Va. 43
Brown, George William 12
Burnside, Ambrose 73, 74, 91, 92, 93, 99, 104, 106–107; resignation of 108

Camp Maxwell, Va. 21, 25
Camp Vernon, Va. 24
Carman, Ezra Ayers 85

Caryl, James 66, 104; court-martial of 109–110
casualties, within the 26th New York 69
Catoctin Mountains 75
Cedar Mountain, Battle of 50–54
Cedar Run 55
Centreville, Va. 67, 69
Chancellorsville, Va. 111; Battle of 116–121
Chantilly, Battle of 70–71
Childs, George H. 22, 37
Christian, Thomas 85
Christian, William H. 5, 6, 8, 10, 13, 16, 20, 23, 24, 25, 28, 30–31, 36, 38, 40, 47, 48, 53, 57, 58, 60, 67, 68, 71, 74, 75–76, 79, 125–126, 127; abandons the field at Antietam 80–81; absence from Second Bull Run 62–63; marriage of 32; Mexican War service 6; resignation of 84–86
Clark, George W. *68*
Cleveland, Anson 10
Cleveland, Charles 81, *129*
Collier, Albert 14
Collins, Hugh 87
Colquitt, Alfred 82
Cosselman, Montgomery 67
Coulter, Richard 80
Coventry, Walter B. 5, *40*, 41, 63, 90, 109
Cowen, Nathan 104
Crigier, Francis 34, 68–69
Culpeper, Va. 50, 54

Dahlgren, James 13
Darla, Charles 9
Davidson, Greenlee 96
Davies, Thomas 26

Davis, Thomas 24–25, 67
Delaplane, Va. 46
desertions, within the 26th New York 106
Doolittle, C. H. 123
Doubleday, Abner 75, 93, 118
Dunham, Martin *8*
Duryea, Abram 62, 75, 79, 80

Early, Jubal 116, 119
East Woods, at the Battle of Antietam 80
Eliot, Washington 8, 22
Ellsworth, Elmer 19–20
Elmira, N.Y. 7, 8; description of camps at 8–9
enlistment bounty 34, *35*
escort duty 39
ethnic enlistees 6–7
Evans, William *101*

Fairfax Court House, Va. 71
Falmouth, Va. 122
Fessenden, Samuel 63
Firman, Warren 50, 55, 64, 74, 85
First Bull Run, Battle of 18–20
Fitzhugh, Norman 116
Fletcher's Chapel, Va. 103, 115
Fort Ellsworth, Va. 20, 21, 25, 32, 35–38, 39
Fort Jefferson (Gulf of Mexico) 24
Fort Lyon, Va. 31, 33–34, 35, 36, 37, 43
Fort Sumter, bombing of 4
Franklin, William 25, 31, 93–94
Frazier, Jerome 101, 128
Frederick, Md. 75

Fredericksburg 44–45; Battle of 93–100; Prospect Hill 93, 96; Twenty-Sixth's casualties at 101–102
Front Royal, Va. 46, 47
Fugitive Slave Act 39–40

Gaffney, Timothy 14, 23, 29, 33
Gainesville, Va. 60
Georgia troops, infantry regiments: 21st 80
German soldiers 6; within the 26th New York 7
Gibbon, John 91, 93, 95, 97, 103, 106
Grand Army of the Republic 129
Groveton, Va. 62

Halleck, Henry 18, 45, 74, 113
Halls' Hill, Va. 71, 74
Hardie, James 93
Harpers Ferry, Va. 78, 89, 91
Harrar, William 16
Hartsuff, George 52, 54, 60, 62, 75, 79, 80, 81
Haymarket, Va. 60, 62
Heintzelman, Samuel 24, 26, 62
Hill, A. P. 51, 91, 119
Hill, D. H. 82
Holstead, William 4, 85, 110, 122, 123
Hooker, Joseph 74, 84, 108–109, 110, 111, 112, 113–114, 116, 117, 119, 120
Hopewell Gap, Va. 60
Howard, Oliver O. 13
Hunting Run 25
Huntley, Thomas 40

Ingersoll, Frank 87

Jackson, James W. 19
Jackson, Thomas J. "Stonewall" 44, 45, 46, 47, 51–54, 62, 70, 93, 116–117, 118
Jennings, Charles 25, 68
Jennings, Gilbert S. 5, 10, 23, 25, 34, 50, 87, 90, *92*, 95, 98, 101, 102, 107, 109, 114, 115, 125, 128
Jennings, John *59*
Jones, Daniel 86
Jones, David 29
Jones, Edward 11–12

Jones, M. M. 15
Jones, Thomas A. *123*

Kane, Edwin *128*
Kearny, Philip 62, 70
Keedysville, Md. 78
Keene, Joseph 99, 129
Kilburn, Henry 111
Kingsbury, John *7*

lack of pay issue 14
Ladies' Soldiers Relief Association 5
Lane, James 97
Lee, Edward 97–98
Lee, Robert E. 49, 56, 71, 79, 90, 116–117, 119; pre–Antietam strategy 73
Lee, Stephen D. 80
Leech, William 97–98
Leesborough, Md. 74
Leonard, Samuel 118
Lincoln, Abraham 16–17, 20, 27, 35, 40, 43, 71, 108, 111, 116; calls for volunteers 4, 49; Emancipation Proclamation 104; visits the army at Antietam 87–88
Longstreet, James 60, 61
Loveland, Albert *122*
Lyle, Peter 85, 91, 94, 97, 98, 106, 109, 111
Lynch, Albert 104, 110
Lyon, Nathaniel 33

Madison County, N.Y. 5
Maine troops, artillery: 2nd 46, 118; 5th 64; infantry regiments: 3rd 13; 5th 24, 30; 16th 102
Manassas Junction, Va. 18, 46, 47, 49, 61, 65
Mansfield, John K. 13
Mansfield, Joseph K. 83
Maryland Campaign; routes of march during 74–75
Mason, Charles 34, 39
Massachusetts troops, infantry regiments: 6th 11–12; 8th 12; 12th 56, 91, 95, 97, 108, 119, 121; 13th 56, 119
Massapomax Creek, Va. 103
McClean's Brigade 65
McClellan, George 20–21, 24, 27–28, 34, 36, 40, 43–44, 48, 71, 73, 75, 78, 86, 87, 120; dismissal of 91
McClenthen, Charles 4, 53,
54, 57, 60, 64–66, 67–68, 71–72, 80, 81, 85, 107, 113, 115
McCunn, John 18
McDowell, Irvin 18, 20, 43–44, 45, 46, 49, 52–53, 54, 67, 74
McQuade, James 63
Meade, George 78, 81, 84, 90, 93, 94, 95, 115
Medal of Honor 82
Meigs, Montgomery 16
Mercer, William 22
Meridian Heights 12, 14
Michigan troops, infantry regiments: 2nd 36, 39
Middletown, Md. 75
Miller, Jabez 68, *129*
Morgan, Edwin D. 4, 10
Mount Vernon, Va. 29
Mount Vernon Road 26, 30
Mud March 106–107, 109, 120
Mumma, Samuel 81
Munson, Buell *102*
Myers, H.C. 49

Neil, William 98
New York State: initial recruiting quotas 4
New York troops: artillery regiments: 3rd Light 125; 16th Heavy 125; cavalry regiments: 12th 125; 24th 125; infantry regiments: 1st 115; 11th Fire Zouaves 19; 14th 5, 8, 16, 23, 122; 14th Brooklyn 77; 15th 19; 16th 24, 26, 30–31; 21st 114; 25th 19; 27th 24, 26, 30–31, 33; 37th 19; 79th 24; 80th 77; 83rd 124; 94th 43, 44, 49, 64, 79, 81, 83, 87, 91, 118; 97th 124
New York Daily Tribune 63
New York Herald 69
New York World 19
Newton, John 33
Nicodemus Heights, Md. 80
North American (steamer) 43
Norton, John 29

Occoquan, Va. 31
Oneida County 49; history of 3; war sentiments 4
Ord, Edward O. 45, 46, 47, 49

Palmer, John 5
Palmer, Norman 68, 80, 102
parole of prisoners 69
Patrick, Marsena 114
Pennsylvania troops, infantry regiments: 11th 80; 88th 44, 49, 52, 55, 56, 61, 63, 81, 83, 91; 90th 44, 49, 50, 56, 61, 64, 74, 80, 81, 95, 97, 99, 111, 116, 119; 107th 100; 136th 91, 95, 97, 100, 108, 113, 120
Pierce, Frank: court-martial of 43
Poe, Orlando M. 36
Poffenberger, Samuel: farm of 78
Pohick Church, Va. 30; skirmish at 30–31
Pollock, William 100
Pollock's Mill Creek 116, 121
Pope, John 48–49, 50, 52, 54, 55, 58, 62, 66, 67, 70, 73
Potomac River 43
Preston, Orlando 6

Quartermasters Department, Union 15

Rapidan River 54
Rappahannock River 44, 50, 55, 63, 100, 117, 119, 120; skirmishing near 56–58
Reno, Jesse L. 54, 74
Reynolds, John 55, 62, 91, 93, 94, 95, 117, 120, 121
Richards, Stephen: court-martial of 37
Richardson, Richard H. 5, 25, 32, 47, 63, 65, 67, 74, 77, 80–82, 90, *91*, 92, 101, 107, 109, 125, 127, 128
Richmond, Hiram 29
Richmond, Fredericksburg & Potomac Railroad 93
Ricketts, James P. 41, 44–45, 46, 49, 52, 55, 56, 60, 74, 78, 80–81, 84, 90–91
Rightmire, Cornelius 19, 21–22
Rightmire, Samuel 67
Ripley, Roswell 81
Ritchie, David 23
Robinson, John 106, 109, 111, 114, 116, 118, 119, 126
Rochester, N.Y. 5, 34

Rogers, William 114
Rome, N.Y. 23
Rome Weekly Sentinel 23
Root, Adrian 50, 53, 87, 97, 100, 118

Salem Church, Va. 119
Sandford, Charles 16
Sandford, William 129
Schubert, Martin *99*
Scott, Winfield 16, 18
Second Bull Run, Battle of 60–69; fighting at Chinn Ridge 63–66
Seward, William H. 40, 128
Seymour, Truman 81, 84
Sherman, William T. 24
Shields, James 45
Shurley, Edmund R. P. 10, 39–40, 46, 57, 58–59
Sickles, Daniel 115
Sigel, Franz 51, 54, 59, 67
Slocum, Henry W. 30–31, 34–35, 84
Smith, Charles A. 22
Smith, David H. 23
Smith, Ira 5, 6, 28
Smith, William F. 93
South American (steamer) 43
South Mountain, Battle of 75–78
Stanton, Edwin 111
Staring, DeWitt 13, 42
Stevens, Isaac 70
Stevenson, Jonathan 6
Stiles, John W. 62
Strasburg, Va. 46
Stuart, J. E. B. 54, 116, 119
Sulphur Springs, Va. 58
Sumner, Edwin 84, 93

Taylor, Nelson 97, 98, 103, 106
Thoburn, Joseph 62
Thomas, Francis
Thoroughfare Gap, Va. 60
Timmerman, Mary H. 32, 37, 63
Tioga County, N.Y. 5
Tomes, Robert 27
Tower, Zealous 49, 52–53, 55, 58, 60, 62, 63, 65–66, 67, 68, 69, 74; privations within his Second Brigade 60–61; wounding of 65–66

Trimble, Isaac 81
Twenty-Sixth New York Infantry: court martials 104; description and presentation of flag 9; dispute over initial enlistment 22–24; homecoming reception 122–123; uniform issue 10, 15
Two-year regiments: disputes over term of enlistment 112–114

United States Ford 118, 120
United States Regular Troops, artillery regiments: 2nd 24, 58; 5th 118
United States Sanitary Commission 27, 36–37, 40–41
Utica Daily Gazette 112
Utica Daily Observer 35, 39
Utica Morning Herald 9

Van Valkenburgh, Robert 12
Vermont troops, infantry regiments: 9th 48
Veterans Reserve Corps 125, 128

Wadsworth, James 31
Wainwright, Charles 86, 120
Walker, Joseph 77
Wandell, Nelson 48
Warrenton, Va. 49, 90
Washington, D.C. 12–13
Washington, George 30
Washington Evening Star 12
Waterloo, Va. 50, 58, 60
West, William 25
Westfall, Eli: court-martial of 37–38
Wetmore, Ezra 66–67, 71, 90, 97, 99, *100*, 101, 107, 109, 119–120, 126, 129
White Oak Church, Va. 106
Williams, John 65
Williams, Seth 35
Williamsport, Pa. 11
Wilson, Charles S. 123
Wilson's Creek, Battle of 33
Winchell, Philip 7

www.ingramcontent.com/pod-product-compliance
Ingram Content Group UK Ltd.
Pitfield, Milton Keynes, MK11 3LW, UK
UKHW050530150426
5217IPUK00026B/1870